Financial and Treasury Management

C I *m* A

Published in association
with the Chartered
Institute of Management
Accountants

Other titles in the CIMA series

Financial and Treasury Management

Stage 4

P. A. Collier, T. E. Cooke
and J. J. Glynn

Heinemann Professional Publishing

Heinemann Professional Publishing Ltd
Halley Court, Jordan Hill, Oxford OX2 8EJ

OXFORD   LONDON   MELBOURNE   AUCKLAND

First published 1988

British Library Cataloguing in Publication Data
Collier, P. A. (Paul A.)
 Financial and treasury management.
 1. Multinational companies. Financial
 management
 I. Title II. Cooke, Terry E. III. Glynn,
 John J. IV. Series
 658.1'599

ISBN 0 434 90266 7

Printed in England by
Redwood Burn Ltd, Trowbridge

Contents

Part Six Public Sector

Part One

Introduction

1 An introduction to financial management

Financial and treasury managers are concerned with administering the provision and use of financial resources. Their decisions are crucial if the firm they represent is to satisfy its financial goals. Such managers therefore require a sound knowledge of the financial markets from which they raise their funds and a clear understanding of the techniques that lead to sound investment decisions. They are therefore concerned with the investment decision, the financing decision, and the dividend decision, i.e. with how the investments required should be financed and to what level.

Each of these decisions has an effect on the value of the firm and hence the wealth of its shareholders. To invest means to acquire an interest in productive opportunities, creating economic value, either directly or indirectly – in other words, the acquisition of tangible assets which produce goods and services or external investment in the financial markets. The financing decision requires determining from what sources funds should be obtained and to what level. These various sources of funds represent the capital structure of the firm. The principal sources of funds are either provided by those who have an equity interest, the shareholders, or those who loan funds at predetermined rates of interest, termed debt capital. If a firm's portfolio of investments fails to generate its predicted levels of return, debt interest takes a higher proportion of available cash inflows, to the detriment of the shareholders. Conversely, if the firm's investment strategy generates greater than predicted cash flows, it is the shareholders who reap the benefit as interest payments are at fixed rates. Dividend policy also represents a financing decision, since to pay out cash in the form of dividends to shareholders reduces the amount available for reinvestment. The optimal dividend policy is that which strikes a balance between current dividends and current growth and thereby maximizes the firm's share price.

These three decisions cannot be taken separately, since it is extremely rare that a firm can undertake all of its possible investment opportunities. For example, capital may be in short supply or additional finance may prejudice the controlling interest of the present owners. Investments need not only be by way of 'in-house' productive opportunities but can also include the acquisition of an existing business for reasons of horizontal or vertical market protection. No book can provide all the answers on one subject, and this one is no exception. However, what we do hope to do is to introduce the concepts on which sound financial decisions are made.

The title of this book is *Financial and Treasury Management*. This title recognizes that, in all but the smaller firms, no one individual is responsible for the administration of the topics discussed in this book. Increasingly these days the functions of corporate finance are being divided into 'Financial Management', with broad responsibility for the investment strategy that best maximizes the value of the firm; and 'Treasury Management', with broad responsibility for obtaining finance, managing the firm's liquid resources and maintaining its relationship with the financial institutions.

Our approach in writing this book has been to highlight these two roles and to examine the principles and practice of corporate finance. Financial theory will be introduced to lay down the foundations of financial and treasury management. To this will be added the constraints of our present-day business environment as provided by government fiscal policy, financial institutions, legislation and practice. We have found that, all too often, many texts consider financial theory in a vacuum, forgetting the UK business and institutional environment.

Corporate goals

In this book we operate on the assumption that management's principal goal is to maximize the value of the firm for its owners, the equity investors. In this context value is reflected by the market price of the firm's equity share capital, which is assumed to be a fair reflection of its investment, financing and dividend strategy. We adopt the concept of value because we assume that rational investors are wealth maximizers who endeavour to maximize, over time, their return on investment either in the form of cash dividends or capital gains. The more traditional goals of maximizing accounting profit or earnings per share are regarded as insufficient targets.

Profit is not as inclusive a goal as wealth maximization. As Lumby (1984, p.7) states:

> Profit, when used in a business sense, is purely an accounting concept introduced by accountants in order to perform their function as auditors for the owners of companies. In very general terms, profit represents the increased wealth of a company that has been achieved by management within

the confines of an arbitrary period of time; the accounting year. But profit is only a very, very rough approximation of increased wealth ... as it is based on a whole range of arbitrary and somewhat inconsistent accounting conventions.

Depreciation and movements on provisions appear in the income statement (profit and loss account) but do not lead to cash flows. As profit is a measure that is not related to the input of resources, it is possible to increase the total level of profits to the loss of existing equity investors. For example, suppose that a company was funded entirely by equity finance and that it had £1 million invested in productive opportunities that yielded a return of 20 per cent or £200,000 per annum. If it were to raise an additional £500,000 of equity investment, its profits would rise to £225,000 per annum. However, while the absolute level of profits has risen 12.5 per cent, the return to the original equity investors would be reduced from 20 per cent to 15 per cent. Accounting profit is ambiguous since it obscures the pattern of cash flows into and out of the firm.

The maximization of earnings per share also suffers from similar defects. It is calculated by dividing accounting profit, defined as earnings before interest and tax, by the total number of equity shares issued. Apart from the fact that, as stated, this is a measure of accounting profit based on arbitrary accounting conventions, the resultant measure of earnings per share only relates to one period of time. Both accounting profit and earnings per share ignore the time value of money (see p. 108). One new project undertaken by a firm might raise earnings per share by 20 pence per annum for 5 years, a total of £1. Another project might have no effect on earnings for 4 years but might increase earnings by £1.25 in the fifth year. Which project is better? The answer really depends on the time value placed on money by investors.

While our goal of maximizing the value of the firm may initially appear somewhat vague, we shall endeavour over the course of this book to show that the price of the firm's equity shares reflects the market's valuation of the projected earnings stream over time, including the riskiness associated with that stream and a variety of other factors. For now, though, we shall examine a normative model that, under a series of restrictive assumptions about the real world, illustrates the micro-economic theory underlying the principles of investment. It is based on two-period graphical analysis, first suggested by Hirshleifer (1958), which adapts the principles laid down by Fisher's (1907, 1930) work on the theory of interest.

Broadly two categories of investment opportunities are available: investment in the external capital market and investment internally in productive opportunities. It could of course be argued that if no productive opportunities are available, the firm should repay its funds to their equity investors and allow them to deal directly with the capital market. (Some investors do of course invest in specialist firms, such as investment trusts, thereby relying upon the expertise of management to spread the risk of investment across a portfolio of firms, each with their own individual risk characteristics.) With respect to investment in internal productive opportunities, this means investment in a range of tangible assets, which extend from plant and machinery to assets such as patents and licences. Productive opportunities are clearly more attractive than investing in the capital market if they provide a greater return.

In the analysis that follows we shall assume certainty and a perfect capital market, i.e. a capital market where both individuals and firms may borrow and lend money at a given rate. The approach adopted is to present this two-period analysis graphically, with the present period denoted as t_0 and the next period denoted as t_1. Any investment therefore requires an immediate cash outlay now (t_0) in return for a cash benefit in the next period (t_1). We do this, firstly, to illustrate the classic economic consumption–investment decision of an individual investor; and, secondly, by incorporating a simple numerical example, to illustrate the 'separation theorem' by which management is theoretically supposed to operate in order to satisfy the needs of all shareholders. Three other basic assumptions are also necessary:

1   Investors are considered to be wealth maximizers whose returns from investment are not affected by distortionary tax rates.
2   All investment opportunities are independent of each other and are divisible.
3   All information regarding these investment opportunities is known with certainty.

While these assumptions are clearly unrealistic, the intention is to isolate some crucial variables that lay down the foundations of optimal project appraisal. In later chapters we shall give some indication of how far we can cope with the problems that arise once these assumptions are relaxed.

This analysis begins with the assumption that there is a given rate at which individuals may borrow and lend on the capital market. Figure 1.1 illustrates the problem of choosing between spending today and spending in the future. An individual's endowment of B could be consumed now (t_0) or invested in the capital market to earn B $(1 + r)$ in the next period (t_1). The downward sloping line represents the rate of exchange in the capital market $(1 + r)$, where r denotes the rate of interest prevailing over this period. If we were to suppose, in Figure 1.2, an endowment of B today (t_0) and F next period (t_1), then one extreme option available to the investor would be to invest all the present endowment in order to increase consumption in the next period by B $(1 + r)$ or FH. Alternatively, the investor could borrow against next period's expected cash flow and increase present consumption by $F/(1 + r)$ or BD. All patterns of consumption, between these two extremes, can therefore be represented somewhere on the line HD.

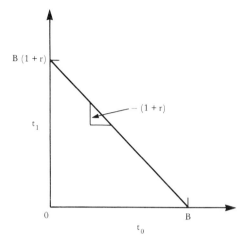

Figure 1.1

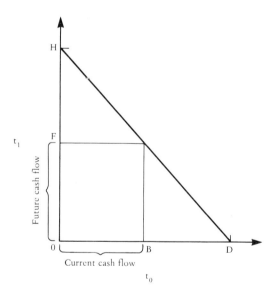

Figure 1.2

Figure 1.3 indicates, by indifference curves, two possible patterns of consumption. Indifference curve I_0, being tangential to HD, indicates that the investor wishes to consume 0W at t_0 with only 0Z available for reinvestment or consumption at t_1. Indifference curve I_0' indicates that the investor wishes to consume more than the present level of endow-

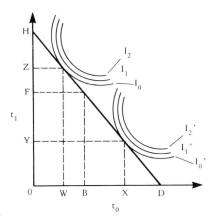

Figure 1.3

ment, that is 0X, by borrowing BX against a known t_1 cash flow of 0F. In this incidence the level of available t_1 funds is drastically reduced to 0Y, since YF will have to be paid out to service the increase in t_0 consumption. Indifference curves, in economic theory, are convex to the origin, thereby indicating that there is diminishing marginal utility attached to consumption at any single point of time. Their basic three properties are therefore that (1) they are positively sloped, that is, they exhibit negative trade-offs; (2) they exhibit diminishing marginal utility; and (3) movements to the right in Figure 1.3 represent increased utility. There are an indifferent number of patterns of indifference curves, of which $I_0 - I_2$ and $I_0' - I_2'$ are examples.

As previously stated, individuals are not only limited to investing in capital market securities but they can also invest in productive opportunities. These opportunities can be represented as a concave investment opportunity line (Figure 1.4). Each productive opportunity is ranked in terms of its return, commencing with that which offers the largest return. In Figure 1.4, projects m_0 and n_0 both have the same level of investment but m_0 produces twice as large a return as n_0. Similarly, if we wished, indifference curves could also be included to show the investor's desired trade-off between consumption and investment in productive opportunities. Rather than do that we will combine investment in productive opportunities with investment in the capital market and then introduce our investor's set of indifference curves; see Figure 1.5, where our investor starts with initial cash resources of 0D (at t_0). As previously stated, by investing all or part of these funds in the capital market the investor can attain any point on the line DH. However, an investment of JD in productive opportunities would produce 0G in the next period (t_1). If the balance of the funds was not consumed, it could return GM on the capital market in the next period (t_1). In other words, by first investing JD in productive opportunities and borrow-

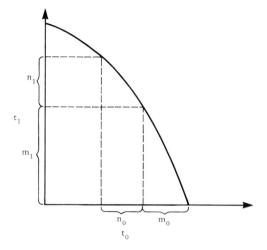

Figure 1.4

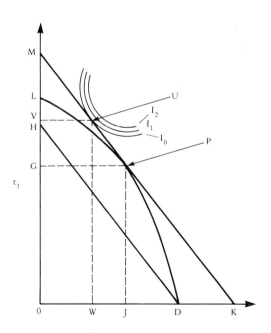

Figure 1.5

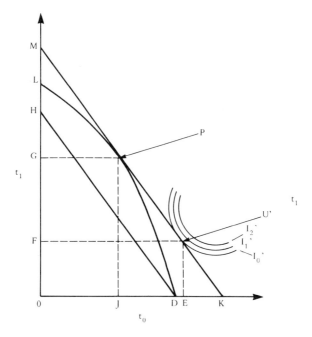

Figure 1.6

ing or lending on the capital market it is possible to attain any point along the line KM. Our investor would only invest JD in productive opportunities, to point P in Figure 1.5, because to invest further would yield a marginal return less than that offered in the market, capital market line KM being moved out parallel to HD until it was tangential to LD.

Figure 1.5 also displays the investor's set of indifference curves. Recall that the objective is for the wealth-maximizing investor to move as far as possible to the right. Indifference curve I_0 is tangential to KM at point U. This means that the investor's consumption pattern is such that 0W is required at t_0, leaving JD invested in productive opportunities and the balance, WJ, to be invested in the capital market. Next period (at t_1) the investor would have 0V rather than 0M for future consumption or reinvestment. Our investor may not be so thrifty and instead may wish to consume more than his t_0 level of funds by borrowing on the capital market. Figure 1.6 replicates Figure 1.5 except that a different set of indifference curves is shown. Here we see that the investor wishes to consume 0E, an increase of DE. However, for our investor to reach this pattern of consumption, productive opportunities must first be undertaken, since they earn more than the cost of borrowing on the capital market. Unfortunately such a high level of current consumption only leaves 0F available in the next period.

The above analysis is based on a two-stage operation. First, the investor selects all productive opportunities that yield returns greater than the market rate of interest. This decision rule makes sense both for individuals who have to borrow funds and those who have sufficient funds for investment. On the one hand the return on borrowed funds exceeds the rate of interest, while on the other hand the opportunity cost of investing surplus funds in productive opportunities is greater than the lending rate available on the capital market. This decision rule merely helps us to establish the level of investment in productive opportunities; it says nothing about how such investments should be financed. This is stage two. Independent of the productive investment decision, individuals should borrow or lend on the capital market to produce the pattern of wealth consumption and distribution that best meets their individual requirements. Misers and spendthrifts alike can all agree on the level of productive opportunities to be undertaken before financing their own desired consumption pattern.

We now introduce a numerical illustration based on Figures 1.5 and 1.6. In so doing, we now suppose that our investor has retired from making direct productive investments and has instead established a firm and appointed a manager to undertake these decisions on his behalf. Our investor has therefore a 100 per cent equity interest in the firm. With a market rate of interest (r) equal to 15 per cent and an initial endowment of £1 million, various assumptions have been made in order to reproduce Figures 1.7 and 1.8. In Figure 1.7 the manager has £1 million to invest or distribute to the owner as required. The manager's first task is to decide on which productive opportunities to undertake. From the graph it can be seen that £0.5 million invested in productive opportunities at t_0 will yield £0.94 million at t_1. Utility curve I_0 reveals that the owner wishes to consume £0.25 million now, so leaving the balance of available funds, also £0.25 million, to be invested in the market at 15 per cent. To invest in productive opportunities beyond point P would provide a return less than that available on the market. This sequence of events is as follows:

	£m	£m
Initial endowment, at t_0	1.00	
less investment in productive opportunities, which yields at t_1	(0.50)	0.94
less dividend distributed to satisfy owner's t_0 level of consumption	(0.25)	
balance invested on the capital market, which yields at t_1	(0.25)	0.29
Endowment available at t_1		1.23

If, instead, the owner wishes to consume £1.2 million at t_0, the manager still undertakes the same level of investment in productive opportunities. As only £0.5 million is available for distribution, the owner will need to borrow £0.7 on his own account on the capital market. Figure 1.8 illustrates this position. Again, the sequence of events is as follows:

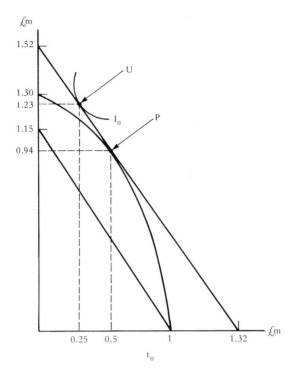

Figure 1.7

	£m	£m
Initial endowment, at t_0	1.00	
less investment in productive opportunities,	(0.50)	
which yield at t_1		0.94
less dividend distributed to owner	(0.50)	
owner borrows on own account,	(0.70)	
in order to consume	(1.20)	
less dividend payable at t_1 sufficient to		
allow investor to repay loan plus interest		(0.81)
Endowment available at t_1		0.13

In both instances the manager has acted in the best interests of the owner. From the information provided in Figure 1.7 it can be noted that to have carried out any other investment plan would have reduced the t_1 endowment below £1.23 million. Equally, had the manager, in Figure 1.8, distributed £1.0 million (thereby leaving the owner with only £0.2 million to borrow), the firm would have to cease trading and there would be no funds available at t_1 to repay the loan. The principle adopted by the manager is to maximize the current wealth of the owner

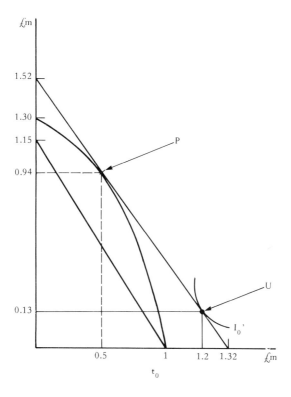

Figure 1.8

who can then transform this wealth into his/her desired pattern of consumption.

This illustration demonstrates what has become known as the 'Separation Theorem' (Tobin, 1958). It is a theorem that has two propositions:

1 Management should invest in all productive opportunities that yield a return greater than that available on the market.
2 Owners (as shareholders) should borrow or lend on the capital market to produce the cash flows that best meet their own individual pattern of consumption.

The market value of the firm today (at t_0) is £1.32 million which is the total funds (£1.52) due to be received in the next period (t_1), discounted at the market rate of interest (15 per cent). If we were to assume that 1 million equity shares had been issued, each with a nominal value of £1.00, then each would have a current market value of £1.32. Our owner/shareholder could either sell parcels of shares for present consumption, if the company was not currently paying a dividend, thereby

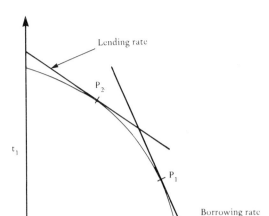

Figure 1.9

reducing his equity interest, or else borrow funds on the capital market. The actual process of issuing equity or raising other forms of long-term capital is discussed in Chapters 10 and 11.

The foregoing analysis assumed that the borrowing and lending rates on the capital market were equal. Figure 1.9 illustrates the more realistic situation where the borrowing rate is significantly higher than the lending rate. Management still must decide on the optimal selection of productive opportunities. Projects should first be selected by reference to the (steeper) borrowing rate, point P_1. If funds are insufficient to accept all these opportunities, the additional funds can be borrowed, as productive opportunities will produce returns that are more than sufficient to cover the cost of borrowing. If, however, the firm has surplus funds available after this exercise, management should then evaluate all remaining opportunities at the lending rate, to point P_2 on Figure 1.9, as these additional projects will earn a return greater than that available on the market.

This two-period analysis can be further developed to accommodate longer time horizons. In fact it is the theoretical basis on which we recommend the 'net present value' discounted cash flow approach to investment appraisal in Chapter 6. As Bromwich (1976, p. 67) states:

> ... a project with a positive net present value covers the opportunity cost of both internal and external funds. Its acceptance, therefore, makes the shareholders better off. Looking at it another way, the net present value of a project is the price at which the firm (and its shareholders) could sell the opportunity to undertake the project to someone else and be no worse off.

Not everyone agrees with the approach of a single economic objective. In reality a firm represents a coalition of groups, each with its own goals. Usually ownership is divorced from the management of the firm and the executive management acts as the trustee or agent, not only for the shareholders but for all parties having an interest in the operations of the concern. Interested parties include (beside equity investors) employees, customers, management, debtors, creditors, government agencies and indeed the public at large.

Alternative views

Simon's (1959) 'administrative man' seeks adequate profit as opposed to maximum profit, and a fair price for products as opposed to a maximum price. Cyert and March (1963) see the organization as one composed of isolated units of interest which combine to form a short-run coalition in response to short-run pressures. Individuals, so the argument goes, make up the membership of any organization, each with their own goals, and so it is meaningless to talk of a single organizational goal. For example, most sales managers probably see their primary role as one of maximizing sales. Such an objective may not necessarily produce the greatest revenue and can lead to conflict within the organization. Contrast this approach with the production manager who would prefer steady production schedules of a narrow range of products. To the production manager, this provides an opportunity to exercise greater control over the production process (implying a reduced incidence of rejects), cheaper tooling costs, less varied amounts of stock and so on.

Empirical evidence suggests that most companies have multiple goals, but that from among these profitability (despite its serious defects) normally receives a high ranking. Pike (1986) conducted a survey which asked financial directors in the largest UK companies to rank specified goals in order of importance. The first choice was the maximization of the return on assets, i.e. an accounting measure – the return on capital employed. This was closely followed by the maximization of earnings per share. Maximization of share price only ranked fourth. US studies also tend to support these findings; see, for example, Petty *et al.*, 1975.

Writers such as Jensen and Meckling (1976) and Fama (1980) view managers as being the agents of owners who act as principals. Jensen and Meckling consider that shareholders need to provide management with a range of incentive packages in order to encourage them to undertake optimal investment decisions. Incentives these days can include share options, bonuses, free holidays, cars, etc. Of all these various incentives, it is argued that managers are more likely to behave in a manner consistent with maximizing shareholder wealth if they too have an equity stake in the firm. Fama (1980) suggests that efficient capital markets not only provide signals about the value of the firm but also, implicitly, provide information on the performance of its managers, which, in turn, increases their own earnings potential in the labour market.

Why consider a theoretical concept?

Corporate finance is not just that of raising funds to finance expenditure; other questions have also to be answered. Which project should be undertaken? What is the cost of finance? The approach outlined is normative, based upon a theory of how rational investors should act. A theoretical framework can present a logical structure on financial affairs so that a link can be made to provide a connection with the pragmatic business environment that operates in the real world devoid of academic conjecture. As Robichek and Myers (1965) state, 'theory is organised to shed light on the complex web of circumstances within which a financial manager must act'.

An optimal allocation of resources leads to the increased value of the firm and the result may have spin-offs for parties other than shareholders. If greater wealth is generated, more finance is available for reinvestment, increases in wages and salaries and so on. Throughout this book financial theory will be introduced to lay down the foundations of sound corporate financial management. To this will be added the constraints of the present-day business environment as provided by government fiscal policy, financial institutions, legislation and practice. The financial and treasury managers' role is to present financially rational proposals to their fellow managers so that they can jointly decide on a course of action (or strategy) which reflects a recognition of possible limiting constraints provided by other competing objectives.

Support for our theoretical concept is reinforced by the Companies Acts, which state that the directors of companies are expected to run them in the best interests of the shareholders. Further, it is the institutions that are the dominant shareholders and they are well placed to influence the direction of corporate management. The Wilson Committee (1980, p. 72) reported that:

> At the end of 1978 the financial institutions as a whole are estimated to have held 50 per cent of listed UK ordinary shares compared with only 21 per cent in 1957. By early 1980 the proportion has probably risen to about 52 per cent. At the end of 1978 the institutions also held just under a half of listed UK company loan capital, three-quarters of listed UK preference shares and about two-thirds of listed public securities.

Indeed Briston and Dobbins (1978) estimate that if present savings habits continue, by 1990 financial institutions will own in the region of 70 per cent of total quoted shares. Even government attempts to get the public to subscribe for shares in various privatized industries seems not to have been successful. Shackleton (1984) points out that the small investor tends only to purchase such shares for a short-term gain and that, within a fairly short space of time, the institutional investors consolidate their control of these industries. He states (p. 67):

When British Aerospace (in 1980) made its appearance on the London Stock Exchange it had 158,000 individual shareholders. Amersham International (in 1981) received 65,000 successful applications for shares. By October 1983 there were 26,000 shareholders in British Aerospace and 7,500 in Amersham International. It seems that the bulk of shares in privatised enterprises are ending up in the portfolios of the major institutional investors who dominate the market.

Privatization has since 1979 become an integral part of the government's economic policy and has expanded from a 5 per cent BP sale in 1980 into a £5 billion a year operation.

Shackleton's pessimism seems at the moment to be only partly confirmed, but the pattern may change over time. Goodway (1987) takes the view that although the government has encouraged wider share ownership, through fringe benefits and its legislation establishing Personal Equity Plans, the City still takes the view that investment advice for the private shareholder is not cost-effective. He points out that in the 1987 BAA flotation seven market-makers turned their back on private investors, choosing not to make a market because they did not want to handle millions of small transactions. Privatization will be further examined in Chapter 20.

Structure of the book

This book is arranged in six parts. Following this chapter the two succeeding chapters consider 'Forecasting and the economic environment' and 'External influences on performance'. All corporate managers should be familiar with basic forecasting techniques in order to understand the significant trends that underlie the performance of the economy. Chapter 2 provides this background, while Chapter 3, recognizing that firms do not operate in a vacuum, considers the diverse external influences that can impact, to a greater or lesser extent, on their performance. The aim of these three introductory chapters is therefore to set the scene in which financial decisions are made.

Part Two has three chapters devoted to measuring performance. Chapter 4 reviews the key ratios that are necessary for analysing annual reports and financial statements. This discussion is carried over to Chapter 5, which deals with sources of information on UK companies, technical analysis, and a framework for ratio analysis, followed by a case study based on Marks & Spencer plc. The chapter also discusses inter-firm comparison schemes. Chapter 6 reviews the main techniques of investment appraisal and follows directly from our discussion in the previous section of this chapter.

Part Three is concerned with capital structure and portfolio theory. In Chapter 7 capital structure theory is discussed from both a normative and practical point of view. Related to this discussion are the important issues of dividend policy and measuring the cost of capital. One approach to analysing the cost of capital is by means of the capital asset pricing model and this provides the link to the discussion in Chapter 8 on the importance of portfolio theory to modern corporate financial control.

Part Four of the book comprises eight chapters on 'Treasury Management', starting at Chapter 9 with the development of the corporate treasury function from within the finance function, and an examination of its main components, which clearly distinguish it from controllership responsibilities. Chapter 10 considers 'long-term funding', including the regulatory role of the stock exchange (going public, flotation methods, and prospectus requirements), USM compared with a full listing, continued debate (from Chapter 7) on the choice between equity and fixed interest finance, and the impact of institutional shareholdings on equity markets. Chapter 11 covers small firms and their financing and Chapter 12 considers funding institutions, and, apart from reviewing Stock Exchange regulations, covers pension funds, insurance companies, the commercial banks, merchant banks, discount houses, Finance Houses Association, Unit Trusts, Investment Trust companies and sources of venture capital. Currency risk management has become increasingly important since the volatility of the economy in the 1970s and it is the topic of discussion in Chapter 13. Definitions of currency risk exposure are provided, together with discussion on forward contracts, options, futures and swaps. This chapter also discusses practical aspects of currency risk management: for example, opinion weighting and the development of econometric models. Medium to short-term sources of funds are also important, particularly for funding the day-to-day operations of the firm, e.g. to pay creditors and to buy stock. Other aspects of what is termed 'working capital management' include stock management, debtor control and the sound management of short-term investments. Chapter 14 considers the advantages and disadvantages of a range of sources for short-term funding. Chapter 15 assesses the importance of working capital management. This section concludes, at Chapter 16, by considering the principles underlying the investment of surplus funds.

Company valuations form the theme for Part Five. Chapter 17 is concerned with 'mergers and acquisitions'. Discussion centres around takeover trends in the UK, motives for merger, and defences against a merger, including reconstruction schemes, disinvestment and management buyouts. This chapter also considers legal control and the City Code, valuation of listed and unlisted companies, and a review of available evidence on the performance of merged firms. Chapter 18 accepts the premise that not all firms will be successful when we discuss 'insolvency', both in terms of the actual process of insolvency and defences against going insolvent.

Part Six of this book considers the public sector where financial management is just as important as in the private sector even though financial goal are often less precise. Rather than seeking to maximize the economic value of their organization, public sector managements are more concerned with seeking to obtain the best value for money from their services, given the resources that they have at their disposal. Only financial management in the nationalized industries can compare to that developed in the private sector, though even then there are some important differences. Many of the topics outlined above are, though, equally important to public sector organizations. For example, the principles of investment appraisal and working capital management are equally applicable; it is just that the economic environment is different. Chapter 19 sets out the public expenditure cycle and the mechanics for considering public expenditure requirements. Chapter 20 considers financial control in the public sector at both central and devolved levels of government. This includes discussion on cash planning and limits, and efforts to attain improved value for money.

Summary

This chapter has introduced the concept that financial managers should endeavour to maximize the current market value of their equity investors' shares, undertaking all productive investment opportunities, provided that their individual returns exceeded that available on the capital market. Under the simplified assumptions outlined, the current market value of the equity investment was also the discounted value of future receipts. The presentation was normative, i.e. the model derived incorporated implicit assumptions about the explicit and varied actions of individual investors. This analysis is not perfect but it is the only one currently available. In the next nineteen chapters we shall endeavour to deal with many of the practical problems surrounding this application.

At the beginning of this chapter we stated that it was our aim to review both the principles and practice of corporate finance. The approach that we have adopted should enable readers to:

1 Take part in the financial management of their organization as a whole and all its activities.
2 Obtain financial resources.
3 Ensure that these are put to profitable and effective use.

References

Briston, R. J. and Dobbins, R., *The Growth and Impact of Institutional Investors*, ICAEW, 1978.

Bromwich, M., *The Economics of Capital Budgeting*, Penguin, 1976.

Cyert, R. M. and March, J. G., *A Behavioural Theory of the Firm*, Prentice-Hall, 1963.

Fama, E., 'Agency Problems and The Theory of the Firm', *Journal of Political Economy*, April 1980.

Fisher, I., *The Rate of Interest*, Macmillan, 1907.

Fisher, I., *The Theory of Interest*, Macmillan, 1930.

Goodway, N., 'Small Investors: Are You Being Served?', *The Observer*, 25 October 1987.

Hirshleifer, J., 'On the Theory of Optimal Investment Decision', *Journal of Political Economy*, vol. 66, no. 4.

Jensen, M. C. and Meckling, W. H., 'Theory of the Firm: Managerial Behaviour, Agency Costs and Ownership Structure', *Journal of Political Economy*, April 1980.

Lumby, S., *Investment Appraisal*, Von Nostrand Reinhold (UK), 1984.

Petty, J. W., *et al.*, 'The Capital Expenditure Decision Making Process of Large Corporations', *The Engineering Economist*, Spring 1975.

Pike, R. H., 'Owner–manager Conflict and the Role of the Payback Method', *Accounting and Business Research*, 1986.

Robichek, A. A. and Myers, S. C., *Optimal Financing Decisions*, Prentice-Hall, 1965.

Shackleton, J. R., 'Privatization: The Case Examined', *National Westminster Bank Quarterly Review*, May 1984.

Simon, H. A., 'Theories of Decision Making in Economics and Behavioural Science', *American Economic Review*, vol. 49, no. 3, 1959.

Tobin, J., 'Liquidity Preference as Behaviour Toward Risk', *Review of Economic Studies*, February 1958.

Wilson Committee Report, *Committee to Review the Functioning of Financial Institutions*, Cmnd 7937, HMSO, 1980.

2 Forecasting and the economic environment

Introduction

A formal view of the future is a key component in a firm's planning and decision-making processes. Forecasting provides this information through the application of selected techniques to relevant available data. In a complex and uncertain world forecasts based upon even the most advanced techniques and widest data sources are unlikely to be accurate and reliable. Nevertheless the future value of key variables and the conditions in which a firm will operate must be considered, and estimates grounded in a rigorous approach are more likely to yield satisfactory results than mere hunches. Further, forecasting requires the relationship between the organization and its environment to be studied, which can only lead management to a better understanding of the business.

Although forecasting is often treated as being synonymous with planning, there are differences. First, planning is essentially subjective and covers controllable factors, while forecasting uses objective techniques and assesses variables over which the firm has no control. Second, forecasts are constructed from the bottom up and grounded in detail, whereas plans start with objectives, which are disaggregated to arrive at plans for various components of the whole. Finally, forecasts, although acknowledging uncertainty, provide a value; in contrast, planning incorporates uncertainties through adopting risk-averse strategies.

An overview of business forecasts

Forecasts for business cover a wide range of variables. A view of the likely factors in forecasts is multi-dimensional. Figure 2.1 shows a possible analysis with four interrelated elements: the level of the forecast, the type of trend, the scope of the forecast and the time period. Let us examine each in turn.

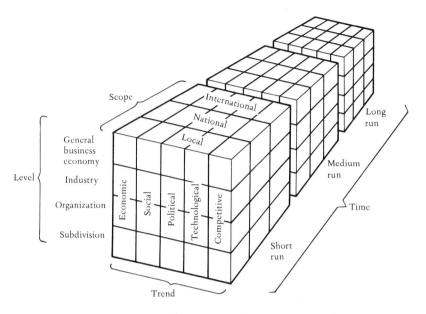

Figure 2.1   Factors in business forecasts

Four levels of variables being forecast are considered. At the highest level is the general business economy. On the basis of past experience firms will be aware of any links between changes in macro-economic factors and its own performances, and it is on these variables, e.g. interest rates in the case of a firm providing credit facilities, that forecasting effort will concentrate. Another level is the industry or industries in which the company operates. Changes in the supply and demand for product categories will be of particular interest and be important in the organization's decision-making process. Forecasts at the organizational level often reflect an aggregation of forecasts at product, territory or other sub-division levels. These last two levels are therefore interdependent.

Another analysis categorizes forecasts in terms of the trends under examination. Commentators, e.g. Argenti (1980), normally refer to five major trends: economic, social, political, technological and competitive. Economic trends closely correspond to the general business economy level and include growth in the economy, foreign exchange and interest rates, money supply, inflation and other related variables. Social trends concern factors affecting potential purchasers of products and employees. For the former the focus will be on changing tastes, habits and behaviour patterns; while for the latter information will be sought on changing attitudes to work, acceptance of new technology and the role of unions. Political trends relate to the impact that legislators and potential legislators might have upon the environment through taxation, and environmental, social and other policies. Technological trends comprise advances in manufacturing and administrative systems, new materials, new products and the impact on the needs of potential customers. Finally competitive trends include the actions of major competitors, opportunities for takeovers, possibility of new entrants and other factors impacting upon the degree of competition facing the firm.

These two dimensions, levels and trends, can be extended by considering the scope of each at local, national and international levels. The relevance of these dimensions will depend upon an organization's interest. For a small firm interest will be in local government with respect to rates and expansion planning consent; while for a multinational concern political trends will impact at a multiplicity of levels, varying from local conditions for each unit to the national situation in countries where there are investments and the wider international field.

Finally there is a time dimension. Figure 2.1 identifies three periods which largely reflect the purpose of the forecast. Short-run forecasts cover short periods, usually in terms of days, weeks or months and aim at the need for forecasts in operational decision-making (for example, exchange rate forecasts in planning hedging strategy). Beyond this, the medium run is concerned with forecasts for the budgeting process and tactical decision-making. The time period covered is usually from months to several years, depending upon a firm's circumstances. Lastly long-range forecasts are necessary for strategic planning and decision-making concerned with facilities, manpower, product changes, market demand and market share at periods of over 3 years. Thus, using interest rate forecasts as an example, purposes for which they are required include short operational decision-making in planning the movement of cash and best borrowing sources, medium-term budgeting, and long-term planning of investments and the timing and nature of borrowings.

Forecasting techniques

A wide range of forecasting techniques are available. All follow the methodology shown in Figure 2.2.

Figure 2.2 Forecasting – the process

The main categories are:

- Time series analysis
- Causal models
- Qualitative approaches
- Marketing methods

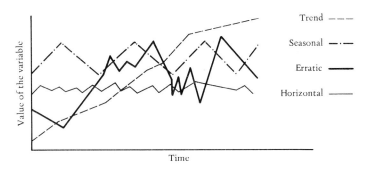

Figure 2.3   Time series patterns

Time series

A time series is a succession of values arranged in date order. The premise underlying time series analysis is that the future value of a variable is related to the past values of the variable arranged in a time series. As might be expected, the technique is useful only in the short run and in the absence of any disturbance to the environment. The type of time series technique used depends upon the past behaviour patterns of variables. Four are distinguished and illustrated in Figure 2.3.

The horizontal pattern lends itself to moving average and exponential smoothing techniques. The former technique and its weighted form rely on combining and averaging several consecutive observations on a continuing basis; while the latter bases its forecast on the previous period plus a proportion of the difference between forecast and actual in this period. Where there is a definite upward or downward trend in the time series data, double exponential smoothing, double moving average and mathematical curve fitting are appropriate. The double systems are closely allied to the techniques for horizontal patterns, whereas curve fitting is only useful when a clear non-linear pattern is observable. Seasonal and cyclical variations to the pattern are tackled by decomposition techniques, which break down the patterns into seasonal, cyclical and trend components. Erratic data require techniques, known as adaptive methods, which in essence 'adapt' themselves as the pattern of data changes.

Causal models

The premise behind this approach is that the value of a variable in the future can be determined by reference to a number of other variables which influence it. For example, the demand for children's toys may depend upon factors such as the population of children (P), advertising expenditure (A), disposable income of parents (I) and the life expectancy of toys (L). This can be expressed as an equation where D is demand for toys

$$D = aP + bA + cI + dL$$

and a, b, c and d are constants determined from statistical regression and correlation procedures. Forecast values of D can be found by inputing values for P, A, I and L.

The advantages of causal models are that they can provide forecasts for a longer time period than time series techniques, and force management to take account of cause and effect in their actions. The disadvantages of causal models relate to their expense and the difficulties of their construction. It is not easy to identify all the factors or gather data about them. Further, as circumstances change, the model will require updating and even then it will not cope with sudden shocks, e.g. VAT increases on the demand for toys.

Qualitative approaches

Time series and causal models require numeric data as might be available in examining economic and competitive trends. Political, social and technological trends do not provide data in this form and hence qualitative techniques have been developed. Although qualitative approaches are primarily aimed at non-numeric areas, they can be applied in determining trends in economic and competitive fields, especially when the situation is volatile.

In essence all qualitative techniques are formalizations of human judgement. Three major techniques exist: scenarios, delphi and trend extrapolation. Scenarios are a creative exercise that take as a starting point the naive extrapolation of data. Alternatives to the observed trend are hypothesized and their likelihood assessed. Finally the impact of the future outcomes on current planning objectives and strategies is determined, along with the actions necessary to achieve a preferred goal. The delphi approach uses a panel of experts to forecast future events or developments through a series of questionnaires. The process is overseen by a coordinator, who analyses the answers, asks supplementary questions and synthesizes the results. Experts are usually drawn from both inside and outside the organization and are kept unaware of each other's answers. The advantage of delphi is that it stimulates creative thinking and arrives at a consensus that is not dominated by any group member. Trend extrapolation is a cruder approach whereby the feasibility of trends continuing is assessed by experts with a view to arriving at an opinion on the limits applying. For example, a petrol company might determine the demand for petrol in the future by extrapolating improving miles per gallon in the light of technological constraints.

Marketing methods

As well as the theoretical forecasting models, there are field-tested techniques developed in the marketing and market research fields. Examples of these include comparative studies, leading indicators and experimental market research. Comparative studies base forecasts upon the performance of a similar venture. Thus a company wishing to assess the demand pattern for a new product would study the launch of comparable products. Leading indicators is akin to causal models but concentrates on the short run. The system depends upon identifying events which are precursors of others: for example, wage increases to a group which set the pace for the whole wage round or building industry activity used as an indicator of the buoyancy in the business sector. Experimental market research uses such techniques as test marketing, advertising, weighting and price adjustment. While there are rarely true experiments, much useful data is collected and forecasts determined from their analysis. Probably in practice it is most useful in establishing causal relationships which can be used in more complex models.

In the last analysis the results of all the techniques require appraisal by experienced staff, but a problem arises as to which techniques should provide information for this stage. No simple answer exists but some guidelines can be provided:

1   Define the degree of accuracy required. Is only a close approximation needed or is the forecast critical, with a direct impact on a number of decisions?
2   The complexity of technique used should match the abilities of forecasting staff. Complex models need to be maintained and output requires skilled interpretation. Without staff of the correct calibre these techniques should be avoided.
3   Users' reaction to forecasts and changes in forecasts should be monitored. Regular and detailed forecasts are only justified if management reacts correctly to them. In many organizations reaction is limited to budgeting and individual decisions. Under such circumstances complex methods may not be justified.
4   Forecasts should be obtained in a cost-effective manner – evaluating the benefits of more costly methods and justifying the increased expenditure is a vital procedure.
5   Forecasting methods must match speed and frequency requirements. For example, forecasts needed today cannot await the construction of a causal model nor is there justification for building a complex causal model and using it only once.

Financial forecasting

From the general overview of business forecasting the emphasis of the chapter moves to the forecasting requirements of the finance function.

Hodson (1984) identified thirteen areas for a treasurer to watch in forecasting. Table 2.1 analyses these into long-run, essentially strategic level forecasts; medium-run, tactical level forecasts; and short-run operational forecasts. Obviously classifications like these are to some extent arbitrary, but readers should gain an appreciation of the elements to take into account.

The format used will vary from purpose to purpose, but it will generally comprise a modified set of the financial accounts, together with key ratios, e.g. gearing for debt capacity and debt: equity ratio for dividend and equity policies. The most intricate part of the process arises from ensuring that the forecasts for different purposes and time scales are consistent with each other. For example, resource allocation and investment strategy will share common forecast variables and impact upon the development of a commercial and financial strategy.

Uncertainty and financial forecasting

So far the approach to forecasting has been deterministic, with each variable having a single value arrived at through human experts subjectively assessing a range of feasible values based upon changing assumptions. An alternative to this is to adopt a probabilistic approach and formally acknowledge that there is a range of values for any particular variable. Three techniques may be identified: sensitivity analysis, scenarios and operational research/statistical methods. Sensitivity analysis acknowledges uncertainty and seeks to identify the impact of changes of one variable upon another. Suppose the cash flow from an overseas subsidiary (C) was identified as being dependent upon market size in the country (M), the subsidiary's market share (S), the exchange rate between the subsidiary's currency, slots, and sterling (E) and the proportion of turnover available as remittable cash flow (P).

$$C = P \left(\frac{M \times (S/100)}{E} \right)$$

If an analysis shows M = 50 million slots
S = 50 per cent
E = 10 slots to £
P = 10 per cent
C can be forecast at £250,000.

Sensitivity analysis explores the forecast by varying key variables in the model, one at a time, by fixed percentages to identify the most critical variable in determining cash flow. Since fixed percentage changes to market and market share will have identical impact Table 2.2 shows them as one variable, with the exchange rate as the other and 5 per cent variations.

Table 2.1   Financial forecasting areas analysed by time period

Finance function	Purpose	Approximate time span	Typical intervals
Long run			
1 Development of commercial and financial strategy	Financial framework, financial targets and financial expression of the strategic plan	3–10 years	1 year
2 Debt capacity	Maximize amount safely borrowable under worst likely circumstances	3–10 years	1 year
3(a) Debt policy	Determine medium- and long-term borrowing requirements	3–10 years	1 year
4 Equity policy	Maintain debt policy	3–10 years	1 year
5 Resource allocation	Identify group cash requirements and availability	3–5 years	1 year
6 Dividend policy	Determine medium-term earnings per share cash flow patterns and debt to equity ratio	3–5 years	1 year
7(a) Investment strategy	Determine level and term of cash available	3–5 years	1 year
8(a) Currency strategy	Determine future currency positions	3–5 years	1 year
9 Tax strategy	Determine potential medium-term tax positions	3–10 years	1 year
10 Investment appraisal	Determine project viability	3–10 years	1 year
Medium run			
3(b) Debt policy	Determine short-term borrowing requirements	1 month–3 years	1 month
7(b) Investment strategy	Determine the level and term of cash availability in the medium term	1 month–3 years	1 month
8(b) Currency risk strategy	Determine currency positions in the medium term	3 months–3 years	1 month
11 Defence	Determine current and future years' profitability	1–2 years	1 year

Table 2.1 continued

Finance function	Purpose	Approximate time span	Typical intervals
12 Budgeting	Provide financial standards against which to measure performance	1 month– 3 years	1 month
Short run			
3(c) Debt management	Determine daily borrowing requirements	1 week– 1 month	1 day
7(c) Investment management	Determine daily level and term of cash availability	1 week– 1 month	1 day
8(c) Currency management	Determine current position	1 week– 1 month	1 day– 1 week
13 Working capital	Determine short-term cash movements	1 week– 3 months	1 day– 1 week

Adapted with the permission of Professional Publishing Limited from *Corporate Finance and Treasury Management*, Gee & Co., 1984.

Table 2.2 Sensitivity analysis – an example

	Sensitivity of cash flows to % changes	
% Change	Market/market share £000s	Exchange rate £000s
+20	300	208.3
+15	287.5	217.4
+10	275	227.3
+ 5	262.5	238.1
0	250	250
− 5	237.5	263.2
−10	225	277.8
−15	212.5	294.1
−20	200	312.5

Since exchange rate changes cause the greatest fluctuation in cash flow – from 208.3 to 312.5 – a percentage inaccuracy in forecasting exchange rate has a slightly greater impact than the same percentage deviation in market or market share. Obviously attention should be directed to variables with the most impact.

Scenarios rely upon the identification, as in sensitivity analysis, of key variables and the range of values which may be expected for them. Thus in the above example exchange rates may be identified as the key variable and a range of 9–11 slots per pound sterling deemed the range.

Forecasts would be prepared for the situation being 9, 10 and 11 slots to the pound sterling respectively and each scenario logically integrated into separate plans.

Operational research and statistical methods require uncertainty to be objectively assessed in terms of probability. This can lead either to an expected value or be an input to a Monte Carlo Simulation approach. Suppose sales are assessed:

£	*Likelihood*
1,000,000	0.2
1,100,000	0.3
1,200,000	0.4
1,300,000	0.1

The expected value of £1,140,000 is calculated by multiplying each value by the associated probability and summing the outcomes. This method helps forecasters assess a likely outcome systematically. A Monte Carlo Simulation approach defines probability distributions for the variables in the model. Suppose in the example of the cash-flow forecast:

Market was defined as a continuous distribution with 45 million slots (likelihood 2), 50 million slots (likelihood 3) and 52 million slots (likelihood 1); market share as a normal distribution mean 50 per cent and standard deviation 5 per cent; and exchange rate as a continuous distribution with a rate of 9 (likelihood 2), 10 (likelihood 5) and 11 (likelihood 3).

Figure 2.4 shows the outcome of 1,000 simulations using the RISK package available from Thorncroft Manor Services, Dorking Road, Leatherhead KT22 8JB.

From the output it can be seen the cash flow will almost certainly exceed £200,000, with the mean value arising from simulations being £242,000. However, the standard deviation of almost £30,000 suggests significant volatility in outcomes.

The greatest value of the techniques described arises from forcing forecasters to confront the uncertainties built into their estimates in a formal way. Nothing can remove the uncertainty of the future, but a proper consideration of the interrelationships and an assessment of a forecast's reliability can only strengthen the planning and decision-making processes.

Forecasting in practice

As with any management procedure, forecasting requires careful planning coordination and control to ensure that forecasts are available as required, are based upon consistent assumptions and are compatible with each other. In practice there are six key stages:

1   Establishing the objective of the forecast – the objective in terms of planning or decision-making use must be clearly specified in order that time horizons and the required degree of accuracy can be determined.
2   Identifying dependencies – forecasts of variables will often be based upon the behaviour of other variables. These explicit and implicit relationships must be specified and causal models established.
3   Identifying sources – once dependencies are established information will be required on the value of variables in any forecasting model. These sources may either be internal to the firm or come from outside.
4   Selecting the appropriate technique or techniques (see pp. 23–6 for the techniques available). The forecaster must select a technique which is compatible with the needs of the forecast.
5   Vetting the output – output from forecasting techniques should not be blindly believed but subjected to reasonableness tests by available experts.
6   Monitoring the performance of forecasters – as part of a continuing process it is important that actual results are compared with forecasts and the reasons for forecasting differences examined. This process should provide for the refinement of forecasting models to enable them to be responsive to environmental dynamics.

The work of forecasters has been greatly assisted by advances in computing. 'Forecasting techniques' (pp. 23–6) indicates that many techniques rely upon repetitive mathematical work of the type that is ideally suited to computerization. Forecasting packaged software is available for most hardware and is a feature in many of the financial modelling packages (for example, FCS–EPS offers curve fitting, moving averages, exponential smoothing, Trigg adaptive smoothing, seasonal analysis and other forecasting techniques). Further, it is feasible to write basic forecasting techniques using spreadsheets and financial modelling software.

Sources of information

Information for forecasts will be gleaned from internal and external sources. Internal sources will comprise information obtained either from the management information system, where the requirement was foreseen, or on an ad hoc basis if it was not. In larger organizations, given increased computer power, the advent of database systems and query languages, it should not be too costly or time-consuming to generate data requirements. However, in smaller organizations where information systems are rudimentary the cost of information and the timescale in which it will be available may well dictate the forecasting approach. For instance, a forecasting model which builds on the last 5 years' sales data analysed by product may well be modified to be based upon 1 year's data if obtaining it requires lengthy analysis.

Figure 2.4 Monte Carlo simulation – an example

No. of simulations:	1000
Minimum value:	159495.5221
Maximum value:	352114.5737
Mean:	242027.7635
Standard deviation:	29752.8965

+ or −   1844.1036
(95% Confidence level)

Probability of exceeding value:

90.0%	205437.7073
75.0%	221094.8494
50.0%	239554.3004
25.0%	260899.3050
10.0%	282833.4280

```
*********
*  NCF  *
*********
```

Cash flow

Values in thousands	0%	10%	20%	30%	40%	50%	
140.000	. 0	.	.	.	.	.	0%
160.000	. <0	.	.	.	.	.	1%
180.000	====<0	.	.	.	.	.	6%
200.000	================<=0>	.	.	.	.	.	17%
220.000	==========================<=0.>	.	.	.	.	.	28%
240.000	=====================<==0.>	.	.	.	.	.	23%
260.000	===============<==0 >	.	.	.	.	.	15%
280.000	=======<=0 >	.	.	.	.	.	8%
300.000	==0>	.	.	.	.	.	2%
320.000	<0	.	.	.	.	.	1%
340.000	0	.	.	.	.	.	0%
360.000	.	.	.	.	.	.	0%
	0%	10%	20%	30%	40%	50%	

Probability distribution derived from 1000 simulations

##########
* NCF *
##########

Cash flow

-----------Chance of not exceeding----------→

Values in thousands	Cash flow	0%	20%	40%	60%	80%	100%	
130.000	100%[1]	0						0%[2]
150.000	100%	0						0%
170.000	99%	0						1%
190.000	94%	0)						6%
210.000	77%		(0					23%
230.000	49%			(0)				51%
250.000	26%				(0)			74%
270.000	11%					(0)		89%
290.000	3%						0)	97%
310.000	1%						0)	99%
330.000	0%						0	100%
350.000	0%						0	100%

100%	80%	60%	40%	20%	0%

-----------Chance of exceeding-----------

Probability distribution derived from 1000 simulations

1 Probability of exceeding the value expressed as a percentage.
2 Probability of not exceeding the value expressed as a percentage.

External sources can be classified into three main areas: (i) government, (ii) outside agencies, and (iii) trade associations.

Government

The government through the Government Statistical Service provides an array of economic and social statistics. An annual guide entitled *Government Statistics – A Brief Guide to Sources* covers all publications, analysing them into general digests, the economy, defence, external trade, transport distribution and other services, society, environment and overseas aid categories. Another annual overview publication is *Key Data*. First produced in 1986, this book aims to provide basic statistics across a wide range of economic and social fields as an introduction to other more detailed sources. Examples of these more detailed sources which might be of interest to forecasters in the business context include:

Economic trends
1 *UK National Accounts* (Blue Book) – published annually with detailed estimates of national production, income and expenditure.
2 *Economic Trends* – published monthly with commentary and a range of statistics aimed at providing a broad background to trends in the UK economy.
3 *British Business* – a weekly digest of economic and trade data published by the Department of Trade and Industry. Subjects covered extend from international comparisons of economic indices through export sales ratios to consumer credit.
4 *Economic Progress Report* – published by the Treasury with articles on government economic policy and Treasury assessments of the economic situation.
5 *Business Monitors* – produced for various industries, services and distributive trades. They contain statistics appropriate to the sector, published at varying intervals. Titles include *Price Index Numbers for Current Cost Accounting* (monthly), *Insurance Business Statistics* (annually), *Classified List of Manufacturing Businesses and Minerals*.
6 *Overseas Trade Statistics of the United Kingdom* – published monthly with detailed statistics of exports and imports through the year.

Social trends
1 *Family Expenditure Survey* – an annual edition with income and expenditure analysed in great detail, including some by region.
2 *Survey of Personal Incomes* – produced annually with analyses of taxable income and income tax by range, source, sex and marital status.
3 *Population Projections* – covers the next 70 years on a biennial basis.
4 *General Household Survey* – a continuous survey of households relating to a wide range of social and socio-economic policy areas on an annual basis.

5 *New Earnings Survey* – relates to earnings of employees by industry, occupation and region. Issued in six parts between October and February each year.
6 *Social Trends* – a selection of statistics plus special interest area studies.

Outside agencies

Various outside agencies provided statistics and forecasts as part of an information service. In addition they will provide research expertise to generate forecasts and other information in areas specific to an individual organization. Examples of these agencies and their publications are:

1 The Economist Intelligence Unit, whose publications include: *Marketing in Europe*, covering a wide range of products and countries; and *Multinational Business*, with news and analysis of multinational companies and their activities. These two publications cover economic and competitive trends respectively.
2 The Henley Centre for Forecasting, which specializes in forecasts of economic and social trends. For example, *Framework Forecasts* for the UK and other countries, *Forecasts of Exchange Data Movements Planning Consumer Markets*, and *Planning for Social Change*.
3 Data Stream is an online information service providing general stock market and economic trend information, plus competitive trend data in the form of accounts for some 14,000 quoted and 10,000 unquoted companies.
4 Extel provides a similar service to Datastream but covers only 3,000 companies. Data provided by Extel in the form of weekly tapes or floppy disks is susceptible to further processing and analysis by a company's own computer.
5 Financial Times Business Information Limited offers a service of information on some 60,000 companies, based upon accounts, cuttings and other published material. This is an ideal source for monitoring competitive trends.
6 McCarthy Information Services supplies a cuttings service covering UK and overseas companies.
7 Income Data Services Limited produces an annual directory of salary comparisons.
8 The International Monetary Fund publishes *International Financial Statistics* and *Balance of Payments Statistics* for a range of countries on a monthly basis.
9 The World Bank produces *World Development Report* and World Debt Tables, covering socio-economic aspects of a number of countries.

The examples given do not mention political or technological trend information specifically. Knowledge of the former can be gained from political intelligence services, newspaper and periodical comments, manifestos and opinion polls; while the latter may be gleaned through technological intelligence services, technological market research and information upon competitors' developments.

Trade associations

Most industry groupings have a trade association to represent their collective interests with government and promote the image of the generic product with customers. Often as part of this activity trade associations will collect data and offer forecasts and statistical information to members. Lists of trade associations are provided in *Henderson's Directory of British Trade Associations*. Examples of publications include:

1 Building industry – *Building, Construction Trends* and *Housing Statistics*.
2 Machine tools – *Machine Tool Review* and *Machine Tool Engineering*.
3 Tobacco – *Tobacco Intelligence* and *World Tobacco*.

Summary

The success of an organization's decision-making and planning activities depends upon the reliability of forecasts. This chapter has examined forecasting in the financial management context and overviewed the increased input from management scientists in determining a rigorous framework for this esoteric art.

However well developed models and statistical procedures become, output must always be subjected to scrutiny for reasonableness from the available pool of human experts. These techniques can assist with judgements on the future but do not remove the final responsibility from those planning and making decisions.

References

Argenti, J., *Practical Corporate Planning*, George Allen and Unwin, 1980.
Hodson, D., 'Internal Organisation', in *Corporate Finance & Treasury Management*, Gee & Co., 1984.

Further reading

OVERVIEW ARTICLES
Hodson, D., 'Forecasting is Essential to Decision-making', *The Treasurer*, September 1983.
Sparkes, J. R. and McHugh, A. R., 'Forecasting Techniques in British Industry', *Journal of Forecasting*, January/March 1984.

RELEVANT ARTICLES

Collier, P. A. and Stacey, R. J., 'Business Forecasting Techniques', in *Practical Financial Management*, Gee & Co., in association with the Institute of Chartered Accountants in England and Wales, 1983.

Goyal, S. K. *et al.*, 'How to Choose Forecasting Software', *Journal of Business Forecasting (USA)*, Summer 1983.

Schulty, R. L., 'The Implementation of Forecasting Models', *Journal of Forecasting*, January/March, 1984.

RELEVANT BOOKS

Firth, M., *Forecasting Methods in Business and Management*. Edward Arnold, 1977.

Granger, C. W., *Forecasting in Business and Economics*, Academic Press, New York, 1980.

Morrell, J., *A Short Guide to Business Forecasting*, The Henley Centre for Forecasting, 1976.

3 External influences on performance

Introduction

Readers should have little difficulty in compiling a list of factors external to an organization which impact upon its performance. Examples include a declining or growing economy, a shrinking or expanding market, high wage costs, competition from cheap imports, adverse or favourable exchange rate movements, tax changes, and import restrictions. Further, rapid travel and ease of communications have led businesses to seek maximum economies of scale through organizing and financing their operations on a worldwide basis. Therefore, for multinational groups, external influences encompass the interaction of these factors on a global scale.

This chapter is not a definitive examination of the multiplicity of interacting factors which affect an organization's performance. Rather, it has the more modest aim of highlighting significant areas to reinforce the message in Chapter 2, that financial decisions cannot be taken without considering the firm's environment. More specifically it covers, from a UK viewpoint, factors in the environment which directly impact upon the decisions made by the finance function. Matters specifically discussed include the UK economy and government policies, government industrial policy, exchange control and taxation.

The UK economy and government policies

Governments have a wide variety of economic policy objectives, including high growth and employment and low inflation. To achieve these, governments can adopt a number of different policy tools, e.g. budgetary and monetary measures, and direct controls over prices, wages and cash spending in the public sector.

Broadly UK government policies have concentrated upon managing demand either through budgetary policies, which adjust the levels of public expenditure and taxation, or monetary policies, aimed at regulating the cost and availability of finance. Up to the 1970s demand management was effected through budgetary policies, which attempted to increase demand in order to encourage economic growth and subsequently reduce unemployment. This approach assumed that the impact of increased demand was not dissipated through imports and that poor economic growth was not related to supply-side phenomena, which may be worsened by crude manipulations of aggregate demand. For example, the 1985 White Paper *Employment: The Challenge for the Nation* proposed that unemployment was caused by a failure of the jobs market rather than a lack of demand.

Following high inflation in the 1970s, greater emphasis was placed on monetary policy, and, in particular, a growing importance was attached to the money stock in the UK. Monetary policy since this period has been designed to restrain inflation by limiting demand in the economy and influencing expectations as to future inflation. However, it is important to recognize that the impact of monetary policy is long-run and that the policy tool is not suited to offsetting short-run variations in demand. Since 1976 it has been common practice to set monetary targets on an annual basis in order to reduce the rate of growth in the money supply gradually, and since 1980 UK monetary and budgetary policies have been linked in the Medium Term Financial Strategy (MTFS).

The MTFS sets targets for growth in the money supply, which, in turn, have implications for the public sector borrowing requirement (PSBR). Since the PSBR represents government borrowing requirements arising from public expenditure exceeding tax revenues, this links directly with budgetary policy (see Chapters 19 and 20).

In practice, the main interests for the finance function of an organization will lie in the level of interest and exchange rates in the economy. Interest rates are determined by internal and external factors. Within the economy, interest rates depend upon the supply of and demand for money. Crucial within this equation is government activity in respect of the size and method of funding of the PSBR. The PSBR can be funded by borrowing either from the banking system, including the Bank of England, or the private non-bank sector through the issue of gilt-edged securities (gilts) and treasury bills by the Bank of England or national savings instruments. When the government borrows from the banking sector, the money stock increases, thereby creating inflationary pressures. However, the alternative of raising funds from the non-bank private sector will put upward pressure on interest rates to persuade investors to hold a higher stock of public sector debt. Consequently, to lessen pressures on inflation and interest rates, in recent years the government has attempted to reduce the PSBR.

Externally the UK monetary system is but one component in the world monetary system. Therefore domestic interest rates must be set in line with the interest rates in other countries. In particular, since 1979, interest rate management has played an increasingly important role in maintaining the sterling exchange rate at predetermined levels. If sterling is too high, interest rates are lowered in order to encourage international investors to move their funds out of sterling, thereby increasing the supply of sterling and reducing the exchange rate, and vice versa if sterling is too low. In general, over the last few years, UK interest rates have been volatile and high in real terms. With respect to the finance function, this has severely restricted the ability of firms to raise medium / long-term fixed interest finance in the UK and encouraged them either to seek short-term funding or go abroad and borrow in the medium / longer-term in markets where interest rates are sufficiently stable to make funds of this nature available.

In 1972 the UK abandoned fixed exchange rates and allowed sterling to float, with the rate being set by supply and demand in the currency markets. This is not to say that the government abdicated all responsibility for the exchange rate but only to imply that the emphasis switched from defending a fixed position to managing supply and demand for the currency. The main techniques that have been used to achieve this are intervention by the Bank of England, using reserves to buy sterling when it is weaker and sell when it is stronger than government policy dictates, controlling flows directly through exchange controls (abolished in 1979), interest rate changes to encourage or discourage sterling investments, control of the balance of payments situation, and prudent economic policies to create 'confidence' in the currency.

Throughout the 1980s sterling has been linked with oil prices, and as these have been volatile, so has sterling. The government policy towards the exchange rate has been to allow sterling to respond to these changes but to attempt to smooth the progress towards a new equilibrium rate. The exact impact of appreciation and depreciation of a currency upon an economy is difficult to determine. In general, when sterling appreciates, imported goods become cheaper, which reduces inflationary pressures and assists the competitiveness of firms whose products have a high proportion of imported raw materials or components. Against this, imported goods being cheaper stiffens competition, thereby reducing margins in the domestic market, while exports become more expensive and therefore less competitive abroad. A currency depreciation will have the opposite effects. From the view of the performance of individual firms within the UK economy the most worrying aspect of the situation is the volatility, which, although coverable in the short run, presents serious problems for medium and long-term planning and decision-making: for example, in deciding whether to fund part of the organization's capital requirements through long or medium-run currency borrowings or whether to set up a manufacturing location abroad or export from the UK.

Beyond concern with interest rates and exchange rates, the main influence on the performance of the firm relates to the general economic climate in the domestic and perhaps world markets. Periods of growth may expand demand for a firm's products, while depressions increase competitive pressures and impact adversely upon a firm's financial results.

Government industrial policy

In the 5 years to 1986 government industrial policy in the UK has concentrated upon increasing the role of market forces. This has been achieved through the relaxation of the referral rules in mergers; the privatization of profitable nationalized concerns; amendments to the tax system, as with the new capital allowance system, which removes artificial incentives to invest in plant and machinery; and a switch in the goals of government assistance away from regional preference towards schemes supporting enterprise, especially in small businesses.

From the standpoint of the finance function the main impact of this strategy has been to cause a revision of investment plans depending upon tax concessions or grants. Readers may wish to contrast this approach with the alternative interventionist strategy. Under such a regime there would be active industrial planning with priorities established and resources mobilized in accordance with them. The finance function's scope for free operation would be curtailed and government dictates and incentives would be key elements in decision-making.

Of the main aspects of government industrial policy, competition and fair trading are discussed in Chapter 17 and taxation later in this chapter (pp. 45–7). Therefore this section concentrates upon government assistance. This is a fast changing area and therefore readers should be prepared to check and ensure that the information given is still current. A good source for such information is the *Guide to Industrial Support* published biannually by the Department of Trade and Industry. Assistance can be categorized into six main areas: investment support, small firms, innovation programmes, advisory services, export promotion, and free ports. An outline of each follows.

Investment support

Investment support is provided in accordance with the Industrial Development Act 1982. Section 8 covers substantial internationally mobile manufacturing projects, which the government wishes to attract to the UK in order to create employment and growth – for example, the Nissan car plant in Tyne and Wear. Section 7 of the Act covers grants to assisted areas through regional development grants. To qualify, projects must create extra jobs and conform with laid down criteria covering expansion of capacity, a change in processes or a change of product. Qualifying activities are widely defined and encompass not only manufacturing but service functions like banking, insurance and business services. While regional assistance might make good social sense, there are several examples, like Chrysler's Lynwood plant in Scotland and the aluminium smelting works in Anglesey, to show that the jobs may only be short-run and prove very expensive. It is difficult for grants alone to overcome geographical disadvantages, especially if the communications network and skilled workforce are missing.

Small firms

There are various small-firm support schemes, with the intention of providing readily available sources of finance to new businesses or existing undertakings wishing to expand. In the 6 years since the venture capital scheme began, a thriving venture capital industry has been created. The scheme encourages the provision of funds by allowing individuals and investment companies who invest in unquoted shares to offset any losses incurred against their income as opposed to it being only available against capital gains. A more generous scheme in the same vein is the business expansion scheme, which also applies to unquoted securities. Under its provisions individuals, not companies, who invest in the unquoted shares of one or more companies engaged in qualifying activities can obtain relief for the investment at their highest rate of personal tax up to an agreed maximum. Obviously there are conditions as to the size of interest in any one company (not greater than 30 per cent), the duration of the investment (minimum 5 years) and the status of the investor (paid directors excluded), but the measure encourages funds for enterprise.

Another form of financial assistance to small firms is the loan guarantee scheme, which enables businesses to obtain loans from participating financial institutions under an arrangement whereby repayment of an agreed portion is guaranteed for the payment of a quarterly premium. The scheme is aimed at encouraging loans to riskier ventures. Finally, small firms are supported by the small firms advisory service and the small firms technical enquiry service, which provide advice of which at least a portion is free.

Innovation programmes

Innovation programmes within the UK have traditionally favoured the defence field. Nevertheless the government has significant schemes in the commercial field – for example, Alvey, covering microelectronics and information technology, computer-aided design / computer-aided manufacture (CAD/CAM) schemes and grants to assist with the application of flexible manufacturing systems.

Advisory services

Advisory services fall into two categories. First, there is the provision of information from services as diverse as the British Standards Institution, which has data on UK, international and individual countries' standards, and IRS–Dial tech, which provides scientific and technical research summaries from a computer database. Second, assistance in the form of free or assisted consultancy is available for specific projects in such areas as heat recovery, corrosion and manufacturing techniques.

Export promotion

Assistance to promote exports is given through two bodies: British Overseas Trade Board (BOTB) and the Export Credit Guarantees Department (ECGD). The BOTB provides an expert intelligence service through its links with commercial attachés at British Embassies and High Commissions. It also has funds to assist with the costs of export market research and the setting up of overseas sales organizations. ECGD has two main functions. It covers the risk that exporters may not receive payment for the goods supplied and provides fixed interest loans to finance the sale of exports.

Free ports

Finally, to remove red tape and encourage exports, the government designated areas in a number of cities (Prestwick, Liverpool, Birmingham, Belfast, Cardiff and Southampton) as free ports. In these areas goods can be imported from outside the European Economic Community (EEC), worked upon and exported to outside the EEC without any customs duties or taxes being payable. The finance function must actively appraise the assistance available from these sources in determining the location, nature and funding of investments.

Exchange controls

Within the ambit of the finance function an important element in the regulatory framework is whether the country in which the group is based or countries where there are subsidiaries, associates or other business interests operate exchange controls. The regulations are imposed by sovereign states with the objective of conserving the nation's gold and currency reserves and improving the balance of payments position. In essence, exchange controls restrict the rights of residents and non-residents in the host country to (i) acquire, hold or dispose of assets or liabilities, either denominated in foreign currency or situated abroad; and (ii) enter into transactions which affect the earning, holding and spending of foreign currency.

Exchange controls are not universal. Countries like the UK, the USA, Canada and West Germany currently permit full convertibility of their currencies, while others operate limited systems such as partial convertibility, which restricts the actions of residents but allows non-residents to convert their currency freely. It is also possible to have the effects attributed to exchange controls without imposing actual exchange controls. For example, if a currency is strong, the taxation of domestic currency deposits held by non-residents can be penal, thus damping down demand for the currency. In contrast, if the currency is weak, the attractiveness of overseas investments can be reduced by special levies or other measures.

For the finance function of a multi-national the impact of exchange controls has two distinct facets: domestic controls and those imposed by governments abroad. The former may insist on the repatriation of investments and profits from overseas, restrict new and supplementary investments, hamper routine payments of pensions, dividends, salaries, fees and royalties to non-residents and impede the importation of goods and services. The latter will impact upon the availability of local funding, the remittance of profits, payment for goods and services and the liquidation and remittance of invested funds.

Obviously the incentive to invest in overseas countries where long-run exchange controls are expected is minimal. Nevertheless, organizations may still wish to make or maintain investments even in territories where they may be caught by existing or newly imposed regulations. Therefore much effort has been devoted towards the legal circumvention of these regulations. Equally governments have done their best to counter such circumventions.

Avoidance techniques fall into two categories: those which enable overseas investments to be funded without introducing funds directly into the country and those which seek to manoeuvre profits into countries without repatriation restrictions. The main techniques for the former are currency swaps and parallel loans. Currency swaps occur when two companies agree to sell each other currency at the spot rate, with an undertaking to reverse the transaction after a specific time. Parallel loans occur when parties make simultaneous and equal loans to each other's foreign subsidiaries. Both are discussed further in Chapter 13 (pp. 288–9). Profit location systems embrace such techniques as transfer pricing, consultancy and royalty payments, invoicing management and spending to group benefit. Transfer pricing works through transactions between group companies. Those in controlled areas buy supplies at high prices and sell their products at low prices when dealing with unrestricted group companies. Consultancy and royalty payments operate in a similar manner to create low profits through high charges. Invoicing management can also reduce profits. If a sharp depreciation of the restricted currency is forecast, it can bill all its sales to group companies in the local currency and provide exchange profits to the purchasers when payments are made, or alternatively group companies supplying could invoice in their own currencies, giving the restricted subsidiary the exchange loss. Spending to group benefit uses blocked funds for research and development, conferences and other expenditure of use to the group.

Therefore exchange controls provide the finance function with opportunities to improve performance through careful planning.

Taxation

As well as being a key element in government fiscal policy, taxation has important implications for financial management and the performance of the organization. At the obvious level taxes on the products of the firm, such as value added tax, car tax and other duties, have a direct effect on consumer demand; while taxes on the income of the organization will impact upon financial decisions and cause the management to adopt tax-avoidance strategies.

In the UK the worldwide profits and capital gains of companies and unincorporated bodies, except partnerships, are subject to corporation tax. Profits for this purpose are calculated by reference to income-tax schedules and principles, while capital gains are assessed under the Capital Gains Taxes Act 1979. In order that the tax charge on capital gains is at the capital gains rate rather than the corporation tax rate (1986–7 30 per cent and 35 per cent full rate respectively) an abatement of one-seventh of the gain (35 − 30/35) is granted. Where payments or receipts have income tax deducted at source, gross amounts are used on the corporation tax computation, with the income-tax element accounted for in arriving at any amount due.

The effects of this regime are numerous. With respect to the performance of the organization's finance function, the discussion can centre upon three areas: funding and distribution from retained profits, the preference for debt finance, and tax planning. Considering each in turn, first, the amount of corporation tax payable by organizations will directly impact upon the funds available from retained earnings for investment or distribution. Ostensibly in the UK this has come down, with the full rate in the 4 years up to financial year 1986–7 falling from 52 per cent to 35 per cent. However, linked with the rate is the level of deductions to reduce the profits that are taxable. At the same time as rates fell, capital allowances, which replace depreciation in tax computations, were drastically cut. The first year allowances at rates up to 100 per cent of expenditure were abolished and replaced by a uniform writing-down allowance on a reducing balance system. Not only did this diminish the incentive for firms to invest in plant and machinery but it also led to industrial companies paying more corporation tax and in consequence reducing retained earnings available to fund investments. Second, the tax system provides an incentive for firms to raise finance from debt rather than equity. This arises because loan interest is deductable in arriving at profits subject to corporation tax, whereas dividends are not. Finally tax planning offers opportunities, through the coordination of tax affairs, especially within groups, to reduce the tax paid. In particular, advantageous elections are available, provided certain conditions are met, to allow the transfer of trades, losses and assets between group companies or permit inter-group interest and dividend payments to be made without the deduction of tax.

Another cash flow benefit, which, following the 1987 Finance Act, will only last until 1990, when corporation tax due dates will have been standardized, arises from the management of mainstream and advanced corporation tax (ACT) payment dates. For the mainstream liability, payment is due 9 months after the accounting period unless the company was trading before April 1965, when pre-existing intervals, which could be up to 21 months, remain. Therefore groups can lengthen the interval to payment of mainstream liability by concentrating profitable activities and manipulating group relief to accumulate mainstream liability in companies with the longest payment interval. Similarly ACT payments can be arranged through elections permitting ACT to be moved within the group in order to minimize the interval between its payment and recovery.

A further ACT avoidance measure is the use of scrip dividends, whereby shareholders are given the option of either a cash dividend or a scrip dividend of shares to the same value. No ACT is due from the paying company for scrip dividends, giving a cash-flow saving to the extent that the scrip option is adopted. Against any gains must be offset increased administration charges (registration, etc.).

For a group with overseas operations further planning opportunities exist. These relate to the organizational set-up and the extent to which overseas taxes can be offset against UK liability. The main choices of organization for overseas operations are overseas resident subsidiary and branch. The taxation treatment is very different. In the former case, defined as when control and management are abroad, no UK tax becomes payable until profits are remitted (but note there is no relief for losses against UK income either), while in the case of branches profits and losses form part of the results of the UK company and are fully liable to UK taxation. However, both branches and overseas subsidiaries will be liable to tax in the location abroad. In effect they are double-taxed.

Normally relief to mitigate this can be obtained through double-taxation agreements, whereby tax paid abroad can be offset against UK liability on the same income up to the limit of the UK tax due. The UK has an extensive network of reciprocal agreements covering over eighty countries, and, further, if no agreement exists, the UK grants unilateral relief. Overseas factors can influence performance and financial decisions through the setting up of holding companies in countries like Switzerland and Holland, which have the best network of double tax agreements; the manipulation of dividends from overseas subsidiaries; and the shifting of profits into tax-favourable locations around the globe by transfer pricing, consignment sales and other techniques.

As well as corporate implications, taxation has consequences for parties external to the firm, who in turn by their actions have an impact upon the organization's performance. For example, personal tax levels will affect disposable incomes. Therefore it is argued that low levels of taxation increase the demand for a firm's products and also provide individuals with more funds to invest. Thus firms benefit from increased sales and more widely available finance. A more certain argument is that differentials between capital gains and income taxes will change investor preferences with respect to dividends versus reinvestment through retained earnings. High taxes on income and low taxes on capital gains might, it could be argued, lead to investors foregoing dividends in order to benefit from an appreciation in the value of the share. This question will be examined further in Chapter 7, but, either way, personal taxation has fairly clear implications for dividend policy.

Summary

As was explained at the outset, this chapter has concentrated upon narrow aspects of a wide subject area. At this point readers should consider what has been omitted. Obvious examples would be the areas of consumerism, environmental issues, employment regulations and the legislative framework. All these have implications for a firm's performance, even if the impact is somewhat removed from the area of financial management.

Within the UK consumerism has developed two distinct aspects, namely the regulation of consumer/trader relations and the broader issue of monopoly power and restrictive practices. A considerable volume of legislation exists both from UK government and EEC sources (for example, see the EEC Directive on Product Liability approved by the Council of Ministers in July 1985) and the whole area is covered by the Office of Fair Trading. As regards environmental issues the impact upon the firm's performance arises from the enforcement of strict planning and pollution controls by government bodies. Employment legislation covering employer/employee relations is another area affecting businesses, especially as regards provisions on minimum wages, equal opportunities and racial equality. Finally, businesses must operate within the law and a wide range of legislation from the Companies Act to the Data Protection Act has implications for a firm's financial results.

The chapter has examined only those areas which directly impact upon the finance function. Later chapters will refer to them in examining decisions made by financial managers.

Further reading

Artes, M. J. (ed.), *Priest and Coppock's The UK Economy – A Manual of Applied Economics* (11th edition), Weidenfeld & Nicolson, 1986.
Guide to Industrial Support, published twice yearly by British Business, Department of Trade and Industry.
Parker, A., *Exchange Control*, Jordan & Sons, 1978.

Part Two

Measuring Performance

4 Ratio analysis

Introduction

Many groups outside a business enterprise – investor, creditors, employees, trade unions, government and regulatory bodies – are interested in its financial affairs. Naturally management within an enterprise is interested in monitoring the performance of the business but it has the great advantage over outsiders of more detailed financial information. Outside groups must therefore rely on published financial statements and other corporate information bulletins to make decisions.

Any figure from the accounts taken in isolation is not particularly meaningful. A profit figure, for example, does not indicate how well the organization has performed unless it is related to another variable, e.g. assets. By comparing one item in the accounts with another a relationship is established in the form of a ratio. However, a ratio in isolation is of limited value unless we have a yardstick to compare it against. One yardstick is to compare ratios for the same company for previous periods. This approach is referred to as time series analysis and is useful in comparing current performance with past performance. However, such an analysis does not provide any information on performance relative to other firms in the same sector, which is referred to as cross-sectional analysis.

This chapter is concerned with demonstrating how to calculate ratios and how to interpret them. The next chapter places ratio analysis in context by providing a framework for analysis. The ratios included in this text are only some of the possible relations that can be calculated. The ratios applicable to any analysis depend upon the type of decision that is being contemplated. Not all the ratios included in this chapter are applicable for all decisions – the analyst must be selective. I recall that as an auditor I visited the chief accountant of a subsidiary of a manufacturing group of companies. I asked how the company had performed over the last 6 months and he produced four pages of ratios with every conceivable manufacturing variance. Being unable to assimilate the information in a few seconds, I repeated the question. The reply given was that he had to complete these four pages for head office and that he presumed that someone there was monitoring progress. This highlights that ratios should be selected carefully in the light of the decisions to be made.

The ratios included in this chapter (summarized on pp. 73–6) have been divided into the following categories, which are the most commonly used in financial statement analysis textbooks:

1 Operating ratios – which analyse revenue and expense items, i.e. the trading results, and the ability of the enterprise to utilize its assets to generate revenue.
2 Liquidity ratios – which measure the ability of the company to meet its debts as they fall due.
3 Capital structure ratios – which reflect how the assets of a company are financed.
4 Stock exchange (investment) ratios – which analyse whether an investment in a listed company is worthwhile.

Operating ratios

The profit and loss account

Ratios based on sales are of considerable value, since revenues and expenses often move in fairly predictable ways. Consequently most items in the profit and loss account bear some relation to sales. Furthermore, most expense items are those incurred during the year and are more objective than some of the valuations in the balance sheet. This is a very general statement, since some of the items in the profit and loss, e.g. depreciation, are a consequence of the valuations in the balance sheet.

It is a requirement of the formats in the Companies Act 1985 that turnover is disclosed. Paragraph 95, Schedule 4 defines turnover as the amount derived from the provision of goods and services falling within the company's ordinary activities. The figure disclosed for turnover should arise after deducting trade discounts but before adding value added tax and excise duty.

Paragraph 55(1), Schedule 4 Companies Act 1985 also stipulates that where a company carries out during the year two or more classes of business which in the opinion of the directors differ substantially from each other, then turnover and pre-tax profit for each class should be disclosed. Furthermore paragraphs 55(2) and 55(5) require turnover figures to be disaggregated into geographical markets unless the directors consider such information to seriously prejudice the interests of the company. There is also a 'continuing obligation' on listed companies to provide, among other things, a geographical analysis of turnover and of material contributions to the trading results of operations carried on outside the UK and Ireland.

Profitability ratios, based on sales or assets, provide very useful information, particularly where the analysis can be undertaken for different classes or divisions of the business. These ratios may be useful in trend analysis and in cross-sectional analysis.

Ratios based on turnover figures

Sales discounts and returns
Sales returns and discounts on sales should be systematically related to sales figures such that any change in the percentage relation over time would need further investigation. A substantial deviation could mean a problem in recording or in the terms of sale or saleability of stocks.

Cost of goods sold
The cost of goods sold ratio is an extremely important measure to the company, the auditor, the analyst and the Inland Revenue, since it normally remains very stable. The relation is even more useful when computed by product line, since cost structures and profit margins for the product mix may be calculated. Where the ratio does not follow the predictable pattern for the industry, management will be alerted to problems and a full investigation undertaken; the Inland Revenue is certainly going to require explanations.

The difference between turnover and cost of goods sold is gross profit, and when related to the sales figure, it provides the gross profit percentage or gross margin. Margins vary from industry to industry and the rate of turnover on stock. For example, a retailer may have a gross margin of only 50 per cent of that prevailing in the manufacturing sector.

Profit margin
Typically trading profit before interest and tax would be used as the numerator in this relation. The ratio measures the efficiency of an organization to generate profits from sales. While the term 'trading profit' is not included in the formats specified in the Companies Act 1985, it is possible to make a good estimate from information disclosed. The formats specify that charges must be analysed by function or by nature. Disclosure by function is to split charges into cost of sales, distribution costs or administrative costs, although these terms are not defined in the Act. Typically cost of sales would include materials consumed, direct wages, depreciation of productive equipment and other production-related expenses. Distribution costs would include wages, expenses and materials directly attributable to this function,

and administrative costs include all other costs that are not required to be disclosed separately.

Profit margin ratios will vary from industry to industry. For example, 8–10 per cent is usual for a manufacturer such as Beecham, whereas a retailer like Marks & Spencer will work on a much lower margin, perhaps 3–4 per cent. Comparisons with other firms in the sector are very useful both over time and at one point in time. Such comparisons can throw light on the company's strategy. For example, empirical evidence suggests that profitability is highly correlated with market share. A company may decide to increase its market share over time with a view to long-run profitability, but it may be at the expense of short-term margins. At the other extreme very high margins may reveal that the company is the market leader, but they could equally lead to increased competition in the sector, with the consequence of reduced long-run profitability.

Productivity margin ratio
This ratio shows the relation between value added and sales and represents the additional wealth created by the organization. Larger companies may prepare value added statements, in which case the figures may be used from the statement. However, such an approach must be treated with caution, since there is no regulation over these statements. Value-added statements can therefore be presented in a number of different ways, depending upon the underlying objective. For example, Marks & Spencer clearly wishes to maximize the figure for contribution to government. Consequently the turnover figure in the value added statement (application of group sales revenue) includes taxes, whereas the figure in the profit and loss account is net of tax.

Productivity margins will vary from sector to sector. For example, a distribution company will have a low added value ratio, whereas a manufacturing unit should have a high added value ratio.

Expense to turnover ratios
A variety of expense ratios can be calculated, and they are likely to be fairly stable over time, provided the expense is variable. However, the formats provided by the Companies Act 1985 are not particularly informative and limit analysis in this area. Some companies, such as Marks & Spencer, recognize this fact and provide additional information, shown below:

Other expenses	1986	1985
	£m	*£m*
Other expenses comprise:		
Staff costs	421.7	384.8
Occupancy costs	89.1	81.6
including – Rentals under operating leases of £28.2 million (last year £26.1m)		

Other costs	120.6	89.0
including – Auditors' remuneration of £.4 million (last year £.3 million) – Hire of plant & machinery of £2.5 million (last year £2.0 million)		
	631.4	555.4
Repairs, renewals & maintenance of properties, fixtures, fittings & equipment	33.6	29.4
Depreciation of tangible fixed assets	53.0	44.7
	718.0	629.5
Less: Other income	26.6	19.8
	691.4	609.7
Interest payable	11.1	12.8
	702.5	622.5

The directors consider that the nature of the business is such that the analysis of expenses shown above is more informative than that set out in the formats in the Companies Act 1985.

Other expense items, such as research and development, would prove to be very useful in providing some limited information on prospects for the future. For example, a high-technology company with low research and development in a particular year might be a cause for concern. However, such useful information is not often disclosed.

Employee costs is an important area to consider and a number of ratios can be developed. For example, staff costs to sales expressed as a percentage is one measure, and others might include sales per employee or staff costs per employee.

Tax ratio
This ratio relates the tax charge to the profit before tax by measuring the proportion of income allocated to taxation.

Profitability based on assets

Return on capital employed
This ratio is probably the most commonly referred to and yet ill-defined relation. It measures a relation between trading profit and capital employed in the business, and is a measure of efficiency and a guide to whether an adequate return is being generated on funds.

Capital employed may be defined as tangible net assets, although some care must be take when undertaking cross-sectional analysis. For instance, a company with a large element of short-term debt will have a lower capital employed than a comparable company with a more prudent balance sheet and higher level of long-term debt. This is because short-term debt is offset against current assets, thereby reducing the figure for capital employed and, other things being equal, increasing return on capital employed. Associates and investments may be excluded from the denominator on the grounds that they are investments rather than assets purchased with a view to earning trading profits, provided that attributable trading profits and dividends are also excluded from the numerator. Another reason for their exclusion is that management may be bolstering returns by investing in other companies rather than in investing in itself. However, inclusion of investments in the denominator and their results in the numerator provides a better measure, but care should be taken in interpretation.

Return on capital employed is particularly useful in identifying strengths and weaknesses within the firm, but often insufficient information is provided for the external analyst to undertake such an analysis. The ratio is useful to management in identifying areas worthy of expansion or divestment, and is also useful in evaluating a potential acquisition. Work by Meeks (1977) found that the return on tangible assets was average, whereas Firth (1976) found that, on average, the ratio was lower than his control group. Firth found that only 16 per cent of the victims had a return on capital employed greater than its paired counterpart in his control group.

Return on total assets

This ratio is a variant on return on capital employed inasmuch as the denominator uses total assets rather than net tangible assets. The figure from the profit and loss account should be profit before tax, so that all investment and other income is included. The ratio measures how efficiently the organization is in utilizing its available assets to generate income. An advantage of this relation is that it attempts to eliminate the different ways in which assets are financed.

Revenue and expense items ratios

Some revenue and expense items may be compared to the relevant asset accounts to provide meaningful results both over time and when undertaking cross-sectional analysis. The extent of such analysis is dependent on disclosure and some of the more useful ratios are as follows:

1 Depreciation charge for the year in relation to gross depreciable assets.
2 Investment income to investments.
3 Interest paid and payable to debt.
4 Interest income to the appropriate investment.
5 Bad debt expense to the provision for doubtful debts.
6 Repairs and maintenance to the appropriate assets, e.g. property, plant or equipment.

A comparison of such ratios over time should provide an insight into their long-run pattern and to managers' policies for that period.

The balance sheet: utilization (turnover) ratios

These ratios relate a balance sheet figure to turnover for the year and measure the extent to which assets are utilized to produce sales. The numerator for each of the following turnover ratios is sales.

Total asset turnover

The ratio total assets to sales measures how efficiently the company's management has been in generating sales from its assets. The implication of this relation is that if assets are increased, they should be used to increase sales. Total assets might be those existing at the year-end, although where there are seasonal fluctuations an average would be more appropriate. The ratio will change if sales are increased without any increase in investments in assets, if selling prices are changed, or if additional assets that are not accompanied by additional sales are purchased.

The total asset turnover ratio may be analysed further into fixed asset turnover and then beyond into the component parts of fixed assets. The fixed asset turnover ratio is used to measure the efficiency with which the firm utilizes its investment in fixed assets.

When comparing companies, the value placed on assets will have important implications, particularly when comparing profitability. With inflation, the historical cost of the assets will usually be lower than current values, so that the age structure of assets must be considered carefully.

Debtors' turnover

This ratio relates sales to average debtors for the year. The appropriate figure for sales is that resulting from credit transactions, since cash sales are never converted to debtors. However, an external analyst will have to resort to the total debtors' figure, since it is very rare for a split to be provided between credit and cash sales.

The ratio is a useful measure of the ability of the company to control its credit policy both over time and compared with relevant industry ratios. In general the higher the ratio, the better the performance, although a company would not wish to adopt a policy that was uncompetitive, since such an action would lead to the loss of customers.

An alternative approach to monitoring a company's credit control performance is to invert the above ratio so that debtors form the numerator and sales the denominator, and multiply by the number of days in the year. This approach is probably easier to understand, since the result measures the number of days it takes to collect the cash from debtors. A variation of this approach is to use 260 days, the approximate number of working days in the year, rather than 365 days.

Using the days it takes to collect the cash from debtors approach, a deteriorating credit policy would be measured by an increase in the ratio. There may be a number of reasons for the deterioration such as:

1   Poor management
2   Credit given to unsatisfactory customers
3   Invoicing section not processing the sales documents quickly enough
4   Late issue of monthly statements
5   Lack of follow-up procedures
6   Fictitious credit sales to improve profitability
7   Fraud
8   Credit might have been increased deliberately to attract sales

Inventory turnover
This ratio measures the numbers of times stock is turned over in the year. Since stock is valued at the lower of cost and net realizable value, it is appropriate to use the cost of sales rather than sales value. As inventories may be affected by seasonal fluctuations, it is appropriate to use an average rather than the year-end stock figure.

The inventory turnover figure will vary from firm to firm and from industry to industry, so that cross-sectional as well as trend analysis is useful. The higher the ratio is a reflection of the degree to which inventories are controlled in relation to sales, although such an outcome would also occur if some of the stock was not properly counted. Care should be taken in interpreting this ratio, because many companies adopt an accounting year that ends when inventories are at a minimum. Carrying too much or too little stock has its costs. Excess stock imposes additional costs of storage and interest on the investment, and increases the possibility that changes in demand will adversely affect the company. The cost of carrying too little stock is that sales may be delayed or lost to competitors.

The inventory turnover ratio can be disaggregated further into a raw material turnover ratio and a work-in-progress turnover ratio. Where the inventory turnover ratio highlights a problem, the disaggregated approach will prove useful in its identification. The inverse of the inventory turnover ratio multiplied by the number of days in the year is a measure of the time it takes to convert stock into sales.

The length of the operating cycle
Details on the working capital cycle are included in Chapter 15.

Creditors' turnover
This ratio is a measure of the amount of credit the company is taking. The numerator is purchases and the denominator trade creditors. Since it is rare for purchases to be disclosed, a substitute would be the cost of sales figure. This provides a comparable ratio in the sense that the numerator and denominator are at cost. In some situations it may be necessary to compare trade creditors with sales, although this is less desirable.

If the inverse of this ratio is multiplied by the number of days in the year, the relation shows the number of days it takes to pay creditors. This ratio is useful in both time-series and cross-sectional analysis, as it can give some indications as to whether the company is able to meet its debts as they fall due and whether it is foregoing profitable discounts being offered. It is surprising that discounts of say 1.5 per cent for payment twenty days earlier are readily foregone, even though the annualized rate is over 30 per cent. Time-series analysis may alert the analyst to changes in the pattern of payment. Cross-sectional analysis is also useful in identifying what is typical for the industry and changes in economic events. For example, during the liquidity crisis of 1973–4 there was a reluctance by some firms to pay anyone unless court action was threatened.

Liquidity ratios

A financial manager will be concerned to ensure that the company can meet its current obligations, such as trade creditors, taxes and short-term loans. As part of his managerial function, he would prepare a cash budget to show the flow of funds on a monthly basis. However, the external analyst will not have access to such information and must rely on reported results. Liquidity ratios are useful in highlighting the possibility of weaknesses in this area. Before these ratios are considered, a number of definitions will be provided.

Liquidity is the ability of the company to meet its debts as they fall due, whereas overtrading occurs when a company has so little finance in relation to its turnover that it cannot meet its debts as they fall due. In contrast, a company is undercapitalized if it cannot carry out its sales at optimum profitability because of insufficient capital. For example, if it has insufficient capital to buy in bulk to take advantage of discounts being offered.

Current ratio

This ratio is calculated by taking current assets and dividing by current liabilities. Current assets includes stocks, work-in-progress, debtors, investments and cash at bank and in hand. The Companies Act 1985 requires creditors to be split between amounts falling due within one year (effectively current liabilities) and amounts falling due after more than one year.

The current ratio is probably the most frequently used ratio in assessing a company's liquidity position, as it shows the extent to which its short-term liabilities are covered by its liquid assets. The ratio varies considerably from industry to industry. For example, a manufacturing concern may have a ratio of about 2:1 or 2.5:1, whereas a retail company may trade on a ratio of 1:1 or less and still be liquid. This occurs because a manufacturing company has substantial investments in stock, with cash not being paid in as regularly as a retail company. A measure of the more immediate liquidity position is provided by the liquid ratio.

Liquid ratio

This ratio is also referred to as the quick ratio or acid-test ratio, since the most illiquid of current assets, stocks and work-in-progress, are excluded from the numerator. The ratio recognizes that where stocks are difficult to realize, financial problems may ensue. The relation provides a measure of the ability of the company to meet its short-term obligations out of its readily realizable assets.

Capital structure ratios for management purposes

Capital structure reflects how the assets of a company are financed in the long run. The structure is segregated into debt and equity and the relation between these two components is referred to as gearing or leverage. The relation between capital structure and valuation of the firm is dealt with in Chapter 7, but it is appropriate here to analyse this interrelation by considering operating and financial leverage. Operating leverage is the extent to which fixed costs are used in the operations of the company. In contrast, financial leverage is a measure of the extent of debt utilization in maximizing shareholders' funds. Note that much of the information included in this section will only be available to internal management since most of it is not published in annual reports.

Operating leverage

An assumption often made in analysing operating leverage is that total revenues and total costs are linearly related and are complete and stable over time and across firms. Rarely are these assumptions met perfectly in practice. Often the cost-accounting concept of a relevant range of activity is considered reasonable so that the impact of fixed costs on the profit structure of the firm may be analysed by means of linear break-even analysis.

Consider, for example, the case where a company A has the following cost structure:

Fixed costs	£20,000
Variable costs per unit	£1.00
Sales price per unit	£1.50
Break-even number of units	40,000

The company is considering its cost structure if it invested in some new machinery that would result in the following:

Fixed costs	£40,000
Variable costs per unit	£0.80

| Sales price per unit | £1.50 |
| Break-even number of units | 57,143 |

The impact of increasing its operating leverage is shown in Figure 4.1. By utilizing new machinery the company would magnify its profits at higher levels of activity but also magnify its losses at lower levels of

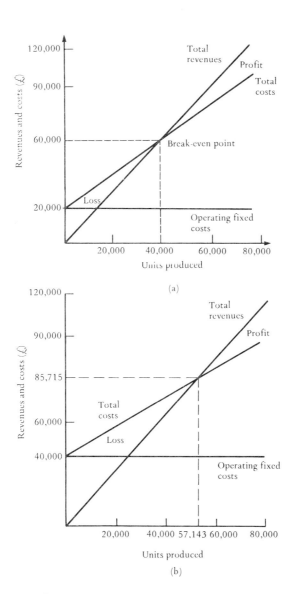

Figure 4.1   The effect of changing operating leverage

activity. For instance, if only 30,000 units were produced, losses would be as follows:

Loss = total costs − total revenues

Before the capital investment:

Loss = fixed costs + variable costs − total revenues
     = £20,000 + (30,000 × £1.00) − (30,000 × £1.50)
     = £5,000

After the capital investment:

Loss = £40,000 + (30,000 × £0.80) − (30,000 × £1.50)
     = £19,000

It is apparent that the capital investment has exacerbated the loss position. However, if 150,000 units were produced, profits would be as follows:

Profit = total revenues − total costs

Before the capital investment:

Profit = (150,000 × £1.50) − (20,000 + (150,000 × £1.00))
       = £55,000

After the capital investment:

Profit = (150,000 × 1.50) − (40,000 + (150,000 × 0.80))
       = £65,000

From the above example it can be seen that increased operating leverage has the effect of magnifying profits at high levels of activity and magnifying losses at low levels of activity. This can be seen more clearly from Table 4.1. The degree of operating leverage can be measured as follows:

$$\text{Degree of operating leverage (DOL)} \text{ at a given level of activity} = \frac{\text{Percentage change in EBIT}}{\text{Percentage change in output}}$$

However, instead of looking at percentage changes in output and earnings before interest and tax it is more common to compute it on a per unit basis. This is illustrated below:

Table 4.1 The effect of leverage on profits

(a) *Before the capital investment*

Units sold	Total revenue (£)	Total cost (£)	EBIT
10,000	15,000	30,000	(15,000)
20,000	30,000	40,000	(10,000)
40,000	60,000	60,000	break-even
57,143	85,715	77,143	8,572
60,000	90,000	80,000	10,000
100,000	150,000	120,000	30,000
150,000	225,000	170,000	55,000

(b) *After the capital investment*

Units sold	Total revenue (£)	Total cost (£)	EBIT
10,000	15,000	48,000	(33,000)
20,000	30,000	56,000	(26,000)
40,000	60,000	72,000	(12,000)
57,143	85,715	85,715	break-even
60,000	90,000	88,000	2,000
100,000	150,000	120,000	30,000
150,000	225,000	160,000	65,000

$$\text{DOL } x = \frac{x(p-v)}{x(p-v)-f}$$

where x = number of units
p = price per unit
v = variable cost per unit
f = fixed costs

Before the capital investment

$$\text{DOL } 60,000 = \frac{60,000(1.50-1.00)}{60,000(1.50-1.00)-20,000}$$
$$= \underline{3}$$

After the capital investment

$$\text{DOL } 60,000 = \frac{60,000(1.50-0.80)}{60,000(1.50-0.80)-40,000}$$
$$= \underline{21}$$

The degree of operating leverage differs considerably in the above example as a result of the capital investment. However, as output increases away from the break-even level of activity, so the degree of operating leverage decreases as a greater contribution is made towards covering fixed costs. For example:

Before the capital investment

$$\text{DOL } 150,000 = \frac{150,000\,(1.50 - 1.00)}{150,000\,(1.50 - 1.00) - 20,000}$$
$$= \underline{1.36}$$

After the capital investment

$$\text{DOL } 150,000 = \frac{150,000\,(1.50 - 0.80)}{150,000\,(1.50 - 0.80) - 40,000}$$
$$= \underline{1.61}$$

The above ratios may be interpreted as follows: if, before the capital investment, the company decided to increase its output by 10 per cent, the expected increase in EBIT would be 13.6 per cent.

$$\text{DOL} = \frac{\text{Percentage change in EBIT}}{\text{Percentage change in output}}$$

$$1.36 = \frac{\text{Percentage change in EBIT}}{0.10}$$

Percentage charge in EBIT = 13.6

If, after the capital investment, the company decided to increase its output by 10 per cent, the expected increase in EBIT would be 16.1 per cent.

Financial leverage

Financial gearing (leverage) is a measure of debt utilization in financing a company's assets and its effect is similar to operating leverage. It is a measure of the extent to which assets are financed by borrowings, and therefore provides information on risk exposure. The effect of financial leverage can be appreciated by considering an example:

Capital structure

	Book value	Market value
Ordinary shares £1 each	£2.5m	£5.0m
8 per cent debenture stock	£2.0m	£1.5m

Profits

Retained profits brought forward at the beginning of the year	= £750,000
Profit after tax this year	= £400,000

Retained profit for the year

	£
Profits after tax	400,000
Dividends (£2.5m × 6%)	150,000
	250,000
Retained profits brought forward	750,000
Retained profits at the year end	£1,000,000

Adjusted capital structure

	Book value	*Market value*
Ordinary shareholder's capital	£3.5m	£5.0m
8 per cent debenture stock	£2.0m	£1.5m
	£5.5m	£6.5m

Capital gearing ratios

(a) on book values $= \dfrac{\text{debt}}{\text{debt} + \text{equity}} = \dfrac{2.0}{5.5} = \underline{36.36}$ per cent

(b) on market values $= \dfrac{\text{debt}}{\text{debt} + \text{equity}} = \dfrac{1.5}{6.5} = \underline{23.08}$ per cent

An ordinary equity investor may view preference shares as being part of debt. This is because a preference share is a hybrid form of security, having some features of both debt and equity. Further details are provided in Chapter 10.

Income gearing ratios
This ratio is calculated as follows, assuming corporation tax as 35 per cent:

$$\dfrac{\text{Debt interest}}{\text{EBIT}} = \dfrac{160,000}{615,385 + 160,000} = \dfrac{160,000}{775,385} = \underline{20.6} \text{ per cent}$$

From the above example it can be seen that gearing may be measured in a number of different ways. The effect of different levels of gearing can be seen from the following example:

		Company	
	A	B	C
Gearing	0%	25%	50%
	£	£	£
Operating profits	500	500	500
Debenture interest	–	100	200
Profits after interest expense	500	400	300

If operating profits were to increase by 10 per cent the position would be as follows:

Operating profits	550	550	550
Debenture interest	–	100	200
Profits after interest expense	550	450	350
Percentage increase in pretax profits	10%	12.5%	16.67%

Thus the higher the level of gearing, the greater the increase in profits, given the same level of profits before interest and taxes. However, if pretax profits had decreased by 10 per cent, the impact would be the same in percentage terms, thereby demonstrating that higher levels of gearing result in greater fluctuations in after-tax profits. The magnifying impact is the same as for operating gearing.

The counterpart to the degree of operating leverage is the degree of financial leverage (DFL), measured as follows:

$$\text{DFL} = \frac{\text{EBIT}}{\text{EBIT} - i} = \frac{x(p-v)-f}{(x(p-v)-f)-i}$$

EBIT = earnings before interest and taxes

i   = annual interest expense or preferred dividend.

In the example shown above the DFL is as follows:

$$\text{DFL} = \frac{775,385}{775,385 - 160,000}$$
$$= \underline{1.26}$$

The degree of financial leverage measures the increase in earnings before interest and tax and earnings per share that would result from an increase in a given level of gearing. For example, a 10 per cent increase in financial leverage would lead to a 12.6 per cent increase in earnings before interest and tax.

The combined effects of operating and financial leverage
In order to show the combined effect we need to multiply the degree of operating leverage by the degree of financial leverage.

$$\text{DOL} \times \text{DFL} = \frac{x(p-v)}{x(p-v)-f} \times \frac{x(p-v)-f}{\{x(p-v)-f\}-i}$$
$$= \frac{x(p-v)}{\{x(p-v)-f\}-i}$$

The application of this formula is shown in Table 4.2, given a per unit sales price of £2.50 and variable costs per unit of £1.50. Using the information provided in column A, the combined effect of operating and

Table 4.2 Combined effects of operating and financial leverage

	A 100,000 units £000	B 120,000 units £000
Sales less total variable costs	100	120
Fixed costs	25	25
EBIT	75	95
Interest	35	35
Profit before taxes	40	60
Taxes at 35%	14	21
Profit after taxes	26	39
Shares outstanding (number)	200,000	200,000
Earnings (pence)	13p	19.5p

$$\text{DOL} \times \text{DFL} \ 100,000 = \frac{100,000 \ (2.50 - 1.50)}{100,000 \ (2.50 - 1.50) - 25,000 - 35,000} = \underline{2.5}$$

financial leverage is calculated as 2.5, reflecting that if output were to increase by 20 per cent, profit after taxes and earnings per share would increase by 50 per cent (2.5 × 20). The split is as follows:

$$\text{DOL} = \frac{100,000 \ (2.50 - 1.50)}{100,000 \ (2.50 - 1.50) - 25,000} = \underline{1.33}$$

$$\text{DFL} = \frac{100,000 \ (2.50 - 1.50) - 25,000}{100,000 \ (2.50 - 1.50) - 25,000 - 35,000} = \underline{1.875}$$

Combined effect = DOL × DFL = 1.33 × 1.875 = $\underline{2.5}$

Other capital structure ratios
In addition to operating and financial gearing, a number of other ratios are often calculated to highlight the debt to equity relationship. For example, an analyst of a company with the following capital structure might calculate one of the following ratios:

Sources of financing (%)		
Preference shares	8	
Ordinary shareholders' funds	62	
		70
Long-term debt	20	
Current liabilities	10	
		30
		100%
Total assets		100%

The *debt ratio* measures the proportion of assets financed through borrowings and the extent of trading on the equity. It is calculated as follows.

$$\frac{\text{Total liabilities}}{\text{Total assets}} = \frac{30}{100} = \underline{30\%}$$

The debt to equity ratio shows the relationship between borrowed capital and capital invested by shareholders, and is calculated as follows:

$$\frac{\text{Total debt}}{\text{Shareholders' funds}} = \frac{30}{70} = \underline{43\%}$$

The equity ratio is a measure of protection to creditors and the extent of trading on the equity and is calculated as follows:

$$\frac{\text{Shareholders' funds}}{\text{Total assets}} = \frac{70}{100} = \underline{70\%}$$

Stock exchange (investment) ratios

The following set of ratios are often referred to as stock exchange or investment ratios, since they are used to analyse whether an investment is worthwhile in a listed company.

Earnings per share

The method adopted in the *Financial Times* to calculate earnings per share (EPS) is to take the last declared earnings figure before extraordinary items, but after deducting tax, minority interests and preference dividends, to obtain earnings attributable to ordinary shareholders from normal activities. This approach is consistent with Statement of Standard Accounting Practice No. 3, which requires that all listed companies publish their earnings per share figure for the current and previous periods on the face of the profit and loss account. The basis of calculation and an explanation thereof should be provided on the face of the profit and loss account or in the accompanying notes.

There are two major practical problems which need to be considered when calculating earnings per share figures. The first involves the treatment of taxation in respect of dividends and the second the number of equity shares, particularly where options exist to enable people to buy new shares for less than their market price, i.e. dilution of share capital.

Under the imputation system companies pay corporation tax based on their profits. The payment of a dividend leads to an advance payment of corporation tax, and shareholders are inputed to have paid their liability to standard rate of taxation. Thus the payment of a dividend does not affect the total amount of corporation tax paid but merely the timing of payment. In these circumstances profits after tax are used to calculate earnings per share without regard to advance corporation tax. Such an approach is called the 'net basis' as it is based after the constant elements of corporation tax have been deducted from earnings. These constant elements include corporation tax on income, tax attributable to dividends received, and unrelieved overseas tax where overseas tax rates exceed those prevailing in the UK.

Sometimes there are problems where advance corporation tax is irrecoverable or when overseas tax is paid but not fully allowable. In the former case the payment of a dividend increases the tax burden. Occurrences such as these are referred to as variable elements that increase the tax burden as a result of vagaries of the system rather than poor decisions by management. SSAP3 provides that earnings per share should be calculated on the net basis but, where materially different, a second figure should be published, one based on the exclusion of additional tax which arises from the payment of a dividend. This approach is called the 'nil distribution basis' and refers to nil distribution of ordinary dividends and not preference dividends.

The second practical problem that needs to be considered carefully concerns changes in share capital that may take the following forms.

An issue at full market price
This would be an unusual approach, since most share issues are in the form of rights issues. It is presumed that once the shares are issued, they contribute to earnings immediately, and as such it is only necessary to weight the share capital to reflect the new shares from the date of issue. No adjustment is made to the previous year's earnings per share figure. For example, if the company had 1.4 million shares in issue and issued a further 350,000 three-quarters of the way through the year, the average number of shares would be

$$= 1.4m + \left(\frac{1}{4} \times 350,000\right)$$

$$= \underline{1,487,500}$$

Given earnings of £180,000, EPS $= \dfrac{180,000}{1,487,500} = \underline{12.1p}$

A capitalization issue
This involves issuing free or bonus (scrip) shares pro rata to existing shareholders by capitalizing reserves. Since there is no effect on profits or the tax charge, the higher number of shares in issue at the date of the report should be used and the previous period should be adjusted for comparability purposes.

Year end	31.12.X1	31.12.X2
Ordinary share capital (£1 each)	100,000	100,000
Bonus issue (1 for 1) in 19X2		100,000
	100,000	200,000
Earnings	£40,000	£60,000
EPS	40p	30p
Adjusted EPS $\dfrac{40,000}{200,000} =$	20p	

A similar situation arises where a company splits its shares into smaller units, i.e. a stock split.

A share exchange
In a takeover situation by issue of shares it should be assumed that the new shares were issued on the first day of the period for which the profits of the new subsidiary were bought into the consolidated profit and loss account. No adjustment should be made to the EPS for the previous accounting period.

A rights issue
Such an issue is made at less than market price, and an adjustment should be made to reflect what is, in reality, a mixture of a capitalization issue and an issue at full market price. For example, if a company has 100,000 shares in issue with a total market value of £200,000, it would receive £100,000 if it had a rights issue of 1 for 1 at £1. The effect of this is the same as if the company had a capitalization issue of 1 for 2, i.e. 50,000 shares, followed by an issue of 50,000 shares at the full market price.

The theoretical share price after the rights issue is the sum of the number of shares in issue before the issue plus the total money received divided by the total number of shares now in issue, as follows:

Market capitalization before the issue 100,000 × £2 = £200,000

Total money received 100,000 × £1	= £100,000
	£300,000
Number of shares	= 200,000
Theoretical market price	£1.50

An adjustment has to be made to both the prior and current years' EPS. In adjusting the prior year's EPS, the new cost would generate a return from the issue date. Since a rights issue is a mixture of an issue at full market price, in which no adjustment is made for the prior year's EPS, and a capitalization issue, which involves a reduction in reported

EPS for the whole year, an adjustment has to be made between these two extremes to correct for the bonus element in the rights issue as follows:

$$\text{prior year EPS} \times \frac{\text{theoretical price after issue}}{\text{actual price before issue}}$$

The actual price to be used is the closing market price for the old shares with the rights, i.e. the cum rights price. Since the theoretical price is less than the actual price before the issue, because of the bonus element, EPS will decrease.

When adjusting for EPS in the current year, the approach adopted must reflect the hybrid nature of the issue, in that it is a mixture of an issue at full market price, which involves a weighted average approach, and a capitalization issue, which involves using the year end number of shares. The adjustment is to divide the actual price before the issue by the theoretical price after the issue to provide the following formula:

$$\frac{\text{Earnings}}{\left(\text{shares before issue} \times \dfrac{\text{cum rights price}}{\text{ex rights price}}\right) + \begin{array}{c}\text{shares in issue after}\\\text{the rights issue}\end{array}}$$

For example, at 1.1 x 2 there were 100,000 shares in issue at £1 each
31.3 x 2 there was a 1 for 1 rights issue

cum rights price = £3
ex rights price = £2

Earnings to 31.12.X1 and 31.12.X2 were respectively £24,000 and £35,000

$$19X1 \quad \text{EPS} = \frac{24,000}{100,000} \times \frac{2}{3} = \underline{16p}$$

$$19X2 \quad \text{EPS} = \frac{35,000}{\left(100,000 \times \dfrac{3}{2} \times \dfrac{3}{12}\right) + \left(\dfrac{9}{12} \times 200,000\right)}$$

$$= \underline{18.67p}$$

Dilution in EPS
In the following circumstances fully diluted EPS should be disclosed at the balance sheet date if the decrease is 5 per cent or more where:

1 There is another class of equity share ranking for dividend in the future.
2 Other securities convertible into equity shares are in issue, e.g. debentures or loan stock.
3 Options or warrants exist to subscribe for equity shares.

In the above circumstances the following adjustments need to be made:

1   Shares not currently ranking for dividend.

$$\text{Fully diluted EPS} = \frac{\text{earnings}}{\begin{array}{l}\text{total of equity shares} \\ \text{ranking for dividend}\end{array} + \begin{array}{l}\text{shares not currently} \\ \text{ranking for dividend}\end{array}}$$

If shares were not issued until after the start of the accounting period in question, a weighted average should be used.
2   Convertible debentures or loan stock. Assume that all such conversions have taken place on the first day of the accounting period.
3   Options outstanding. The fully diluted EPS should be calculated as though the options have been taken up on the first day of the accounting period or date of issue of the option, if later. If the option had been taken up, it would have led to an inflow of cash to the company which would be used to generate extra earnings. In these circumstances the net profit should be increased by the interest generated if such funds had been invested in 2.5 per cent consolidated stock on the first day of the accounting period (price is the closing price of the previous day). Since income has been assumed to increase, it is appropriate that a notional deduction be made for corporation tax on the extra income.

Earnings yield

The earnings return on market price, or earnings yield, is the reciprocal of the price/earnings ratio and is measured as earnings per share divided by market price. The yield figure published in the *Financial Times* is the gross equivalent, calculated as follows:

$$\left(\frac{\text{EPS} \times 100}{\text{price}}\right) \times \left(\frac{100}{100 - \text{standard rate of tax}}\right)$$

An earnings yield figure can be calculated on current prices or using the year-end market price. Market price is more informative than book value, since market price reflects money foregone at any given time by a decision to continue to hold the stock.

Price – earnings ratios

This ratio is calculated by dividing the current middle market price of the share by the company's earnings per share. A high ratio indicates that the market considers that its earnings are likely to grow quickly, and a low ratio indicates that earnings are expected to stagnate in the future. The ratio represents the number of current year's earnings it would take to earn the equivalent of its current price. From a market perspective, the ratio reflects its views on a company's future return as reflected by its earnings and dividend potential and on its business and financial risk. However, such statements represent generalizations. For example, if a company has performed badly in the past, but is expected to recover quickly, the price–earnings ratio of that firm may be abnormally high for the sector in which it operates. The converse may also be true.

The ratio is used extensively in acquisition analysis and the price–earnings ratio of the acquiree is called its exit price–earnings ratio. The higher the ratio an acquirer is willing to pay reflects the extent to which it is prepared to go in order to gain control of the acquiree.

In the 1960s and 1970s the price–earnings ratio was considered to be the most important stock–market indicator of performance. Although price–earnings ratios must now be treated with considerable caution because of accounting problems, particularly with respect to extraordinary items and deferred tax, they remain an important influence on takeovers. The reason for this is that, with a share-for-share exchange, a company can increase its earnings per share and share price by acquiring another company with a price–earnings ratio lower than its own, provided that the earnings of the victim are capitalized at a rate above its existing capitalization rate (further details are provided in chapter 17).

Dividend yield

Dividends are paid net of tax at the standard rate and carry a tax credit which satisfies the requirements for basic rate tax. As with all yield figures, they reflect a relationship between a variable and market price. Dividend yield reflects the distributed return on its current investment. The gross equivalent of the net dividend paid is used for the dividend yield calculation as follows:

$$\left(\frac{\text{Dividend per share} \times 100}{\text{market price}}\right) \times \left(\frac{100}{100 - \text{standard rate of tax}}\right)$$

Dividend cover

Dividend cover is calculated by dividing earnings per share by net dividend per share and the relationship reflects the extent to which dividends are protected or covered by earnings.

Summary of ratios

Ratio Operating ratios	Method of computation	Significance
1 Sales return ratio	$\dfrac{\text{Sales returns}}{\text{Sales}} \times 100$	Measures the saleability of stock.
2 Sales discounts ratio	$\dfrac{\text{Sales discounts}}{\text{Sales}} \times 100$	Measures the extent to which the terms of sale affect turnover.

3	Cost of goods sold ratio	$\dfrac{\text{Cost of goods sold}}{\text{Sales}} \times 100$	Shows the relationship between costs and sales value of items sold.
4	Gross margin	$\dfrac{\text{Sales} - \text{cost of goods sold}}{\text{Sales}} \times 100$	As for 3. The ratio usually remains fairly stable.
5	Net profit margin	$\dfrac{\text{Trading profit before interest and tax}}{\text{Sales}} \times 100$	A measure of efficiency of the organization to generate profits from sales.
6	Productivity	$\dfrac{\text{Value added}}{\text{Sales}} \times 100$	Measures the additional wealth created by the organization.
7	Tax ratio	$\dfrac{\text{Tax charge}}{\text{Profit before tax}} \times 100$	A measure of the proportional tax charge.
8	Expense items	$\dfrac{\text{Expense}}{\text{Sales}} \times 100$	Relates individual expenses, e.g. research and development, to sales.
9	Return on capital employed	$\dfrac{\text{Trading profit}}{\text{Tangible net assets}} \times 100$	A measure of efficiency
10	Return on total assets	$\dfrac{\text{Trading plus other income}}{\text{Total assets}} \times 100$	Measures efficiency in utilizing its available assets.
11	Revenue and expense item ratio	for example, $\dfrac{\text{Depreciation charge}}{\text{Gross depreciable assets}} \times 100$	Identifies depreciable assets and the extent of the provision for depreciation.
12	Total asset turnover	$\dfrac{\text{Total assets}}{\text{Sales}}$	A measure of the utilization of assets to generate sales.
13	Debtors' turnover	$\dfrac{\text{Sales}}{\text{Average debtors}}$	Measure of the control of credit.
14	Inventory turnover	$\dfrac{\text{Sales}}{\text{Average inventory}}$	A measure of the control of inventories in relation to turnover.
15	Creditors' turnover	$\dfrac{\text{Purchases}}{\text{Trade creditors}}$	Indicates reasonableness of trade creditors and the speed of payment.

Liquidity ratios

16	Current ratio	$\dfrac{\text{Current assets}}{\text{Current liabilities}}$	Measures a company's liquidity position.
17	Liquid ratio	$\dfrac{\text{Current assets} - \text{inventories}}{\text{Current liabilities}}$	Measures the ability to meet short-term liabilities.
18	Cash days to sales ratio	$\dfrac{\text{Short-term investments plus cash} \times 100}{\text{Sales}}$	Indicates the reasonableness of liquid assets in relation to sales.
19	Gross funds to debt ratio	$\dfrac{\text{Gross funds from operations} \times 100}{\text{Current liabilities and loans}}$	Measures the extent to which short-term obligations are covered by gross funds.
20	No credit interval	$\dfrac{\text{Debtors plus short-term investments plus cash} \times 365}{\text{Operating expenses less depreciation}}$	Measures the number of days the most liquid assets could support operating expenditures.

Capital structure ratios

21	Degree of operating leverage	$\dfrac{\text{Percentage change in EBIT}}{\text{Percentage change in output}}$	Measures the extent to which fixed costs are used in the company's operations.
22	Degree of financial leverage	$\dfrac{\text{EBIT}}{\text{EBIT} - \text{interest expense}}$	A measure of debt utilization in financing assets.
23	Debt ratio	$\dfrac{\text{Total liabilities}}{\text{Total assets}}$	Measures the proportion of assets financed through borrowings and the extent of trading on the equity.
24	Equity ratio	$\dfrac{\text{Shareholders' funds}}{\text{Total assets}}$	Shows the protection to creditors and the extent of trading on the equity.
25	Debt to equity ratio	$\dfrac{\text{Total debt}}{\text{Shareholders' funds}}$	Shows the relationship between borrowed capital and capital invested by shareholders.

26	Total debt to total assets	$\dfrac{\text{Debt} + \text{current}}{\text{liabilities} \times 100}$ $\overline{\text{Total assets}}$	Measures the percentage total funds provided by creditors.
27	Interest cover	$\dfrac{\text{Profit before interest}}{\text{Interest}}$	Measures the extent to which interest charges are covered by profits.

Investment ratios

28	Earnings per share	$\dfrac{\begin{array}{c}\text{Earnings before}\\ \text{extraordinary items but}\\ \text{after deducting tax,}\\ \text{minority interests and}\\ \text{preference dividends}\end{array}}{\begin{array}{c}\text{Number of ordinary}\\ \text{shares}\end{array}}$	Shows the amount of earnings attributable to each ordinary share.
29	Earnings yield	$\dfrac{\text{EPS}}{\text{Price}} \times 100$	Shows earnings return per share based on the current share price.
30	Price/earnings ratio	$\dfrac{\text{Market price per share}}{\text{Earnings per share}}$	Measures whether the price of an ordinary share is in line with earnings.
31	Dividend yield	$\dfrac{\text{Dividend per share}}{\text{Market price per share}}$	Measures the return to ordinary shareholders on current price of stock.
32	Dividend cover	$\dfrac{\text{Earnings per share}}{\text{Net dividend per share}}$	Measures the extent to which dividends are protected by earnings.
33	Return on equity	$\dfrac{\begin{array}{c}\text{Profit after tax before}\\ \text{extraordinary items}\\ \text{but after deducting}\\ \text{minority interests and}\\ \text{preference dividends}\end{array}}{\begin{array}{c}\text{Equity shareholders'}\\ \text{investment}\end{array}}$	Measure of efficiency in earning a satisfactory return on equity shareholders' investment.
34	Payout ratio	$\dfrac{\begin{array}{c}\text{Ordinary and}\\ \text{preference}\\ \text{dividends} \times 100\end{array}}{\text{Retained profit}}$	Shows the relation between dividends and retained profit.

Summary

The purpose of financial statement analysis is to assist the decision-making process. The analysis consists of selecting suitable information for the appropriate user group to enable them to allocate their resources efficiently. Ratio analysis is the primary method of financial statement analysis, consisting as it does of comparing variables both over time and between companies. Ratios in this chapter were classified into operating ratios, liquidity ratios, capital structure ratios and investment ratios. Ratios calculated were computed as though the figures in the financial statements were accurate and objective. However, many of the figures are in fact subjective and should be considered in the context of the accounting policies adopted by the firm.

References

Firth, M., *Share Prices and Mergers*, Gower, 1976.
Meeks, G., *Disappointing Marriage: A Study of the Gains from Merger*, CUP, 1977.

ADDITIONAL REFERENCES
See references at the end of Chapter 5.

5 The interpretation of reports and financial statements

Introduction

In Chapter 4 ratios were classified into four groups – operating ratios, liquidity ratios, capital structure ratios, and investment ratios. This chapter aims to utilize those ratios to interpret annual reports and financial statements. This is to be achieved by introducing the techniques of analysis and by providing a framework within which that analysis can be undertaken. The techniques are used to analyse the accounts of Marks & Spencer Plc, a well-known UK retailer. A retailer was chosen in preference to a manufacturing company to reflect changes in the British economy. Since 1979 there has been a devastating reduction in the manufacturing capacity of UK industry that has not yet filtered through to many textbooks. Indeed, most management accounting texts concentrate, almost exclusively, on the manufacturing sector, as though management accountants were only employed in that sector.

Cross-sectional analysis is the comparison of one company with others in the same sector, but in order to undertake such an analysis information must be available. Sources of information on UK companies are therefore dealt with before the techniques of analysis.

Sources of information on UK companies

Information may come from the following sources:

1 Newspapers and periodicals
2 The City
3 Specialist guides and reference books
4 Computer databanks
5 Inter–firm comparison schemes

Newspapers and periodicals

A considerable amount of information on listed companies can be obtained from publications such as the *Financial Times*, *The Economist*, *Euromoney*, and the *Investor's Chronicle*. These publications often undertake special surveys on particular industries. In addition, there are many industries that have specialist trade publications which provide coverage of both listed and unlisted companies.

The City

A requirement of listing is that information, e.g. audited financial statements, should be disclosed to particular information services such as Extel. In addition to information services, many brokers have specialist research departments that offer detailed market reports for clients or potential clients. The research reports are only on quoted companies, since the market reports are offered as a 'sweetener' to trade.

The *Stock Exchange Official Year Book* is an annual publication providing information on all listed companies on the London Stock Exchange, including a summary of the financial statements. Other useful guides on listed companies include *The Extel Book of Market Lenders* and the *Hambro Company Guide*.

Specialist guides and reference books

Specialist guides and sources of reference material include *Who Owns Whom*, a book which identifies ownership of subsidiaries in alphabetical order. There are UK, US and European editions of this publication. *The Times 1000* provides information on turnover, capital employed, profit margins and returns on capital employed for each of the top 1000 UK industrial and commercial companies. *Kompass Guides* classify companies by size, product, service and by standard industry classification codes. The guides cover France, West Germany, the UK and other European countries.

Other guides include those published by Graham and Trotman on quoted and unquoted companies and include information on turnover and profitability. *Financial Reporting*, by the Institute of Chartered Accountants in England and Wales, provides a detailed analysis of the reporting practices of 300 industrial and commercial companies. *Crawford's Directory of City Connections* gives information on those who provide the financial services to major UK quoted and unquoted companies.

Computer databanks

Datastream
Datastream is a UK organization owned by Dun and Bradstreet that provides access to the London computer on daily share prices on all

listed companies in the UK and some other companies in France, West Germany and Japan. The service provides instantaneous access to share price data, and some terminals have the facility for providing information in graph form.

Textline
The UK computer can be accessed, for a fee, via the telephone system, and provides information on a company or industry that has been published in the press, primarily the UK press, although there are some contributions from international publications.

London Business School data tapes
Provides share price and returns information on a monthly basis on two data tapes that are available annually. In addition, there is a quarterly Risk Management Service report that provides investment data on UK listed companies.

Companies House, London and Cardiff
Companies House is run by the Department of Trade and Industry. Audited financial statements and company registers are available on microfiche on all UK registered companies. For a small fee searches may be undertaken for duplicates of the microfiche or photocopies, such a service taking about two days.

Inter-firm comparison schemes

The Centre for Interfirm Comparison
This is a non-profit-making organization established by the British Institute of Management and the British Productivity Council. The centre undertakes inter-firm comparisons and provides advice on the use of those ratios with the aim of being of service to management.

Inter Company Comparisons Ltd
This commercial organization offers a number of services, and the main ones are listed below:

1   *ICC Business Ratio Reports.* These reports cover 180 industries and each one provides 26 ratios and 6 growth rates for up to 100 leading companies in an industry. A commentary is included in each report, along with data sheets for each company and sector averages. The annual reports provide 3 to 4 years' data for a cost of £155 each (1987).
2   *ICC Financial Surveys.* Each annual survey contains details of up to 600 companies in 200 industries, including principal activities and key financial data for the last 3 years. They cost between £125 and £185, depending on the number of surveys.
3   *Industrial Performance Analysis.* This annual publication provides

average performance statistics, using 13 ratios for 140 sectors, covering a 3-year period. The 1986 edition costs £42.
4   *USM*. This report contains detailed profiles of all companies on the USM and compares their performance with competitors in the quoted and private company sectors. Sector-by-sector comments are provided by stockbrokers.
5   *Key Note Publications*. These publications provide an overview of the industry's structure, market background, recent developments and future prospects for 130 market sectors.

Extel publications

Extel cards provide a source of information on over 7,500 UK and international companies. The following are the major card services:

1   *The UK Listed Companies Service*. This service covers over 3,000 companies listed on the UK and Irish Stock Exchanges. The service consists of an annual card for each company and includes addresses, activities, balance sheets, board members, capital, chairman's statement, dividend record, profit and loss accounts, subsidiaries, yields and earnings. In addition, News Cards provide cuumulative information on dividends, interim and preliminary results and other corporate news.
2   *The Analyst's Service*. This publication provides a source of reference to more than 1,250 companies for a period of 10 years, on capital changes, balance sheets, profit and loss accounts, share prices, dividends and selected ratios.
3   *The Unlisted Securities Market Service*. Provides information on all USM companies.
4   *The Over the Counter Service*. This service comprises Annual and News cards for companies traded on the OTC markets.
5   *The Unquoted Companies Service*. This service covers 2,000 of the larger unquoted companies in the same detail and format as for the listed service.

Jordan & Sons Ltd

This firm offers the following information services, among many others:

1   *Industrial Surveys* are produced for 20 industries, with each one covering between 50 and 150 companies. Each survey covers the extent of disclosure of information, an analysis of important areas, and a commentary by an industry expert. The surveys cost between £50 and £150 each and they provide selected information over the past 4 years.
2   *The Top 4,000 Privately Owned Companies* is an annual publication split into two volumes containing the top 2,000 companies and the second 2,000 companies respectively. The aim of the publication is to provide up-to-date financial information, and it includes tables of leading performers, financial data on each company, and details

of the type of business, name of chief executive, addresses and telephone numbers. In addition, there are quarterly updates for an additional charge.

3   *Top Companies in Regions* surveys major companies on a regional basis. Each survey provides a profile of major companies, including information on both balance sheet and profit and loss account figures, together with additional features such as the type of business, the names of directors, telephone numbers, ownership information and audit details.

Techniques of analysis

Financial analysis is not primarily a matter of making an inordinate number of calculations. Once the calculations are completed, the process of analysis can begin, but before this is undertaken a number of analytical procedures may be adopted to enable the salient features to be gleaned quickly. However, a distinction should be made at the outset between an analysis of data over time, which is often referred to as horizontal analysis, and an analysis of data for one year, usually referred to a vertical analysis. The main techniques of analysis are trend analysis, financial ratio analysis, common-size statement analysis, and funds flow analysis – summarized below.

Trend analysis

Trend analysis is a common review technique whose sophistication varies greatly. In its simplest form it compares the current year's balances with those of the previous year. More sophisticated techniques, e.g. regression analysis, can be applied, the greater the number of observations, although monthly balances will only be available internally. Since such information will not be available to the external reviewer, only those techniques appropriate to his needs will be considered here.

The simplest form of trend analysis is to find the percentage change in the figures over the last 12 months. Once this has been undertaken, the analyst will need to ask himself questions so that each of the material changes are satisfactorily explained.

An alternative approach is to calculate ratios for a number of years, based on the last 5 or 10 years. The aim of such an approach is to provide a reasonable landmark against which current performance may be compared and to provide a greater insight into what may happen in the future. If an analyst asks 'What should the amount be this year?', a casual approach is being adopted. In contrast, if the analyst merely looks at the previous year's figures and wonders if the current year is out of line with previous periods, the approach is often referred to as a diagnostic approach.

Techniques for trend analysis can be categorized into single variable

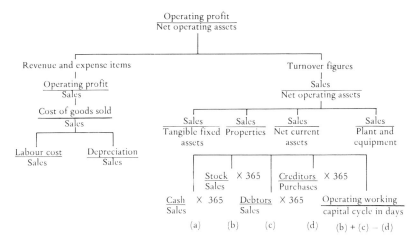

Figure 5.1   Pyramid of operating ratios

or multiple variable models. A single variable model aims to predict an amount based on previous time series data for that account. In contrast, a multiple variable model utilizes a number of variables to predict a single variable. Single variable models include the graphical method, the period-to-period change method, the weighted average method, the moving average method, and statistical time series analysis, including regression and Box-Jenkins time-series analysis. Multiple variable techniques include linear regression. All these approaches are covered in standard statistics books or in managerial mathematics textbooks.

Financial ratio analysis

Financial ratio analysis has the advantage over trend analysis that knowledge of a number of variables and their interrelations provides a greater insight into understanding financial statements than the prediction of one variable. Ratio analysis enables stable relations to be isolated and provides a useful approach to comparing one company with another, i.e. cross-sectional analysis, even though the companies may differ in size.

An example of the use of operating ratios is shown in Figure 5.1, as a pyramid in order to analyse events more effectively. The apex of the pyramid is return on net operating assets, thereby eliminating non-trading events such as investment income. A low return on net assets may be the result of low or falling profit margins or a low rate of asset turnover, so that a fuller investigation into the cause of the difficulty will necessitate a review of both revenue and expense items relative to sales and turnover figures. Readers will notice that the return on net operating assets is the cross product of the profit margin and asset turnover figures, i.e.

$$\frac{\text{Operating profit}}{\text{Net operating assets}} = \frac{\text{Operating profit}}{\text{Sales}} \times \frac{\text{Sales}}{\text{Net operating assets}}$$

As the pyramid of ratios is completed, it should be easier to identify the problem areas. For example, lower margins may be the result of high wage inflation or reflect increased competition in the industry, or may even be the result of government policy, such as a prices and incomes policy. In contrast, a lower asset turnover may reflect increased investment in assets that has not yet produced the expected income. The pyramid is a useful approach in highlighting problem areas, although it must be borne in mind that ratios are interrelated and should not be looked at in isolation.

Common-size statement analysis

This approach includes converting each item in the accounts to a percentage of an appropriate aggregate amount. For example, items of expense and revenue would be converted to a percentage of turnover, whereas balance sheet items might be converted to a percentage of total assets. Such an approach may be applied to the profit and loss account, the balance sheet and the funds statement. However, a common-size profit and loss account statement is more meaningful than the other two statements, because most revenue and expense items bear some relation. In contrast, many items on the balance sheet do not have any relation with, say, total assets, or indeed many items in the funds statements may not have any relation with, say, total funds. However, this type of analysis applied to the balance sheet and funds statement is not without its uses, since trends in major items are highlighted. Such an analysis may prompt the analyst to raise additional questions.

A common-size statement is normally prepared in time-series format, although it can be produced in a cross-sectional layout. The former highlights changes in capital structure and asset composition whereas the latter permits comparisons with other firms' expenses, assets, and capital items.

Funds flow analysis

Funds flow analysis is a neglected form of evaluation, principally because of a lack of consensus as to the purpose and format of the statement. The problem is not unique to the UK, and many countries in the world wait until the leading countries in standard setting move to a consensus. At present there is a movement away from the all-financial-resources or working capital concept toward a cash concept. Such a movement is desirable, because for many sectors of the economy, e.g. the building industry, cash is more important than accounting profits.

The objective of SSAP 10 in the UK is to show the way in which a company's operations have been financed and how its financial resources have been utilized. The funds flow statement is designed to provide a link between the opening and closing balance sheet and the profit and loss account for the period. It is prepared by selecting and reclassifying items in the final accounts and is intended to supplement these final accounts. The funds flow statement is intended therefore to assist the user to link the profit and loss account with the balance sheets and to provide information not highlighted in those statements. For example, the balance sheet provides a snapshot of assets and liabilities at a particular time and the profit and loss account only provides a partial explanation of flows as they affect items such as purchases, sales etc. These statements ignore the purchase and sale of fixed assets and funds from borrowings or issue of shares. The funds statement is designed to highlight such information, to deal with changes in figures between accounting periods, and to explain increases and decreases in assets and liabilities.

Since a source and application of funds statement is prepared by most companies, it may be accepted at face value or converted to a common-size statement to analyse trends. The funds statement should be used to raise additional questions such as:

1 Are funds generated adequate to pay dividends and taxation?
2 How have profits been used?
3 How have funds from capital issues been utilized?
4 How has working capital changed and is it reasonable?
5 Why have some major assets been sold and what have the funds been used for?
6 What assets were purchased in the recent acquisition?
7 How was the acquisition paid for?
8 How have increases in fixed assets been financed?
9 What other important sources or applications are there?

The funds statement is a useful source of information, particularly when trend analysis is applied, but it often prompts further questions rather than resolving those questions. Its analysis forces the reader to ask those important questions and seek explanations which may or may not be provided elsewhere in the accounts.

A framework for ratio analysis

When analysing financial statements, it is helpful if the analyst has a framework within which to consider the issues. The following framework may be helpful:

1 Identify the decisions for which the analysis is to be made. The analyst should identify the information and ratios relevant to the decision that has to be made; and adopt a commonsense approach in which a select number of ratios, about six, might be calculated in the first instance. If the selected ratios emphasize areas of concern,

further analysis might be undertaken. The type of decision that needs to be made can probably be categorized as follows:

(a) To provide information for the purchase, sale/or retention of securities. These share trading decisions might be based, in the first instance, on a comparison of investment ratios. Further analysis would comprise a consideration of both profitability and the financial stability of the company.

(b) To provide information for a creditor, including a banker. Creditors will be interested in liquidity ratios with a view to assessing the firm's ability to cover its current liabilities and service its future debt. However, creditors will also be interested in future profitability, since this provides information on the firm's ability to generate future profits. Note that both investors and creditors will be interested in the firm's ability to remain solvent. This involves the prediction of future events. An approach to predicting insolvency using ratios is described in Chapter 18.

(c) To provide information on the ability of a company to raise debt or equity. A company should combine equity with borrowings of varying maturities. The appropriate combination depends to a large extent not only upon the type of business and its future prospects but also on the country in which the firm operates. For example, in the UK and US it is not usual for a first-class industrial business to be financed by borrowings considerably more than 35 per cent. In other words, it is usual for equity and reserves to finance 65 per cent of the net assets of the business. These guidelines do vary from time to time, depending upon economic conditions. In other countries, such as Germany, where banks have a substantial equity stake in the business, the level of gearing may be substantially higher than that prevalent in the UK and US.

As an initial guide, gearing ratios do provide a measure, if somewhat crude, of the financial stability of the company. However, owing to distortions which can occur in its measurement other ratios such as interest cover and asset cover are important. When consideration is being given to raising equity, initial guidance may be obtained by scrutinizing trends in earnings per share, dividends per share, and price–earnings multiples.

(d) To provide information to managers. From a managerial point of view a balanced perspective is required, with the consequent consideration of probably one or two ratios from each of the categories. If this analysis shows areas of weakness, a more extensive evaluation will be required.

In undertaking any analysis it is important that the accounting policies of the company are scrutinized and particular attention paid to policies that are not consistent with other firms in the sector. In addition, the analyst should try to evaluate the implications of any changes in the company's accounting policies that have occurred over the year.

2   Identify specific ratios that will assist the evaluation of relevant information. Once the decision for which the analysis is being made is decided upon and the relevant information selected, it is appropriate to identify specific ratios that will assist the evaluation process. It is important to emphasize that the essence of ratio analysis is selectivity – to be able to select which ratios are relevant to the particular circumstances. It is all too easy to provide too much irrelevant information. For example, when using the pyramid of ratios, there is no point in calculating sub-divisions of ratios when the main ratios do not highlight anything useful for answering the problem set.

3   Undertake a limited ratio analysis, consider the results and carry out any further ratio analysis that appears relevant. This may comprise a comparison with information for prior periods, a comparison with similar information on the industry in which the entity operates and a consideration of relevant non-financial information.

4   On the basis of the information and analysis, reach a decision. This is the final stage after all relevant information has been carefully considered and evaluated.

A case study – Marks & Spencer Plc

In order to demonstrate a full range of ratios the following analysis provides an overview of the performance and financial position of the company.

Background information

Marks & Spencer Plc (M & S) has an outstanding post-war record and a reputation for being the UK's leading retailer. It is the only retailer in the world that has been given a 'Triple A' rating by both Standard and Poors and Moodys.

Its field of operations are centred around clothing and food and to a lesser extent homeware. Its food is normally of very high quality, and this is reflected in the price charged. Indeed M & S often insists that it has first choice of wholesalers' produce before other retailers. In the clothing area the company has been very successful in children's and ladies' clothing, both outerwear and underwear. The company has also been successful in extending its range of clothes for men but has been less successful in moving into casual wear and fashion for both sexes.

The company's traditional customer clientele may be described as middle-aged and middle-class, i.e. the group that can readily afford its products. However, the company is trying to diversify its product range and customer clientele, and is undertaking development of three out-of-town sites with Tesco and Asda–MFI, specialist shops for children's clothes, and is experimenting with furniture sales and mail-order sales.

M & S does not accept traditional credit cards such as Access and Visa, presumably on the grounds that it reduces its margins. However, in 1985 it introduced its own chargecard, which has proved very successful. In the first 14 months some 1.2m cards were issued and the company estimated that it created some £65m of additional sales.

In 1987 the company was in the middle of refurbishing its stores at an estimated cost of £1.5bn, a programme that it hopes will increase selling space by over a quarter. The 1986 annual report provides the following information on total sales area and number of outlets:

	1985	1986
Year ended 31 March		
Total sales area (000 sq. feet)		
UK	7216	7486
Europe	266	269
Canada	2304	2394
Number of outlets		
UK	265	269
Europe	9	9
Canada	227	243

The traditional strength of the firm is in the UK, but after initial difficulties in trading in Europe performance has improved. Indeed profits in Europe in 1986 increased by 47 per cent, with a pre-tax profit margin of 11.3 per cent, which exceeded that of the UK. Recent success in France and Belgium has renewed interest in expanding in Europe.

Substantial difficulties have been encountered in Canada, although in the year ended 31 March 1986 a 21 per cent increase in sales had the effect of showing a profit of C$ 3.2m compared with a loss of C$ 1.2m in the previous year. D'Allaird's, which specializes in ladies' clothing increased its sales by 14 per cent, with operating profit increasing by 49 per cent to C$ 9.4m. In contrast, the Peoples Division, which sells a wide range of merchandise, suffered a decrease in profits from C$ 10.3m to C$ 7.9m, although sales increased by 8 per cent. The decrease in profits was attributed to price reductions implemented in order to clear unwanted stock.

Database

Since M & S does not provide information over a 5-year period, the data in Tables 5.1 and 5.2 has been extracted from the MicroExstat service.

Table 5.1

Marks and Spencer Plc

Income statements Actuals million	1982 March 31	1983 March 31	1984 March 31	1985 March 31	1986 March 31	*Average*
Total sales	2,198.70	2,505.50	2,854.50	3,208.10	3,734.80	2,900.32
Labour costs	255.00	296.00	338.70	391.30	429.30	342.06
Depreciation	22.70	30.30	39.90	44.70	53.00	38.12
Other operating costs	1,712.40	1,957.10	2,212.40	2,468.90	2,889.90	2,248.14
Total operating expenses	1,990.10	2,283.40	2,591.00	2,904.90	3,372.20	2,628.32
Profit from sales	208.60	222.10	263.50	303.20	362.60	272.00
Investment income	27.10	34.90	34.50	19.50	25.80	28.36
Operating profit	235.70	257.00	298.00	322.70	388.40	300.36
Profit before interest	235.70	257.00	298.00	322.70	388.40	300.36
Short-term interest	10.50	14.80	12.30	15.20	20.50	14.66
L & M interest	3.20	3.20	3.20	3.70	2.90	3.24
Total interest	13.70	18.00	15.50	18.90	23.40	17.90
Profit before tax	222.00	239.00	282.50	303.80	365.00	282.46
Tax payable	100.20	79.70	90.10	120.80	134.00	104.96
Deferred tax	0.10	22.80	22.70	−0.20	7.30	10.54
Total tax charge	100.30	102.50	112.80	120.60	141.30	115.50
Profit after tax	121.70	136.50	169.70	183.20	223.70	166.96
Exceptional charges	−0.10	−0.30	1.50	−0.30	−0.80	0.00
Minority interests	1.10	1.60	1.80	2.10	2.10	1.74
Preference dividend	0.10	0.10	0.10	0.10	0.10	0.10
Profit attributable to ordinary shareholders	120.60	135.10	166.30	181.30	222.30	165.12
Ordinary dividend	60.20	67.00	82.30	89.70	103.10	80.46
Retained earnings	60.40	68.10	84.00	91.60	119.20	84.66
Earnings per share	9.21	10.28	12.63	6.87	8.40	9.48

Table 5.2

Balance sheets Actuals million	1982 March 31	1983 March 31	1984 March 31	1985 March 31	1986 March 31	Average
Properties	1,021.50	1,075.70	1,115.70	1,178.40	1,243.90	1,127.04
Plant and equipment	92.00	150.20	237.60	167.10	201.40	169.66
Tangible assets	1,113.50	1,225.90	1,353.30	1,345.50	1,445.30	1,296.70
Intangible assets Related companies	–	–	–	10.70	18.30	14.50
Other fixed assets	40.40	33.30	41.30	52.80	55.80	44.72
Fixed assets	1,153.90	1,259.20	1,394.60	1,409.00	1,519.40	1,347.22
Stock	143.70	163.30	194.10	229.70	235.30	193.22
Debtors	46.40	50.50	40.00	34.80	81.00	50.54
Securities	85.40	108.90	61.90	108.30	75.70	88.04
Cash	80.70	77.80	73.60	83.80	96.60	82.50
Current assets	356.20	400.50	369.60	456.60	488.60	414.30
Creditors	167.00	176.70	186.10	183.30	214.00	185.42
Current tax due	116.60	100.50	115.00	141.80	162.00	127.18
Proposed dividends	37.30	42.70	55.30	61.20	70.10	53.32
Current liabilities	320.90	319.90	356.40	386.30	446.10	365.92
Working capital	35.30	80.60	13.20	70.30	42.50	48.38
Capital employed	1,189.20	1,339.80	1,407.80	1,479.30	1,561.90	1,395.60
Ordinary shares	327.40	328.40	329.10	659.90	661.30	461.22
Reserves	736.30	814.80	896.30	664.00	789.70	780.22
Ordinary equity	1,063.70	1,143.20	1,225.40	1,323.90	1,451.00	1,241.44
Preference shares	1.40	1.40	1.40	1.40	1.40	1.40
Minorities	4.90	7.30	8.80	10.80	10.50	8.46
Deferred liabilities Deferred tax	8.40	12.90	24.20	2.90	17.30	13.14
Debentures and bonds	45.00	45.00	45.00	45.00	45.00	45.00
Other L & M loans	2.90	7.40	8.60	4.30	1.10	4.86
Long and medium liabilities	62.60	74.00	88.00	64.40	75.30	72.86
Net assets	1,126.30	1,217.20	1,313.40	1,388.30	1,526.30	1,314.30
Short bank loans	62.90	122.60	94.40	91.00	35.60	81.30
Capital employed	1,189.20	1,339.80	1,407.80	1,479.30	1,561.90	1,395.60

Table 5.3 M & S Plc (31 March year-end)

	1982	1983	1984	1985	1986
Return on equity	11.3	11.8	13.6	13.7	15.3
Tax ratio	45.2	42.9	39.9	39.7	38.7
Return on capital	19.8	19.2	21.2	21.8	24.9

Table 5.4 Multiple stores sector to 31 December 1985

	1981	1982	1983	1984	1985
Return on equity	12.9	11.6	10.3	12.2	13.4
Tax ratio	40.1	38.9	39.9	37.8	38.7
Return on capital	18.4	16.7	15.1	17.0	16.8

Measurement of profitability

Shareholders invest in a company provided the return is adequate to compensate for the risk attached to that investment. One measure of the return on investment is profit attributable to ordinary shareholders divided by the book value of equity investment. In the case of M & S for 1986 this is calculated as follows:

$$(\text{£m}) \quad \frac{223.70}{1451.00} \times 100 = \underline{15.42 \text{ per cent}}$$

Table 5.3 provides a 5-year summary of the return on equity investment and Table 5.4 provides information on average returns in the multiple stores sector over a similar period of time. The return on equity investment is higher in 1986 than in the previous four years and M & S has come from a below-average performer in 1981 to a consistently better than average performer. An analysis of the return on equity investment (for 1986) is provided below:

1 Return on net operating assets

$$\frac{\text{Operating profit before tax}}{\text{Net operating assets}} = \frac{388.40}{1561.9 - 75.70} \times 100 = \underline{26.13 \text{ per cent}}$$

2 Return on external investments

$$\frac{\text{Investment income}}{\text{Outside investments}} = \frac{25.80}{75.70} \times 100 = \underline{34.08 \text{ per cent}}$$

3 Return on net assets employed (capital)

$$\frac{\text{Profit before interest and tax}}{\text{Net assets employed}} = \frac{388.40}{1561.90} \times 100 = \underline{24.87 \text{ per cent}}$$

4   $\dfrac{\text{Interest on loan capital}}{\text{Loan capital}} = \dfrac{23.40}{45.0 + 1.10 + 35.60} \times 100 = \underline{28.64 \text{ per cent}}$

5   Return on equity shareholders' investment before tax

$\dfrac{\text{Net profit before tax}}{\text{Equity shareholders' investment}} = \dfrac{365.00}{1451.00} \times 100 = \underline{25.16 \text{ per cent}}$

6   Tax ratio

$\dfrac{\text{Corporation tax}}{\text{Net profit before tax}} = \dfrac{141.30}{365.00} \times 100 = \underline{38.71 \text{ per cent}}$

The return on net assets employed of 24.87 per cent differs from the return on equity shareholders' investment before tax of 25.16 per cent as a result of gearing. That the difference between the two ratios is not great is the result of the company's low level of gearing. The tax ratio of 38.71 per cent gives a return on equity shareholders investment of 15.42 per cent, i.e. the return on equity shareholders' investment before tax of 25.16 per cent multiplied by $(1 - 0.3871)$, where 0.3871 is the tax ratio.

M & S has a higher return on equity, on capital and on operating assets in 1986 than in the previous 4 years. Furthermore, its perform-ance exceeds the average for the multiple stores sector for all 5 years, and it therefore represents an excellent long-term investment.

Analysing return on net operating assets

Return on net operating assets is a key measure of efficiency, as it represents the ability of the company to utilize its assets to generate profits. The ratio is also a useful starting point to analyse the operations of the company in more detail by using a pyramid of ratios as shown in Figure 5.2. The 1986 figure is calculated as follows:

$$\text{Return on net operating assets} = \frac{\text{Operating profit}}{\text{Net operating assets}}$$

$$= \frac{388.40}{1561.90 - 18.30}$$

$$= \underline{25.2 \text{ per cent}}$$

The average return on net operating assets for companies in the multi-ple stores sector was 17 per cent in 1986, considerably less than the comparable figure for M & S. In order to analyse the reason for this it is necessary to disaggregate return on net operating assets into its compo-nent elements of profit margin and asset turnover.

$\dfrac{\text{Operating profit}}{\text{Net operating assets}} = \dfrac{\text{Operating profit}}{\text{Sales}} \times \dfrac{\text{Sales}}{\text{Net operating assets}}$

$\qquad 25.2 \qquad = \qquad 10.4 \qquad \times \qquad 2.42$

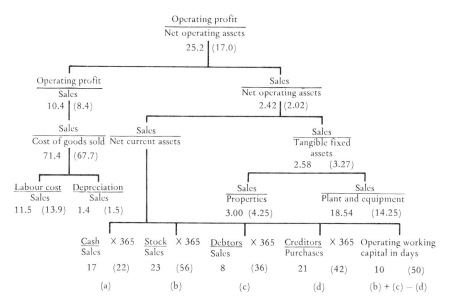

Figure 5.2 Pyramid of operating ratios for 1986 (percentages in brackets refer to the average for multiple stores)

The high return on net operating assets in 1986 is the result of above-average profit margins and a high rate of asset turnover. Tables 5.5 and 5.6 show the comparable ratios for M & S and the multiple stores sector for the period 1981–6. Over the period the profit margin of M & S has been consistently above 10 per cent, some two to three percentage points above the average for the sector. However, it is noticeable that M & S's turnover in 1982 was considerably below the average, and measures were taken to rectify this. While M & S's asset turnover has improved considerably over the period, the average for the sector has been declining.

With a reasonably constant profit margin over the period the increased utilization of its assets to generate sales accounts for the improved return on net operating assets. In fact if the multiple stores sector did not include M & S, this feature would have been highlighted even more.

The cost of goods sold ratio was higher in 1986 than the average for the sector, reflecting the higher gross margins earned by M & S. It is noticeable that gross margins in both M & S and the sector as a whole have been improving since 1982. The labour cost ratio of M & S in 1986 was lower than in the previous 4 years, whereas for the sector as a whole it has been increasing. Thus, while wage costs have been increasing at rates above the level of the retail price index, M & S has been more effective in ensuring that productivity has also increased.

Throughout the period under consideration the depreciation ratio of

Table 5.5   Marks and Spencer – 31 March

	1982	1983	1984	1985	1986
Return on net operating costs	19.8	19.2	21.2	22.0	25.2
Profit margin	10.7	10.3	10.4	10.1	10.4
Asset turnover	1.85	1.87	2.03	2.18	2.42
Cost of goods sold ratio	72.3	72.1	71.8	71.1	71.4
Labour cost ratio	11.6	11.8	11.9	12.2	11.5
Depreciation ratio	1.0	1.2	1.4	1.4	1.4
Sales to tangible fixed assets	1.97	2.04	2.11	2.38	2.58
Sales to properties	2.15	2.33	2.56	2.72	3.00
Sales to plant and equipment	23.90	16.68	12.01	19.20	18.54
Cash days	28	27	17	22	17
Stock days	24	24	25	26	23
Debtor days	8	7	5	4	8
Creditor days	28	26	24	21	21
Operating working capital days	4	5	6	9	10

Database: MicroExstat

Table 5.6   Multiple stores – 31 December

	1981	1982	1983	1984	1985
Return on net operating assets	18.8	16.9	15.2	17.1	17.0
Profit margin	7.7	7.6	7.2	7.9	8.4
Asset turnover	2.44	2.23	2.10	2.17	2.02
Cost of goods sold ratio	n/a	n/a	68.9	67.2	67.7
Labour cost ratio	12.0	12.4	14.4	14.0	13.9
Depreciation ratio	1.6	1.6	1.7	1.7	1.5
Sales to tangible fixed assets	3.95	3.44	3.18	3.35	3.27
Sales to properties	5.39	4.57	4.23	4.60	4.25
Sales to plant and equipment	14.74	13.91	12.86	12.31	14.25
Cash days	18	21	21	22	22
Stock days	53	52	52	49	56
Debtor days	39	36	33	32	36
Creditor days	44	42	41	41	42
Operating working capital days	48	46	44	40	50

n/a = not available
Database: MicroExstat

Table 5.7 Analysis of turnover in 1986

	UK	Europe	Canada
Turnover (£m)	3,395.4	94.1	181.5
Total sales area			
(000 square feet)	7,486	269	2,394
Sales per square foot	453.57	349.81	75.81
Percentage of UK	–	77	16.7

M & S has been consistently higher than the sector, reflecting either a policy of writing-down assets quicker than competitors or reflecting high capital spending. Without a considerable amount of other information it is not possible to comment on the former proposition, but a scrutiny of the accounts does reveal a high level of capital spending:

> The modernisation programme is proceeding vigorously and 44 stores have been converted. The new layout includes walkways and more space for customers to select their purchases. We believe this modernisation has resulted in a more attractive, comfortable and convenient shopping environment and in all the stores which have been modernised sales have increased substantially. The capital investment programme last year was over £140 million and plans made during the year will enable significant acceleration of investment in the year ahead. We will modernise a further 2.7 million square feet of selling space and plan capital expenditure for the year 1986/87 of over £300 million. In the four years ahead to 1990, we are planning a total capital expenditure of over £1,500 million ...

The above demonstrates how to analyse the profit-margin of a company. The pyramid of ratios shown in Figure 5.2 has disaggregated cost ratios into labour cost and depreciation, but it is possible to extend the analysis to all cost ratios.

The other aspect of the return on net operating assets is to analyse the asset turnover position. As already mentioned, M & S has a higher than average asset utilization ratio. A feature of the sales to tangible fixed assets ratio is that while M & S has been improving its turnover over the period, the ratio has been consistently lower than the average for the sector. This reflects the heavy investment the company makes in store development and the problems it has encountered, particularly in Canada. Table 5.7 shows sales per square foot analysed by geographical area. Sales per square foot in Europe amount to 77 per cent of those of the UK whereas in Canada they are only 16.7 per cent. Indeed such a deduction is confirmed by an analysis of the sales to tangible fixed assets ratio. The sales to property ratio of M & S is consistently lower than the average for the sector, whereas the sales to plant and equipment ratio is consistently higher.

The operating working capital cycle in days shows some unusual features. Firstly, cash relative to sales has declined over the period at a rapid rate, demonstrating that cash requirements have been reduced, and M & S has been utilizing its liquid assets more effectively. Compared with the multiple stores sector, the number of days' sales held as cash is now below average. Similarly M & S's stock turnover is very high relative to the sector, reflecting tight control and quick through-put. Since the business is essentially a cash business, the number of days it takes debtors to be converted to cash is very low, particularly when compared with the average for the sector. However, relative to the sector, M & S pays its creditors considerably more quickly than the average for the sector, and in fact over the period the company has increased the speed of payment. The net effect of this is that M & S's operating working capital in days is extremely low relative to the sector, although in terms of days the cycle has been increasing over the period.

Return on net operating assets is an important measure reflecting the ability of the company to generate profits by utilizing its assets effectively. This measure is often used by management as a key performance indicator. However, some companies stress other ratios as being of more importance. For instance, BTR, one of the UK's most acquisitive companies, stresses return on sales as being more important, as it ensures good cash flow. The company argues that return on net operating assets places insufficient emphasis on profits. With such an approach it needs to look to other ratios for control of its capital, especially its working capital. For example, doubtful debts are quickly transferred to its specialist debt collection company, Clear-a-Debt, to ensure early settlement of overdue accounts.

One element of operating efficiency that has not yet been discussed in this chapter is the productivity of the labour force. Efficiency demands effective utilization of human as well as physical assets. One way of measuring the efficiency of the labour force is by calculating value added, i.e. the company's sales less bought-in materials and services – its net output. One of the problems of a value added statement is that there is no standard format. This allows companies to manipulate a statement, if prepared, to demonstrate a particular point. For example, M & S prepares a type of value added statement that it calls the 'Application of Group Sales Revenue'. It is clear that one of the objectives of the statement is to emphasize taxes, since group sales revenue includes sales taxes, whereas the figure in the profit and loss account must be net of value added tax. However, only the costs of collection to M & S is a real burden, since the tax is borne by customers. Similarly income tax on salaries is not a burden to the company, other than the cost of administration, but rather it is a levy on employees. The 'Application of Group Sales Revenue' statement may be reclassified to show a more traditional value added statement, with sales revenue being shown net of taxes. By showing turnover net of VAT the contribution to government figure is £267.2m in 1986 as opposed to the figure in the 'Application of Group Sales Revenue' statement of £589.8m.

Value added represents the wealth created by the company and the

Table 5.8   Marks and Spencer value added statement

	1985 (£m)	1986 (£m)
Turnover, excluding VAT	3,208.1	3,734.8
Bought-in goods and services	2,434.1	2,852.8
	774.0	882.0
Employees	291.7	322.0
Government	241.6	267.2
Providers of capital	101.6	113.3
Replacement of assets	139.1	179.5
	774.0	882.0

statement shows how it is divided among the team. It is possible to create a pyramid of ratios, using value added as the starting point. Unfortunately we do not have any figures available other than those shown in Table 5.8. A typical ratio would be value added per employee:

$$\frac{\text{Value added}}{\text{Number of employees}} \quad 1985 = \frac{\pounds 774\text{m}}{53,963} \quad 1986 = \frac{\pounds 882\text{m}}{56,444}$$
$$= \underline{\pounds 14,343} \qquad = \underline{\pounds 15,626}$$

An alternative or additional method of analysis is to convert the profit and loss account items to a percentage of sales. Such an approach is called common-size analysis, since pounds are converted to a common proportion. Table 5.9 shows the common-size profit and loss account for M & S for the period 1982–6. There are no unusual features over the period. Labour costs were brought back under control in 1986 after they moved upwards sharply in 1985. Depreciation, and other operating costs, interest, exceptional items, minority interests are all reasonably stable over the period. Investment income and the tax charge have fallen slightly and with a fairly constant dividend it has enabled retained earnings to be increased in 1986.

Investment ratios

Table 5.10 shows the important investment ratios for the period for M & S and Table 5.11 shows those for the multiple stores sector. Great care needs to be taken to interpret these ratios. For example, earnings per share has grown at an average compound rate of 12.8 per cent p.a. This is deduced as follows:

$$\frac{\text{EPS at time } t_{1986}}{\text{EPS at time } t_{1982}} = \frac{8.4}{4.6} = 1.826 \text{ or a growth of 82.6 per cent}$$

Table 5.9   Marks and Spencer Plc common-size analysis –
Profit and loss accounts for years ending 31 March

	1982 (%)	1983 (%)	1984 (%)	1985 (%)	1986 (%)	1986 £m
Sales	100	100	100	100	100	3,734.8
Labour costs	11.60	11.81	11.87	12.20	11.49	429.3
Depreciation	1.03	1.21	1.40	1.39	1.42	53.0
Other operating costs	77.88	78.11	77.51	76.96	77.38	2,889.9
Investment income	(1.23)	(1.39)	(1.21)	(0.61)	(0.69)	25.8
Interest	0.62	0.72	0.54	0.59	0.63	23.4
Tax charge	4.56	4.09	3.95	3.76	3.78	141.3
Exceptional items		(0.01)	0.05	(0.01)	(0.02)	(0.8)
Minority interests	0.05	0.06	0.06	0.07	0.06	2.1
Preference dividend	–	–	–	–	–	0.1
Ordinary dividend	2.74	2.67	2.88	2.80	2.76	103.1
Retained earnings	2.75	2.73	2.95	2.85	3.19	119.2
	100.00	100.00	100.00	100.00	100.00	

Table 5.10   Marks and Spencer (31 March year-end)

	1982	1983	1984	1985	1986
EPS	4.60	5.14	6.32	6.87	8.4
Dividends per share	2.30	2.55	3.13	3.40	3.9
Dividends cover	2.0	2.00	2.0	2.0	2.2
Price–earnings ratio	16.7	18.7	20.9	21.0	25.3
Valuation ratio	1.9	2.21	2.84	2.87	3.88

Table 5.11   Multiple stores sector (31 December)

	1981	1982	1983	1984	1985
EPS	8.62	9.61	10.41	12.13	12.92
Dividends per share	3.22	3.61	4.02	4.36	4.57
Dividends cover	2.7	2.7	2.6	2.8	2.8
Price–earnings ratio	7.0	6.7	8.1	9.8	13.9
Valuation ratio	0.91	0.77	0.84	1.19	1.86

Using compound interest tables for year 5 the factor of 1.826 is at 12.8 per cent p.a. The same approach can be adopted for the multiple stores sector:

$$\frac{\text{EPS at time } t_{1985}}{\text{EPS at time } t_{1981}} = \frac{12.92}{8.62} = 1.5 \quad \text{or a growth of 50 per cent}$$

The annual average compound rate of growth for M & S is 12.8 per cent, which compares very favourably with that of the sector growth of 8.5 per cent. However, looking at the actual earnings per share figures one might conclude that M & S has consistently underperformed the sector. This is undoubtedly explained by the fact that many companies in the multiple stores sector have shares with a £1 par value, whereas M & S has shares with a £0.25 par value. Consequently, as a result of having low par value shares, individuals can buy small holdings in the company, but this has the effect of producing a large number of shareholders.

Also as a result of low par valued shares, dividends per share, dividend cover and the price–earnings ratio are distorted and not comparable between M & S and the sector. However, a comparison of valuation ratios is still valid. This ratio compares market capitalization to equity shareholders' funds, expressed as a percentage.

Capital structure ratios

Capital structure ratios for M & S are shown in Table 5.12 and the same variables have been calculated for the multiple stores sector (Table 5.13).

Normally financial reports do not contain any information on fixed costs and variable costs, or indeed output levels, so it is not possible to assess the degree of operating leverage. However, it is possible to ascertain financial leverage by using book or market values. By comparing ratios of M & S with the multiple stores sector it is evident that the former has a lower level of gearing in relation to equity and total assets, with the consequence that interest cover is that much greater. Income gearing and capital gearing are two ways of dealing with the same problem – the former through the profit and loss account and the latter through the balance sheet.

Liquidity ratios

Liquidity ratios measure the ability of the company to meet its debts as they fall due. Table 5.14 summarizes the key ratios for M & S and Table 5.15 shows comparable information for the multiple stores sector.

A company's short-term financial strength is measured by its liquidity (working capital) ratios and the speed with which it generates liquid assets (turnover ratios). Turnover ratios have already been dealt with in

Table 5.12   Marks and Spencer (31 March year-end)

	1982	1983	1984	1985	1986
Equity ratio (%)	70.53	68.96	69.46	71.04	72.33
Debt to equity ratio (%)	41.78	45.00	43.81	40.77	38.25
Total debt to total assets (%)	29.47	31.04	30.45	28.96	27.67
Interest cover	17.20	14.28	19.23	17.07	16.60

Table 5.13   Multiple stores sector (31 December)

	1981	1982	1983	1984	1985
Equity ratio (%)	59.16	62.15	60.12	60.33	55.66
Debt to equity ratio (%)	69.22	61.03	66.18	65.63	79.38
Total debt to total assets (%)	40.95	37.93	39.78	39.59	44.18
Interest cover	10.99	10.79	7.61	11.10	10.70

Table 5.14   Marks and Spencer (31 March year-end)

	1982	1983	1984	1985	1986
Current ratio	0.93	0.91	0.82	0.96	1.01
Liquid ratio	0.55	0.54	0.39	0.48	0.53
Cash days to sales (%)	7.55	7.45	4.75	5.99	4.61
Gross funds to debt	59.9	58.1	67.0	69.8	83.6
Net cash to debt	12.1	9.7	25.5	18.8	29.7
No credit interval	39.42	38.43	25.11	28.96	27.85

Table 5.15   Multiple stores sector (31 December)

	1981	1982	1983	1984	1985
Current ratio	1.60	1.61	1.52	1.50	1.42
Liquid ratio	0.82	0.83	0.77	0.78	0.71
Cash days to sales (%)	4.88	5.71	5.73	6.07	6.09
Gross funds to debt	42.3	42.9	37.9	43.4	38.5
Net cash to debt	22.1	11.9	3.7	25.1	9.6
No credit interval	62.17	61.85	58.01	58.87	63.27

this chapter. What remains is a consideration of working capital, which is often defined as the difference between current assets and current liabilities.

Two key measures of the ability to meet its short-term obligations are the current ratio and the liquid ratio. It is noticeable that while the current ratio of M & S improved marginally, it manages consistently to operate on a lower level of liquidity than the average for the sector. It is also true that the liquid ratio is lower for M & S than the sector. M & S is able to operate at lower levels of liquidity because it is more success-ful than the average for the sector in turning over its assets to generate cash.

The no credit interval or defensive interval is a measure, in terms of days, that the company could continue without further cash inflows. As with all the other liquidity measures, M & S operates at a consistently lower level than the average for the sector.

Common-size analysis

An alternative or complementary approach to analysing the trends of ratios is to prepare a common-size statement for the balance sheet. A common-size balance sheet statement for the years 1982–6 is shown in Table 5.16.

The common-size balance sheet statement shows no major changes over the period other than a bonus, or capitalization issue of shares, which occurred in 1985. This analysis confirms the stability of M & S. A point worth reiterating is that the common-size profit and loss account is often more useful than a common-size balance sheet, because most revenue and expense items do have some relation to turnover, whereas assets and liabilities may include no operating items, which will reduce the comparability of the percentages both over time and cross-sectionally.

Funds analysis

An approach not common in practice is to reclassify the funds state-ment to present a common-size statement. Each source is expressed as a percentage of total sources and each application is shown as a percen-tage of total applications (Table 5.17). By far the largest source of finance is M & S's operating profits, demonstrating that the company rarely goes to the capital markets for debt or equity – indeed the *Investors Chronicle* (25.7.86) stated that the company was still 'deeply distrustful of City and press'. In contrast, many of the applications of funds are variable from year to year. For example, stock as a proportion of total applications declined considerably in 1986, reflecting the small-est stock increase during the year when compared with previous years. Other investments, such as those made in plant and equipment, are also lumpy, with major investments being made in 1984. Changes in invest-

Table 5.16   Balance sheets as at years ended 31 March

	1982 (%)	1983 (%)	1984 (%)	1985 (%)	1986 (%)	1986 (£m)
Properties	67.64	64.81	63.24	63.16	61.95	1,243.9
Plant and equipment	6.09	9.05	13.47	8.96	10.03	201.4
Related companies	–	–	–	0.57	0.91	18.3
Other fixed assets	2.68	2.01	2.34	2.83	2.78	55.8
Total fixed assets	76.41	75.87	79.05	75.52	75.67	1,519.4
Stock	9.52	9.84	11.00	12.31	11.72	235.3
Debtors	3.07	3.04	2.27	1.87	4.03	81.0
Securities	5.66	6.56	3.51	5.81	3.77	75.7
Cash	5.34	4.69	4.17	4.49	4.81	96.6
	100.00	100.00	100.00	100.00	100.00	2,008.0
Ordinary shares	21.68	19.79	18.65	35.37	32.93	661.3
Reserves	48.76	49.09	50.80	35.59	39.33	789.7
Preference shares	0.09	0.08	0.08	0.08	0.07	1.4
Minorities	0.32	0.44	0.50	0.58	0.52	10.5
Deferred tax	0.56	0.78	1.37	0.16	0.86	17.3
Debentures and bonds	2.98	2.71	2.55	2.41	2.24	45.0
Other non-short-term loans	0.19	0.45	0.49	0.23	0.05	1.1
Short-term loans	4.17	7.39	5.35	4.88	1.77	35.6
	78.75	80.73	79.79	79.30	77.77	1,561.9
Creditors	11.06	10.65	10.55	9.83	10.66	214.0
Current tax due	7.72	6.06	6.52	7.60	8.08	162.0
Proposed dividends	2.47	2.56	3.14	3.27	3.49	70.1
	100.00	100.00	100.00	100.00	100.00	2,008.0

ment in securities, cash and short-term loans should be looked at together to reflect movements in liquid assets.

Summary of the case study

M & S is highly efficient in utilizing its assets to generate sales and profits, and its performance in terms of return on equity, on capital and on operating assets exceeds the average for the multiple stores sector. Furthermore, since M & S is included in the multiple stores sector, its performance against the sector excluding itself would be even more dramatically demonstrated.

The company achieves a high return on net operating assets by its high rate of asset turnover and high profit margins. It has also been more successful than its competitors in achieving productivity gains to offset increases in wage costs.

The company is financially sound and its modernization programme is being funded, at present, out of its operating cash flows. It has a low level of gearing in relation to equity and total assets and so it has the

Table 5.17   Marks and Spencer – common-size analysis

| | Funds statement for years ending 31 March | | | | |
	1982	1983	1984	1985	1986
Sources (%)					
Operating profit	77.61	68.26	91.19	87.24	90.35
Depreciation	7.47	8.05	12.20	12.08	12.33
Exceptional income	0.03	0.08	(0.98)	0.08	0.19
Fixed asset dividends		0.55	1.50	0.54	1.28
Sale of investments	0.10	2.10			
Shares issued	1.65	1.32	1.47	1.74	1.60
Non-short-term loans		1.20	0.37		
Short-term loans	4.25	15.86	(8.63)	(0.92)	(12.89)
Creditors	8.89	2.58	2.88	(0.76)	7.14
	100.00	100.00	100.00	100.00	100.00
Applications (%)					
Interest paid	4.51	4.78	4.74	5.11	5.44
Tax paid	20.94	30.31	26.10	31.12	24.32
Dividends paid	17.45	16.39	21.36	22.68	21.94
Extraordinary charges	24.04	8.42	7.56	4.76	9.30
Stock	8.99	5.21	9.42	9.62	1.30
Debtors	0.92	1.09	(3.21)	(1.41)	10.75
Property investment		7.41	6.27	5.62	9.26
Plant and equipment		20.92	40.88		18.03
Purchase of investments			2.55	6.03	3.02
Non-short-term loans	4.31			1.16	0.74
Investment in securities	5.73	6.24	(14.38)	12.55	(7.58)
Cash	13.11	(0.77)	(1.29)	2.76	2.98
	100.00	100.00	100.00	100.00	100.00

potential to go to the market to borrow for any future developments. Its short-term liquid position is not as secure as many of its competitors – a reflection that the company does not wish to have large under-utilized cash balances.

The prospects for the company are good, although not without problems. While the Canadian operations produced a profit for the first time in many years, it still has a poor return on its investment in North America. At home there is pressure on selling space, which has led to some satellite store developments, although this does not appear to be a long-term consistent policy. The company is also trying to diversify both its product range and clientele and is developing fashion-wear, furniture, carpets, soft furnishings and other household textiles.

Ratio analysis in perspective

No single group of ratios is suitable for all purposes; rather our analysis should be developed according to the specific ratios required for specific purposes. Once the appropriate ratios have been selected, they may be used for comparison. However, any comparison requires a yardstick; the use of prior years is of limited validity in the sense that the ratios provide information on performance, etc., relative to what has happened previously, and that yardstick may or may not be a representative base. Another approach is to compare a given ratio with 'ideal' or 'desirable' ratios, but this may lead to questionable results. For example, if a current ratio of 2.1 is considered to be 'ideal', then one might come to the conclusion that Marks & Spencer consistently has financial problems. That this is not the case is due to the nature of the business – this area of retailing generates considerable cash flows that enable firms to operate on lower levels of liquidity than other sectors.

Another source of comparison is with firms in the same industry. A participating company may also enrol in an inter-firm comparison scheme, but this course of action is not without its problems.

Problems and limitations in using ratio analysis may be categorized into the following groups:

1   Practical accounting problems.
2   Lack of information.
3   The assumed nature of the ratio.
4   The determination of material deviations.

Unless ratios are calculated in a uniform manner from uniform data, comparisons can be misleading. This may occur because of differing year-ends of participants, because of lack of comparable information in some key areas such as bad debts, and details on future orders which will affect future earnings, and, in particular, differences in accounting bases and policies. Firstly, there is the problem of a lack of uniformity in the way in which ratios are computed – this is demonstrated by the fact that one organization in business offering such a service does not calculate ratios in the same way as another organization. Consequently in comparing one company with the average for the sector it is important to ensure that the ratios are computed in a consistent manner. Furthermore, differences in accounting policies between companies exacerbate the problems of comparability. Differences may arise in the accounting policies adopted for stock valuation, for the allowance for doubtful debts, depreciation, the allocation of overheads and the recognition of income. The analyst must be alert to these differences and make adjustments where necessary.

For a ratio, the relation between two variables should be variable, linear, complete, be stable over time and be consistently computed if cross-sectional analysis is to be meaningful. In practice such assumptions are not perfectly met although, often they are reasonably approximated.

Finally, if deviations between companies are found, the analyst must consider whether the deviation is material. This is a matter of judgement in the light of knowledge of the firm and the sector in which it operates. In practice auditors sometimes consider a deviation in excess of 5 per cent to be material.

As far as the company itself is concerned, cross-sectional ratio analysis can be useful to identify strengths and weaknesses relative to competitors. However, a few simple ratios do not provide an automatic means to run a company, since business problems have complex patterns. Ratios help to ask the questions but do not say why a particular event has occurred.

Inter-firm comparison schemes

Organizations offering inter-firm comparison schemes have been mentioned earlier in this chapter. An excellent summary of the requirements of such schemes and problems encountered is provided by Sizer (1974). This section summarizes some of the points mentioned in that article.

Requirements of the scheme

The first requirement to ensure comparability is to establish detailed definitions and principles of valuation and agree with each participating company the methods for following them. The required information is then collected and the scheme's organizers check the figures. The next stage of the process is to calculate, tabulate and circulate ratios for the participating firms. The scheme's organizers continually develop their comparisons with a view to improving comparability and to assist management to interpret the ratios.

Problems encountered

One of the main problems encountered was a lack of comparability of the data, particularly because of differences in accounting policies adopted by firms. As mentioned under the section on framework for analysis, it is important that financial data is considered in the light of the accounting policies adopted by the company. A second problem encountered was a lack of information in some key areas, such as bad debts, which made comparability difficult. Other problems included the variable impact of inflation on firms and of transfer pricing within a vertically integrated group of companies.

From an interpretative point of view comparisons in themselves only raise questions as to why differences between firms exist rather than to explain why they differ. Further practical problems were encountered because of differences in accounting year-ends, and in keeping participants anonymous and confidential. In addition, a large drop-out rate occurred, exacerbating all the above-mentioned problems.

Reasons why participants withdraw

One of the reasons put forward for withdrawal from the scheme was a lack of comparability and therefore usefulness of the data to participants. Furthermore companies performing poorly are likely to withdraw from the scheme, making comparisons even more difficult if participants change each year. A second reason was that once weaknesses had been identified by a company and action taken to remedy the situation, there was no need to participate further in the scheme.

Summary

This chapter has covered sources of information on UK companies, techniques of analysis, an application of such techniques to a company, Marks & Spencer Plc, and has tried to place ratio analysis into perspective. The techniques of analysis of financial statements include trend analysis, financial ratio analysis, common-size statement analysis and funds flow analysis. All these techniques were applied to Marks & Spencer Plc. In order to analyse financial statements it is important that the information selected is relevant to the decision to be made. Specific ratios should be identified and calculated and where necessary further analysis should be undertaken. On the basis of the information collected and analysis undertaken a decision should be made.

No single group of ratios is suitable for all purposes. Any comparison requires a yardstick, which may be information on prior years, 'ideal ratios', or inter-firm comparisons. There are many problems inherent in comparing one company with another. Ratios must be calculated on a uniform basis and accounting policies should be consistent. Since these conditions are not often found in practice, a great deal of judgement is required in reaching decisions.

References

Sizer, J., *Insight into Management Accounting*, Penguin, 1985.

Further reading

Bird, P., *Understanding Company Accounts*, Pitman, 1979.
Blake, J. D., *Interpreting Accounts*, Van Nostrand Reinhold, 1984.
Foster, G., *Financial Statement Analysis*, Prentice-Hall, New Jersey, 1986.
Holmes, G. and Sugden, A., *Interpreting Company Reports and Accounts*. Woodhead-Faulkner, 1986.
Ingham, H. and Taylor Harrington, L., *Interfirm Comparison*, Heinemann, 1980.

Kennedy, R. D. and McMullen, S. Y., *Financial Statements – Form, Analysis and Interpretation*, Irwin, 1969.

Lee, C. F., *Financial Analysis and Planning*, Addison-Wesley, Reading, Massachusetts, 1985.

Lev, B., *Financial Statement Analysis: A New Approach*, Prentice-Hall, New Jersey, 1974.

Morley, M. F., *Ratio Analysis*, Van Nostrand Reinhold, 1984.

Parker, R. H., *Understanding Company Financial Statements*, Penguin, 1986.

Westwick, C. A., *How to Use Management Ratios*, Gower, 1987.

6 Investment appraisal

Introduction

In Chapter 1 it was stated that the principal role of financial management is to maximize the welfare of the equity investors (or owners) of the businesses, on whose behalf it manages. In practical terms the economic principle of welfare maximization equates to the maximization, over time, of dividend payments. The more profitable the company in cash terms, the greater the investments that can be undertaken. This, in turn, should lead to increased dividend payments and a rise in share price. From Chapter 7 it will be appreciated that there is a direct correlation between share price and company performance as measured by dividend payments.

This chapter is principally devoted to the use of discounted cash flow (DCF) techniques for the sound evaluation of potential investments. It is a technical chapter that points out which project is to be preferred to another, mutually exclusive, project; that ranks the acceptability of projects if investment funds are limited; and assists in deciding when the economic life of a project has come to an end. Readers should be aware that the process of evaluation is but one stage of deciding for or against a particular project. Pinches (1982) warns against focusing too much attention on the selection phase to the exclusion of the identification, development, and control phases. Indeed management would also be well advised to institute an ex-post/review stage. Important though these phases are, lack of space precludes their further discussion. Simon (1960) and Ansoff (1968) both provide useful insights into the general framework of decision theory.

Non-discounting appraisal techniques

Though the concern of this chapter is with the net cash flows generated by alternative projects over time, we briefly discuss two traditional non-discounting appraisal techniques as, historically, they have been commonly used in business. The two techniques in question are the Accounting Rate of Return and the Payback Method.

The Accounting Rate of Return is also referred to as the return on investment or return on capital employed. There are many ways in which this measure can be derived, its base being the ratio of some measure of accounting profit to a corresponding measure of capital outlay. One of the more common ratios is to calculate average profit after depreciation but before any allowance for taxation and divide by the average capital employed. If significant, it would also be usual practice to include in capital employed any increases in working capital, should the project be accepted. Let us consider a simple example: Project A requires an initial capital outlay of £50,000 and has a life of 5 years, at the end of which it can be sold as scrap for £5,000. The expected annual profits over this period for the project are:

Year	£
t_1	4,000
t_2	10,000
t_3	16,000
t_4	12,000
t_5	3,000

Average capital employed:

$$\frac{£50,000 - £5,000}{2} = £22,500$$

Average annual profit:

$$\frac{£(4,000 + 10,000 + 16,000 + 12,000 + 3,000)}{5} = £9,000$$

Account rate of return:

$$\frac{£9,000}{£22,500} \times 100 = 40 \text{ per cent}$$

A simple accept/reject decision is then made on the basis of the accounting rate of return achieved. Providing the result obtained, 40 per cent, exceeds some predetermined 'target' rate of return, it is accepted; otherwise, it is rejected.

The advantages of this technique are ease of calculation, consideration of profit flows over the whole life of the project, and producing a percentage rate of return which is a ratio commonly used by market analysts and others when measuring the profitability of a company. The disadvantages do, however, outweigh these advantages. As alluded to earlier, there is no standard measure of capital employed and profit. Being an accounting ratio, non-cash items such as depreciation are included, the production of a ratio in percentage terms fails to reflect the absolute size of investment, and although the whole life of individual projects are considered, this method fails to distinguish between the differing length of lives of mutually exclusive projects. Finally, and most fundamentally, the accounting rate of return ignores the time value of money.

The second commonly used non-discounting appraisal technique is the Payback Method. Strictly speaking this method is more of a liquidity measure than a profitability method. As with the Accounting Rate of Return, its calculation is simple but it concentrates on cash flows and not accounting measures. Individual projects are accepted provided they 'pay back' within a target period, while mutually exclusive projects are ranked by speed of repayment. Let us consider two further projects, B and C:[1]

	Project B	Project C
Investment (t_0)	− £20,000	− £20,000
Cash flows:	£	£
t_1	+ 12,000	+ 8,000
t_2	+ 8,000	+ 8,000
t_3	+ 8,640	+ 4,000
t_4		+ 8,000
t_5		+ 6,000

If the target cut-off return period was 3 years, then both projects would be acceptable. If, however, Projects B and C were mutually exclusive, Project B is preferred to Project C, since its payback period is 2 years compared to C's 3-year period. The Payback Method can also be discredited because it fails to take account of any cash flows arising after the payback period and, as with the Accounting Rate of Return, it too ignores the time value of money.[2]

Discounted cash flow techniques

The notion of the time values of money, introduced in Chapter 1, stems from the concept that the receipt of £1 today is more valuable than the receipt of £1, say, in a year's time. This notion becomes clearer if we consider the simple example of a project that requires an outlay of £100 in order to produce £105 one year later. Is this a worthwhile project? Well, the answer depends on the alternative use to which this money could have been applied. Suppose that, instead, a finance house would have paid interest of 10 per cent per annum on all deposits. That being the case, this investment would have produced £110 in one year's time and would clearly be preferable. Each of these investment opportunities earns a different rate of return: the first 5 per cent and the latter 10 per cent. In a more complicated example we would have to consider cash flows arising over several years, but again the concept is a simple one, as we merely institute the principles of compound interest. £100 invested at 5 per cent for, say, 3 years would earn £15.76 and the same amount would earn £33.10 if invested at 10 per cent for the same period. This analysis is rather simplified, and for a more detailed introduction see Levy and Sarnatt (1986, Chapter 3).

Two approaches to accommodating the time value of money in investment appraisal have been developed: the Net Present Value and the Internal Rate of Return. The former technique imputes a known discount factor, which is based on the market-determined opportunity cost of capital. Projects under this approach that have a positive net present value are accepted. The latter technique solves for that discount rate that equates future cash flows to the cost of the initial investment, i.e. a net present value of zero. Providing that the Internal Rate of Return for each project exceeds a known, predetermined hurdle rate, they too are accepted. We consider each of these approaches in turn.

Net Present Value (NPV)

The Net Present Value (NPV) can be found from the following expression:

$$NPV = \frac{Cf_1}{(1+r)^1} + \frac{Cf_2}{(1+r)^2} + \frac{Cf_3}{(1+r)^3} + \cdots \frac{Cf_n}{(1+r)^n} - INV_0, \text{ or}$$

$$NPV = \sum_{t=1}^{n} \frac{Cf_t}{(1+r)^t} - INV_0, \text{ where}$$

Cf_t = the net cash flow at the end of year t
INV_0 = the initial investment outlay at $t = 0$
r = the discount rate based upon the opportunity cost of capital
n = the project's expected life-cycle

The net cash flow for each year is expressed in present value terms by dividing by $(1+r)^t$ as appropriate. The following illustration represents the present value factors for a discount rate of 10 per cent:

$$\frac{1}{(1+r)} = \frac{1}{(1.1)} = 0.909$$

$$\frac{1}{(1+r)^2} = \frac{1}{(1.1)^2} = \frac{1}{(1.21)} = 0.826$$

$$\frac{1}{(1+r)^3} = \frac{1}{(1.1)^3} = \frac{1}{(1.33)} = 0.751$$

$$\frac{1}{(1+r)^4} = \frac{1}{(1.1)^4} = \frac{1}{(1.46)} = 0.683$$

$$\frac{1}{(1+r)^5} = \frac{1}{(1.1)^5} = \frac{1}{(1.61)} = 0.621$$

At this point it might be useful to reconsider the cash flows for Projects B and C from the previous section. Let us now assume that the company's opportunity cost of capital is 10 per cent. This would probably be based upon either the weighted average cost of capital, as discussed in Chapter 7, or perhaps a risk-adjusted measure such as derived from the capital asset pricing model, as discussed in Chapter 8. The relevant calculations for Projects B and C are now:

		Project B				*Project C*	
	£	*PVF (10%)*	*PV (£)*	£	*PVF (10%)*	*PV (£)*
t_0	− 20,000	1.000	− 20,000	− 20,000	1.000	− 20,000
t_1	+ 12,000	0.909	+ 10,908	+ 8,000	0.909	+ 7,272
t_2	+ 8,000	0.826	+ 6,608	+ 8,000	0.826	+ 6,608
t_3	+ 8,640	0.751	+ 6,489	+ 4,000	0.751	+ 3,004
t_4				+ 8,000	0.683	+ 5,464
t_5				+ 6,000	0.621	+ 3,726
			NPV £ + 4,005			NPV £ + 6,074

NB: PVF = present value factor
PV = present value

Both projects have positive net present values, but if they were mutually exclusive, Project C would be prefered. This is the reverse situation to the advice given by the Payback Method. The difference between these two methods is that the NPV approach considers those cash flows arising after the cut-off period and also considers the time value of the funds so invested.

The Internal Rate of Return (IRR)

The Internal Rate of Return (IRR) can be found by solving for i in the following expression:

$$INV_0 = \frac{Cf_1}{(1+i)^1} + \frac{Cf_2}{(1+i)^2} + \frac{Cf_3}{(1+i)^3} + \cdots + \frac{Cf_n}{(1+i)^n}, \text{ or}$$

$$INV_0 = \sum_{t=1}^{n} \frac{Cf_t}{(1+i)^t}, \text{ where}$$

i = the discount rate that equates the sum of future cash flows to the initial investment (or IRR), with the other notation as previously defined.

While the calculation of IRRs may call for the solution of complex polynomial equations, there are several computer software packages and some financial calculators that can quickly expedite their solution. An alternative approach, which provides a good approximation of a project's IRR, can be found by using the mathematical technique of linear interpolation. We can calculate the IRR for Project B by means of linear interpolation as follows:

(*a*)   let i = 20 per cent.

	£	*PVF (20%)*	*PV (£)*
t_0	− 20,000	1.000	− 20,000
t_1	+ 12,000	0.833	+ 9,996
t_2	+ 8,000	0.694	+ 5,552
t_3	+ 8,640	0.579	+ 5,003
		NPV £ +	551

This result indicates an IRR greater than 20 per cent

(*b*)   let i = 25 per cent.

	£	*PVF (25%)*	*PV (£)*
t_0	− 20,000	1.000	− 20,000
t_1	+ 12,000	0.800	+ 9,600
t_2	+ 8,000	0.640	+ 5,120
t_3	+ 8,640	0.512	+ 4,424
		NPV £ −	856

This result indicates an IRR less than 25 per cent.

With these two results we can now interpolate to find an exact value:

$$0.20 + \frac{551}{551 + 856} \times (0.25 - 0.20) = 0.22 = 22 \text{ per cent}$$

We can now test the 'soundness' of our approximation by letting i = 22 per cent:

	£	*PVF (22%)*	*PV (£)*
t_0	− 20,000	1.000	− 20,000
t_1	+ 12,000	0.820	+ 9,840
t_2	+ 8,000	0.672	+ 5,376
t_3	+ 8,640	0.551	+ 4,761
		NPV £ −	23

Only a small rounding difference of £23 is left. This approximation can be compared with the author's calculation via a programmable financial calculator which produced an IRR or 21.89 per cent, a difference of only 0.5 of 1 per cent.

Readers should confirm their familiarity with the technique of linear interpolation by calculating the IRR for Project C. The result should also work out to be 22 per cent, meaning that, if these two projects were mutually exclusive, management might be indifferent between them. It could be argued that a marginal preference be given to Project B, since it has the shorter life-cycle, and because the further into the future we go, the more difficult it is to forecast our cash flows.

While it is true that usually the NPV and IRR approaches produce the same recommendation, there are important occasions when these two approaches can provide conflicting advice. Bromwich (1976, p. 87) states that 'knowledge of a project's internal rate of return is neither necessary nor sufficient for optimal investment decisions'. On its own the IRR of a project gives no information about either a project's present value or the effect of its acceptance on the value of the firm. Whereas the NPV provides an absolute value, the IRR does not. The above consideration of Projects B and C is a case in point. While the NPV approach favours Project C with an absolute net present value of + £6,074, the IRR approach was indifferent between the two.

The NPV v IRR

The NPV approach is both theoretically and technically superior to the IRR approach, and is therefore the preferred discounted cash flow technique. Lumby (1984, p. 56) states:

> The fact that, in a decision choice involving mutually exclusive projects, selecting the project with the highest positive NPV will give a correct decision but selecting the project with the highest IRR will, *only by chance*, give the correct decision, has been explained on the basis that the IRR ranks projects in an order of preference which is independent of the capital market rate.

But why is this so? The reason is a fundamental one, based on the underlying reinvestment assumption of each approach. The NPV decision rule assumes that the cash flows resulting during the life-cycle of a project have an opportunity cost equal to the discount rate used. By contrast, the IRR decision rule assumes that the cash flows resulting during the life-cycle of a project have an opportunity cost equal to the IRR which generated them. The theoretical basis for the NPV approach is that the discount rate used is determined by the capital market. No such theoretical basis exists for the IRR approach. Can we really suppose that surplus cash flows arising from one investment will earn the same IRR in the next investment. Levy and Sarnatt (1986, p. 41) suggest that there is an economic rationale for the IRR rule. They suggest that all projects should be accepted providing that, under our notation, i > r. However, their argument ignores the unrealistic reinvestment assumption implicit in the IRR approach. Further, if we need to calculate r for the purposes of comparison, why not simply use the NPV approach? The NPV approach will provide an absolute measure that fully represents the increase in value of the company if a particular project is undertaken. The IRR approach simply provides a percentage figure that can express no such measure of wealth. In addition, the IRR fails to distinguish between the proposed scale of investment from competing projects. Consider, for example, the cash flows of two mutually exclusive Projects D and E:

	Project D	*Project E*
	£	£
t_0	− 5,000	− 8,000
t_1	+ 2,505	+ 3,750
t_2	+ 2,505	+ 3,750
t_3	+ 2,505	+ 3,750
NPV (when r = 10%)	£+ 1,230	£1,326
IRR	24%	19%

As can be seen, the IRR approach favours Project D, while the NPV approach favours Project E. Which project do we choose? They are after all mutually exclusive: perhaps, for example, they both require to use the same parcel of land or group of skilled labour. One way to clarify this situation is to consider the incremental cash flows between Projects D and E. In other words, we are asking is it really worth investing an additional £3,000 on Project E? The decision rule under the IRR approach is to accept the larger project, providing the IRR on the incremental cash flows exceeds the cost of capital (that is, if i > r as previously explained). Let us see:

	Project (E–D)
	£
t_0	− 3,000
t_1	+ 1,245
t_2	+ 1,245
t_3	+ 1,245
NPV (when r = 10%)	£ + 96
IRR	12%

Our calculations show that the incremental Project (E–D) has an NPV of £+ 96 (which is the difference between the individual NPVs for Projects D and E) and an IRR of 12 per cent. Since i is greater than r, we should decide upon Project E, since our IRR decision rule holds for both Project D and Project (E–D) and Project D plus Project (E–D) equals Project E. In this example initial confusion was presented by the IRR rule. No such confusion was presented by the NPV approach. Figure 6.1

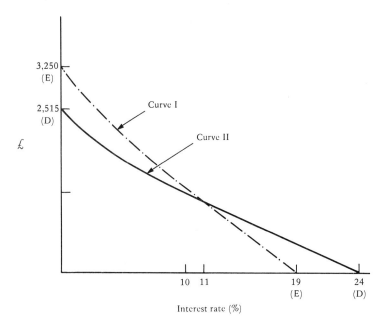

Figure 6.1

explains how this confusion can arise. Curves I and II represent the net present values at different rates of interest of the two projects. The present value rule would advise Project E if the company's cost of capital is below 11 per cent and Product D if it is higher. As the cost of capital (r) is less than 11 per cent, Project E is to be preferred.

The IRR approach is also unable to provide solutions to those potential projects that have unconventional cash flows. In such situations an IRR may not exist, or if it does, it may not be unique.

Such situations could occur, for example, when a project has an expansion option which would lead net cash outflows a few years into the life of the project. Another example could occur in the extractive industry, when net cash outflows often occur at the end of a project's life, due to landscaping costs incurred to restore the environment. Levy and Sarnatt (1986, p. 87) provide an illustration of a non–conventional cash flow which has no IRR. The numbers are $t_0 = +100$; $t_1 = -200$ and $t_2 = +150$. Rather than waste time, accept their assertion that no solution is to be found. By the way this sequence, if discounted at 10 per cent, produces a positive NPV. An alternative sequence of $t_0 = -20,000$; $t_1 = +51,000$ and $t_2 = -31,500$ produces two IRRs, 5 per cent and 50 per cent. Bromwich (1976, p. 103) provides further analysis and discussion of this phenomenon. Suffice it to say for our purposes, where multiple rates of return exist, there are no mathematical or economic grounds for specifying any one IRR over another. One final problem with the IRR approach is that it is also impossible to use when projects have different lives, see Cooke and Glynn (1981) and p. 120.

Readers should by now be aware that the authors strongly favour discounted cash flow appraisal techniques to non-discounted cash flow appraisal techniques, and that our conclusion, from the foregoing paragraphs, is we also strongly favour the NPV decision rule for investment appraisal. The NPV approach is theoretically justifiable on three grounds. It is an approach that:

1   Seeks to maximize the welfare of individual investors.
2   Considers the scale of investment.
3   Reinvests interim cash flows at the appropriate rate.

By contrast, the IRR approach may produce different recommendations to those by the NPV approach, owing to the scale of investment, the timing of cash flows and the difference in reinvestment assumption. The IRR approach is also unable to deal with projects having non-conventional cash flows and mutually exclusive projects that have different lives.

Although, from Chapter 1, the concept of NPV allows for the efficient separation of ownership and management of the company, there are some *real-world* difficulties with this approach. In the real world capital markets are not perfect. Management and investors also have imperfect knowledge and are uncertain over the future prospects of potential projects. In defence of what some might argue is a naive model, we can at least say that we are able to isolate some important variables that form part of the decision-making process. Pike (1982) and Klammer and Walker (1984) have confirmed an increasing acceptance of DCF techniques by business, so that utilization rates of more than 75 per cent among the surveyed firms are commonplace. Kennedy and Sugden (1986, p. 37) cite an additional five surveys that have been carried out in both the UK and USA during the 1970s and 1980s. The remainder of this chapter considers some practical applications of the NPV approach.

Replacement decisions

A company may keep some items of plant and machinery indefinitely, but as their age increases, so do their operating and maintenance costs, while their residual value declines. Management needs to decide when it should replace an existing machine with a new one and also estimate the optional life of the replacement. This can never be a one-off decision, as technology and product enhancements occur constantly. Not only are capital outlay costs to be considered, but also a difference arises in working capital requirements between operating and maintaining current operating capacity compared to replacement technology. In this section we are concerned to find the *economic life* of an asset rather than its physical life.

Let us consider the situation where a firm has a machine which could be sold now for £1,500. In a year's time it is estimated that it would realise £750 and in 2 years' time only £300. Its operating costs would be as follows: year 1, £2,000; year 2, £3,000. Should the machine be replaced by a more modern machine with the following cash flow details?

Purchase price, £6,000. Operating costs (including any adjustments to working capital requirements) are expected to be as follows:

Year 1	£1,200	Year 4	£1,950
Year 2	£1,500	Year 5	£2,250
Year 3	£1,700	Year 6	£2,950

The new machine is expected to have a residual (net resale) value of £3,000 at the end of 1 year, £1,800 at the end of 2 years, £1,600 at the end of 3 years, £1,100 at the end of 4 years, £800 at the end of 5 years and £600 at the end of 6 years. The cost of capital will be taken as 10 per cent.

The first stage is to decide upon the economic life of the new alternative. On its own, the net present value tells us little, since each alternative is for a different length of time. The results are shown in Table 6.1, which indicates that the 5-year alternative provides the lowest annual equivalent cost. The annual equivalent (AE) cost is found by dividing the NPV of a project by an annuity factor to give an equivalent cash flow. We need a measure that enables us to consider projects over different economic horizons. The AE method achieves this by the conversion of NPV to annual equivalent terms. An annuity can be defined as an annual constant amount of cash which arises for a given number of consecutive years. To repeat this replacement cycle into perpetuity would therefore require a present value of costs of £31,230, i.e. an annuity that continued indefinitely:

$$\frac{NPV}{r} \quad \text{or} \quad \frac{£3,123}{0.10} = £31,230$$

The next stage is to incorporate this value into the cash flows relating to the present machine (Table 6.2). The solution would appear to be to retain the existing machine for one further year and then replace with the technically superior machine.

Earlier it was stressed that companies should continually reassess their decisions with respect to equipment. It could be that in one year's time an alternative replacement is available. At such time therefore we would need to reappraise the situation. It could be argued that we should be able to predict the impact of future technological change now, but any resultant forecast cash flows would probably be of dubious value.

Table 6.1 The economic life of the replacement machine*

Net cash flows	Replacement period (years)					
	1 (£)	2 (£)	3 (£)	4 (£)	5 (£)	6 (£)
Year 0	− 6,000	− 6,000	− 6,000	− 6,000	− 6,000	− 6,000
1	+ 1,800	+ 1,200	− 1,200	− 1,200	− 1,200	− 1,200
2		+ 300	− 1,500	− 1,500	− 1,500	− 1,500
3			− 100	− 1,700	− 1,700	− 1,700
4				− 850	− 1,950	− 1,950
5					− 1,450	− 2,250
6						− 2,350
(a) NPV (r = 10%)	− 4,364	− 6,843	− 8,404	− 10,186	− 11,838	− 13,660
(b) $a_{n/r}$	0.909	1.736	2.487	3.170	3.791	4.356
(a) ÷ (b) A.E	− 4,800	− 3,942	− 3,379	− 3,213	− 3,123*	− 3,136

Table 6.2 The optimal solution**

Net. cash flows	Replacement period (years)		
	Now (£)	1 (£)	2 (£)
Year 0	1,500		
	− 31,230		
1	−	− 1,250	
		− 31,230	− 2,000
2	−	−	− 2,700
			− 31,230
(a) NPV (r = 10%)	− 29,730	− 29,528**	− 29,858

The replacement problem has been discussed under some rather simplifying assumptions to highlight the basic principles of evaluation. We will briefly discuss two of the more complicated issues – inflation and taxation. The use of real cash flows or money cash flows is a problem universal to all NPV calculations. Suffice to say that when evaluating any project, management should either prepare all cash flow forecasts in real terms, i.e. today's pounds, or else use money cash flows (estimated to be applicable at some future date) discounted by a money rate of discount (estimated at some future time period). The former ignores the incidence of inflation on future cash flows but the latter has the merit that different inflation rates are considered for different costs. If a specific index was used for, say, labour rates and a newer machine required less labour, then a clearer distinction is drawn on cost savings between the two alternatives. Our example has assumed that all cash flows and discount factors are net of tax. This is clearly a simplifying assumption and the financial appraisal should be undertaken in the

Table 6.3   Single-period capital rationing

Project	NPV £000	I_0 £000	NPV/I_0	I	Ranking II	III
F	152	400	0.38	2	1	*
G	72	200	0.36	3	2	2
H	168	600	0.28	5	4	4
I	240	600	0.40	1	*	1
J	140	400	0.35	4	3	3
	£ 772	£ 2,200				

light of the taxation position of the individual company. A further example on p. 126 will incorporate aspects of taxation when a financial lease evaluation is considered.

Capital rationing   SCARCE RESOURCES

One of the conditions of a perfect capital market is that companies can obtain unlimited amounts of funds, providing that they are prepared to pay the prevailing market rates for these funds. In practice funds are not generally freely available to this extent and a situation of capital rationing exists. Capital rationing may not only be enforced by the capital market, but there may well be internal rationing as part of a management strategy: for example, a divisionalized company may limit the amounts available between its various divisions (see Bromwich, 1976, Chapter 10). Funding may be limited for one period or for several (multi-) periods, and we shall consider each of these situation in turn.

Single-period capital rationing

With single-period capital rationing the normal procedure is, firstly, to select these projects with positive NPVs and then to rank them in order of unit contribution per £1 of available investment outlay. Consider the following example, which concerns five projects, F, G, H, I and J, whose total required investment outlay is £2.2 million but there is only £1.2 million of funds available in this period. The relevant calculations are shown in Table 6.3, where column four calculates the NPV per £1 of investment outlay and columns 5–7 provide alternative rankings. Ranking I assumes that all five projects are independent. As only £1.2 million is available, it is suggested that only three projects be under-taken – I, F and G, which collectively provide a combined NPV of £464,000 or 60 per cent of the combined NPV in the absence of capital rationing.

Rankings II and III consider the situation when projects F and I are, for some reason, mutually exclusive. The procedure in such circumstances is to re-rank all projects, but on each occasion excluding one of the mutually exclusive projects. Ranking II excludes project I and ranking III excludes F. Ranking II suggests that projects F, G and J be undertaken, with the surplus funds being invested in project H. This combination produces a combined NPV of £420,000. Ranking III suggests that projects I, G and J be undertaken, with a combined NPV of £452,000.

One problem with this approach is that it is assumed that projects are divisible, i.e. that fractions of projects can be undertaken, such as one-third of project H in ranking II above. If this condition cannot hold, then the only alternative is to rank by inspecting alternative combinations of investment opportunities. Our example is so constructed that our choices do not rely on divisible projects. If all five projects are independent, then the feasible solution is offered by ranking I. With projects F and I being mutually exclusive, ranking II offers the preferred option. Note that, with reference back to p. 115, the ranking by IRR approach would not be of any use, because this would only provide a ranking in terms of absolute percentage rates of return, whereas what is required is a measure of performance relative to the available investment funds.

Multi-period capital rationing

The more normal business situation is that capital rationing situations persist over several years. Contractual commitments recently signed will require future funding, the company may be restructuring in size and direction and so on. All these demands dictate the amount of residual investment available to undertake productive investments in any one year. In order to reach our objective of maximizing shareholders' welfare we need to employ mathematical programming. Although pioneered by Weingartner (1963), it is only in recent years that computer software packages have become readily available tools for the financial manager. Such packages are not solely restricted to capital rationing situations but can also incorporate other limitations, such as a shortage of a particular material or class of skilled labour. Carsberg (1969) provides a useful introduction to mathematical programming, while Mepham (1980) provides a guide to the detailed application of linear and matrix algebra.

Financial lease evaluation

One example of a NPV calculation where the cash flows and the discount rate are known with certainty is a financial lease evaluation. Unlike our earlier examples, it is assumed that an investment decision has been made but that, in the absence of available funds, a decision has now to be made between leasing the assets and borrowing the necessary funds. Leasing has become one of the most important sources of finance for companies in the UK. Figures 6.2 and 6.3 provide recent statistics on the cost and type of leased assets. Assets acquired during 1985, at cost, amounted to £5,757 million. These statistics have been compiled by the Equipment Leasing Association, and it is estimated that its seventy-five companies are the major providers of lease finance to industry and commerce, and between them provide some 20 per cent of all new UK investment in plant, machinery, ships, vehicles and aircraft. From Figure 6.2 it can be seen that there was in 1985 a 43 per cent increase in business on the 1984 level, which itself had been 39 per cent up from 1983. The compound 2-year increase between 1983 and 1985 amounted to no less than 99 per cent, or about 80 per cent after allowing for inflation.

The new corporate tax system introduced over the 1984–6 period had a major impact on the trend of leasing business from its announcement in March 1984. Many industrial companies were unable to make full use of 100 per cent first-year allowances on plant and machinery acquisitions. The impact of the allowances themselves, together with the pre-1984 scheme of stock appreciation relief and the relatively poor profitability of the industrial company sector at the time, meant that many of these companies were not in a taxpaying position, or at least lacked the taxable capacity to take full advantage of capital allowances. Thus leasing companies in the banking and financial sectors acquired plant for leasing, using their own taxable capacity to make use of the first-year allowances, and passing on the benefit of this to lessee companies through the terms of lease rentals. The phased reduction in tax rate encouraged leasing companies to write more business in this transitory period, while allowances could still be claimed against a relatively high rate of tax. Given a reasonably good performance in the UK economy, leasing could resume a pattern of long-term growth in the future, though from a rather lower base than in the exceptional year of 1985.

Financial leasing is, in essence, just another form of instalment purchase, though for the lessor to be able to claim all available allowances it is not permissible for eventual ownership to pass to the lessee. That being the case, in the absence of taxation, it is only necessary to compare the interest rate implicit in the lease with the alternative borrowing rate. (The implicit rate is the IRR of the lease.) When tax benefits can be obtained by the deduction of lease rentals, these need to be incorporated into a full evaluation in order to contrast the benefits with those waived by the capital allowances foregone had the asset(s) been purchased. In such an evaluation care should be taken to select a discount rate which reflects the cost, on an after-tax basis, of alternative borrowing. All taxation receipts and payments should be included in the cash flows and the evaluation carried out on a net of tax basis to ensure that any timing differences on tax receipts and payments are incorporated into the analysis. To illustrate these points consider the following information:

	1984 (£m)	1985 (£m)
Assets acquired during year (at cost)	4,012	5,757
Rentals received during year	2,622	3,586
Leased assets owned at year-end (at cost)	16,307	20,921

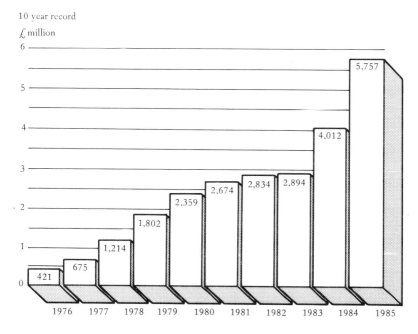

Figure 6.2   Summary of the leasing business of ELA members

Machinery at cost	£48,000
Date of acquisition	1 January 1987
Primary lease period	5 years
Rental	£225 per £1,000 payable annually in advance
Marginal borrowing rate	10 per cent
Corporation tax rate	35 per cent
Capital allowance	25 per cent p.a.
Company year end	31 December
Tax payment date	12 months after year end
Economic life of machinery	5 years
Residual value	nil

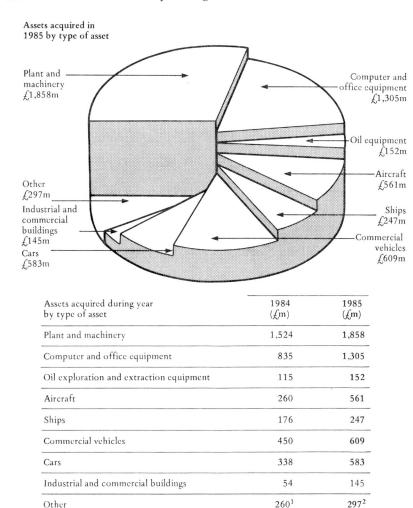

**Assets acquired in
1985 by type of asset**

Plant and machinery £1,858m

Computer and office equipment £1,305m

Oil equipment £152m

Aircraft £561m

Other £297m

Industrial and commercial buildings £145m

Cars £583m

Ships £247m

Commercial vehicles £609m

Assets acquired during year by type of asset	1984 (£m)	1985 (£m)
Plant and machinery	1,524	1,858
Computer and office equipment	835	1,305
Oil exploration and extraction equipment	115	152
Aircraft	260	561
Ships	176	247
Commercial vehicles	450	609
Cars	338	583
Industrial and commercial buildings	54	145
Other	260[1]	297[2]
Total	4,012	5,757

1   Of which £139 million identified as films
2   Of which £99 million identified as films

Figure 6.3   **Assets acquired in 1985**

Should this financial lease be undertaken or should the company borrow funds in order to buy this machinery? Assume that the company has taxable income. Table 6.4 provides the solution that it is better to lease the machinery rather than borrow the necessary funds. Readers should note the need to time-lag the after tax discount factor, that tax benefits/liabilities arise 12 months after a company's year-end. To ignore this fact would be, quite wrongly, to assume that corporation tax operated on an accruals basis. The absence of taxable capacity means that tax benefits can be deferred for a number of years. This in turn means that in the earlier years of a lease appraisal the discount factor can be materially higher. Consider a company that will not pay tax for the next 3 years, i.e. 1987 to 1989, but will pay tax in 1990 on 1989's profits. If the purchase takes place on the first day of the financial year, the company's effective tax delay will be 4 years at the start of 1987, then 3 years at the start of 1988, then 2 years from the start of 1989 onwards.

A short note on risk analysis

For the majority of investment appraisals, future cash flows and the cost of capital are rarely known with certainty. A number of simple methods have been devised and are widely used, to make some allowance for the risk of such productive ventures. None of these methods are perfect, though they do have the advantage of easy application. We use the term *risk* rather than *uncertainty*, because, unlike the latter term, it is assumed that some measure of probability distribution is known (for example, future sales based on previous patterns) or is available (for example, by market surveys).

Probably the simplest approach is to raise the discount rate to incorporate a measure of risk. The problem is, though, that there is a disproportionate impact on the present value of the cash flows. For example, raising the discount factor from 10 per cent to 20 per cent lowers the present value of the cash flow in year 1 (t_1) by about 11 per cent, whereas by year 50 (t_{50}) it has reduced the cash flow by about 1 per cent.

It would also seem that the initial raising of a discount rate is nothing more than a simple *rule of thumb* approach. In this example an extremely risk-averse individual might have doubled the discount factor. Another person might have thought a 2 per cent premium sufficient. Who is to tell which rate is correct and whether the effect of such a premium should be compounded over time? Other approaches include the *range method*, where cash flows are broadly categorized into groups such as 'most optimistic', 'best estimate' and 'most pessimistic'; and the application of probabilities or certainty equivalents to future cash flows. The notion of certainty equivalence is simple. It is a measure, based on the economic concept of utility preference, which represents investor indifference between a certain return and a risky return. For

Table 6.4   Solution to financial lease evaluation

Year	Lease rental (£)	Tax benefit (£)	Purchase price saved (£)	Capital allowances foregone[a] (£)	Net cash flow (£)	DF[b] (6.93%)	DCF (£)
0	− 10,800		+ 48,000		37,200	1.00	+ 37,200
1	− 10,800				− 10,800	0.94	− 10,152
2	− 10,800	+ 3,780		− 4,200	− 11,220	0.87	− 9,761
3	− 10,800	+ 3,880		− 3,150	− 10,070	0.82	− 8,257
4	− 10,800	+ 3,780		− 2,363	− 9,383	0.76	− 7,131
5		+ 3,780		− 1,772	+ 2,008	0.72	+ 1,446
6		+ 3,780		− 5,315	− 1,535	0.67	− 1,028
						NPV £	+ 2,317

Workings

(a)
Year	Written-down value brought forward	Capital allowance (25%)	Written-down value carried forward	Tax on capital allowance (35%)
2	48,000	12,000	36,000	4,200
3	36,000	9,000	27,000	3,150
4	27,000	6,750	20,250	2,363
5	20,250	5,063	15,187	1,772
6	15,187	15,187*	−	5,315

*Balancing allowance 15,187 × 35% = 5,315
(Assuming sale proceeds = zero)

(b) One year lag in tax payment

$$r^* = 10\% - \frac{10\%\,(0.35)}{(1 + r^*)}, \text{ where } r^* = \text{after-tax borrowing rate}$$

By a process of approximation $r^* = 6.72\%$[3]
A two-year lag is therefore:

$$r^* = 10\% - \frac{10\%\,(0.35)}{(1.0672)(1.0672)} = 6.93\%$$

The resultant discount factors necessary to calculate the discounted cash flows.

Year	r^*		
1	6.93%	$\frac{1}{1.0693}$	= 0.94
2	6.93%	$\frac{0.94}{1.0693}$	= 0.87
3	6.93%	$\frac{0.87}{1.0693}$	= 0.82
4	6.93%	$\frac{0.82}{1.0693}$	= 0.76
5	6.93%	$\frac{0.76}{1.0693}$	= 0.72
6	6.93%	$\frac{0.72}{1.0693}$	= 0.67

illustrations of these fairly basic concepts see, for example, Levy and Sarnatt (1986) or Lumby (1985).

A variety of mathematical models are also used to aid decision-making, e.g. methods such as decision trees, network planning and Monte Carlo simulation. Palmer (1979) reviews these and other forecasting models, together with some useful case studies. More recently increasing attention has been given to the application of portfolio theory to investment appraisal (see Chapter 8).

Summary

The technique of discounting future cash flows to arrive at a net present value are relatively straightforward; it is the underlying assumptions that are important. Firstly, all costs and benefits should only be in monetary terms. Non-cash items such as depreciation are irrelevant. Secondly, only differential or opportunity costs should be used. Past costs are irrelevant costs. The relevant cost of a particular stock item, for example, is either its replacement cost, the opportunity cost of a substitute material or its scrap value, the value depending on the alternative(s) available. Thirdly, the discount rate should reflect the relevant opportunity cost to the firm's equity investors. This is a cost that should incorporate both financial and business risk (see Chapter 8).

Notes

1 For ease of expression, initial investments are denoted as being made at time t_0. Thereafter cash flows are taken at the end of each year, commencing at t_1. Investments and negative cash flows are denoted by a negative $(-)$ sign, while net positive cash flows are denoted by a positive $(+)$ sign.
2 A variation to the payback method is the discounted payback method. While this latter approach is an improvement, in that it discounts cash flows in arriving at the payback period, it too ignores cash flows arising thereafter.
3 For further analysis of the need to use a tax-lagged discount rate see Hubbard G., *Finance Leasing*. CIMA.

References

Ansoff, H. I., *Administrative Behaviour*, Penguin Books, 1968.
Bromwich, M., *The Economics of Capital Budgeting*, Penguin Books, 1976.
Carsberg, B. V., *Introduction to Mathematical Programming for Accountants*, George, Allen and Unwin, 1969.

Cooke, T. E. and Glynn, J. J., 'Fixed Asset Replacement in a Recession', *Accountancy*, November, 1981.

Kennedy, J. A. and Sugden, K. F., 'Ritual and Reality in Capital Budgeting', *Management Accounting*, February 1986.

Klammer, T. P. and Walker, A. C., 'The Contingency Increase in the Use of Sophisticated Capital Budgeting Techniques', *Californian Management Review*, Fall 1984.

Levy, H. and Sarnatt, M., *Capital Investment and Financial Decisions*, (2nd edition), Prentice-Hall, New Jersey, 1986.

Lumby, S., *Investment Appraisal*, Van Nostrand Reinhold, 1984.

Mepham, M. J., *Accounting Models*, Polytech Publishers, 1980.

Palmer, C. F., *Quantitative Aids for Management Decision-Making*, Saxon House, 1979.

Pike, R. H., *Capital Budgeting in the 1980s*. CIMA Occasional Paper No. 112, 1982.

Pinches, G. E., 'Myopia, Capital Budgeting and Decision-Making', *Financial Management*, Autumn 1982.

Simon, H. A., *Administrative Behaviour*, Macmillan, New York, 1960.

Weingartner, H. M., *Mathematical Programming and the Analysis of Capital Budgeting Problems*, Prentice-Hall, New Jersey, 1963.

Part Three

Capital Structure and Portfolio Theory

7 Capital structure and dividend policy

Introduction

An essential factor in the financing decisions of the firm is the cost of capital. It is important to understand this concept in order to design a logical approach to deciding the extent to which the firm should undertake productive opportunities.

Because we live in an uncertain economic environment, different sources of capital have different costs due to different risks. With certainty and perfect capital markets, there would be no difference between the cost of equity and debt financing. The requirements of perfect capital markets have been summarized as follows (Modigliani and Miller, 1961, p. 412):

> In 'perfect capital markets' no buyer or seller (or issuer) of securities is large enough for his transactions to have an appreciable impact on the then ruling price. All traders have equal and costless access to the information about the ruling price and about all other relevant characteristics of shares ... No brokerage fees, transfer taxes and other transaction cost are incurred when securities are bought, sold or issued.

In such a world investors (present and potential) would know with certainly the effect of their transactions. Alas, ours is the real world in which we have risk/uncertainty, transaction costs and a distortionary taxation system. These factors influence management's choice of capital.

Long-term capital for investment is either generated internally or raised externally through the medium of the various forms of security (see Chapter 10). The financial manager must understand the market influences on each source in order to attract new investors, retain the interest of present investors and perceive why other investors have moved their funds elsewhere.

In this chapter the cost of each separate source is first derived, ignoring any effect its use may have on the price of other funds. This is followed by an examination of the effects of using different mixes of funds. Once a firm has decided upon its optimal capital structure, it must decide how much equity it will obtain externally, through the issue of new equity capital, and what proportion internally, through the retention of earnings. This is an important area of discussion, since retained earnings constitute by far the largest single proportion of funds used by UK companies.

The cost of capital

In this section we firstly consider the individual costs of equity shares, retained earnings, preference shares and debt. We then consider combinations of funding in order to arrive at some weighted average cost of capital.

Cost of equity capital

This is the most difficult source to measure, as the forecasting of future earnings, dividends, share prices and required rates of return is exceedingly difficult. Unlike other forms of security, discussed below, the return to the investor is not set at a constant figure. Indeed, if the company prospers, equity investors expect that increasingly large dividends will be paid in the future. The price an investor will pay to secure a particular share depends upon his assessment of the cash flows expected, either in the form of expected future dividends or expected future sales price, and the riskiness attached to these expectations. Two ways of measuring the equity cost of capital are commonly used: the capital-asset pricing model and the dividend valuation model.

From Chapter 8 we know that the capital-asset pricing model implies that the required return on an equity share is:

$$E_{rj} = rf + \beta_j(E_{rm} - rf)$$

where rf = the risk-free rate

        E_{rm} = the expected return for the market portfolio

        βj = the beta-coefficient (as described in Chapter 8) for equity share j.

There it was stated that the opportunities to hold linear combinations of risk-free assets and portfolios of risky securities are available to managers and shareholders alike, and provide a rational opportunity cost for alternative investments.

Another, more traditional way of measuring the equity cost of capital is to find that rate of return which equates the expected future dividend stream to the market price of the share. Let us consider a simple example by asking what is the required rate of return for a share with a current market value of £2.00 in a static economic environment where a constant annual dividend of 20p is anticipated? With this information we can show how the required rate of return is derived. Taxation is ignored.

The relevant stages are:

(i) Market value of share, P_0 = present value of expected future dividends.

(ii) $P_0 = \dfrac{d_1}{(1 + k_e)} + \dfrac{d_2}{(1 + k_e)^2} + \dfrac{d_3}{(1 + k_2)^3}$ ———— into perpetuity (∞),

where, d = expected future dividends
k_e = required rate of return.

Rewritten as,

(iii) $P_0 = \displaystyle\sum_{t=1}^{\infty} \dfrac{d_t}{(1 + k_e)^t}$, which simplifies to,[1]

(iv) $P_0 = \dfrac{d_1}{k_e}$

Remember that values for d_1 and P_0 are observable, so that by rearrangement the equity cost of capital is:

(v) $k_e = \dfrac{d_1}{P_0} = \dfrac{20p}{£2.00} = 0.10$ or 10 per cent.

This basic model can be further developed to allow for a growth in dividends. In similar fashion to the stages first outlined, the perpetuity valuation model reduces to:[2]

(vi) $P_0 = \dfrac{d_1}{(k_e - g)}$, and the equity cost of capital becomes

(vii) $k_e = \dfrac{d_1}{P_0} + g$.

If dividends are expected to grow by about 5 per cent compound per annum, the equity cost of capital is:

$k_e = \dfrac{20p}{£2.00} + 5$ per cent $= 15$ per cent

For k_e to be realistic, market expectations must be such that dividends are believed to grow at a rate of g. One method of projection would be to examine the past history of dividend payments as a guide to future expectations. Such an approach would mean that investors expected past performance to provide a suitable proxy for future performance. If anything other than a constant growth of dividends is expected in the future, the model must be sub-divided into periods, each spanning an expected growth pattern. For example, if dividends were expected to grow at a 5 per cent compound for 5 years and then grow at 10 per cent into the foreseeable future, we would have the following expression:

$$P_0 = \sum_{t=1}^{5} \frac{d_1(1+g)^t}{(1+k_e)^t} + \sum_{t=6}^{\infty} \frac{d_5(1+g)^{t-5}}{(1+k_e)^t}$$

$$£2.00 = \sum_{t=1}^{5} \frac{20p\ (1.05)^t}{(1+k_e)^t} + \sum_{t=6}^{\infty} \frac{25.53p\ (1.10)^{t-5}}{(1+k_e)^t} \quad (t_{1-5}: R_e = 15\%;$$

$$t_{6-\infty}: R_e = 20\%)$$

Cost of retained earnings

Earnings reinvested by companies account for approximately 75 per cent of their total investment in productive opportunities. It would be wrong to regard retentions as a free cost; there is certainly no contractual cost but plainly an opportunity cost. If funds are retained by the firm, the investors forego their use and they should therefore be compensated. Retained earnings should earn a return sufficient that higher future dividends at least compensate for the forgone opportunities available to investors had they received their dividends earlier. Investors are not a homogeneous group and the extent of the opportunities foregone relates closely to the operation of the corporation tax system and its interrelation with income tax and/or capital gains tax. Again, a simple example should suffice to explain the principles. Capital gains tax will be ignored as a proper analysis would require knowledge of exactly when each shareholder wishes to realize his gains.

Let us suppose that a firm retains profits of £25,000 after the deduction of corporation tax. Had these profits been paid out, then their recipients would have reinvested their dividends at a market rate of 10 per cent. The question is, at what rate will the firm need to reinvest this sum in order to preserve the best interests of its investors? By taking two extremes we can compute this required rate of return. In the first instance all investors will be assumed to have no liability for income tax. Had the £25,000 been distributed, investors would have received dividend warrants to this value plus tax credits totalling £10,715 (assuming a basic rate of 30 per cent for income tax, $\frac{3}{7}$ths). That is £35,715 altogether. A 10 per cent return yields £3,571.50 p.a. In contrast, the firm would need to reinvest these funds at a rate of almost 15.38 per cent before corporation tax, i.e. 10 per cent $\frac{1}{(1-c)}$,

where C denotes corporation tax at 35 per cent.
The proof is:

£25,000 at 15.38 per cent = £3,845
£3,845, less corporation tax at 35 per cent = £2,499
£2,499, plus tax credit (3/7ths) ≃ £3,571.5

Note that figures, where necessary, have been rounded off to give greater clarity to the argument presented.

In the second instance, let us assume that there is only one investor, who has a marginal tax rate of 60 per cent. Had he received a dividend, this would have resulted in the payment of additional income tax of 30 per cent on the grossed up dividend of £35,715, leaving £14,286 for reinvestment to produce £1,429 p.a. To satisfy this investor the firm could afford to undertake any opportunities earning above 6.15 per cent before corporation tax. In this situation it would be in the investor's best interests not to remove his funds from the firm. The proof is:

£25,000 at 6.15 per cent = £1,538
£1,538, less corporation tax at 35 per cent = £1,000
£1,000 plus tax credit (3/7ths) = £1,429

As stated above, this example is somewhat unrealistic in its assumptions, but it does at least indicate the effect of the taxation system on investment decisions. Several papers have been written which have also incorporated the effects of capital gains tax.[3]

Given the diverse interests of investors, it can be broadly stated that an investor with a large income, assessable at a high marginal rate of income tax, would prefer companies with a low payout policy because of the difference between his personal rate of income tax and the effective rate of tax on capital gains.

Because investors do not represent a homogeneous group, it is impossible for a firm to satisfy all needs. Some authors, for example Elton and Gruber (1970), have discussed what is termed the 'clientele effect', whereby investors having similar characteristics with similar expectations are attracted to particular companies. Quirin 1967 argues that, where shareholders are subject to differing tax rates, the correct discount rate to use is that based on the preferences of tax-free individuals. As Bromwich (1976, p. 123), states:

> All those equity-holders who are subject to tax will have lower costs of capital than this, and therefore, using this rate will ensure that all accepted projects covers the minimum requirements of all shareholders, and that at least the tax-free ones are made better off.

The assumption is that firms face at least the same opportunities as investors with a nil liability to income tax. Solomon (1963) follows a similar line of argument when he suggests that to overcome this difficulty of conflicting interests, the minimum cost of retained earnings should be equated with that of the market rate of return – this amounts to an opportunity cost concept.

Cost of preference shares

The cost of a preference share is related closely to its stated dividend, even though payable at the discretion of the directors. If a £1 nominal value preference share had a dividend of gross 7½ per cent and a market value of 90p, its cost would be 8.33 per cent, i.e.

$$k_p = \frac{d_p}{Ps_0} = \frac{7.5}{90} = 8.33 \text{ per cent,}$$

where k_p = cost of preference shares,
d_p = fixed dividend based on nominal value,
Ps_0 = market price of preference shares.

Over recent years there has been a marked drop in the popularity of preference shares on the part of the issuing company. Kirkman and Usher (1971) relate this primarily to the introduction of corporation tax in 1965. The Finance Act of that year stated that interest on debentures, discussed next, should be an allowable expense for taxation purposes, but that dividends on shares, whether ordinary or preference, would not be accepted for such purposes. Following on from this many firms arranged schemes whereby preference shares were converted into debentures, providing that such shares were classified as redeemable in the Articles of Association. Those preference shares that presently remain in circulation are mainly in the hands of corporate bodies that have felt unwilling to give up the advantages of franked investment income (as opposed to unfranked investment income).

Cost of debt

Normally debt is regarded as having a lower cost to the firm than equity, as interest payments are less uncertain. A similar framework to that for equity capital is used – first without taxation:

$$D_0 = \frac{I_1}{(1 + k_d)} + \frac{I_2}{(1 + k_d)^2} + \cdots \frac{I_n + D_n}{(1 + k_d)^n}$$

where D_0 = current market price
I_n = interest payment in time n
D_n = amount payable on redemption
k_d = cost of debt capital

Suppose that a debenture has a fixed rate of interest of 8 per cent and a current market price of £100, and that it will be redeemed in 10 years' time. The cost of finance will be 8 per cent. If the market price dropped, say, to £90, then the rate of interest required would rise to above 10 per cent, i.e.,

$$£90 = \frac{8}{(1 + k_d)} + \frac{8}{(1 + k_d)^2} + \cdots \frac{(8 + 100)}{(1 + k_d)^{10}}$$

Readers can verify for themselves the exact value of k_d to satisfy this equation.

Interest charges are a tax deductible expense for corporation tax purposes, but any rate computed should not be adjusted to a net of tax basis. This is because the tax advantage of debt is reflected in the cost of equity, because dividends are higher than would otherwise be the case. In the example outlined below readers can confirm for themselves that the equity return to shareholders is (in cash flow terms) 7.8 per cent, with corporation tax at 35 per cent. If debt interest was not a tax deductible expense the net of tax equity return would only be, on an average cost basis, 6.4 per cent.

While individual debt instruments are repaid from time to time, the firm naturally replaces a given proportion of debt in its capital structure. For this reason the appropriate formula for calculating the cost of debt is in the form of a perpetuity:

$$k_d = \frac{I_0}{D_0}$$

Combining debt with equity

The discussion so far has related to individual sources of capital. Following on from this we have to consider whether the costs that we calculate, should be average costs (based on the existing capital structure) or marginal costs of capital (based on raising additional/new funds).

In practice it is generally regarded as impossible to allocate specific funds to specific projects. Rather funds for projects are thought of as coming from a central 'pool'. To this extent it has commonly been the practice to use a weighted average cost of capital (WACC) for project evaluation. When new projects are considered, the WACC could be based on individual existing average costs of capital if no additional funds are required. Otherwise, if additional funds must be raised, it would be more appropriate to use a WACC based on marginal costs. The weightings used, regardless of whether based on average or marginal costs, will be those appropriate to the firm's desired capital structure.

Let us suppose that we have the following (hypothetical) estimates for a certain company:

Source of finance	Current market value	Average cost	Marginal cost
Equity	£2 million	12%	12%
Debentures	£1 million	8%	10%

The two measures for WACC would therefore be based on the formula:

$$k_0 = k_e \frac{P_0}{V_0} + k_d \frac{D_0}{V_0}$$

where $V_0 = P_0 + D_0$, that is the total market value of the firm, and K_0 is the WACC. The average WACC is 10.67 per cent and the marginal WACC is 11.33 per cent. Note also that by using the market value of equity, such valuation is believed to include an allowance for retained profits. If difficulty is encountered in obtaining individual market values, then book values must be used, though as rather a secondary measure. In this situation a weight must be applied to retained earnings.

Use of the WACC as a cut-off rate for project evaluation has the advantage of simplicity, but the assumptions which underlie it should not be forgotten. Firstly, there is the assumption that all projects are of the same risk class. It may be that a firm which is currently diversifying its activities should require different rates of return for particular ventures. Secondly, there is the assumption that the firm maintains constant proportions of debt and equity. Changes in the capital structure may alter the financial risk of individual sources of capital as well as altering the relevant weights of each source. Finally, it has been argued that certain projects may be eligible for particular sources of 'cheaper' finance, and the discount factor should reflect the cost of these 'cheaper' funds.

Just now it was stated that the weightings used for calculating the WACC should be appropriate to the firm's desired capital structure. What ought now to be apparent is that, given a world of risk and uncertainty, a judicious mix of debt and equity can result in a lower cost of capital than if the firm was financed solely by equity. The measure or yardstick usually referred to here is that of leverage or gearing. The standard textbook approach to financial leverage is to state that the optimal degree of financial leverage is that degree which minimizes the WACC. This is a compatible objective to maximizing the market value of shares for our equity investors.

Consider an all equity financed company. It currently has 1,000 shares outstanding with a market price of £10 each, and earnings are currently £1,000 per annum. (Earnings per share, EPS, is therefore £1.) Suppose that this firm wished to embark upon a major investment costing £10,000 and expects to double its annual earnings from £1,000 to £2,000. Should it issue an additional 1,000 shares, at market price, or raise £10,000 of 8 per cent loan stock? (For simplicity of illustration, taxation is ignored.)

The choice of finance is as follows:

	Equity-financed	*Debt-financed*
Number of shares in issue	2,000	1,000
Debentures (at 8% p.a.)	–	£10,000
	£	£
Earnings before interest and tax	2,000	2,000
Interest	–	800
	£2,000	£1,200
Earnings per share (EPS)	£1	£1.20

Shareholders are better off if loan stock is issued. Note that if earnings increase further, the interest charges will take a decreasing proportion of earnings and the attraction of debt finance is enhanced. On the other hand, if earnings do not attain management's expectations, then debt financing will take an increased share of the company's profits and EPS could be reduced. If the above earnings forecast dropped to only £1,000, the EPS for the all equity company would be 50p and only 20p for the firm employing debt capital. This example serves to illustrate that it is desirable to study how the financial structure of the firm relates to the equity's investor's wealth.

The optimal capital structure debate

Much has been written on the effect that capital structure has on the cost of capital. There is in fact a rather complex relation between capital structure and the cost of capital. If the cost of capital is to be based on some weighted average of a number of sources, each with a different cost, does one suppose that different structures lead to different costs? It is perhaps useful to remember that the various components of capital depend upon market factors which in turn take account of commercial and financial risk. Having examined the effect of leverage we now look at three theories of its implication for the cost of capital. These three theories are (a) the net income approach, (b) the traditionalists' view, and (c) the net operating income approach. For each the following assumptions are made:

1 No income and corporation tax.
2 Changes in capital structure are instantaneous and are affected without transactions costs.
3 The firm pays out all earnings in the form of dividends. The earnings are constant and continue into perpetuity.
4 The earnings streams of the two firms to be examined below are the same in terms of business risks in the eyes of the shareholders. Further, business risk is assumed to remain constant over time.

In terms of notation previously introduced, the following discussion examines the effect of each theory on k_e and k_0 for varying amount of debt in the capital structure.

The net income approach

The net income approach assumes that the value of the firm increases as increasing amounts of debt are added to the firm's capital structure. Neither the cost of debt or equity is expected to change as the level of leverage increases. Financial risk is ignored. As will be seen from Figure 7.1, as leverage increases k_0 decreases, i.e. the higher the proportion of debt employed, the lower the WACC.

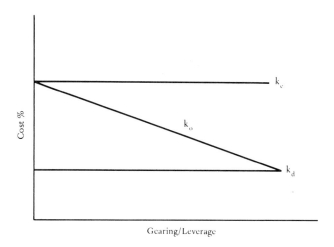

Figure 7.1

This model is over-simplistic in that equity investors are assumed not to require a higher return as more and more of the net earnings fall due to the providers of the debt capital. Equally the providers of debt capital are expected to accept the same rate of interest. By utilizing low-cost debt finance, the WACC is reduced and the value of the company is increased.

The traditionalists' view

This viewpoint is argued more from observation than from any vigorously tested model. Traditionalists would contend that to begin with (in agreement with the net income approach) leverage should be increased by the introduction of debt, because the financial risk caused by the introduction of this source is more than compensated for by the gains to the equity from its use. As debt is added to the firm's financial structure, the average cost of capital will fall.

Later, as the proportion of debt increases, the cost of equity will increase to take account of increasing risk arising from the deployment of debt and will be offset. This stage will vary between firms, owing to individual differences in commercial and financial risk. Beyond this point the cost of equity will increase rapidly, as will the cost of debt, so that the cost of capital will likewise increase. Figure 7.2 depicts the traditionalists' viewpoint. Initially, to point X increases in debt lower k_0, but after point Y even the providers of debt require a higher return.

The net operating income approach

This third view is frequently associated with Modigliani and Miller (MM hereafter). Their 1958 paper first challenged the more traditional

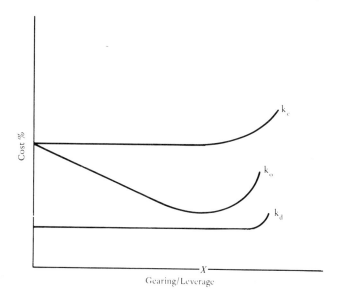

Figure 7.2

approach to the firm's capital structure and created a lively academic debate which has continued ever since.

MM's view stated (in summary) that, given the conditions of perfect capital market, two companies with the same productive potential, yielding identical cash flows and of the same risk 'complexion', must have the same aggregate capitalization value, regardless of their capital structure. They further assumed that distortionary taxes did not exist. A market mechanism called 'arbitrage' was expected to interpose, such that investors would act to equate the two values of the companies in all respects except that of leverage. (Arbitrage, in this sense, can be defined as the switching of funds by the investor from one investment to another so as to obtain a better return for the same risk level.) The attraction of this theory is that the WACC, being constant, could be used as an accepted discount factor for project appraisal.

In the perfect capital market envisaged by MM information is freely available to all investors; further, they are expected to act in a rational manner and to have similar expectations. All investors are also expected to agree on the expected future stream for each firm. Finally, all firms can be classified into equivalent or homogeneous risk groups. With these assumptions three propositions are derived:

1 The total market value of a company is independent of the amount of debt in its financial structure.
2 As leverage increases, the equity cost of capital of a levered corpora-

tion will rise in order to offset advantages flowing from the lower cost of debt relative to equity.
3   In order to maximize equity holders' wealth the firm should use its weighted average cost of capital as a cut-off rate.

The essence of this argument hinges on the assumption (examined below) that arbitragers are able to substitute personal for corporate leverage. Before examining these propositions further, let us introduce a simple numerical example. We consider two companies. Company A has 100 per cent equity, whereas Company B has 80 per cent equity and 20 per cent debt. Total capitalization, in the short term, is summarized thus:

	Co.A	*Co.B*
Earnings	£10,000	£10,000
less interest on debt (5%)	–	1,000
Earnings available to equity holders	£10,000	£9,000
Equity capitalization rate	10%	11%*
Market value of equity	£100,000	£81,818
Market value of debt	–	£20,000
Total market valuation	£100,000	£101,818
Weighted average cost of capital	10%	9.8%

*Pay 1% higher to allow for financial risk.

MM maintain that, while this position might persist in the short term, in the long term the two companies' cost of capital will equalize. MM argue that investors in Co.B are able to obtain the same return with no increase in financial risk by investing in Co.A for a smaller investment outlay. Because of less outlay, they would sell their shares in Co.B and invest in Co.A. Let us consider one particular investor with a 1% share of Co.B's shares, with market value of £818. He should:

1   Realize his investment in Co.B for £818.
2   Borrow £200 at 5 per cent interest, the same rate applicable to corporate borrowers, to give his own portfolio the same leverage as Co.B.
3   Buy 1 per cent of the unlevered Co.A for £1,000.

Before this transaction his expectation in Co.B was £818, earning 11 per cent, i.e. £90 annum. Now it is £1,000, earning 10 per cent, which is £100. From this must be deducted debt interest (£10), also to give £90. However, this outlay is £800 (£1,000 – £200), compared with the £818 invested in Co.B. The investor is able to gear the equity of Co.A by taking on personal debt. MM's view of leverage can be shown graphical-

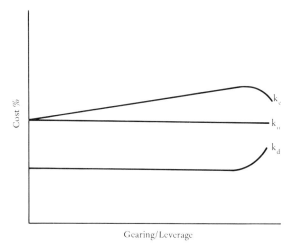

Figure 7.3

ly in Figure 7.3. A glance back to Figure 7.2 highlights the differences between MM and the more traditional approach. Appendix 7.1 (p. 153) considers MM's propositions more closely in algebraic terms. Figures 7.4 and 7.5 illustrate the value of a geared/levered firm with respect to the traditional and net operating income theories.

MM propositions and the real world

Under the restrictive assumptions developed by MM, their conclusion that leverage cannot affect the total market value of two similar firms must be true. It also follows that the cost of capital will remain constant. Such assumptions are, though, too restrictive for applicability in the real world. It is in this area of applicability that most attacks have been made against MM's propositions.

MM initially ignored the distortionary effect of corporate taxation, whereby debt is more favourably treated than equity. This point was later accepted by MM (1963), when they decided that, owing to the deductibility of debt interest before computing the tax liability, the weighted average cost of capital would continuously decline as more and more debt is added to the firm's capital structure. Tax savings of $C.k_d.I$, where C denotes the rate of corporation tax, would be available to equity holders. The value of a levered company would therefore be:

$$V_0 = \frac{Y(1-C)}{k_e} + \frac{Ck_dI}{k_e}$$

Where Y = firm's expected annual earnings, before the deduction of debt interest and other notation is as previously defined.

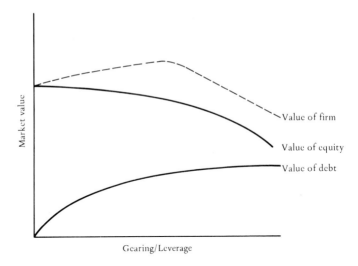

Figure 7.4   Traditional view of optimal capital structure

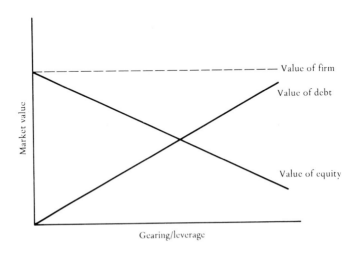

Figure 7.5   Modiglani and Miller's view of optimal capital structure

Solomon (1963, p. 114) argues that the tax savings on debt should instead be capitalized at the same rate as debt payments, k_d. This is because tax savings on debt are assumed to be more certain than equity payments, as the former accrue every time debt interest is repaid.

Could it now be argued that, given the tax deductibility of debt interest, firms should strive to use as much debt finance as possible? Most authorities would say not, suggesting instead that the cost of debt is more likely to rise to a level which outweighs its attractiveness over equity if excessive leverage is pursued. One needs also to consider the interplay of personal taxes. It would seem that firms should strive to secure the best net-of-all taxes returns for their equity investors.

Criticism is also raised against MM's assumptions with respect to the arbitrage process. No difference is drawn between corporate debt and personal debt, i.e. the inference is that personal and corporate leverage are equivalent. Is it really true that individuals have ready access to all funds available to corporations? Is it also true that individuals and firms are equally risky? Certainly individuals could never have as high a credit rating as large corporations. The limited liability which companies enjoy mean that the investor is safer if the firm borrows on his behalf. If firms can secure larger funds and borrow at lower rates than individuals, then the notion that personal leverage can replace corporate leverage collapses. As Bromwich (1976, p. 156) points out: 'In England the managers of institutional funds could, if they wished, "arbitrage" by changing the leverage within their portfolios. That they do not seem to do so has been cited as an argument against MM's views.'

In the previous chapter discounted cash flow techniques were introduced. The appropriate discount factor (required rate of return) was assumed to be based upon the opportunity cost of capital. We now realize that different sources of funds, by having different costs, present management with the problem of how best to attain some optimal balance of funds–capital structure. Three approaches to this problem were examined. The first, the net income approach, can generally be ignored as being too simplistic. We are left with two opposing theories, neither providing a definitive solution. Empirical studies which have been carried out have been inconclusive. Apart from MM's (1958, 1966) empirical evidence, work has also been carried out by Barges (1963), Gordon (1967) and Weston (1963, 1967).

Can we attempt to reach some middle ground position? MM, as previously stated, have modified their original conclusions and conceded the distortionary effects of corporation tax. Perhaps one important issue arising out of their work is that we do at least arrive at an important check-list of factors which all contribute to management's thoughts concerning the capital structure of their particular firm. Equally traditionalists would nowadays accept the MM view that capital structure, while important, is not the overriding determinant of the cost of capital. In recent years a significant proportion of the finance literature has moved away from the WACC concept, advocating instead separate procedures for the timing of cash flows and their uncertainty.

What is apparent from both viewpoints is that extreme positions are to be avoided. The debate on the optimal capital structure question remains open.

Dividend policy

Two views can be taken on the relevance of dividend policy; one is the obverse of the other. The first view is that the firm decides upon the amount of earnings it wishes to invest, leaving any residual to be distributed as dividends. In theory it could be argued that earnings should be reinvested, provided that the resultant earnings exceed those required. Only if funds remained after accepting all such projects would residual earnings be paid out as a dividend. With such a policy the payment of cash dividends constitutes a 'passive residual' (Solomon, 1963). The rationale of this theory follows on from ideas developed earlier in the book but could result in a wide fluctuation in the level of payment from year to year. The second view is one that is often observed in practice, that the firm decides upon a dividend and then uses residual funds for reinvestment. The differences between these two views arise because of market imperfections.

It is impossible to derive precise rules on dividend policy which could be universally applied by all firms. Instead, we isolate the basic elements which constitute the most favourable policy. This chapter begins by reviewing the debate of whether or not dividend policy affects the market value of a firm's equity shares. The question is material if we recall that the objective of the firm was previously taken to be that of maximizing the value of the equity investors' investment.

Dividends and valuation

Considerable attention has been devoted to the question whether or not dividend policy influences the value of the firm. Two alternative schools of thought have arisen over this matter. The more traditional school advocates that dividend policy plays a vital role in determining the market value of the firm. This school contends that, for a variety of reasons, dividends are preferred to capital gains. Proponents, such as Gordon (1959) and Lintner (1956), suggest that capital gains (which arise when retained earnings are reinvested by the firm) are seen as more risky than present dividends. Walter (1967) states that dividends have an effect on equity share prices because they communicate information about the company's profitability. If a company has a stable dividend policy and this is altered, investors could interpret this as a change in management's expectations for the future and the market price of the shares will adjust accordingly. A reduction in dividend could, for example, be said to reflect pessimism.

There is an alternative school, one which adheres to the notion that dividends ought only to be considered as a passive residual. Modigliani and Miller (1961) argue that in a tax-free world the market is indifferent between receiving a specific sum of money in the form of dividends or capital gains. In other words, dividend policy is irrelevant. What is important is the net operating earnings of the firm. In conditions of certainty and perfect capital markets it is expected that the firm undertakes what it believes to be its optimal investment policy and that the investor will enter the market if he wishes to generate a cash flow different to that offered by the firm. More specifically their assumptions are:

1 Perfect capital markets in which all investors are rational. Information is available to all at no cost, transactions are instantaneous and without cost, securities are infinitely divisible; and no investor is large enough to affect the market price.
2 An absence of flotation costs on securities issued by the firm.
3 A world of no taxes.
4 A given investment policy for the firm, not subject to change.
5 Perfect certainty by every investor as to future investments and profits of the firm. MM also extend their argument to an uncertain world.

MM's view is best explained by means of a simple example. (A more rigorous proof is provided in Appendix 7.2, p. 154)
   Let us assume that an all-equity firm wishes to undertake a productive opportunity which requires an initial outlay now, at t_0, and returns £125 per annum into perpetuity. It will be assumed that equity investors will forgo one current dividend of £1,000 in anticipation of future increased dividends of £1,125 all following years. Taxation and transaction cost are ignored.
   The cost of capital, for this all-equity firm, is assumed at 10 per cent. The current value of the firm is thus:

$$V_0 = 0 + \frac{d_1}{k_e}$$

$$= 0 + \frac{£1,125}{0.10} = £11,250$$

where V_0 is the market value of the company, d_1 the dividend to be received in perpetuity from time t_1, and k_e the equity cost of capital. (Note: 0 simply denotes a 1-year postponement in receipt of dividends.) As an alternative, let us assume that the project was financed by issuing additional equity to new investors, therefore enabling the £1,000 to be paid to current investors by way of a dividend. If dividend policy is irrelevant, the firm has the same value as that when the current dividend is withheld. Existing equity holders can value their investment as the sum of the current dividend, d_0, now and in the future, plus the new project's attributable dividends ($d_p = £125$ per annum) net of the return required by the new equity investors, d_n.
   This is represented by:

$$V_0 = d_0 + \frac{d_0}{k_e} + \frac{(d_p - d_n)}{k_e}$$

If we assume that all new equity investors have the same expectations as original investors, we can substitute our assumed values, thus:

$$V_0 = £1,000 + \frac{£1,000}{0.10} + \frac{£(125 - 100)}{0.10} = £11,250$$

With our assumptions it can be seen that the choice between dividends and retentions is irrelevant.

What if, instead of raising additional equity, an equivalent amount of debt was raised: Dividend policy again is irrelevant, as, under MM's certainty assumption, the cost of debt is also 10 per cent. Earlier in this chapter it was noted that MM argued that, by using low-cost debt, equity investors would increase their required rate of return, such that any gain from debt was exactly offset. It is apparent that MM's view of dividend policy follows on from their capital structure theory and that opposing views on dividend policy will not be finally resolved until the capital structure debate is settled.

As Bromwich (1976) points out, this rather academic debate is not about whether investors use dividends or earnings' figures in their company valuation models. Rather it is whether a given sum of money is valued differently when paid out as dividends or as capital gain. Real world complications and imperfections cause dividend policies to affect the wealth of equity investors differently. These we now examine.

Risk
One the more serious charges levelled against MM by the 'traditionalists' is that they ignore risk. There are those who believe that, if a present dividend is 'safe' (i.e. certain) and a capital gain is risky, it is preferable to receive a current dividend – the bird in the hand argument. Gordon (1959) contends that investors, being risk–averse, are willing to pay a higher price for equity shares that offer a greater current dividend, all other things held constant. MM would argue that as long as investment policy and borrowing are held constant, a firm's cash flows are the same. It is distant earnings, they contend, that are uncertain, and this uncertainty will be the same whether earnings are distributed as dividends or capital gains.

Taxation
MM are also accused of ignoring problems with regard to a differential tax structure. The individual tax position of equity investors greatly influences their desire for dividends, their interest being to receive the largest possible 'net of all taxes' return. There is a bias in favour of capital gains, as these are taxed at a lower rate than dividends. Moreover, the capital gains tax is deferred until such time as the investment

is sold. This bias remains despite the introduction of the imputation system of corporation tax in April 1973. Because of the varying tax positions of investors, any decision made by the firm is a compromise, and therefore, to a certain extent, a firm's dividend policy determines the composition of its equity investors. This is known as the 'clientele effect', whereby high marginal income-tax payers are attracted to firms with a low payment policy and vice versa. An algebraic analysis of these tax implications is provided in Appendix 7.3, p. 157.

It ought not to be forgotten that many equity investors are financial institutions rather than individuals. Corporations receiving dividends from other corporations, termed franked investment income, are allowed to offset the accompanying income-tax credit against their own liability to pay advanced corporation tax. Surplus franked investment income, i.e. the amount left after franking the distributions, can be rolled forward to subsequent accounting periods. Other bodies, such as pension funds and charities, would be unaffected by tax considerations in their preference for dividends or capital gains, such receipts being exempt from income-tax and capital-gains tax.

As with the argument concerning the optimal capital structure, investors are assumed to be able to borrow and lend in the market in order to obtain a desired income pattern; this may not be so and transactions costs would also arise. There is also the assumption that all equity investors are in agreement as to the risk class and future prospects of the firm. Some investors may either have access to different information or may evaluate such information differently.

Apart from this unresolved academic debate, other considerations have also to be resolved by management when deciding the level of dividend to distribute. These considerations include the legal framework, the firm's desired payout ratio, liquidity needs, the level of fixed interest payments and so on.

Dividends and earnings

It is fairly well documented that, while profits may fluctuate considerably, dividends are usually paid at a fairly constant level. In a classic paper Lintner (1956) interviewed about thirty corporate managers about their dividend policy. Most of the managers thought that it was more a problem of paying out a proportion of earnings rather than deciding what was needed for investment and distributing any residual. As such, most decided upon a long-term target ratio. However, with fluctuating earnings this would result in fluctuating dividends, which was felt undesirable. The general contention was that equity investors preferred a steady progression in the level of dividends. There was therefore a policy of conservatism, one that tended to lag behind the level of earnings. Dividends are only increased once a sustained increase in earnings has been ascertained. Dividend stability is thought desirable because equity investors, being generally risk-averse, prefer stable to fluctuating dividends. When a firm retains a proportion of its earnings, equity investors will value its shares more highly if they anticipate that current reinvestments will yield larger dividends in the future. A stable policy encourages this anticipation.

Dividends and liquidity

While earlier discussions have considered whether a firm retains or distributes net operating earnings, nothing has been said of the liquidity position of the firm. Retained earnings could very well be invested in assets necessary for the continuance of the business. It is perfectly possible for a firm to have a reasonable record of earnings, yet be unable to pay out dividends; this could be particularly true when a firm has embarked on a programme of expansion. Given the situation of a firm with part of its capital composed of debt, a decision has to be made as to how such funds are to be serviced. At maturity debt can be repaid by issuing additional new debt, or else retained earnings/additional equity could be used. A firm is better able to predict what its earnings will be if earnings are relatively stable. Such a firm therefore is more likely to pay out a higher percentage of its earnings than a firm whose earnings fluctuate. An unstable firm is not so certain that in subsequent years the hoped for earnings will be realized, so that it is more likely to retain a higher proportion of current earnings. A lower dividend will in such circumstances be easier to maintain if earnings should fall off in the future.

Brief mention should be made of scrip dividends. A scrip dividend is paid in the form of additional shares rather than cash. The shareholder pays no extra cash for such shares and the company preserves its liquid resources, as no cash leaves the company. Such an issue should not normally depress the share price to any great extent, provided that the firm has good future prospects and that the number of new shares is not too great.

Inflation

In periods of severe inflation, as recently witnessed in the UK, management must also have regard to the fact that even larger retained earnings are required to maintain the current operating capacity of the firm. Historic cost depreciation provisions become insufficient to replace existing assets as they wear out or become obsolete, and additional funds are required to maintain operating capacity. An examination of dividend policy in recent years has suggested that companies are not yet taking inflation-adjusted profit information seriously. While, in the short term, companies appear to do their utmost to maintain dividend payments in money terms, in the longer term it is questionable if such payments can be maintained. It could be that share prices can be maintained. It could be that share prices may decrease in the short term due to lower profits and consequent reduced dividends. The long term prosperity of a company (and therefore its future profits, dividends and share price) must be more assured if financial decisions are based on more relevant information.

Dividends: other economic factors

Access to capital markets is also an important consideration. Large, well established firms with a good record of profitability and stable earnings should have easier access to capital markets and other forms of external financing than small and new firms, which may well be regarded as riskier by potential investors. If ability to raise equity or debt from the capital market is restricted, then a firm must retain more earnings to finance its operations. A well established firm is thus likely to have a higher dividend payout rate than a new or small firm, although a small firm's distribution policy may be dictated by 'Close Company' regulations.

Alternative sources of finance can also affect the retention situation in the firm. Some companies, as a matter of policy, will expand only to the extent of their internal earnings. Such a policy is defended on the grounds that raising additional funds, even in the form of additional equity, could dilute the control of the dominant group in the company. Issuing debt may also increase the risks of fluctuating earnings to the present owners of the company. As mentioned previously, the tax position of equity investors influences their desire for dividends.

In past times governments have restricted the level of dividend payments made by companies as part of their fiscal policy for restricting wage demands. Dividend controls were removed in July 1979. Since that time only a minority of UK firms have rushed to raise their level of dividend payments. In discussing the level of dividend payments readers should remember the current economic climate, one in which British industry's profits are under pressure from falling exports, increasing imports, high domestic interest rates and drastic cuts in public expenditure.

Does dividend policy really matter? Most of the empirical work concerning dividend policy has been carried out in the US. Reference has already been made to the work of Lintner. Further comprehensive attacks against MM's view have been offered by Gordon (1962) and Benishay (1961), both of whom support a dividend model of the firm. Additionally, they suggested that the size of the firm, its liquidity position and previous stable record of earnings all contributed to the share price. MM, in addition to producing empirical evidence with their original paper, later produced a second study (1966) in support of their arguments. They reasoned that unadjusted earnings figures used in some studies produced a bias in favour of a dividend policy. MM proposed an alternative measure of expected earnings, using elaborate econometric methods. To date, empirical evidence of the effect of dividends and retentions on share prices remains inconclusive.

Dividend policy is basically a trade-off between retaining earnings within the firm or else paying out cash dividends and seeking to raise additional equity or long-term debt. One unresolved consequence of dividend policy is the effect on the market for equity shares by such announcements. This valuation debate hinges on the degree to which market imperfections impinge, the most obvious and serious of these being the different tax treatment of dividends and capital gains.

It is generally recognized that sudden changes in dividend policy can cause sudden changes in equity share prices. Accordingly it would make sense for firms to follow a conservative approach to the payment of dividends, one that lags behind the earnings pattern of the firm, so that once payments are increased, they are likely to continue at this level. Dividend policy may affect the financial structure, the flow of funds, the firm's liquidity, share prices and investor satisfaction. It remains an important aspect of financial management.

Notes

1   Proof: $P_0 = \dfrac{d_1}{(1+k_e)} + \dfrac{d_2}{(1+k_e)^2} \dfrac{d_3}{(1+k_e)^3} + \cdots \cdots \underline{\hspace{1cm}} \infty$

(a) rewrite $P_0 = d\left[\dfrac{1}{(1+k_e)} + \dfrac{1}{(1+k_e)^2} + \dfrac{1}{(1+k_e)^3} + \cdots \dfrac{1}{(1+k_e)^t}\right]$

(b) multiply both sides by $(1+k_e)$ $P_0(1+k_e) = d\left[1 + \dfrac{1}{(1+k_e)} + \dfrac{1}{(1+k_e)^2} + \cdots \dfrac{1}{(1+k_e)^{t-1}}\right]$

(c) subtract (b) from (a) $P_0(1+k_e-1) = d\left[1 - \dfrac{1}{(1+k_e)^t}\right]$

(d) as $t \to \infty$, so $1/(1+k)^t$ approaches 0, therefore (c) approaches $P_0 k_e = d$ and $P_0 = d/k_e$

2   $P_0 = \dfrac{d_0(1+g)}{(1+k_e)} + \dfrac{d_0(1+g)^2}{(1+k_e)^2} + \cdots \dfrac{d_0(1+g)^\infty}{(1+k_e)^\infty}$

Multiply both sides of the equation by $(1+k_e)/(1+g)$ and subtract from the product –

$\dfrac{P_0(1+k_e)}{(1+g)} - P_0 = d_0 - \dfrac{d_0(1+g)^\infty}{(1+k_e)^\infty}$

Because k_e is greater that g, the second term on the right-hand side will be zero. Consequently –

$P_0 \dfrac{(1+k_e)}{(1+g)} - 1 = d_0$

$P_0(k_e - g) = d_0(1+g)$

$P_0 = \dfrac{d_1}{(k_e - g)}$

3   A detailed analysis of taxation and corporate financial policy is outside the scope of this chapter. References are provided at the end of this chapter.

Appendix 7.1 *An algebraic analysis of the net operating income approach to capital structure*

In order to consider MM's propositions more closely, the following notation is introduced:

Let $\bar{Y}$ = firm's expected annual earnings, before the deduction of debt interest

V_0 = firm's total market value

V_e = total market value of equity

I = total market value of debt

k_0 = cost of equity capital in a non-levered firm

k_d = cost of debt

k_l = cost of equity capital in a levered firm

Each proposition is now considered in turn.

Proposition 1. The total market value of a company is independent of the amount of debt in its financial structure. The acceptance of this proposition requires acceptance of two correlated hypotheses about the behaviour of a firm's weighted average cost of capital:

(*i*) the company's overall cost of capital will be unaffected by changes in its debt/equity ratio, $k_0 = \dfrac{\bar{Y}}{V_0}$

(*ii*) following on from (i), the weighted average cost of capital of a levered firm must equal the equity cost of an unlevered firm in the same risk class, irrespective of the degree of leverage used by the firm with debt in its financial structure, $k_0 = k_e$

The equity cost of an unlevered firm is expressed as $k_0 = \dfrac{\bar{Y}}{V_e}$

The cost of a levered firm is expressed as $k_0 = \dfrac{\bar{Y}}{V_e + I}$

It, therefore, follows that $k_0 = \dfrac{\bar{Y}}{V_0} = k_e = \dfrac{\bar{Y}}{V_e}$

Proposition 2. As leverage increases, the equity cost of capital of a levered corporation will rise in order to offset the advantages flowing from the lower cost of debt relative to equity. This can be expressed as:

$$k_l = \frac{(\bar{Y} - k_d I)}{V_e} \quad \dots\dots\dots\dots\dots\dots\dots\dots\dots\dots\dots\dots\dots \text{(a)}$$

Acceptance of Proposition 1 leads to a basis for proving the second proposition. Proposition 1 stated that the combined value of debt and equity of a levered firm must have the same value as an otherwise identical all-equity company.

This can be alternatively stated as asserting that the identical annual income of the two companies can be derived by multiplying by the market value of the levered firm, i.e.

$$\bar{Y} = (V_e + I) k_e \dots\dots\dots\dots\dots\dots\dots\dots\dots\dots\dots\dots \text{(b)}$$

We can now express expression (a) as:

$$k_l = [(k_e (V_e + 1) - k_d I] \dots\dots\dots\dots\dots\dots\dots\dots\dots \text{(c)}$$

Expression (c) simplifies to:[1]

$$k_l = k_e + \frac{(k_e - k_d)}{V_e} I \dots\dots\dots\dots\dots\dots\dots\dots\dots\dots \text{(d)}$$

This final expression for the levered company's equity cost of capital states that this cost of capital is equal to the equity cost of all-equity company plus a premium related directly to the proportion of debt used by the company. This premium is the difference between the all-equity cost of capital and the cost of debt weighted by the proportion of debt in the company's financial structure, i.e.

$$\frac{(k_e - k_d)}{V_e} I$$

Such gains are identical to the premium which equity holders would require in a levered company if Proposition 1 is accepted.

Proposition 3. In order to maximize equity holders' wealth the firm should use its WACC as a cut-off rate. In other words, for the unlevered company, k_e is the correct cut-off rate; whilst for the levered company, k_0 is the correct rate (remembering that for two such companies in the same risk class, $k_e = k_0$).

Note 1
Multiplying out the first element on this right-hand side of the expression, $k_e (V_e + I)/V_e$, and substituting this in equation (c).

Appendix 7.2   *Proof that the dividend policy adopted by a firm is irrelevant and in no way influences the value of the firm or the return to shareholders*

Perfect certainty and perfect capital markets are assumed.

Consider an equity investor who purchases a share at price, P_0, and holds it for a certain period at the end of which time he receives a dividend, d_1, and the market price of the share changes to P_1. His return for the period, k, may be calculated as:

(1) $k = \dfrac{d_1 + (P_1 - P_0)}{P_0}$

By rearrangement of terms, the prices at which a share will sell at the beginning of the period may be expressed as:

(2) $P_0 = \dfrac{1}{1+k}(d_1 + P_1)$

If n_0 is the number of shares outstanding at the beginning of the period and m_1 is the number of new shares issued at the end of the period at the ex-dividend closing price P_1, then the number of shares outstanding at the end of the period n_1 may be expressed as:

(3) $n_1 = n_0 + m_1$

from which,

(4) $n_0 = n_1 - m_1$

The value of the firm at the beginning of the period V_0 is the number of shares outstanding at that time multiplied by their beginning of period prices. Thus, from equation (2):

$$n_0 P_0 = \dfrac{n_0}{(1+k)}(d_1 + P_1)$$

$$= \dfrac{1}{(1+k)}(n_0 d_1 + n_0 P_1)$$

(5) $V_0 = \dfrac{1}{(1+k)}(D_1 + n_0 P_1),$

where D_1 is the aggregate dividend paid by the firm at the end of the period on those shares outstanding at the beginning of the period, i.e. is, $D_1 = n_0 d_1$. By substituting equation (4) for n_0 in equation (5):

(6) $V_0 = \dfrac{1}{(1+k)}(D_1 + V_1 - m_1 p_1),$

where $V_1 = n_1 p_1$, the value of the firm at the end of the period. That is to say, the value of the firm is equal to the present value of the total dividend paid at the end of the period plus the value of the firm at the end of the period less the value of additional shares sold at the end of the period.

(To avoid any problems associated with financing policy, it is assumed that any new funds raised by the firm are by means of a new share issue. This in no way detracts from the value of the analysis, as alternative forms of finance can be incorporated within this framework, without altering the conclusions.)

If I is the cash outflow at the end of the period required for the firm's investment programme and X is the net cash savings of the firm at the end of the period generated by investments of prior periods, then the amount of funds which have to be raised externally in order that the firm is able to undertake its desired investment I_1 is equal to $I_1 - (X_1 + D_1)$. It has already been assumed that m_1 is the number of shares which the firm has to issue at a price P_1 to raise the required volume of new funds. Therefore:

(7) $m_1 P_1 = I_1 - X_1 + D_1$

Equation (7) illustrates an extremely important functional relationship. It reveals the complete cash flow interdependence of financial management's three main decisions – the financing decision $(m_1 P_1)$, the investment decision $(I_1 - X_1)$, and the dividend decision (D_1). The equation simply says that funds raised externally equal net investment plus dividends paid, or, more intuitively, cash inflows for the period equal cash outflows for the period. (A decision to hold cash is considered to be an investment decision, so any cash balances at the end of the period are included in the I_1 term.)

Therefore, it can be seen from equation (7) that a change in any one of the three main financial decisions of the firm must result in a change in at least one of the other two financial decisions. Thus a decision to change the firm's dividend policy by increasing dividends by £100,000, say, must result in a fall in investment of £100,000 or, if investment is to remain unaltered, an increase of funds raised externally by £100,000, or some combination of the two. If it is assumed that the investment policy of the firm is predetermined, then any change in D_1 must be exactly offset by a change in $m_1 P_1$, i.e. for any given policy, a change in the firm's dividend policy will have a one-for-one relationship with a change in the firm's financing policy.

By reference to equation (6) the impact of a change in the firm's dividend policy on the value of the firm can now be determined. Since the right-hand side of equation (6) contains the expression $(D_1 - m_1 P_1)$, the effect of a change in a firm's dividend policy, and the investment policy being unchanged, I is zero.

The conclusions of the above analysis become more apparent if equation (7) is substituted for $m_1 P_1$ in equation (6). The value of the firm can then be expressed as:

(8) $V_0 = \dfrac{1}{(1+k)}(X_1 - I_1 + V_1)$

which is independent of D_1, the current dividend decision. This equation holds for any period of time and could be extended ad infinitum:

$$\text{(9)} \quad V_0 = \sum_{t=1}^{} \frac{1}{\prod_{j=1}^{} } + \frac{X_t - I_t}{(1+k)}$$

Thus, under perfect certainty and perfect capital markets, the value of the firm depends upon the investment opportunities available to the firm, I_t, their profitability, X_t, and the market rate of discount, k. It is independent of the dividend policy of the firm, and dividend policy is irrelevant.

Appendix 7.3 *Dividend policy: personal taxation considerations*

The question which an equity investor wishes to know is, am I better off receiving a current dividend or should I accumulate a capital gain instead? This is but one question from the whole area of corporate financial policy and taxation. The following notation is introduced:

P = amount of earnings available for reinvestment or distribution
r = required rate of return (before tax)
C_u = corporation rate on undistributed earnings
C_d = corporation rate on distributed earnings[1]
t = marginal rate of income tax
g = capital gains tax rate

Consider the effect on the equity investor's wealth at the end of one period if the company, instead of paying $P(1 - C_d)$ by way of a dividend, retains $P(1 - C_u)$ and reinvests such earnings to get a return of r before corporation tax. It is assumed that this gain is taxed (implying a sale of equity) at the end of the period. After one period with reinvestment the equity investor has:

(1) $P(1 - C_u)(1 + r)(1 - g)$

after capital gains tax.

This policy can be compared with one of paying a dividend of $P(1 - C_d)$ to the equity investors, having it taxed at rate t, and then investing $P(1 - C_d)(1 - t)$ to earn in a second company. After one period with reinvestment, which is itself subsequently paid out as a cash dividend, the equity investor will have:

$\quad P(1 - C_d)(1 - t) + rP(1 - C_d)(1 - t)(1 - C_d)(1 - t)$ or
(2) $P(1 - C_d)(1 - t) + rP(1 - C_d)^2(1 - t)^2$

The advantage of retention taxed at a capital gains rate, compared to dividends taxed at a marginal rate of income tax, is:

(1) − (2) $P(1 - C_u)(1 + r)(1 - g) - P(1 - C_d)(1 - t) + rP(1 - C_d)^2(1 - t)^2$

which reduces to

$$P[(1 - C_u)(1 + r)(1 - g) - (1 - C_d)(1 - t)[1 + r(1 - C_d)(1 - t)]]$$

As an example, let us compute the deferral advantage of a corporation reinvesting likewise to earn a similar return on external reinvestments. Assume the marginal income tax rate, t, to be 60 per cent; g = 30 per cent; C_u = 35 per cent; C_d = 7 per cent; r = 10 per cent
   Using the last expression we have:

£100 [(0.65)(1.10)(0.70) − (0.93)(0.40) [1 + .10(0.93)(0.40)]]
a £34.83 advantage

Note (1)
C_u and C_d could be said to result from the present UK imputation system of corporation tax, which is effectively a two-rate system, one for retentions and the other (lower) for distributions.
   Let us consider a company with a before-tax profit of £100 which is either fully distributed by way of a dividend or fully retained. Corporation tax is at 35 per cent and the imputation credit is ³⁄₇ths (given, for ease of illustration, a basic rate income tax of 30 per cent). The situation would be as follows:

	Profit retained	*Profit fully distributed*
	£	£
Profit	100	100
Corporation tax: 35%	35	35
	£65	65
Imputation credit: ³⁄₇ths		28
		£93

   If fully distributed, shareholders receive £93 and the effective tax rate is only 7 per cent. We have in effect a two-rate system and denote corporation tax on retained profits as C_u (35 per cent) and for distributed profits C_d (7 per cent).

References

Barges, A., *The Effect of Capital Structure on the Cost of Capital*, Prentice-Hall, 1963.
Benishay, H., 'Variability of Earnings-price Ratios of Corporate Policy', *American Economic Review*, Vol. 51, 1961.
Bromwich, M., *The Economics of Capital Budgeting*, Penguin Books, 1976.

Elton, E. J. and Gruber, 'Marginal Stockholders Tax Rates and the Clientele Effect', *Review of Economics and Statistics*, February 1970.

Gordon, M. J., *The Investment, Financing and Valuation of the Corporation*, Irwin, 1959.

Gordon, M. J., *The Investment, Financing and Valuation of the Corporation*, Irwin, 1962.

Gordon, M. J., 'Some Estimates of the Cost of Capital to the Electricity Industry 1954–7: Comment', *American Economic Review*, December 1967.

Lintner, J., 'Distribution of Incomes of Corporations Among Dividends, Retained Earnings and Taxes', *American Economic Review*, May 1956.

Modigliani, F. and Miller, M. H., 'The Cost of Capital, Corporate Finance and the Theory of Investment', *American Economic Review*, June 1958.

Modigliani, F. and Miller, M. H., 'Dividend Policy, Growth and the Valuation of Shares', *Journal of Business*, October 1961.

Modigliani, F. and Miller, M. H., 'Corporation Income Taxes and the Cost of Capital: A Correction', *American Economic Review*, June 1963.

Quirin, G. D., *The Capital Expenditure Decision*, Iruin, 1967. Press, 1963.

Walter, J. E., *Dividend Policy and Enterprise Evaluation*, Wadsworth, 1967.

Weston, J. F., 'A Test of Cost of Capital Propositions', *Southern Economic Journal*, October 1963.

Weston, J. F., 'Valuation of the Firm and its Relation to Financial Management', in Robichek, A. A. (ed.), *Financial Research and Management Decisions*, Wiley, 1967.

8 Portfolio theory and the capital asset pricing model

Introduction

Business risk or uncertainty is probably one of the most important elements that need to be considered in project evaluation. Traditionally crude 'rule of thumb' approaches have been adopted in order to provide a safety margin before an investment is undertaken. For example, if a company determined its cost of capital to be, say 15 per cent, a safety margin could be added in order to accommodate any riskiness in future cash flows. Such a risk premium reflects a subjective assessment of risk. Raising the discount rate from 15 per cent to 20 per cent lowers the present value of the cash flows occurring in year one by about 4 per cent, whereas cash flows occurring in year thirty will be reduced by 73 per cent. Simply increasing the discount rate presupposes that risk can be measured by a simple uplift in the discount rate. However, there is no empirical evidence to support the proposition that risk increases with time at a compound rate.

Recently, greater attention has been given to examining whether there are any lessons to be learned from those who trade on the stock exchange. It is increasingly being recognized that the same principles of risk apply not only to managers of portfolios of shares but also to diversified companies considering how best to replace their product lines or diversify into new markets. If a portfolio manager was, for the sake of illustration, managing a pension fund there would be two broad objectives to be borne in mind, first the need for certain funds to be invested for long-term growth, and second the need for certain investments to be current high income earners in order to service current pension commitments. For those concerned with investment within a firm there is a need to be sure that products earn an appropriate return. Appropriate in the sense of each particular product, its competitors and the specific risks associated within the market in which it is sold. To suggest that a divisionalized company should expect each of its divisions to contribute equally to corporate goals is to ignore the fact that one particular market has inherent risk characteristics that are different from other markets. These risks arise from many varied sources. There may be problems associated with the supply of basic raw materials; technological innovation may provide competitors with a market advantage; export sales may be subject to currency fluctuations and so on.

This chapter first considers risk in relation to investments on the stock exchange. It illustrates that the relevant characteristics for any investment are its expected return, the variation in that return and the relationship between the return for each investment and that for every other investment. This is primarily illustrated within a portfolio framework. This framework is then adapted and simplified with the introduction of the capital asset pricing model. We then consider the implications of financial investment for project appraisal within the firm.

An introduction to risk

Before continuing further it is important to recognize that there is a theoretical difference between the terms *risk* and *uncertainty*. Risk is normally defined as when the probability distribution of an event or outcome is known. Uncertainty, on the other hand, is when such a probability distribution is not known. Despite this technical distinction, this chapter will treat uncertainty as being synonymous with risk.

It is no simple matter to estimate the probability of a set of outcomes. One way might be to provide broad categories of outcomes, for example, pessimistic, most likely and optimistic. Possibilities might be introduced by asking the forecaster to provide a *single best* measure within a broad band of possibilities. Consider Table 8.1 which illustrates the forecasted sales of a particular product. Using a single best probability criterion would suggest that expected sales are at a level of £700,000 per annum, this being the single most likely outcome. Such a set framework of probabilities is both undesirable and limiting. An analyst may often have available historical data or detailed market projections, via surveys for example, that would enable probabilities to be formulated more accurately. Let us suppose that there is more detailed information concerning these sales forecasts. Table 8.2 provides this information, but note that while an expected value (or mean) of forecasted sales is produced it still remains a fairly crude single measure of risk. This time the individual probabilities are simply aggregated.

A second measure needs to be considered, that is the variation in the expected return. This is particularly important when one considers that most firms have to consider a variety of alternative investment strategies. Again, this is best illustrated by means of a simple example.

Consider a firm with two mutually exclusive projects, X and Y; each

Table 8.1   Single best criterion

		(£000)
Pessimistic	1 in 10 chance	500
Most likely	8 in 10 chance	700*
Optimistic	1 in 10 chance	1,000

*single best outcome

Table 8.2   Expected value (mean) sales forecast

(a) Probability	(b) Possible target sales (£000)	(a) × (b) Expected value (£000)
0.1	500	50
0.3	700	210
0.4	800	320
0.1	900	90
0.1	1,000	100
		770 Expected value (mean)

involves an investment outlay of £500,000, each has an expected life of three years with no residual values. Figure 8.1 shows that, when annual cash flows are considered, each has an expected annual cash inflow of £300,000. However, Project Y is more risky than Project X as measured by the dispersion of each project's probability distribution. The method of dispersion traditionally used is the standard deviation. The standard deviation is defined as the square root of the mean of the squared deviation from the expected value. It is not possible to have a simple measure, such as the average deviation from the expected value (or mean), since it is a quality of an arithmetic mean that positive and negative deviations from it just balance out each other. A better way of avoiding the cancelling of the plus and minus signs would be to *square* the deviations. The mean is a representative value and, if expressed graphically, gives some idea where the part of a distribution lies on the horizontal axis of a bell-shaped normal distribution curve. The spread of the normal curve is controlled by the standard deviation. A measure of standard deviation for competing projects is only reasonable when their expected values are broadly similar. When they differ substantially a measure of relative dispersion is required. This may be achieved by relating the standard deviation to the expected value, generally referred to as the coefficient of variation:

$$\partial = \frac{\sigma}{\bar{A}t} \quad \frac{\text{(standard deviation)}}{\text{(expected value)}}$$

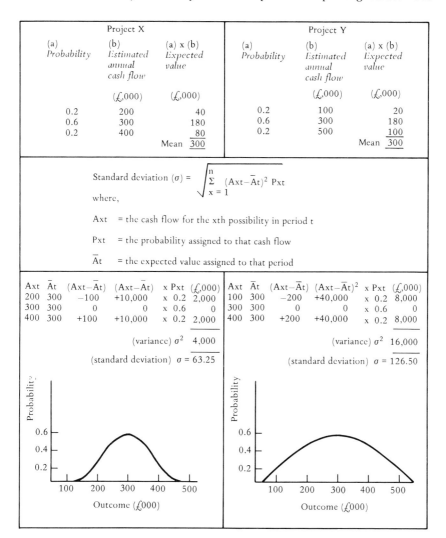

Figure 8.1 Measuring the mean and standard deviation

Using the information provided in Figure 8.1, the results for Project X and Project Y are 0.211 and 0.422. Once again demonstrating that Project X is half as risky as Project Y.

This simple example illustrates the mean–variance approach for evaluating investments on the basis of their expected return and standard deviation. It was first developed by Markowitz as early as 1952. This rule states that Project I will be preferred to Project II if one of the two following combinations holds true:

1 The expected return of I exceeds (or is equal to) the expected return
   of II and the variance of I is less than the variance of II.
2 The expected return of I exceeds that of II and the variance of I is
   less than (or equal to) that of II.*

Thus the expected return is taken as an indicator of a project's profitability and the standard deviation serves as an index of risk. In our
previous illustration Project X is preferred to Project Y. Both have the
same expected annual cash inflows but Project Y is more risky in terms
of its variance. With this simple summary of basic statistical concepts
we can now consider the fundamentals of portfolio theory.

Portfolio selection

Most investors would generally agree with the rule of not putting all
their eggs in one basket. More technically one could say that diversification reduces risk in an economy in which every asset's returns are
subject to some degree of uncertainty. The idea being that if one investment fails then others will provide some measure of protection against
extreme loss. Portfolio selection is devoted to the investigation of project (or investment) selection in the presence of risk. Portfolio theory
can be simply understood by considering the simple case of a two-share
portfolio. It can be shown that, given two shares S and T, even if T is
considerably more risky than S, a portfolio composed of some of S and
some of T *may* be less risky than a portfolio composed exclusively of the
less risky share S. That is, it is possible to reduce the risk of a portfolio
by incorporating an asset whose risk is greater than any of the investments held initially. Suppose that Share S has a 50/50 chance of the
probability of an average return of 8 per cent or 12 per cent; Share T
has a 50/50 chance of the probability of an average return of 6 per cent
or 14 per cent. Also, further suppose that when S's return is high, T's
return is low and vice versa. With a portfolio composed of two-thirds S
and one-third T the average expected return is 10 per cent.[†] Investing
funds in the riskier share (T) reduces the overall risk of the investor. In
fact shares S and T are perfectly negatively correlated. The theory for
portfolio selection can therefore be summarized as follows:

1 The two relevant characteristics of a portfolio are its expected return
   and its risk.
2 Rational investors will choose to hold efficient portfolios which are
   those which maximize expected returns for a given degree of risk, or
   alternatively, minimize risk for a given expected return.

*Note however that Markowitz leaves open the question of which project to choose when
Project I provides a higher return than Project II but also has a greater variance than
Project II.
[†]When S has a high return = 2/3 (12%) + 1/3 (6%) = 10%
When S has a low return = 2/3 (8%) + 1/3 (14%) = 10%

3 It is theoretically possible to identify efficient portfolios by the proper analysis of information for each security on its:

- Expected return.
- The variation (or variability as measured by the standard deviation) in that return.
- The relationships between the return for each share and that for
  every other share.

Given the large number of shares traded on the stock exchange it
would also be a necessary corollary to have the use of an appropriate
computer program capable of utilizing these three kinds of information
in order to specify a set of efficient portfolios. The relationship or
association between the return for each share and that for every other
share is provided by the coefficient of correlation. This is the covariance
taken not as an absolute value, but relative to the standard deviations
of the individual balances. The covariance by itself is not an adequate
measure of association because it is influenced by the magnitude of the
original deviation. Correlation coefficients range from $+1.0$ to -1.0.
Perfectly negatively correlated shares could theoretically lead to the
total elimination of risk. However, such relationships are almost never
found in the real world. Diversification into uncorrelated shares can,
though, significantly reduce risk. Perfectly positively correlated shares,
at the other extreme, do not reduce risk at all.

An extended example should usefully illustrate the three measures
introduced in point 3 above. Suppose that the shares of two companies
F and G have the following (simplified) probability distributions:

Probability	Returns on F (%)	Returns on G (%)
0.2	30	5
0.6	15	15
0.2	0	−5

Their individual expected returns and standard deviation of returns
are shown in Table 8.3. They were calculated in line with the principles
previously illustrated in Figure 8.1. Also calculated is the covariance of
returns between shares F and G, Cov $(r_F r_G)$. This is an important element when considering the standard deviation of the portfolio. While
the expected return of the portfolio is simply the weighted average of
the proportions held in each share, the standard deviation is slightly
more complex in that it considers the variance of each individual share
and the covariance between the returns of F and G. Appendix 8.1
provides the derivation of the formula for the standard deviation of a
two-asset portfolio. Table 8.3 illustrates that if we know the expected
return and standard deviation for the return of each individual asset
and if we know the covariance figures for each pair of returns, then
there exists sufficient data to enable us to calculate the expected return
and standard deviation for any portfolio. For a portfolio composed of 60

Table 8.3   Example of a two-asset portfolio

(a) Probability	(b) Estimated return share F (%)	(a) × (b) Expected return	(a) Probability	(b) Estimated return share G (%)	(a) × (b) Expected return
P	r_F		P	r_G	
0.2	30	6	0.2	5	1
0.6	15	9	0.6	12	7.2
0.2	0	0	0.2	−5	−1
	$E(r_F)$	15		$E(r_G)$	7.2
	σ_F^2	90		σ_G^2	44.56
	σ_F	9.48%		σ_G	6.675%

Covariance of F with G:

$$\Sigma\,[r_F - E(r_F)]\,[r_G - E(r_G)]P$$

$$(30 - 15)\,(5 \quad - 7.2) \times 0.2 = \quad - 6.6$$
$$(15 - 15)\,(12 \quad - 7.2) \times 0.6 = \qquad 0$$
$$(\ 0 - 15)\,(-5 - 7.2) \times 0.2 = \quad \underline{36.6}$$
$$\text{Cov}\,(r_F . r_G) \qquad\qquad 30$$

Given that Cov $(r_F . r_G) = \sigma_F . \sigma_G . \rho_{FG'}$ then

$$\rho_{FG} = \frac{\text{Cov}\,(r_F . r_G)}{\sigma_F . \sigma_G .} = \frac{30}{9.48 \times 6.675} = \underline{0.474}$$

Expected return for a portfolio composed of 60% (x) Share F and 40% (1–x) Share G

$$r_P = x_F . E(r_F) + (1 - x)_G . E(r_G)$$
$$r_P = 0.6(15) \ + (0.4)7.2 \qquad = \underline{11.88\%}$$

Standard deviation of this portfolio:

$$\sigma_P = \sqrt{x^2{}_F . \sigma^2{}_F + (1 - x)^2{}_G . \sigma^2{}_G + 2x_F . (1 - x)_G\ \text{Cov}(r_F . r_G)}$$
$$\sigma_P = \sqrt{(0.36 \times 90) + (0.16 \times 44.56) + (2 \times 0.6 \times 0.4 \times 30)}$$
$$\sigma_P = \quad \underline{7.34\%}$$

per cent shares in Company F and 40 per cent shares in Company G it is calculated that the expected return should be 11.88 per cent with a standard deviation of only 7.34 per cent.

In this illustration the correlation coefficient, 0.474, is less than +1; this is the normal case when the risk of the portfolio is *less than* a weighted average of the risk of the individual components. The further away the correlation coefficient is from + 1, the greater will be the risk reduction effect.

Earlier it was stated that should shares be perfectly positively correlated there is no reduction in risk at all. In fact this is the only case when the risk from a two-asset portfolio would simply be a weighted average. This can be illustrated by substituting the correlation co-efficient derived in Table 8.3, for + 1.0. The covariance now becomes:

$$\sigma_F . \sigma_G . \rho_{FG} \qquad \text{or}$$
$$9.48 \times 6.675 \times + 1.0 = \underline{63.28}$$

If we substitute this value into the end term of our two-asset formula the revised standard deviation becomes 8.36 per cent. (You should verify this calculation for yourself.) This figure is equal to the simple weighted average of the standard deviation for each individual share, that is:

$$0.6(9.48) + 0.4(6.675) = \underline{8.36\%}$$

Also recall that, theoretically, it is possible to construct a portfolio with zero risk. That is, if two shares exhibit perfect negative correlation. If such were the case with shares F and G the make-up of this formula would be found by solving for x in the expression:

$$\sigma_p = x(\sigma_F) - (1 - x)(\sigma_G) = 0$$

In this case the solution for x is 0.52. In other words, if 52 per cent of the portfolio's funds are invested in share F and the balance in share G, then the risk of the portfolio would be zero and the expected (certain) return would be:

$$rp = 0.52(15) + 0.48(7.2) = \underline{11.26\%}$$

The various results obtained from considering a two-asset portfolio, composed of shares in F and G, are illustrated in Figure 8.2.

Although we have only considered two share portfolios, the analysis can be extended to portfolios consisting of infinite combinations of shares. Two expressions can be derived from portfolios consisting of n shares:

$$E(r_P) = \sum_{i=1}^{n} x_i . E(r_i)$$

$$\sigma^2_P = \sum_{i=1}^{n} \sum_{j=1}^{n} x_i . x_j . \sigma_i . \sigma_j . \rho_{i.j.}$$

where x_i represents the proportion of funds invested in component i. Rather than consider further detailed examples of portfolios we will concentrate on the remaining principles involved by means of further graphical representation.

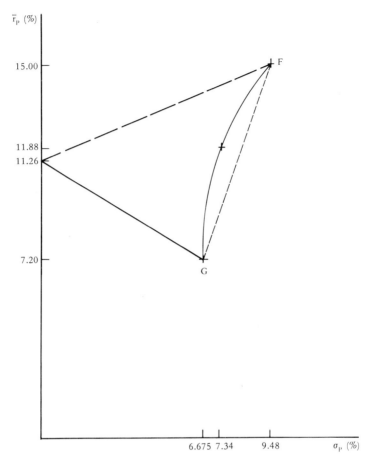

Note: In this and subsequent figures $\bar{r}_p$ = expected return: σ_p = standard deviation

Figure 8.2

A graphical representation

Figure 8.3 provides a summary to date of the theory of portfolios. Figure 8.3(a) depicts three individual portfolios, I, II and III – their relationships are important. Portfolio III should be preferred to portfolio II by an individual who is prepared to gamble. Portfolio I would be preferred by a more conservative investor, there being a lower return but being more certain. Readers should readily appreciate the two assumptions implicit in Figure 8.3(a) with respect to risk and return:

1   Investors are assumed to prefer more return than less, other things being equal.

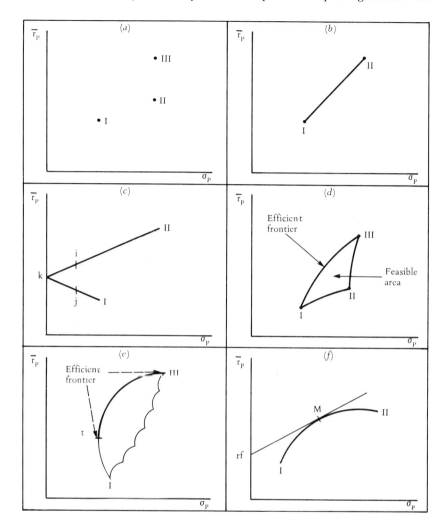

Figure 8.3

2 Investors are said to be risk-averse in the sense that they prefer lower rather than higher risk.

From these two suppositions two rules can be derived:

1 The portfolio with the lowest standard deviation of return will be selected from any two sets of securities offering the same expected return.
2 The choice between two equally risky portfolios will fall to that having the higher return.

Figure 8.3(b) depicts perfect positive correlation with a portfolio of two shares. Because both are perfectly correlated neither can help offset the risk of the other. A risk-averse investor would be better to put all his/her funds in share I, while a gambler would place all his/her funds in share II. Perfect negative (or inverse) correlation is depicted in Figure 8.3(c). When two assets are perfectly inversely correlated, it is always possible to make up a portfolio with a standard deviation of zero; that is, where risk has been totally eliminated (shown here as point k). Also note that a rational investor would always choose point i in preference to point j.

The multi-share portfolio is depicted in Figure 8.3(d). While only three shares are plotted the principle applies regardless of the number of shares. The shaded area depicts all feasible combinations of these three shares. The arc I.III represents the *efficient frontier*. All rational investors would choose portfolios along this curve since all other portfolios are inferior. Figure 8.3(e) also depicts a multi-share portfolio (now composed of several shares). Note that this time the arc I.III does not depict the efficiency frontier. Observe the shape of the curve. Only the portion t.III represents the efficiency curve.

Readers should now understand the basic principles of portfolio theory. This analysis is now completed by introducing the possibility of a risk-free asset (or investment). With such an investment, the return is known for certain and exhibits no variability. Government bonds held to maturity are usually credited with being such an investment. Such investments are held to be risk-free as it is expected that there is no chance of default either on the interest payments or on redemption since if the government ran out of money it could always print some more. However, it is important to note that this assumption only holds in the absence of inflation. If inflation is expected to be present then only a monetary return is certain, the real return remains uncertain. Figure 8.3(f) depicts the situation where an investor could place all, or part, of his/her funds with government bonds, or all, or part, of such funds in a portfolio of shares on the stock exchange. Only portfolios on the arc I.II are considered since all other combinations are inferior. If the investor invests part of his/her funds in government bonds with the balance being invested in risky assets on the stock market the combined portfolio will be plotted somewhere on the straight line rf through M, where rf represents the risk-free rate of interest. Point M is the point at which a straight line is drawn from rf until it is tangential to the efficiency frontier I.II. The point M is known as the market portfolio and all rational investors would now wish to be somewhere on the line rf.M rather than I.M. The line rf.M, in Figure 8.3(f) is also known as the *capital market line* (CML).

If you wish to check that rf.M is a straight line then rewrite the formula for a two-asset portfolio when the second security is riskless.

By way of illustration let us introduce some simple numbers into the situation depicted in Figure 8.3(f) – this is illustrated in Figure 8.4. Suppose that portfolio M has an expected return of 15 per cent and that

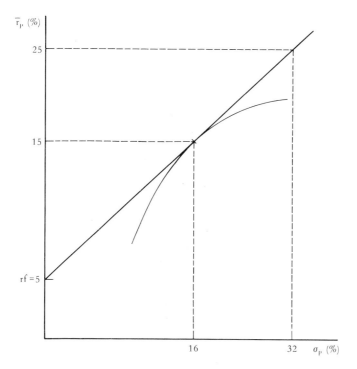

Figure 8.4

a suitable risk-free rate (rf) is 5 per cent. The standard deviation of portfolio M is 16 per cent while the risk-free rate has a zero standard deviation. If an investor places half of his/her funds in portfolio M and the remainder in government bonds the investor's expected return is halfway between points rf and M:

$$E(r_P) = (0.5 \times 15\%) + (0.5 \times 5\%) = 10\%$$

likewise the standard deviation is linearly reduced to half that of portfolio M, thus:

$$\sigma_P = (0.5 \times 16\%) + \text{zero} + \text{zero} = 8\%$$

If instead it were possible to borrow, at the risk-free rate, an amount equivalent to the investor's present endowment – that is you invest twice as much in portfolio M – the position would be:

$$E(r_P) = (2 \times 15\%) \text{ less interest } (1 \times 5\%) = 25\%$$
$$\sigma_P = (2 \times 16\%) - (1 \times \text{zero}) + 0 = 32\%$$

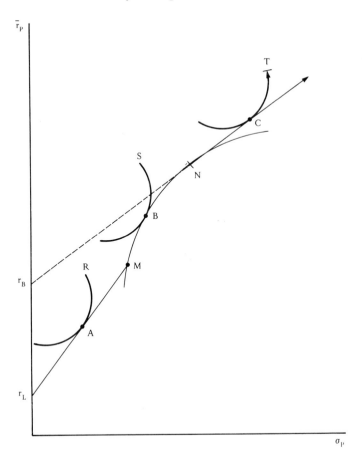

Figure 8.5

This analysis could be further extended by releasing the risk-free assumption and having different borrowing and lending rates. Figure 8.5 combines the possibility of borrowing money at an interest rate of r_B and the possibility of lending money at an interest rate of r_L by buying government bonds. Also depicted are the indifference curves of three investors, R, S and T. Investor R will hold portfolio A, which consists of placing a proportion of his investment funds in government bonds and the balance in the risky portfolio M. Investor S holds portfolio B. Finally, investor T holds portfolio C which consists of placing all available funds in risky portfolio N, plus borrowing additional funds at rate r_B and placing these also in portfolio N.

Returning to the situation of an equal borrowing/lending rate we will give further consideration to the CML. Before so doing though it would be useful to remember that the assumptions necessary for the conclusions reached in the foregoing analysis are exactly those that arose earlier, in Chapter 1, when we considered a normative framework for investment appraisal. While certain of these assumptions are clearly unrealistic this analysis is a necessary prerequisite for considering the capital asset pricing model (CAPM) below.

The slope of the CML denotes the trade-off between risk and return. The relationship can be written as:

$$[E(r_m) - rf] / \sigma_m,$$

where $E(r_m)$ and σ_m represent the expected return and risk of the market portfolio and rf is the risk-free return. It represents the market price of risk. As an example consider the following situation:

$$\frac{E(r_m) - rf}{\sigma_m} = \frac{16\% - 8\%}{4\%} = 2$$

which indicates that every 1 per cent rise in risk (standard deviation) is compensated by an increase of 2 per cent above the risk-free return.

The final stage of analysis is to derive a general expression to measure the risk/return trade-off of a portfolio that lies along the CML. In general terms, this portfolio (termed j) is calculated thus:

$$E(r_j) = rf + [E(r_m) - rf]\sigma j$$

or simply:

$$E(r_j) = rf + \lambda \sigma j$$

where $\lambda = [E(r_m) - rf] / \sigma_m$, the market price of risk. The formula reflects that an efficient portfolio should be well diversified since the market does not reward investors for taking on unnecessary risk. As such, the expected return reflects the extent to which the market will reward investors for taking on risk which may not be diversified away from holding efficient portfolios. Thus, the expected return on an efficient investment portfolio is equal to the risk-free return, rf, plus a risk premium, $\lambda . \sigma_j$. The premium is a reflection of the portfolio's own risk, σ_j, together with the market's risk attitude, λ.

This analysis, or model, of portfolio theory is theoretically robust but only of rather academic interest. (It is however a necessary prerequisite to what follows.) Recall that one of the necessary conditions for operating this model was a manageable computer program. Readers will readily appreciate this necessity when they consider that a portfolio of 1000 shares would require 1000 expected values, 1000 variances and a staggering 499,500 covariances to be calculated. However, there is a satisfactory simplification to the portfolio model. Sharpe (1964) suggests the abandonment of the covariances of each share and the substitution of information concerning the relationship of each security to the market. The foundation of his work is nowadays termed the capital asset pricing model (CAPM).

The capital asset pricing model

With CAPM, instead of measuring/estimating the correlation between returns for a security and all other securities, it is only necessary to estimate the correlation between a particular share's return and that for some market index.

Sharpe thought of the market as providing two prices:

1 The price of time (or the pure rate of interest).
2 The price of risk; the additional expected return per unit of risk borne.

Risk is considered to consist of two elements: *unsystematic* risk, caused by events unique to a firm, and *systematic* risk. Events unique to a firm could, for example, be concerned with the quality of management or the fact that one firm may have a technological advantage over its competitors. Systematic risk relates to factors that affect all firms to a greater or lesser extent, for example, the state of sterling or the possibility of an oil embargo. The theory is that unsystematic risk can be diversified away by investors holding a diversified portfolio so that the relevant risk measure is systematic risk. Some authors refer to these elements as being market risk and unique or specific risk.

Sharpe's relationship can be expressed as:

$$E_{rj} = rf + \frac{[E_{rm} - rf]}{\sigma^2_m} \, Cov_{jm}$$

where $Cov_{jm} = \sigma_m.\sigma_j.\rho_{jm}$ and j = an individual share and m = some recognized market index. Therefore:

$$E_{rj} = rf + \frac{[E_{rm} - rf]}{\sigma^2_m} \, \sigma_m . \sigma_j . \rho_{jm}$$

$$E_{rj} = rf + \frac{[E_{rm} - rf]}{\sigma_m} \, \sigma_j . \rho_{jm}$$

$$E_{rj} = rf + \beta_j \, [E_{rm} - rf], \text{ where } \beta_j = \frac{\sigma_j . \rho_{jm}}{\sigma_m}.$$

The beta coefficient, β_j, measures the systematic risk for share j relative to the systematic risk in the market. The term $(E_{rm} - rf)$ denotes the systematic (market) risk premium, that is the difference between the pure rate of interest and the average return on the market. Figure 8.6 presents a graphical representation of the CAPM. All shares

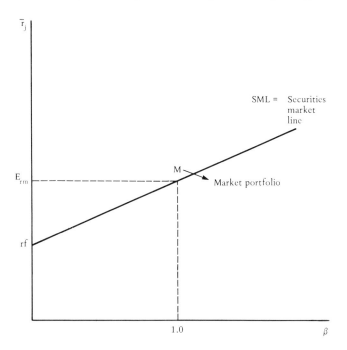

Figure 8.6

have measures of systematic risk that lie on the *securities market line* (SML). Though superficially similar to Figure 8.4, note that the horizontal axis has a different measure of risk. Rather than add further complicated analysis to the main body of this chapter, Appendix 8.2 provides, with the aid of calculus, the derivation of the SML from the CML – both are linear functions of three variables.

From Figure 8.6, it will be noted that the return of the market index (or portfolio), E_{rm}, has a beta coefficient of 1. All shares that move exactly in line with the market will also have a beta coefficient of 1. Remembering that:

$$\beta_j = \frac{\sigma_j \cdot \rho_{jm}}{\sigma_m},$$

this means that share j must be perfectly correlated with the market and that the riskiness of the individual asset, σ_j, is equal to that of the market, σ_m. Hence the beta coefficient of shares that are generally riskier than the market as a whole will have higher beta coefficients ($\beta_j > 1.0$), while the converse is true of less risky investments ($\beta_j < 1.0$). A zero beta coefficient implies zero risk as with government bonds. If a share had a beta coefficient of 0.75, it would be exactly the same as the weighted average beta coefficient of a portfolio that is invested 75 per cent in the market index and 25 per cent in government bonds.

Beta coefficients can be calculated by plotting the returns for an individual security against some market index and then drawing in a line of 'best-fit' (characteristic line). To use such a beta for purposes of evaluation means that the investor accepts past performance as a guide to future expectation.* Fortunately such calculations are unnecessary if a specialist statistical service is used, such as the 'Risk Measurement Service' provided by the London Business School which measures quoted equities on the London Stock Exchange.

On the basis that we are using a risk measurement service we consider the following simplified illustration:

Data $rf = 8\%$
$E_{rm} = 18\%$
$\beta_j = 1.5$

The expected return for share j is therefore:

$$E_{rj} = 8\% + 1.5(18\% - 8\%) = 23\%$$

This indicates that a rational investor requires a higher return from a share that is riskier on average than the market. A 0.5 rise in risk premium raises the required return by 5 per cent, namely from 18 per cent to 23 per cent. As with all simple expressions, if we know various investor requirements simple decision rules can be made. For example, suppose that an investor wished to select for investment shares that earned 20 per cent per annum then, retaining values for rf and E_{rm} as above we can solve for the value of β_j that produces a return of 20 per cent. In this case $\beta_j = 1.2$ and our investor could use the risk measurement service to select shares with a beta coefficient of at least 1.2.

Adaptation of the CAPM to project appraisal

Basic micro-economic theory states that each project should be evaluated by its own opportunity cost of capital. Under conditions of certainty and perfect capital markets, the appropriate rate is the market borrowing/lending rate as this is the rate by which the firm will either borrow further funds or lend surplus funds. Releasing these assumptions to allow for a different borrowing and lending rate, the firm should first assess all available projects at the borrowing rate as this is the appropriate rate should additional funds be required. If, however, the firm has surplus funds available, remaining projects should be

---

* Rather than illustrate this point here, readers are advised to refer to Lintner, 1965(a), 1965(b).

assessed at the lending rate, as those yielding a positive net present value will return more than if the funds had been lent on the market.

When risk is introduced, we require an appropriate risk-adjusted discount rate. This necessitates the calculation of a required rate of return *tailored* to the riskiness of the individual project. The model developed in the previous section can only serve as a suitable measure providing the projects undertaken by a firm fall within the present risk class of that entity, and are also financed solely by equity capital. Both conditions are now elaborated as follows.

It has already been established that the more risky a firm the higher the required return. For example, a food manufacturer might have an equity beta of 0.9, while a retail store chain might have a beta of around 1.3. Investors, given a risk-free rate of 8 per cent and a market premium of 10 per cent, would require a return of 17 per cent from the former and 21 per cent from the latter. The retail store group should either use its own beta measure or an industry average when calculating the expected return on a new shop development. The question arises: should the same risk measure be applied if the firm wished to diversify its activities into, say, the manufacture of household goods?

If the average industry sector beta coefficient for household goods is taken as 0.8, then the required return is 16 per cent. This is the required return for equity investors in this sector of the market, based upon the riskiness of the business sector relative to overall market performance. Unquoted companies could also estimate required rates of return by comparison with similar quoted firms.

So far, we have only discussed equity beta coefficients. These are, after all, the only statistical measures available. Under the assumptions of the CAPM, an equity beta is composed of two constituents – business risk and financial risk. For individual project evaluation we need employ only that proportion related to business risk. If the firm has debt in its capital structure (as is the usual case) we need to 'ungear' the equity beta coefficient, thus:

$$\beta_e \frac{E}{(E + D)} + \beta_d \frac{D}{(E + D)} = \beta_{project}$$

where:

β_e = the equity beta coefficient
    (available via market evaluation)
β_d = the debt beta coefficient
E = the proportion of equity finance
D = the proportion of debt finance

The term on the right hand side of the equation, $\beta_{project}$, measures the business risk borne by the firm's equity investors. The difference between β_{equity} and $\beta_{project}$ represents the additional financial risk borne as a result of the firm's deployment of debt.

In the example that follows, it is assumed that the debt beta co-efficient, β_d, is zero. This is not normally the case, but the value of β_d is small due to the security coverage normally required by the providers of debt capital. Buckley (1981) discusses this further.

Suppose that a firm has £10 million of capital, financed 60 per cent by equity and 40 per cent by debt. If the firm's equity beta is 1.5, then the project beta is:

$$1.5(0.6) + 0(0.4) = 0.9 = \beta_{project}$$

and the firm's required return for its project is:

$$E_{project} = R_f + \beta_{project} (E_{rm} - Rf),$$
$$E_{project} = 8\% + 0.9 (18\% - 8\%) = 17\%$$

Readers may wish to confirm these results as follows:

	£m
	£m
£10 million invested in projects earning 17%	1.7
less interest on debt (taken at 8% on £4m)	0.32
Balance attributable to equity investors	£1.38

$$\text{Return to equity investors} = \frac{£1.38m}{£6.00m} \times 100\% = 23\%$$

If we utilize our basic equation, the expected return by the equity investors is:

$$E_{rj} = 8\% + 1.5(10\%) = 23\%$$

If only the financial structure of the firm changes, then the company cost of capital remains unaltered. To continue with the present example, if the company replaced £3 million of debt with equity capital then only the equity beta coefficient would alter i.e. due to the reduction of gearing employed. The revised equity beta coefficient becomes:

$$\beta_e(0.9) + 0(0.1) = 0.9$$
$$\beta_e = 1.0$$

Again, these results can be confirmed as follows:

	£m
£10 million invested in projects earning 17%	1.7
less interest on debt (now 8% on £1m)	0.08
Balance attributable to equity investors	£1.62

$$\text{Return to equity investors} = \frac{£1.62m}{£9.00m} \times 100\% = 18\%,$$

and the expected return to equity investors is:

$E_{rj} = 8\% + 1.0(10\%) = 18\%$

where E_{rj} denotes the expected return to equity investors from a revised capital structure.

If the firm were to diversify, then it would be more appropriate either to select an equity beta coefficient for a particular firm in that industry sector, or one based on the average of firms in that market sector.

Of course such a beta would represent the equity risk of either a particular firm or for that industry sector. In such situations one 'ungears' using the appropriate weightings relative to that firm or industry sector. The resultant measure for business risk is then incorporated in the above formula.

The analysis so far has not considered the tax advantage arising from the deployment of debt in a firm's capital structure. It is a relatively straightforward matter to incorporate the impact of corporation tax into our earlier discussion. Our basic equation can be re-expressed as:

$E_j = [rf\,(1 - c) + \beta_j(E_{rm} - rf)]\,(1 - c),$

where c denotes corporation tax. To ungear an equity beta we still multiply β_j by:

$$\frac{E}{E + D}$$

in order to provide the firm's pre-tax required return for each project:

$E_{project} = rf + \beta_{project}\,(E_{rm} - rf)$, as above.

Traditionally, many firms have used only one rate of return for project evaluation. Figure 8.7 depicts the notion that different rates should be selected, depending upon the riskiness of the individual project.

The criteria developed in the CAPM mean that projects should be accepted if their expected return, when plotted, is on or above the securities market line. This means that some projects are accepted that would otherwise have been discarded, had a single discount rate been employed, while others are rejected.

A single discount rate for all levels of risk would be a horizontal line which would dissect the securities market line at or below the point E_j.

Although the model provides a useful way of valuing risky investments, it is important to appreciate the assumptions on which it is based and hence its limitations as an appraisal technique, especially when adapted for capital project appraisal. These assumptions are basically those that were introduced into our portfolio model:

1 Share (asset) values are determined according to expected rates of return and variances.

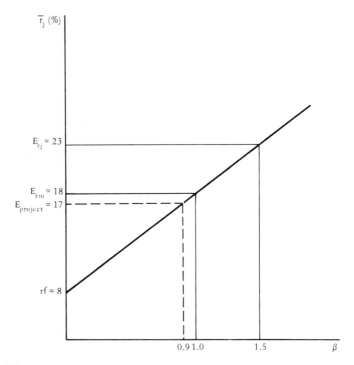

Figure 8.7

2 A lower variance is preferred to a higher variance for the same mean
   rate of return; a higher mean rate of return is preferred to a lower
   mean rate of return for the same variance.
3 All investors have the same expectations regarding the expected
   returns, variances and covariances of all shares.
4 Borrowing and lending opportunities are available to all investors at
   a publicly quoted risk-free rate of interest.
5 Fractional holding of investments is permitted.
6 There are no transaction costs.
7 A perfect market exists, open to all investors and with a free supply
   of information.
8 There is no taxation.

   Are these assumptions important? Unfortunately yes. In changing the
composition of a portfolio there may exist substantial transaction costs
and so marginal changes in a portfolio may no longer become profitable. Fama (1965) has shown that where portfolios are not explicitly
based on means and variances, the CAPM holds, provided that the
return on shares are normally distributed or at least symmetrical. With
respect to the borrowing/lending assumption; not only may some firms
or individuals borrow at more favourable rates than others, but also

with inflation it is impossible to have a known risk-free rate of interest in real terms. The CAPM has been extended to deal with different borrowing and lending rates (Black, 1972). Personal taxation is ignored in the model but is important. Since different investors have different rates of tax they may choose portfolios peculiar to their personal tax situation. The question of the effect of taxation on investment decisions is a complex one and was discussed in detail in Chapter 6. If the rate of return determined by the SML is used as a discount rate for more than one time period, then the investor implicitly assumes that the beta coefficient, the risk-free rate of interest, and the mean rate of return on the market are constant throughout the life of the project (unless adapted as above).

If the CAPM is too restrictive as a single period model it is possible to adapt the model. Consider the following expression:

$$NPV = \sum_{t=0}^{n} \frac{Ft}{(1+r_{j1})\,(1+r_{j2})\cdots(1+r_{jt})}$$

together with the following data:

cash flows: $t_0 = -£220,000$; $t_1 = £100,000$; $t_2 = +£200,000$
$r_f = t_1 = 7.75\%$; $t_2 = 8\%$
$r_m = t_1$ and $t_2 = 17.5\%$
$\beta_j = t_1{:}1.5$; $t_2{:}1.6$

therefore: $r_{j1} = 7.75\% + 1.5\,(17.5\% - 7.75\%) = 22.38\%$
$r_{j2} = 8\% + 1.6\,(17.5\% - 8.0\%) = 23.20\%$

$$NVP = -£220,000 + \frac{£100,000}{(1.2238)} + \frac{£200,000}{(1.2238)\,(1.232)} = -£5,637$$

With the availability of this information this project would be rejected. If at t_0 we had made a normal NPV calculation using a discount rate of, say, 19 per cent and used this figure at t_1 and t_2 then the project would have had a positive NPV of $+£5,267$.

Summary

Although a tremendous amount of detail has been presented in this chapter it is possible to summarize the key points covering portfolio theory and its adaptations for use in determining a risk-adjusted discount rate for project appraisal.

It was demonstrated that investors, or their managers, can reduce the risk of their portfolios by a judicious mix of risky investments, having taken into account not only their individual risks and expected returns but also the covariances or correlation coefficients of their expected returns to those of the other risky investments in the portfolio. By introducing the ability to lend and borrow at some risk-free rate of interest, the range of efficient portfolios of interest to the investor is reduced to just one – the market portfolio. As all the risky investments in a market must be held by someone, it follows that the market must contain all risky investments. All rational investors will wish to hold an efficient portfolio, which is efficient both in the sense of providing the greatest possible level of expected return for a given level of systematic risk. The expression for the CML provides the level of return to be expected from an efficient portfolio, given the amount of risk chosen by an investor.

Having outlined the basic tenets of portfolio theory, the capital asset pricing model (CAPM) was introduced in order to provide a more manageable approach to determining the required return of individual shares. The CAPM was then adapted in order to provide a theoretically acceptable discount rate for the purposes of project appraisal. It is important though to remember that we have been discussing a model. By definition a model is based on assumptions. The limitations briefly presented clearly highlight the fact that care needs to be taken when using beta adjusted discount rates. Such an approach is most certainly to be preferred to some of the less complex 'rule of thumb' approaches introduced at the beginning of this chapter. Most of the empirical research into the CAPM tends either to provide evidence that the model does not work in efficient conditions or does little more than confirm the assumptions on which the model is based, some which do not apply in the real world. While accepting this we suggest that, despite these defects, the development of portfolio theory (and in particular the introduction of the CAPM) provides a most useful approach to demonstrating the relationships involved. To dismiss models such as the CAPM would be to dismiss other useful, though equally imperfect, tools such as break-even analysis charts.

The CAPM is being increasingly adapted by market analysts as a means of measuring the performance of individual shares. It seems highly probable that it will become more widely adopted by industry in the years to come since it is clearly better to use a model with known flaws rather than leave risk adjustment to subjective judgement.

Appendix 8.1 *The derivation of the formula for the standard deviation of a two-asset portfolio*

When comparing share F with share G the business risk is measured by:

$$\sigma_F{}^2 + \text{Covariance (Cov)}_{FG}\ x_F.(1-x)_G$$

likewise, comparing share G with share F produces:

$$\sigma_G{}^2 + \text{Cov}_{GF}\ x_F.(1-x)_G$$

the precise mix of these two shares is found by taking a weighted average of variances and covariances which can be written as:

$$\sigma p^2 = x_F^2 . \sigma_F^2 + (1-x)^2{}_G . \sigma^2{}_G + Cov_{FG} x_F . (1-x) + Cov_{GF} x_F . (1-x)_G$$
$$\sigma p^2 = x^2{}_F . \sigma^2{}_F + (1-x)^2{}_G \sigma^2{}_G + 2 \; x_F . (1-x)_G . Cov_{FG}$$

with the standard deviation being simply the square root of this last expression.

Appendix 8.2 *The derivation of the securities market line (SML) from the capital market line (CML)*

The general expression to measure a portfolio that lies along the CML is:

$$E(r_j) = rf + [E_{rm} - rf] . \sigma_j$$

where

$E(r_j)$ = the expected return of share j
rf   = the risk-free rate of interest
E_{rm} = the expected return on the market
σ_j = the standard deviation associated with share j

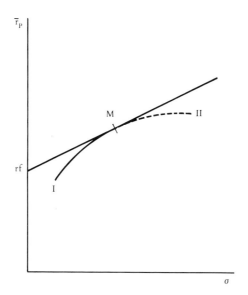

The CML gives the market's relationship between risk and return. The relationship between risk and the expected return for an individual security is, however, of more interest. An individual share will be plotted somewhere on the efficiency frontier I.M.II, as depicted in the graph below. Consider that I represents a particular share. A portfolio lying along the arc I.M will therefore contain a larger proportion of I than the market portfolio, M. Similarly portfolios containing a smaller proportion of I than that in the market portfolio will lie on the dashed extension M.II.

The equation of the curve I.M can be found and, using calculus, the slope of the curve I.M at M can be calculated; if this is denoted by S_m, then it can be shown that:

$$S_M = \frac{(E_I - E_M)}{Cov_{IM} - \sigma^2_M} \cdot \sigma_M$$

where E_I is the expected return of share I, and Cov_{IM} is the covariance of return between share I and the market portfolio M.

As the slope of the arc I.M must be tangential to the CML at M, S_M can be set equal to:

$$\frac{E_M - rf}{\sigma M}$$

giving:

$$\frac{(E_I - E_M)}{Cov_{IM} - \sigma_M^2} \cdot \sigma_M = \frac{E_M - rf}{\sigma M}$$

This expression can be simplified and rearranged such that E_I is the value of most interest, thus:

$$E_I = rf + \frac{(E_M - rf)}{\sigma^2_M} \cdot Cov_{IM}.$$

Hence, the expected return on any security is equal to the risk-free rate, a constant, plus a term for bearing risk. This latter term is equal to some constant:

$$\frac{E_M - rf}{\sigma^2_M}$$

multiplied by a variable, Cov_{IM}. So under CAPM, risk is measured in terms of the covariance of return between the security and the market as a whole, and not solely in terms of the standard deviation.

The covariance is an absolute measure and it is more convenient to convert this to a relative measure by dividing by σ^2_M. The beta coefficient (here β_I) is defined as:

$$\frac{Cov_{IM}.}{\sigma^2_M}$$

If β_I is substituted into the earlier expression for E_I, then:

$E_I = rf + \beta_I (Em - rf)$

which is the straight line equation known as the SML.

References

Black, F. *et al.*, 'The Capital Asset Pricing Model: Some Empirical Tests', in Jensen, M., *Studies in the Theory of Capital Markets*, Praeger, New York, 1972.

Buckley, A., 'Beta Geared and Ungeared', *Accounting* and *Business Research*, Spring 1981.

Fama, E. F., 'The Behaviour of Stock Market Prices', *Journal of Business*, January 1965.

Further reading

OVERVIEW ARTICLES

Boys, P., 'The Capital Asset Pricing Model-Underlying Theory', *Accountancy*, September 1984.

Boys, P., 'CAPM's Implications for Investment', *Accountancy*, October 1984.

Glynn, J. J., 'Capital Budgeting: Risk Assessment with the Capital Asset Pricing Model', *Certified Accountant*, December 1980.

Pitt, Francis, D. and Jollyfield, R. J., 'The Capital Asset Pricing Model: A Simple Approach', *Certified Accountants Studies' Newsletter*, May 1985.

RELEVANT ARTICLES

Alderfer, C. and Bierman, H., 'Choices with Risk: Beyond the Mean and Variance', *Journal of Business*, July 1970.

Blume, M. E., 'Portfolio Theory: A Step Towards its Practical Application', *Journal of Business*, April 1970.

Fama, E. F., 'Risk, Return and Equilibrium: Some Clarifying Comments', *Journal of Finance*, March 1968.

Friend, I. *et al.*, 'New Evidence on the Capital Asset Pricing Model', *Journal of Finance*, June 1978.

Levy, H., 'The Capital Asset Pricing Theory and Empiricism', *The Economic Journal*, March 1983.

Levy, H., 'Equilibrium in an Imperfect Market: A Constraint on the Number of Securities in the Portfolio', *American Economic Review*, September 1978.

Lintner, J., (a) 'The Valuation of Risk Assets and the Selection of Risky Investments in Stock Portfolios and Capital Budgets', *Review of Economics and Statistics*, February 1965.

Lintner, J., (b) 'Security Prices, Risk, and the Maximal Gains from Diversification', *Journal of Finance*, December 1965.

Markowitz, H., 'Portfolio Selection', *Journal of Finance*, March 1952.

Sharpe, W. F., 'Capital Asset Prices: A Theory of Market Equilibrium Under Conditions of Risk', *Journal of Finance*, September 1964.

Stapleton, R. C., 'Portfolio Analysis, Stock Valuation and Capital Budgeting Decision Rules for Risky Projects', *Journal of Finance*, November 1971.

RELEVANT BOOKS

Markowitz, H., *Portfolio Selection: Efficient Diversification of Investments*, New York, Wiley, 1959.

Sharpe, W. F., *Portfolio Theory and Capital Markets*, McGraw-Hill Book Co., 1971.

Part Four

Treasury Management

9 Functions of treasury management

Introduction

The function and structure of the finance department and the role and duties of its officers will vary according to organizational characteristics, for example size, complexity of the group and degree of centralized management. The chapter accepts this diversity and therefore concentrates on discussing these matters in terms of a representative group finance department.

While treasury management gained a higher profile in the UK with the formation of the Association of Corporate Treasurers in 1979, it is not a new phenomenon. Some UK companies have employed treasurers for many years and in the US the finance function has long been split between a controller and a treasurer. However since 1967, when Tricker observed the beginnings of a division of the chief accountant's role between a financial controller and a treasurer, there has been a gradual evolution in UK multi-national companies towards the US model with a financial controller and a treasurer reporting to a finance director at group centre.

The reasons for the rise of the corporate treasurer are diverse. Important influences would include:

1 *Floating exchange rates* – sterling commenced to float in June 1972. This decision increased the risks associated with borrowing, investing and trading in foreign currencies.
2 *1970s financial environment* – this era saw oil price rises in 1977 and 1979. These, together with floating exchange rates, began a trend towards generally higher and more volatile interest rates. Simultaneously world recessions brought pressure upon cash flows and increased the need for extra funding. In the context of a collapse of the market for corporate long-term debt and difficulties in raising new issue finance, companies moved towards short-term bank bor-

rowing which in effect became part of the company's permanent capital. This greater dependence on short-term finance with consequent vulnerability to greater interest rate volatility has increased the emphasis upon managing borrowings and controlling cash flows.

3   *Financial innovation* – greater financial risks led to the growth of eurocurrency and other secondary markets with new opportunities for raising finance and covering risk. As a result, corporate financial management became more complex and required greater attention if advantage was to be taken of these new devices.

4   *Financial image* – the riskier financial environment, especially in the light of the dramatic falls in stock market values of late 1987 and the periodic bouts of turbulence on the foreign exchanges, has prompted an increased emphasis by UK companies on their corporate image with providers of capital and the markets generally. Therefore liaison with bankers, financial analysts, shareholders and others has become an important activity for the finance function.

5   *Technology* – the availability of online information regarding financial markets, through Reuters, Telerate and others, has extended the scope for real time decision making and consequently promoted a demand for specialist personnel capable of working in such environments.

In sum, the background to the development of the corporate treasury function in the UK reflects the response by companies to environmental changes, which have increased financial risks and made more policy options available.

An overview of the finance function

Finance functions are ubiquitous and exist to some extent at virtually all levels of a business organization. Members of the finance function have dual responsibilities in organizational terms. First there is line responsibility with each finance officer reporting to an executive (for example at head office, the group finance director reporting to the group managing director) and second a functional responsibility with subsidiary and divisional finance executives reporting to the group finance director. The latter relationship denotes the all pervading nature of finance and the importance of coordinating and centralizing, to some degree, financial planning, control and information systems to meet internally and externally imposed requirements.

The contribution of the finance function is at two levels – strategic and routine. At the strategic level there is a threefold role for the finance function in the development of overall group strategy:

1   Quantification of group strategic plans into financial terms (for example return on capital employed, earnings per share and cash flow) and the monitoring of actual performance against the strategic plan targets.

2 Development of strategic plans for individual financial areas. This process involves interaction with group strategic plans (for example funding plans depend upon acquisition and investment strategies). Areas where the finance function might be expected to develop strategic plans would include funding, dividend policy, financial image, currency risk management, allocation of funds, investment of surplus funds, taxation and working capital management.
3 Provision of information into the strategic planning process including historic financial data and financial forecasts covering a range of scenarios.

The routine level would encompass the numerous day-to-day activities which might typically be classified under the finance function. The following list is not exhaustive but covers the routine responsibilities of a representative finance function:

1 *Finance* – financial structure of the group, funding management, currency management, cash management, management of an investment portfolio and relationships with financial institutions.
2 *Management accounting* – budgetary control system, costing analysis, provision of management information on a regular and ad hoc basis, investment appraisal, working capital management and forecasting.
3 *Financial accounting* – records of transactions, preparation of regular financial accounts for internal and external use, collection and payment of cash and financial analysis.
4 *Auditing* – liaison and assistance to external auditors and control of the work of the internal auditors.
5 *Other* – secretarial (maintenance of statutory books, making periodic returns, meetings and procedural legality), taxation, insurance and pensions.
6 *Computerized information* – in some organizations the computer department will report to the finance director while in others it is a distinct department.

Having briefly outlined the function and activities of a typical finance department, the next section discusses the role of the treasurer.

Role of the treasurer

In discussing the functions of treasury management it is useful to examine the role of the treasurer. Information on the typical treasurer's role can be derived from two main sources – the Association of Corporate Treasurers (its pronouncements and entry requirements) and the Davis and Collier (1982) research project. Both sources agree that there are four core areas in the role of the treasurer, although the depth of involvement will vary widely:

1 *Currency risk management* – responsibility for those decisions which affect the foreign currency risk exposure of the company. At a strategic level the treasurer will provide forecasts of long-run exchange rate movements; while at the routine level the involvement will be in carrying out the day-to-day implementation of currency risk management within the policy guidelines laid down. Typically this would comprise the forecasting of short-run exchange rates, netting currency flows, reporting exposure on a regular basis, dealing in the foreign exchange markets, and managing the functions with a view to reducing exposures. These matters are examined in detail in Chapter 13.

2 *Funding management* – essentially responsibility for funding the group's short, medium and long-term cash requirements. At a strategic level involvement with the capital structure of the group, forecasting interest rates and advising on the future state of the financial markets. On a routine basis management of interest rates and interest rate risk, monitoring of daily short-run borrowing positions, advising on the choice of borrowing instrument when longer run finance is required and operational responsibility for the raising of funds by debt or equity issues. These matters are examined in detail in Chapters 10 and 14.

3 *Cash management* – the efficient transmission of money inside the group and to third parties, management of the group's surplus funds in an investment portfolio and some role in working capital management. The role in working capital management arises because responsibility for cash management, surplus funds and funding generally inevitably implies an interest in collections and payments. This interest may express itself in terms of having an input to policy within the group, centralization of these functions under a treasurer or a position between these extremes. The investment of surplus funds is dealt with in Chapter 16 while cash (liquidity) management is covered in Chapter 15.

4 *Banking* – the management of relationships with the banks including negotiation of facilities, and acting as a channel of communication generally. Although treated separately here, it could be argued that banking is really an integral part of currency risk management, funding management and cash management rather than a separate role. However, the majority of treasurers in the Davis and Collier survey perceived it as a distinct duty, hence its inclusion.

Appendix 9.1 contains a summary of various views of the treasurer's role to provide support for the contentions in this section.

Treasurer versus financial controller

Table 9.1 shows a possible division of the finance function between treasury and controllership responsibilities. As has been repeatedly

Table 9.1   Treasurer versus controller

Controller/accounting department	Treasurer/treasury
Accounting and financial control	Banking – organization of money
Management information – provision	handling
and interpretation	– relationships with the
Regular internal and external	financial community
reporting	Currency management
Audit – internal and relationships	Raising long-term permanent capital
with external	Borrowing – short, medium and
Working capital management	long-term
Asset security – internal control and	Advising on capital structure
insurance	Investment of surplus funds
Taxation	Cash management – collections and
Secretarial	payments, policy and cash forecasts
	Pension funds

Note: Audit, taxation and secretarial are often distinct areas not the responsibility of the controller

stated no precise definitions exist; however it may aid readers to consider two broad generalizations. First that the treasurer is the manager of cash as a productive resource, while the controller is concerned with planning and controlling its use. Second that the treasurer is a financial risk manager while the controller is the information handler, provider and interpreter. Difficulties of definition reflect the ad hoc way in which treasury departments have been set up as responsibilities of the finance function have become sufficiently complex to require a division into two distinct areas.

Organization of the treasury management function

At present treasury departments are confined to large companies and typically are small head office organizations. Research shows that the majority have fewer than five full-time non-secretarial staff and suggests that a typical organization chart resembles Figure 9.1.

It might be thought that treasury management is essentially a centralized function, whose *raison d'être* is an ability to manage the aggregate of surplus funds, borrowing and currency in a more efficient manner than could be achieved by individual operating unit initiative. However, the structure of treasury departments varies and it is possible to envisage two extremes. On the one hand there is a fully centralized department with global responsibility for decision making in all treasury areas where operating units merely report to the treasury and handle transactions in accordance with treasury instructions. On the other treasury responsibility may reside at the operating units with the central treasury function merely advising and providing policy guidelines. The practice of the majority of UK companies falls between these

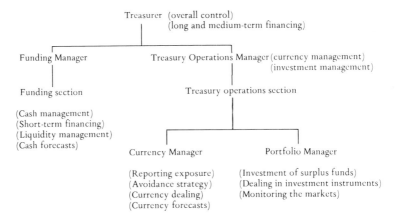

Figure 9.1   Treasury department organization

extremes. Factors involved in deciding upon a suitable treasury organization include:

1   *Group structure* – the composition of the group and the relative importance of individual operating units will be important. For example, a group with a strong home market bias and few overseas subsidiaries may well be strongly centralized, whereas if overseas operations exceed domestic involvement there could be strong arguments for the autonomy of powerful satellites.
2   *Extent of risk* – wherever risk is significant in group terms it is probable that the centre will want direct involvement in decision taking. Therefore, for example, operating units involved in long-run contracts with significant exchange exposure may expect the central treasury to maintain close control.
3   *Evolution* – management structures evolve in response to internal and external stimuli. Treasury functions are relatively new and therefore organizational structures involving them exhibit considerable variety as systems are developed and the treasury function becomes integrated.
4   *Management philosophy* – some groups have a philosophy of centralized control while others encourage decentralization as a means of motivating operating unit management.
5   *Quality of management* – treasury management requires highly skilled staff who are difficult to recruit. It is unlikely that groups can obtain sufficient manpower to staff all operating units with trained treasurers.
6   *Economies of scale* – central treasuries are able to borrow, invest and deal in larger amounts than individual operating units. Such transactions will obtain better rates and lower costs than would be

Table 9.2   Analysis of treasury responsibilities between the centre and operating units

Key functions	Centre	Operating units
Currency risk management		
Exposure reporting	Summary of group position	Notify centre of all exposures over agreed limits
Dealing	Full group responsibility	Only transactions to an agreed limit
Policy	Full group responsibility	Advice
Forecasts – exchange rates	Overall responsibility and summary of fore-	Advice and local information
– flows	cast currency flows	Budget information
Funding management		
Long and medium-term	Full group responsibility	Advice
Short-term	Full group responsibility for significant amounts	Action within agreed limits
Forecasts of requirements	Summary of group position	Budget information
Cash management		
Money transmission	Swap systems and policy	Action within agreed limits
Working capital	Policy input	Day-to-day management
Cash forecasts	Summary of group position	Budget information
Banking		
Operating unit bank relations		
– existing	Review/advice	Direct contact
– new	Approval	
Group banking relationships	Full group responsibility	None

available to local units. Further centralization permits netting and other offset systems to be operated.

Table 9.2 shows an example of a split of treasury function responsibilities between the centre and operating units for a few of the more common activities. It is for illustrative purposes only and not intended to suggest best practice.

The final aspect of treasury management organization to be discussed in this section is control over bank accounts. Given the fundamental importance of cash to a business it is probable that its management will be centralized through the consolidation of group bank accounts. Two basic schemes exist for this. First, the netting approach whereby

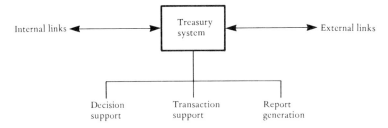

Figure 9.2 Features of a typical treasury system

account balances throughout the group are pooled and interest paid or received based upon the net figure. Thus an overdrawn balance on one operating unit's account can be offset against credit balances elsewhere. The group obtains interest savings by this device but will obviously incur charges from the bank for this service. Alternatively there is the zeroizing approach by which group operating unit bank accounts are organized in a hierarchical structure and the balance of each account is cleared daily up the hierarchy into one central group account. The operating unit is compensated for this zeroizing by an adjustment to the inter-company account. In either instance separate arrangements will be required with each banking group and the analysis will be by currency as it makes no sense to mix different currencies.

Treasury information systems

Treasurers are required to react speedily to changes in the economic environment. To do this successfully they require systems giving online information regarding these movements and the organization's position. Such information can only be provided by a computerized system and increasingly there has been a trend towards automation of the treasury function. This section describes a possible multi-function system based around a treasury workstation (a terminal or number of terminals linked to a computer facility). Systems for treasury departments may result from in-house development but are more likely to have been obtained through banks or from software houses. Figure 9.2 shows the main features of a system.

Features of a typical treasury system are as follows:

1 *Internal links* – this represents connections with the organization's other computer systems. Principally this will be into the accounting system with an interface ensuring that the accounts are automatically updated as treasury transactions occur and providing the facility to obtain internal information on matters such as billing. It is also conceivable that the treasury system links with the organization's

electric office system with access to word processing and electronic mail.

2 *External links* – there are two major links: to banks and to financial information services. The links to the banks will provide balance information services and access to electronic funds transfer systems. The balance reporting function may require a link to each banking group or could make use of an intermediary such as ADP or GEISCO, which will collect balance information from all banks and consolidate it by customer. Balances reported are normally those cleared at the close of business on the preceding day but many systems offer a forecast of the opening position which takes account of uncleared items and automated transactions in process. Electronic funds transfer services enable the bank's customers to initiate transactions with the effect of transmitting same day or forward value payments to any beneficiary whose bank account details are known. Obviously there are serious security implications involved and it is normal for password controls and checks on the identity of the terminal to be in force. Financial information services are provided by a range of companies on either a continuous or periodic update basis. The information covers stock, commodity, foreign exchange and money market and is usually paid for by an annual charge. Examples of online continuous update services include Extel's – Esprit Service, Reuters – Money Manager and Telerate's – Basic Service; while periodic update services are provided by Datastream, Reuters – Pocketwatch and television based Ceefax and Oracle.

3 *Decision support* – these are based on spreadsheet systems and covering the areas of cash flow forecasting and cost analysis on foreign currency positions. This facility enables the treasurer to undertake sensitivity analysis as changes in rates and circumstances become apparent from the internal links. In particular the cost analysis will provide input data for standard worksheets to enable the costs and benefits of various hedging positions to be continuously assessed.

4 *Transaction support* – computer systems provide a menu of transaction types with specific input formats. Supporting vouchers, confirmation letters and a transaction log will automatically be produced. By reference to treasury database information, checks are obtained on the actions of treasury in terms of transaction size, or placement, with a particular institution.

5 *Report generation* – exactly which reports are produced and their frequency will depend upon the circumstances of individual organizations. Examples of reports include:

(a) Bank balance reports covering sterling and foreign currency accounts with details of ledger and cleared balances.
(b) Balance history reports with information on balance movements over a period.

(c)   Foreign currency exposure reports showing current and forecast exposures.

(d)   Hedging contract monitoring giving a list of existing contracts and an evaluation at current rates to highlight profit potential.

(e)   Interest accruals estimating the interest accrued on borrowings at any point in time.

(f)   Maturity ladders analysing borrowings by maturity date and providing information on the net position at future dates.

(g)   Investment portfolio valuations listing the investment portfolio and valuing it at current rates.

Treasury information systems have peculiar design problems. These arise from combining the requirement for real-time information from internal and external sources with an ability to interpret the data in an appropriate timescale. The former prerequisite poses difficulties in interfacing with other computer systems while the latter needs sophisticated modelling routines. In practice, while there is a range of treasury management software available, few packages provide all the facilities discussed above.

Summary

The rise of treasury management as a separate functional area within the finance director's sphere of influence can be linked to the increased complexity of the financial environment since 1970. The objectives of this new function may be summarized as:

1   The provision of funds for the business at minimum cost.
2   The management of cash within the organization with a view to transmitting funds efficiently and investing surplus funds within laid down criteria.
3   The management of exchange rate risks.
4   Liaison with the banks and other financial institutions in order to promote a good pecuniary reputation for the organization.
5   Advice on corporate financial objectives such as capital structure, gearing and dividend policy.

The mechanics behind achieving these objectives will be discussed in later chapters; however at this stage the reader should be aware of the role of the treasurer, treasury management's position within the wider context of the finance department and the information systems requirements of the treasurer.

References

Davis, E. W. and Collier, P. A., *Treasury Management in the UK*, Association of Corporate Treasurers, 1982.

Appendix 9.1 *Role of the treasurer – sources*

Davis and Collier (1982)	Association's Part II examinations*	Association's experience requirement categories*
Main treasury functions: Banking Investment of surplus cash Borrowing Currency management and some involvement in: Short-term cash forecasts Funds flow forecasts Taxation	1 Corporate finance – financing of the corporate entity, raising debt and equity cost of capital, financial control, acquisitions and investments 2 Funding management – sources in the international and domestic markets, risks for lenders and borrowers and their management 3 Liquidity management – short-term borrowings, surplus funds investment, banking and cash forecasting and budgeting 4 Currency management – market practice, managing currency transactions and covering risk 5 Treasury management – integrative paper	1 *Corporate financial objectives* I.1 Financial aims and strategies I.2 Financial and treasury policies I.3 Financial and treasury systems 2 *Liquidity management* II.1 Working capital and transmission management II.2 Banking relationships and arrangements II.3 Money management 3 *Funding management* III.1 Funding policies and procedures III.2 Sources of funds III.3 Types of funds 4 *Currency management* IV.1 Exposure policies and procedures IV.2 Exchange dealings including futures and options IV.3 International monetary economics and exchange regulations 5 *Corporate finance* V.1 Equity capital management V.2 Business acquisitions and sales V.3 Project finance and joint ventures 6 *Related subjects* VI.1 Corporate taxation VI.2 Risk management and insurance VI.3 Pension fund investment management

*Association of Corporate Treasurers

Further reading

Brandenberg, M., 'The Money Manager: A New Type of Executive', *Accountancy*, April 1986.

Donaldson, J. A., *The Corporate Treasury Function*, ICAS, 1988.

Hodson, D., 'Why Industry Needs its (Professional) Company Treasurer', *The Director*, May 1981.

Tricker, R. I., *The Accountant in Management*, B. T. Batsford, London, 1967, Chapter 3.

RELEVANT ARTICLES

Donaldson, J. A., 'What Price Treasury Management?', *The Accountant's Magazine*, May 1980.

Long, G., 'Staffing a Treasury Department', *The Treasurer*, October 1984.

RELEVANT BOOKS

Giannotti, J. B. and Smith, R. W., *Treasury Management*, J. Wiley & Sons, New York, 1981.

Ross, D., *International Treasury Management*, Woodhead-Faulkner Ltd, 1987.

10 Long-term funding

This chapter deals with long-term funding and some of the surrounding issues. Types of security are considered, the functions of the Stock Exchange, its composition and system of trading, 'Big Bang' and 'Mini Bang' are dealt with followed by a discussion of the listing structure, the role of advisers, and the secondary issues. The chapter then deals with the choice between equity and debt and a consideration of the impact of institutional shareholdings on equity markets.

Types of security

While there are many types of security, a broad distinction exists between equity capital and loan capital. Equity capital normally refers to ordinary shares with preference shares forming a hybrid form of security with features of both debt and equity. Table 10.1 provides an analysis of applications for listing granted by the Stock Exchange Council.

Equity capital

Equity capital of a company constitutes the greatest risk to an investor since there is no security of either income or capital. However, equity shareholders have the right to appoint and dismiss directors and have the right of dividends as recommended by the board of directors. Furthermore, if a company is liquidated, shareholders have the right to receive any surplus once preferential creditors have been paid in full. Thus, shareholders fully participate in the risks and rewards of a company. If profits are high the return can also be high – both in terms of dividend yield and capital gains. The corollary is also true so that equity shares may be more volatile than other securities.

Table 10.1 Analysis of applications for listing granted by the Council of the Stock Exchange

	Total (£m)	Equities (£m)	Preference (£m)	Participating redeemable preference (£m)	Loans (£m)	Convertibles (£m)	I.I.I. (£m)	Eurobonds (£m)
1973	335	276	15	—	13	31	—	—
1974	214	175	14	—	10	15	—	—
1975	1,783	1,521	55	—	12	120	75	—
1976	1,269	1,157	22	—	—	90	—	—
1977	1,204	1,083	50	—	—	1	70	—
1978	1,396	1,324	49	—	10	1	12	—
1979	1,608	1,170	35	35	55	36	45	232
1980	1,647	1,098	62	193	2	222	43	27
1981	2,909	2,493	60	60	30	253	13	—
1982	3,120	1,776	49	231	891	73	—	100
1983	4,581	2,569	108	1,274	461	99	—	70
1984	9,001	6,899	61	858	490	173	—	520
1985	13,846	4,775	9	431	597	795	—	7,239
1986	23,250	14,019	33	528	1,243	320	—	7,107

Source: Stock Exchange

Some companies issue 'A' shares which have reduced, or even no voting rights and others issue 'B' shares which offer fully paid shares in lieu of dividends. A further variation are deferred shares which are sometimes, although not often, issued. These defer dividend payments until some future predetermined threshold, such as a particular date or level of profits is reached.

Preference shares

A preference share is a hybrid form of security since it has some features of both debt and equity. In practice preference shares have a fixed dividend which is paid prior to the claims of ordinary shareholders but after interest has been paid to debenture and loan stock holders. Thus from a creditor's point of view preference shares are normally viewed as part of the equity base. However, from an ordinary shareholder's perspective, preference shares have features of debt since obligations to preference shareholders must be met before those of ordinary shareholders.

A preference shareholder has a claim on income and assets and one or both of these claims conveys preferential rights before ordinary shareholders. A prior claim to income means that a preference dividend must always be paid before an ordinary dividend is paid although it is a characteristic of equities that there is no obligation to pay dividends at all. A shareholder has no legal redress if a dividend is not paid.

A cumulative preference share differs from a non-cumulative preference share. For example, if a company does not pay preference dividends for a number of years because of financial problems it cannot, of course, pay ordinary dividends. If the company recommences dividend payments it must pay the arrears to cumulative preference shareholders but it will not do so to non-cumulative preference shareholders.

Another variation of a preference share is a participating preference share which has a fixed rate of dividend plus a variable element depending upon the level of company profits.

In addition to, or alternatively, a preference share may have a prior claim on assets in a situation where the company is wound up.

With respect to influence on management, the voting rights of preference shares may vary according to whether the shares are non-cumulative or cumulative. Non-cumulative preference shareholders are likely to have some voting rights at all times to compensate for the possible loss of a dividend. In contrast, a cumulative preference shareholder will probably have his or her rights restricted in some respect. For example, a restriction may be imposed which only permits a vote at an annual general meeting, when its dividend is in arrears or when its legal rights are under review.

Another feature of preferred stock is that they sometimes have rights of conversion into ordinary shares which make them a viable financing instrument. Furthermore, while most preference shares are irredeemable and therefore constitute permanent capital, it is possible to issue preference shares that are redeemable at a prearranged redemption date or redeemable at the company's option, provided the articles of association so permit.

Since ordinary shares have a higher risk, preference shares may be issued at a lower cost. Provided the funds raised from preference shares are used profitably the earnings thereby generated should exceed their cost and increase both earnings per share and wealth of the ordinary shareholders. However, in practice preference shares are relatively cost-ly when compared to debt. The reason for this is that since the introduction of the imputation tax system in 1973 a payment to a preference shareholder is deemed to be a dividend – an appropriation of profits – whereas a payment to a debenture holder is deemed to be interest and therefore tax deductible. Furthermore, advance corporation tax (ACT) is payable on preference dividends so that companies with low tax charges may not be able to offset ACT against their mainstream corporation tax liability.

Another advantage of preference shares is that if the company is in a loss-making situation there is no obligation to pay a dividend. However, failure to pay a preference dividend is a sign of severe financial problems that could mean that the company would be unable to issue further preference shares for a considerable period of time. Furthermore, failure to pay a preference dividend is likely to be seen by the financial community and by creditors to be showing a red warning signal.

Since preference shares normally have some restrictions on voting rights, they are sometimes popular with private companies as a means of realizing some of their investment without diluting control over the business. This is sometimes achieved by a capitalization issue in which the bonus element is in the form of non-participating, non-voting shares which can be sold to institutions. Such an approach can also be used by a listed company which is majority owned by family members.

Long-term debt

Corporate bonds is a generic term which refers to bonds, debentures, debenture stock or loan stock which fulfil a number of conditions. The bond must be quoted on a recognized Stock Exchange in the UK or on the Unlisted Securities Market, must be marketable and must be a normal commercial loan. Corporate bonds have not been particularly attractive in the early 1980s, since high rates of interest have been obtainable on gilt-edged stocks and they are free from capital gains tax if held for more than twelve months. Section 64, Schedule 13 of the Finance Act 1984 redressed this imbalance by placing qualifying corporate bonds, issued after 13 March 1984, on the same footing as gilt-edged stocks. In addition, bonds issued on or before 13 March 1984 may become qualifying bonds, provided that the acquirer did not obtain the bond as a result of a no gain/no loss transaction such as between husband and wife, or if holdover relief had been claimed under the provisions relating to gifts.

A debenture is a general term for long-term debt that normally has a total life of at least ten years. In effect a debenture is a piece of paper acknowledging indebtedness. Normally a debenture is secured by a trust deed which sets out the contractual terms between the company and debenture holders. A trustee, normally a bank or insurance company, is appointed to safeguard the interests of debenture holders and to ensure that the terms of the contract are adhered to.

Typically a debenture will be secured by either a fixed or floating charge (or both). A fixed charge is secured on a specific asset of value, normally property, and the terms of the charge should ensure that no prior charge is made on that asset without the consent of debenture holders. In contrast, a floating charge literally floats over a group of assets, such as fixed or current assets, and in the case of default the lender chooses the assets to crystallize from that group. The advantage of a floating charge is that in the case of a breach in the debenture trust deed an administrative receiver can be appointed to run the business until the breach is remedied. In contrast, a fixed charge only confers rights over a specific asset with no rights over other assets.

Normally a debenture is issued at par and is redeemable at par, interest being paid each year on nominal values. The redemption period is often spread so that management may redeem the loans at their discretion. For example, 10 per cent debenture stock might be redeemable between 1992 and 1996 in equal instalments or in a lump sum at any time over that period. Management will compare the net present value of alternative courses of action to determine whether redemption is profitable. A number of factors will be taken into consideration in determining redemption. For example, changes in taxation might encourage refunding or a change in capital structure may become desirable. Other reasons might include a wish for the company to release an asset upon which there is a fixed charge or to repay debt as cash flows are better than anticipated or simply because interest rates are falling. The redemption may be made either out or current cash flows, or by raising new capital, or by setting aside profits each year in a sinking fund.

An alternative to the redeemable debenture is the perpetual or irredeemable debenture. As the name suggests the company does not repay the loan except in the case of a liquidation. A further variation is the mortgage debenture which has security on property.

Convertible loan stock

The main feature of convertible securities is that the holder has the option to convert his stock within a given time period into equity shares at a specified price. If the conversion option is not taken the loan stock continues on its redemption path. However, if the majority of stock-holders wish to convert them the company may take powers to convert the remaining stock or to repay at a predetermined price.

Convertible securities are normally debentures but occasionally they are preference shares. Once converted into equities it is not possible to convert back into a fixed return security. The value of a convertible consists of the fixed coupon rate, based on the risk of the investment, and the value of the conversion right. The right of conversion from debt to equity is usually stated as a conversion price or conversion ratio and the conversion premium is the difference between the issue price of stock and conversion value at the date of issue. For example, if a company has issued £500,000 10 per cent convertible loan stock at par with the option to convert at a future date on the basis of £100 nominal convertible loan stock for ninety ordinary shares with a market value of £1, the conversion price and conversion ratio are as follows:

$$\text{Conversion price} = \frac{\pounds 100}{90} = \pounds 1.11$$

$$\text{Conversion ratio} = \frac{90}{100} = 0.90$$

The conversion price shows that £1.11 of loan stock is required to obtain each ordinary share and its reciprocal is the conversion ratio which shows the number of shares that will be obtained from the conversion of each £1 of loan stock.

Convertibles are always issued at a yield which is higher than the yield currently available on ordinary shares, otherwise it would be worthwhile to convert immediately, if possible. It becomes beneficial to convert when the issue yield on equities is at least as good as the yield on the convertible security.

An important feature of convertible issues is that it is assumed that the share price will increase sufficiently to allow the conversion to take place. If this does not occur the company is committed to both interest payments and repayment of the debt on the due date. If the convertible issue was not converted it would jeopardize any further issues of this type of financial instrument.

The valuation of a convertible debenture depends upon its value as a pure debt instrument and the value of the option to convert into equities. For example, if the debt has a twenty year maturity, a 6 per cent coupon rate with a coupon value of £100, the value of a pure debt instrument is as follows:

$$V_0 = \frac{6}{(1.08)^1} + \frac{6}{(1.08)^2} + \cdots \frac{6}{(1.08)^{20}} + \frac{100}{(1.08)^{20}}$$

$$V_0 = 6(9.9181) + 100(0.2145)$$

$$V_0 = \pounds 80.36$$

The discount rate used in this example (8 per cent) is equal to the coupon rate that would be required for a non-convertible debenture. The justification for this is that both convertible and non-convertible loan stock have the same perceived risk. The reduced coupon rate reflects the fact that there is a convertible element to the financial instrument. The above valuation is at $t = 0$, when the debenture was issued. If the debenture is valued at $t = 10$ the calculation would be as follows:

$$V_{10} = \frac{6}{(1.08)^1} + \frac{6}{(1.08)^2} + \cdots \frac{6}{(1.08)^{10}} + \frac{100}{(1.08)^{10}}$$

$$V_{10} = 6(6.7101) + 100(0.4632)$$

$$V_{10} = 40.26 + 46.32$$

$$V_{10} = £86.58$$

Generalizing:

$$V_t = \sum_{t=1}^{n} \frac{I_t}{(1+r)^t} + \frac{RP}{(1+r)^n}$$

V_t = value of a straight debt instrument
t = time running from issue to maturity (n)
I_t = the coupon interest rate at time t
RP = the redemption price or coupon value
r = the market rate of interest, or required rate of return on a pure debt instrument

It is noticeable from the above example that the value of the pure debt instrument increases over time as it approaches its redemption rate.

In addition to the value as a pure debt instrument there is a value to be attached to the option to convert into equities. One of the objectives of issuing convertible loan stock is that it will be converted into equity at a price which exceeds its current price. The value of equities will grow to:

$$P_n = P_0(1 + g)^t$$

P_n = share price at time t_n (conversion value)
P_0 = share price at time t_0
g = expected growth rate of the share price

The conversion ratio is the number of shares to be received on conversion of the loan stock. The valuation of convertible loan stock becomes:

$$V_0 = \sum_{t=1}^{n} \frac{I_t}{(1+r)^t} + \frac{P_0(1+g)^n CR}{(1+r)^n}$$

where

V_0 = current market value of the security, convertible in year 'n', and
excurrent year's interest
I   = annual interest payment
K_d = required rate of return
P_n = projected market value, in year 'n' of the security
CR = the conversion ratio
P_0 = the price of an equity share at t_0
g   = expected growth rate of the share price

For example, a company issued an 8 per cent irredeemable debenture on 31 December 1987. The coupon value (face value) of the debenture is £100 and it is being sold for £95. The loan stock has the option to be converted into 75 equity shares at any time between 1 January 1992 and 31 December 1994. The price of equities on 31 December 1987 was £1.10 and the expected rate of growth is 6 per cent per annum. Calculate the yield on the convertible loan stock assuming redemption at the earliest possible date:

$$95 = \frac{8}{(1+r)^1} + \frac{8}{(1+r)^2} + \frac{8}{(1+r)^3} + \frac{8}{(1+r)^4} + \frac{1.10\,(1+.06)^4 \times 75}{(1+r)^4}$$

This is an internal rate of return calculation that can be solved by trial and error – the yield is 10.5 per cent. In contrast the value of the stock as pure debt which is irredeemable in this case can be calculated as follows:

$$\text{interest yield} = \frac{\text{interest}}{\text{market value}}$$

If the yield of a similar security without convertible rights is 11 per cent then the market value of the pure debt is:

$$\text{market value} = \frac{\text{interest}}{\text{interest yield}} = \frac{8}{0.11} = \underline{£72.73}$$

The conversion rights premium which represents the value attached to the convertible element of the security, is therefore:

$$\frac{£95 - £72.73}{75} = £0.30 \text{ per share}$$

The conversion premium at 31 December 1987:

$$= \frac{£95}{80} - £1.10 = £0.09 \text{ per share}$$

This premium represents the difference between the market value of the security and its conversion value at a particular point in time.

In determining the terms of issue of a convertible, a company will estimate its dividend growth and determine a coupon rate and conversion price so that the conversion timescale matches the firm's needs. An advantage to the company of a convertible loan stock issue is that, provided the enterprise has good prospects, the rate of interest should be lower than that needed for an issue of straight debt. Furthermore, the issue may be useful when a business is developing a new product or a new line of business so that the conversion can be made to coincide with anticipated extra profits.

A further advantage to the company of a convertible issue is that where the current share price of a company is depressed it avoids issuing cheap equity and the enterprise will hope that the conversion period will coincide with higher share prices thus giving the company as much money as possible per share issued. Furthermore, whereas the alternative of a rights issue would need to be issued at a discount to the current market price, a convertible is effectively issued at a premium.

Convertible bonds have become more popular in the mid-1980s with UK companies such as Hanson Trust and Tricentrol making successful issues. However, while these issues have proved successful the stock market is not particularly keen on this hybrid form of security.

A variation on a national convertible bond is a eurocurrency bond. While the conversion period on nationals may extend a number of years after issue it is unusual for a eurocurrency bond issue to have a first conversion date in excess of six months from the issue date and once the exercise date is reached it is normal for the conversion right to remain open for the life of the bond.

While there are advantages of convertible loan stock issues there are also disadvantages. Their unpopularity on the stock market must be taken into consideration in deciding upon issue terms but there are other disadvantages. Since the exercise period may extend for several years the company registrar will be faced with the administrative task of constantly registering small parcels of equities. One way of alleviating the administrative burden is to arrange for conversion to take place during a specific month in each year of the conversion period. Furthermore, the conversion of debt into equity dilutes existing equity, although prior approval by shareholders must have been obtained before a convertible issue since shareholders in the UK have pre-emption rights.

Loan stock with warrants

Loan stock with warrants is a variant of a convertible security and its main feature is that the loan stock remains outstanding until the date of redemption and the warrant becomes a separate negotiable security. The warrant gives the holder the right to obtain a certain number of shares at a fixed future date at an agreed price and the loan stock is maintained until the redemption date, when, if conditions are suitable, it can be replaced by a further issue.

The advantages to a company are similar to those attributable to convertible securities and in fact if the equity warrant is held with the bond the two are very similar. However, an important difference is that with convertible loan stock the treasurer is able to predict, with reasonable accuracy, the period over which the stock will be converted. With the equity warrant the treasurer is less able to predict when the option will be exercised.

The Stock Exchange

The origins of the Stock Exchange can be traced back to the seventeenth century when buyers and sellers used to congregate in coffee houses to undertake share transactions in joint stock companies. The early joint stock companies were primarily involved in overseas trade that involved considerable risks. Merchants found it convenient to raise money from a number of individuals who, in return for accepting part of the risk, received part of the profits. Thus the capital of these companies was divided into shares and a market developed in these securities as individuals wished to change their liquidity positions. These were the origins of the primary market, a source of long-term finance for the company, and the secondary market, a market in second-hand securities.

Functions of the Stock Exchange

The functions of the Stock Exchange have not changed from its early seventeenth century origins. Obviously the markets are now highly sophisticated and the role of the Exchange is to provide a framework within which investors can feel confident to undertake transactions. This framework permits companies to come to the market to raise capital and provides investors with the opportunity to purchase new issues and second-hand securities. The market thereby provides a link between the company wishing to obtain long-term funds and investors who wish to move quickly to maintain their liquidity positions. However, the Stock Exchange is not only the medium for providing capital to companies it also provides money (via the Bank of England) to governments through the issue of securities. The split between the public sector and the companies sector is shown in Table 10.2. There were arguments in the 1970s that the corporate sector was being crowded-out of the new issues market by the public sector. Companies complained that so much government borrowing was being undertaken that interest rates were forced up thereby making it uneconomic for the corporate sector to make debt issues. Indeed one response to this was that some companies repaid their fixed interest rate debt early. Table 10.2 shows that the proportion of total issues attributable to the public sector does vary from year to year although it is noticeable that the percentage has been declining quite rapidly in the 1980s. This is due to a reduction in the rate of increase in government borrowing and an

Table 10.2 New issue proceeds

Year	Total (£m)	Public sector (£m)	Public sector (%)	Companies sector	Companies sector (%)
1974	3,557	3,343	94	214	6
1975	9,043	7,260	80	1,783	20
1976	10,291	9,022	88	1,269	12
1977	16,487	15,283	93	1,204	7
1978	10,855	9,459	87	1,396	13
1979	17,886	16,510	92	1,376	8
1980	19,623	18,003	92	1,620	8
1981	17,408	14,499	83	2,909	17
1982	18,922	15,902	84	3,020	16
1983	24,390	19,879	82	4,511	18
1984	32,427	23,637	73	8,790	27
1985	41,556	27,710	67	13,846	33
1986	49,521	26,271	53	23,250	47

Source: *The Stock Exchange Official Yearbook* 1986–7

upsurge in corporate issues in 1985 and 1986 due to buoyant world stock markets.

The public sector issues consist of British and Irish government securities, corporation and county authorities, public boards and the overseas public sector. Interestingly the overseas public sector has risen from virtually nothing in 1975 to £8,309m in 1985 representing nearly 30 per cent of the public sector issues. The proportion of British government issues to total issues has declined from 88 per cent in 1980 to 62 per cent in 1985.

Composition of the Stock Exchange

The Federation of Stock Exchanges was formed in 1965 and in 1973 the exchanges of the UK and the Republic of Ireland were merged into one exchange. The main trading floor is in London but there are other floors in Birmingham, Dublin and Glasgow. In addition, there are regional centres with administrative offices in Belfast, Bristol, Leeds, Manchester and Newcastle.

There are over 5000 members of the United Exchange and all must comply with the rules and regulations laid down by the Council. The Council consists of elected members (forty-five in 1987), who are normally elected for a period of three years, and five lay members. It is the responsibility of the Council to elect a chairman and deputy chairman who are appointed on an annual basis.

The system of trading

The traditional system of trading which made a clear distinction between the role of the broker and that of the jobber was terminated on 27

October 1986 and replaced by a new dealing system for both securities and government stocks – the 'Big Bang'. The new system permits all member firms of the Exchange to act as brokers and dealers. Thus a member firm can act as both broker (agent) and as dealer (principal). The principal can either sell stock from its own inventory or take a stock on to its own book.

The role of market makers is to make a market by competing for the business of other brokers and dealers rather like the traditional role of the stockjobber. One important difference is that market makers can deal directly with clients whereas pre-Big Bang stockjobbers could not.

A new information source, the Stock Exchange Automated Quotations System (SEAQ), was introduced as part of the changes in the dealing system introduced in autumn 1986. SEAQ is a screen-based computer system which provides information about the market itself and dealings in it. The system provides some protection to investors in that competing market makers are obliged to provide information on their bid and offer prices and the amount of sharedealing they are prepared to accept at these prices. This information thereby becomes available to all subscribers to the system both in the UK and overseas. Once a bargain is struck the market maker is obliged to enter details of the deal, in terms of price and number of shares involved, into the computer system within five minutes.

As part of the SEAQ system securities have been divided into four main categories:

1 *Alpha securities* – these are securities in large companies that are heavily traded and in which a large number of market makers deal. Transactions in these securities are shown immediately on the screen.
2 *Beta securities* – these are securities in companies that are not as heavily traded as alpha stocks and although trades must be recorded within five minutes of execution the details do not appear on screen. The details are reported later in the Stock Exchange Daily Official List.
3 *Gamma securities* – these are securities that are less traded than the previous two categories. Prices appearing on the screen are indicative rather than firm quotations.
4 *Delta securities* – these are securities that are thinly traded and no prices are provided on the screen although market makers interested in the shares display their interest.

The SEAQ classification of UK equities at 31 December 1986 is shown in Table 10.3.

The SEAQ system provides information at three different levels:

1 *The investor screen (SEAQ 1)* – this provides the best buy and sell prices for each security at a given time, the price of the last two

Table 10.3 SEAQ classification of UK equities

Category	Number of equities as at 31 December 1986
Alpha	76
Beta	534
Gamma	1,296
Delta	244
Total	2,150

deals in alpha stocks, and the cumulative volume of turnover during that trading day.

2 *The dealing screen (SEAQ 2)* – this is the one providing details of each market maker's quotes.

3 *The input facility (SEAQ 3)* – this is available only to market makers and enables them to input their trading information.

Information appearing on screens is not lost once it disappears but is stored so that the Surveillance Division can recreate the market at a particular time with the aim of ensuring a fair market.

The 'Big Bang'

'Big Bang' came about at the time it did because in 1983 the Office of Fair Trading was threatening to take action against some of the restrictive practices of the Stock Exchange. However, before the Director General of the Office of Fair Trading could take action in the Restrictive Practices Court, Mr Cecil Parkinson, the then Secretary of State for Trade and Industry, intervened and a deal was arranged with the Stock Exchange whereby commission scales would cease to exist by December 1986. While the action of the Director General precipitated action at the time it did, some believe that it would have occurred anyway because of competitive pressures and the internationalization of markets.

The delay of three years in the complete abolition of fixed commission charges was due to other fundamental changes that the Stock Exchange decided to introduce at the same time. Whereas the US Stock Exchange moved to unfixed commissions in 1975, the move in the UK was accompanied by the change from single capacity roles to dual capacity roles. There lay the advent of the new financial conglomerates that now dominate the City.

In addition to the abolition of fixed charges and the abolition of single capacity roles, 27 October 1986 also saw a major revolution in access to information. As already mentioned the SEAQ service was introduced and delivered, in the main, through the Stock Exchange's own information service called TOPIC. While some teething problems were encountered in this system it can now cope with the demands placed upon it.

These demands include daily trading volumes in excess of 50,000 trades involving 500 million shares with a value in excess of £16 million. While the settlement system, TALISMAN, also had problems initially it now appears capable of handling the increase in turnover in securities that has occurred since 27 October 1986.

The effect of these changes in technology has been that transactions are undertaken through dealing screens rather than on the Stock Exchange floor. Dealing has become simpler and cheaper although unofficial minimum charges still seem to exist. Prices are now often handled net rather than the old price-plus-commission basis. The cheaper commissions have benefited the institutional investors more than any other group because of trading in large volumes. For example, commission charges to the largest institutions have fallen in general from about 0.35 per cent before Big Bang to 0.2 per cent in early 1987. The charge to medium-sized institutions, those managing less than £56 million in funds, has fallen to about 0.25 per cent. However, being able to generalize about commissions raises the question of the variability of the charges. It seems that while commission charges have fallen they have settled to a new level which is being maintained by the new cartels.

In contrast, charges for small deals may have actually increased for both the private investor and the institutions. Dealers no longer offer a 'continuation' service to institutions which permit them to link several small deals into one large transaction in order to keep the transaction costs down.

One concern expressed about the reduction in the jobbers' turn and reduced commission charges was that research output and quality might deteriorate. At the time of writing it is too early to make an assessment although it appears not to have occurred. Perhaps increases in trading volumes and the bull market assisted in maintaining output but this might change in a bear market.

One of the features that reforms in the market has precipitated is a new regulatory framework for investor protection – the 'Mini Bang'.

The Financial Services Act 1986 – 'Mini Bang'

In 1983 Professor Gower was commissioned by the government to prepare a report on investor protection. Part I of the report entitled 'Review of Investor Protection' was published in January 1984 with the objective of offering solutions and generating debate. It was originally envisaged that Part II would be published as a draft bill, implementing the recommendations advocated in Part I of the report. However, due to the publication of the White Paper on investor protection in January 1985, Part II was used as a response to comment on the government's proposals.

The main points of the White Paper were as follows:

1   There should be two practitioner-based regulatory bodies to supervise financial services. A 'securities and investments board' and a

'marketing of investments board' should be formed, which would be responsible to the Secretary of State for Trade and Industry. The framework within which these boards may operate will be laid down by legislation and enforced by the Secretary of State.

2 The definition of investments will be extended to include financial and commodity futures contracts, and certain other products, in addition to those covered by the Prevention of Fraud (Investments) Act 1958.

3 An investment business will include any business which affects transactions in investments with or for others, arranges investments or gives advice about them. It will be an offence to carry on an investment business, as defined, without authorization.

4 The Secretary of State or approved regulatory bodies may grant, vary, make subject to conditions, suspend or revoke such authorization.

Part II of Professor Gower's report welcomed the government's proposals with two major reservations. First, he considered that there should be only one regulatory body and, second, that success would be dependent on support from the financial services secretary in terms of manpower and financial resources.

After considerable debate in Parliament, the Financial Services Act 1986 received Royal Assent on 7 November 1986 with the implementation of the Act being phased over 1987. The first impact of the Act is that any investment business must register with, and obtain approval from, the Securities Investment Board (SIB) or one of its delegated self-regulatory organizations. The SIB is responsible to the Secretary of State for Trade and Industry and each self-regulatory organization (SRO) is responsible directly to the SIB. The main self-regulatory organizations and their roles are shown in Table 10.4.

In 1986 the new structure of investor protection was marketed as a self-regulatory system but by early 1987 it was being described as a self-regulatory body with the full force of the law behind it which will provide it with powers equivalent to that of the Securities and Exchange Commission (SEC) in the US. The reasons for this change in marketing by the chairman of the SIB, Sir Kenneth Berrill, was because several scandals emerged over the winter period 1986/7, principally Guinness and cases involving insider dealing. Further major scandals will only enhance the case for an equivalent of the SEC and in the long run this appears to be inevitable. However, the Guinness affair probably does not reinforce the case either way since it was an anonymous tip off from Caracas to the SEC which started the investigation. Furthermore, it has not been the Stock Exchange that has failed to report prima facie cases of insider dealing but rather the government which has not pursued such cases with any vigour.

Another area of considerable concern, arising from dual capacity, has been conflicts of interest and so-called 'chinese walls'. A chinese wall has been described as an 'arrangement whereby information known to

Table 10.4 The main self-regulatory organizations and their roles

Name	Regulatory role
1 Association of Futures Brokers and Dealers	Firms dealing and broking in futures and options, incidental investment management and business advice
2 The Stock Exchange	Firms dealing and broking in securities and related options and futures, incidental investment management and business advice
3 Life Assurance and Unit Trust Regulatory Organization	Life companies and unit trust managers and trustees
4 International Securities Regulatory Organization	Firms dealing and broking in securities, international money market instruments, forward agreements and related futures and options
5 Financial Intermediaries Managers and Brokers Regulatory Association (FIMBRA)	Will regulate the markets formerly covered by the National Association of Dealers in Securities and Investment Managers and the Life and Unit Trust Intermediaries Regulatory Organization
6 Investment Managers Regulatory Organization	Will regulate investment managers and advisers, including managers and trustees of collective investment schemes and in-house pension fund managers

persons involved in one part of a business is not available (directly or indirectly) to those involved in another part of the business and it is accepted that in each of the parts of the business so divided, decisions will be taken without reference to any interest which any other person in any other such part of the business may have in the matter'.

The problem is that if one group, say in the research department, produces a buy recommendation when, if at all, should it inform the market maker within the same firm? Should clients be provided with the information before, at the same time, or after the information has been provided to the market makers? The SIB recommends, but only recommends, synchronization. Furthermore, the chinese walls must extend to computer systems if they are to be effective. As part of the regulatory process each financial conglomerate has set up its own compliance department to try to ensure that transactions are conducted within the bounds of best market practice – whatever that might be.

The listing structure

The Stock Exchange has a five-tier structure for dealings:

1 *Listing* – highly regulated established companies.
2 *Unlisted securities market* – regulated smaller companies.
3 *Third tier* – smaller untested companies in a market regulated by the exchange.
4 *Rule 535-3* – an unregulated market in unregulated mineral exploration companies.
5 *Rule 535-2* (formerly Rule 163(2)) – occasional deals in unregulated companies.

Before 1977 there was really only one market for securities – the listing tier. However, in December 1977 the Stock Exchange gave publicity to the fact that occasional bargains in unlisted securities could be undertaken under Rule 163(2) (now Rule 535-2) or, where applicable, bargains in mineral exploration could be completed under Rule 163(3) (now Rule 535-3). Considerable interest was generated in undertaking such transactions especially when permission to trade was given more frequently. The most important difference between trading in listed companies and under these rules is that the former is a regulated market in which a formal relationship is entered into with the Stock Exchange, by acceptance of the continuing obligations requirement, whereas the latter involves trading in the securities of companies that are not regulated by the Exchange.

As a result of interest in trading in unlisted shares the Stock Exchange formed the Unlisted Securities Market (USM) in November 1980. Trades under Rule 535-2 are now less common and at 31 December the USM had 368 companies on the market. Although the number of companies coming to the market has exceeded 500 some have been taken over, temporarily suspended, or graduated to a full listing.

The formalities involved in a full listing are more onerous than the USM. Whereas a listed company must comply with the requirements of continuing obligations, USM companies need only comply with the less onerous general undertaking.

In the mid 1980s concern was expressed that many of the companies on the USM were very large and that there might be a case for a third market in shares of smaller untested companies. In May 1986 the Stock Exchange provided details of its proposals for a third market. The new market opened on 26 January 1987 and provides a means by which high-risk investments might obtain funds from the public within the framework of regulation by the Stock Exchange. The procedures for admission to this market are less onerous than either the first two tiers, with most of the responsibilities being dealt with by a company's sponsoring institution, which must be a member of the Stock Exchange. It is the responsibility of the sponsor to assess whether the company is suitable for the third market in terms of its trading record, the nature of its business, the composition of the board of directors and its memorandum and articles of association. In addition, the sponsor must try to ensure a liquid market and that at least two market makers are willing to register that they will deal in those securities. Thus the role of the sponsor is crucial in deciding whether a company is suitable or not for the third market. Responsibility has thereby been transferred from the Stock Exchange to the sponsor. Once a company has entered the third market the requirements for publication of information are less oner-ous. For example, the company must publish annual accounts but it need not produce interim or six-monthly financial results. Furthermore, if a company wishes to make an acquisition or disposal of companies it need not circularize its shareholders although such information should be publicly announced.

Most third market shares will be classified as gamma stocks on SEAQ although some may be included in the delta category – the least liquid of securities.

The two most important tiers of the market are the full listing cate-gory and the USM and these will be considered in further detail and compared. The rules and regulations applying to these two tiers are set out in the Yellow Book (Listing), the Green Book (USM) and Companies Act 1985. The overall objective of the Stock Exchange is to ensure that all shareholders, both existing and potential, are provided with all relevant material information about the company and its affairs.

There are requirements for entering the two main markets and these consist of both those prescribed by the Stock Exchange and those that are considered to be best practice. These requirements are summarized in Table 10.5. While some of the minimum levels are given, for example profit levels and capitalization, in practice they are much higher. In the case of USM companies the Green Book states that in exceptional circumstances a company may be brought to the market where the funds to be used are for a product or project that has been fully re-searched and costed and where income will be generated fairly quickly.

While the requirements for a full listing and entry to the USM differ, the post-admission requirements are very similar. The objective of both the Yellow Book and Green Book is that an informed market in its shares is maintained. However, the costs involved in a USM flotation are cheaper to arrange. For example, the costs of a placement on the USM and for a full listing are shown in Table 10.6.

Advantages of a quotation

One of the major reasons for going to the markets is to raise capital for expansion and/or to realize some of the investment made by manage-ment. Directors can buy and sell shares as they wish, subject to their responsibilities as directors, rather than being locked into their invest-ment or when selling from suffering delays which arise in obtaining a valuation for private negotiation.

Once a quotation is obtained it becomes easier and cheaper to raise

Table 10.5   Requirements for full listing and entry to the USM

	Full listing	USM
Minimum market capitalization	£700,000	£500,000
Minimum proportion of shares in public hands	25%	10%
Minimum level of annual profits	£1m	£0.5m
Minimum profit record in years	5	3
Number of years of unqualified (material) audit reports	5	3
Long-form accountants' report	Required	Normally required by the sponsors.
Short-form accountants' report	Required	Required when new shares issued
Adequacy of working capital	Required from directors and sponsors	Directors' declaration
Extel service	White and yellow cards	Green card
Advertisments in national newspapers		
Introduction	2 small boxes	1 small box
Offer for sale	2 full prospectuses	2 small boxes
Placing	1 full prospectus 1 small box	1 small box

Table 10.6   Costs of a placement

	Full listing (£000s)	USM (£000s)
Professional fees		
Broker	30	20
Banker	40–60	25–40
Solicitors	25–40	20–30
Accountants	30–80	25–60
Expenses		
Advertising	70	10
Printing	15–30	15–20
Fees	1–15	–
Additional costs		
Capital duty	1% of value of new shares	
Placing fee	0.5% of amount placed plus a fee	

Source: Arthur Young

equity or debt from the capital markets. Easier because investors are more aware of the company and they are able to buy and sell their securities on the secondary market, and cheaper because a rights issue can be undertaken.

Since the company will have been vetted by the quotations department of the Stock Exchange, investors may reasonably rely on the information published by the company. Thus, a consequence of a quotation is that a company often enhances its credit-rating. Furthermore, the publicity surrounding the share issue often improves public awareness of the company, its products, and its suppliers and customers.

A further advantage of a quotation is that it facilitates growth by acquisition since its shares can be used as purchase currency. An acquisition may be completed, therefore, without the necessity to increase gearing or use cash resources.

Share participation schemes also become more viable since shareholders are quickly able to realize their investment if they so wish. Naturally the aim of such a scheme is to involve employees more in the corporate organization in the hope that it will improve relations and performance.

Disadvantages of a quotation

One of the main disadvantages of a quotation is the initial cost. This has already been discussed. The second most important disadvantage is that directors become responsible to the shareholders which means increased responsibilities, accountability and public scrutiny. The release of information must be carefully considered to ensure that a fair market exists in the company's securities. Information may not, therefore, be partial or selective. Furthermore, the Stock Exchange's model code for securities transactions ensures that a director notifies other members of the board before dealing, and deals are restricted to certain time periods thereby avoiding periods when price sensitive information may be more readily available.

As part of the increased publicity surrounding a quoted company, a poor trading performance can have a disastrous impact on the share price of the enterprise. Thus, there is considerable pressure on directors to improve profits and dividends.

Since some of the company's shares are in the hands of the public, the company may become more vulnerable to an unwelcome takeover bid. Naturally this depends on the distribution of shares.

In addition to the initial costs of a quotation, other costs may a rise to ensure that control systems and reporting systems will be adequate to meet the increased administrative demands placed upon the company.

The role of advisers

The main professional advisers who will be used in obtaining a quotation will be stockbrokers, a merchant bank, solicitors, accountants and a sponsor.

Stockbrokers
Every company seeking a full listing or a quotation on the USM is required by Stock Exchange regulations to have a firm of stockbrokers to act for it. The stockbroker acts as an intermediary between the company and the Stock Exchange and ensures that all the appropriate regulations are complied with. The stockbroking firm will advise on the appropriate price at which to offer shares, on the marketing aspects of the flotation and will ensure that an adequate secondary market will exist.

The merchant bank
There is no necessity for a merchant bank to be appointed for an initial quotation. The main benefit of an appointment is to obtain sound financial advice which may enable the issue to be more widely accepted. However, this benefit must be weighed against the costs and usually the accountants and stockbrokers can provide all the advice necessary at this stage.

Solicitors
Normally two firms of solicitors are appointed – one acting for the company and the other acting as solicitor to the issue. The one acting for the company will prepare the directors' service contracts, amend the articles of association as appropriate and advise on matters dealing with the sponsor. The second firm of solicitors is appointed to supervise the issue and ensure verification of statements made in the prospectus. The procedure is important to the directors because directors are jointly and severally liable for the contents of the prospectus. Additionally, this firm of solicitors will protect the interests of the sponsor and shareholders.

Accountants
Sponsors to an issue will only endorse a full flotation after a detailed report has been prepared on all the major aspects of the company. Usually a 'long-form' accountants' report is prepared which consists of a very detailed and confidential review of all the key aspects of the business. The purpose of the review is to ensure accuracy of the reported figures, to assess the strengths and weaknesses of the business and the management team. While there is no standard format for such a report the contents will trace the development of the business and contain information on the following:

1   The history and development of the business
2   Historical financial data
3   Products, suppliers and marketing
4   Future plans and developments
5   Management and employee structure
6   Accounting and management information systems
7   Capital structure and level of borrowing
8   Tax

While there is no requirement to have a long-form accountants' report for USM companies there is a requirement to have a short-form accountants' report in the case of an introduction. The report provides a historical financial record of the company and it is included in the prospectus. In practice, however, sponsors usually do insist on having a long-form accountants' report and eventually if the shares are offered to the public a short-form accountants' report will be included in the prospectus. In addition to this, the accountants will need to assess whether the company has adequate working capital, and scrutinize its indebtedness and any profit forecast.

Sponsor
A broker or merchant bank may act as a sponsor to an issue. The role of the sponsor is initially to assess whether the company is suitable for a proposed flotation and whether a full listing or the USM is appropriate. This is often achieved by preparing a preliminary report. If this report is satisfactory it is then usual, in the case of a full listing, for a long-form report to be prepared by one of the large firms of practising accountants. A large firm of accountants is employed to provide added comfort. Provided this report is satisfactory the sponsor coordinates all future planning and preparations to ensure a successful flotation.

Other advisers
Other interested parties will include the company's bankers and valuers and additional advice may be required from a registrar and a public relations firm.

Methods of flotation

Where shares are already widely held it may be possible to bring a company forward for a flotation by an introduction. The Stock Exchange requires that there must be a minimum of 100 shareholders and at least 25 per cent of the shares must already be held by the public if a full listing is envisaged and 10 per cent for a USM quotation. The number of shareholders stated above must exclude directors and connected persons and any shareholder with in excess of 5 per cent of the equity.

An introduction involves releasing existing shares onto the market rather than issuing further shares. It is the cheapest form of flotation for USM companies because no accountants' report is required. However, sponsors will probably require some work to be undertaken by accountants to provide added comfort. Furthermore, all the information necessary for the Extel card must be checked thoroughly.

A placing
In a placing the sponsor places shares among its clients, usually City institutions, thereby effectively excluding the individual investor from the issue. In essence, the company sells the new shares to the issuing house and the latter then places them with clients. There was, before 27

October 1986, a provision which restricted the distribution to clients to 75 per cent of the issue with the residual being allocated to other brokers.

Big Bang heralded a change in the placing limits. The placing for a full listing was raised from £5m to £15m and for a USM quotation from £3m to £5m. Furthermore, the 25 per cent residual allocation can be distributed in two ways. The sponsor can advertise the shares to the general public or distribute them to one or more other brokers. Since the costs become higher if shares are advertised it has become common practice to distribute the 25 per cent to one or two brokers. Thus, it has become more difficult, if not impossible, for the private investor to purchase new issues when there is a placement. Since the thresholds for a placement have been raised, by far the majority of new issues have been by this method because of the lower costs when compared with the offer for sale. Since most new issues go to a premium the gains have largely accrued to institutions – hardly the provision of a fair market!

Offer for sale
An offer for sale is a flotation of shares to the general public. The shares can be offered directly by the company – an offer for subscription – or by the sponsor who purchases the shares either from the company or existing shareholders. An offer for sale by subscription is relatively rare and is usually confined to investment companies. There is no restriction on the size of an offer for sale so that a company can easily fulfil the minimum requirement for equity capital held by the public.

A variation on this method of issuing shares is the offer for sale by tender. Investors are invited to tender for the shares and the price determined is that which ensures that all the issue is sold. In the UK, the price determined applies to all shareholders so that those offering to purchase shares at a higher price are able to purchase them at the striking price. In practice, the price determined is one where demand marginally exceeds supply so that an allocation is undertaken in the hope that shares will go to a premium on issue.

The prospectus

Any offer which invites the public to subscribe for shares must contain a prospectus. The contents of the prospectus are prescribed in Companies Act 1985 and by the rules of the Stock Exchange. Thus, whenever there is an offer for sale, a placement or subscription it is necessary for a prospectus to be prepared which provides the public with a proper understanding of the company, its business and its prospects. For a placement of shares there is no requirement for a full prospectus to be published but instead a 'particulars document' is prepared for circulation to the institutions – a mini prospectus. The level of disclosure of information is similar to the short Extel card and is normally satisfactory provided a certificate of exemption is granted by the Stock Exchange.

Once the sponsors receive a first draft of the accountants' long-form report they will prepare a full prospectus, where necessary, which must receive prior approval from the Stock Exchange. The contents of the prospectus fall under the following headings:

1   Summary of financial information
2   Directors and advisers
3   Directors, management and staff
4   Trading record, forecast and dividends
5   Reasons for, and use of, the issue proceeds
6   Prospects
7   Accountants' short-form report
8   Profit forecast
9   Statutory and general information

The choice of new issue method

The choice of new issue method depends upon a number of factors including the size of the offer, the issue costs, the expected performance of the share after issue, and the desirability of wider share ownership. For small companies, and since 27 October 1986 medium-sized companies, a placement is the favoured way of small issues because of the lower levels of costs. Cost savings are made on advertising and sub-underwriting in particular. Furthermore, a relatively small issue by an offer for sale can lead to excess demand for shares leading to a high initial share price that sometimes cannot be sustained in the long run. For example, offers for sale in May and June 1987 included those shown in Table 10.7.

Table 10.7   Offers for sale in May and June 1987

Name	Value or offer (£m)	Amount attracted (£m)	Times subscribed
Computer People	3.9	78.2	20
Pickwick	8.5	487.5	51
Sock Shop	4.9	257.8	53
Tie Rack	12.5	1,060	85
Barry Wehmiller	21.4	674	31

Source: Financial Times

In the short run the companies mentioned in Table 10.7 did maintain their initial share price although in the long run the price will be determined by the fundamental attributes of the companies.

The choice with an offer for sale is whether to fix a price or whether to allow the market to determine it by tender. A tender method might be used where markets are volatile or where there are unusual features about the company which makes it difficult to determine a price accurately. In determining an issue price the buoyancy of the secondary market will be taken into consideration.

The type of new issues made over the period 1983–5 is shown in Tables 10.8 and 10.9. Over the period 1983 to 1985, 351 companies entered the Stock Exchange by raising new equity capital; 102 companies obtained a full listing and 249 obtained a quotation on the USM. These figures exclude introductions, transfers from the USM and vendor placings. The amount raised over that period totalled £6,155.8m for a full listing and £539.9m on the USM. The full market figure is somewhat distorted by the issue of £3,916m for British Telecom in 1984 which leads to a distortion in the percentage figures. However, an offer for sale was more popular for a full listed quotation than for USM quotations where placements are the norm.

Secondary issues

It has been traditional for existing companies to raise additional equity capital funds by making a rights issue which is an offer to existing shareholders to purchase shares. Provided all shareholders take up their rights the proportionate ownership of the company remains constant. This pre-emption right is specified in the Stock Exchange rule book and also in Companies Act 1985 (589). Section 95 of the Companies Act permits the disapplication of pre-emption rights if power is given to the directors of the company by the articles or by a special resolution

There has been much discussion in 1986 and 1987 about vendor placings since they raise arguments over pre-emption rights and bought deals. For example, in June 1986 controversy surrounded a £686m vendor placing by the Dee Corporation which was used to acquire Fine Fare and Shoppers Paradise supermarket chains. Such a large deal involved selling shares to outside shareholders rather than to existing ones thereby diluting the shareholding of the latter group. Both Prudential Assurance and M & G Investment Management objected to the terms of the Dee Corporation vendor placing and forced amendments to it. This in spite of the issuance of a discussion paper in February 1987 entitled 'Flotations and Pre-emption' which favoured some relaxation of existing rules. Opposition to changes in pre-emption rights has come from the National Association of Pension Funds which sees relaxation as a threat to the enshrined right to prevent a major dilution in their shareholding by placements to third parties.

In contrast to the UK position, there are no pre-emption rights in the US. The US favours bought-deals by which the whole of a company's new share issue goes to a securities house which then offers them to the highest bidder.

Some of these issues have been considered by Wolff (1986):

In the last decade placings, vendor placings and the like have become increasingly important methods for issuing new equity. The private placing is a very flexible and efficient method for issuing new equity. Placings do

Table 10.8 New issue methods – full listing for equity

	1983			1984			1985		
	Amount raised (£m)	Percentage of total	Number of issues	Amount raised (£m)	Percentage of total	Number of issues	Amount raised (£m)	Percentage of total	Number of issues
Placings	–	–	–	19	0.4	7	11.3	1.4	4
Offers for sale	100.2	40.6	9	4,417.5	86.8	19	670.0	81.6	32
Tenders	146.5	59.4	15	635.7	12.5	5	102.8	12.5	6
Subscriptions	–	–	–	15.8	0.3	2	37.0	4.5	3
	246.7	100	24	5,088.0	100	33	821.1	100	45

Source: Bank of England Quarterly Bulletin

Table 10.9 New issue methods – USM quotation for equity

	1983			1984			1985		
	Amount raised (£m)	Percentage of total	Number of issues	Amount raised (£m)	Percentage of total	Number of issues	Amount raised (£m)	Percentage of total	Number of issues
Placings	66.8	41.1	57	112.6	63.8	75	142.5	71	77
Offers for sale	36	22.2	7	58.6	33.2	10	53.0	26.4	10
Tenders	38.6	23.7	7	5.2	3	2	5.3	2.6	2
Subscriptions	21.2	13.0	2	–	–	–	–	–	–
	162.6	100	73	176.4	100	87	200.8	100	89

Source: *Bank of England Quarterly Bulletin*

Table 10.10　Typical expenses on a £100m rights issue

	£	*Percentage of amount raised*
Capital duty	1,000,000	1.00
Stock Exchange listing fee	14,000	0.01
Printing costs	23,000	0.02
Distribution costs	14,000	0.01
Receiving bank's charges	42,000	0.04
Accountants' fees	50,000	0.05
Legal fees	17,500	0.02
Issuing house's fees	2,000,000	2.00
Total	3,160,500	3.15

Note:　These expenses do not include the 15 per cent VAT charged on the fees but this may be recovered by most trading companies and is not usually a cost.
Source:　*Bank of England Quarterly Bulletin*, December 1986

have their drawbacks, however. A discount on a placing involves a transfer of wealth from existing shareholders to new ones. Scenarios in the spirit of the one we referred to as the 'Coalition Hypothesis' (that a relatively small number of institutional investors who hold a small majority of the shares in a certain company conspire to transfer wealth from smaller individual shareholders and others to themselves) could do great harm to smaller shareholders and would reduce the proportion of shares that is held private-ly. Thus, the Government's objective of promoting the growth of holdings by small individual shareholders may well be undermined by a move to abolish pre-emptive rights.

Rights issues have been the most important method of raising new equity in the UK and one of the advantages is that a prospectus does not have to be published and there is no requirement for an accoun-tants' report or publication of the latest annual accounts. However, a statement must be made regarding the adequacy of working capital and level of current borrowings. In addition, the details of the offer, the purpose for which the funds are required, the arrangements for sub-scribing and the technical constraints on residents of specific territories must all be disclosed.

Typical costs of a rights issue are shown in Table 10.10. The two major costs are the capital duty and the issuing houses' fees. The latter includes sub-underwriting and brokers' fees. All the costs are not vari-able so that in the case of a small rights issue the accountants' fees and legal fees will assume a greater significance of the total amount raised.

While rights issues are common for companies with a quotation, alternatives include vendor placings and vendor rights. A vendor plac-ing is an arrangement whereby an acquirer takes over a target company by the issue of shares although the victim's shareholders actually re-quire cash. An agreement is made by the acquirer for the target com-pany to pass on these shares to a merchant bank, which places them primarily with financial institutions. In return for giving up the shares, the target company receives cash. Vendor rights is another method of achieving the same advantages. The acquirer issues shares in consideration for the shares of the target company. Since the target company's shareholders require cash, there is a prior arrangement for a merchant bank to obtain the acquirer's shares from the target company. The shareholders of the target company obtain cash from the merchant bank for giving up the shares and the merchant bank then offers the shares to the shareholders of the acquirer as a rights issue.

The choice between equity and debt

One of the key considerations in choosing between debt and equity will be their relative costs. Since equities confer the greatest risk to investors they will expect a higher return than that obtained by debtholders. Tax plays an important part in deciding between the two sources of funding because dividends are deemed to be appropriations and are not deductible against tax whereas debt interest is allowable. Provided the company is in a tax-paying position the real cost of debt is considerably lower than the nominal cost.

Another factor is that companies will normally like to achieve a balance between debt and equity to retain flexibility. For example, if a company was all-equity financed it could lead to periods of excess funds and surplus cash balances. The company may not wish to distribute the funds as a dividend because of its level of distributable profits. However, if a reasonable level of debt exists with varying maturities it can repay it when surplus cash arises.

The type of business is also important since some sections of the economy have higher levels of gearing than others. A highly geared company may not make an attractive investment because of the risk element.

Security will also be important so that if the company has an asset of considerable value it can use it as security for a loan. The asset must be of reasonably assured value, for example lending on the strength of a potential oil well may well be highly risky for a bank if the well fails to produce oil.

When raising additional debt, covenants in trust deeds must be carefully scrutinized to avoid a breach of regulations accompanying existing loans. Often covenants will be inserted in these deeds to ensure that excessive levels of debt are not permitted or any prior security is not given.

In deciding on the timing of an issue the current share price and current rates of interest must be taken into consideration. For example, it is advantageous to issue debt when rates of interest are relatively low and to issue equities during periods of high share prices.

A further factor is the relative costs of issuing debt and equities. In addition, a view will need to be taken on expected levels of inflation and on future rates of interest.

The impact of institutional shareholdings on equity markets

Institutional shareholders consist of insurance companies, private pension funds, public pension funds, investment trust companies, banks etc. and they hold somewhere between 40 per cent and 50 per cent of listed securities in the UK. Their role is to raise funds from individuals and companies, to invest in the stock market and to employ professional management to maintain their portfolios.

There is considerable evidence that over the period 1965–83 there was a gradual decrease in the number of private investors in equities as a result of institutional growth. There are a number of reasons for this. First, the advantage of diversification has led to growth in unit trusts, as large funds are more able to achieve this objective. Second, institutional investors have a preference for equities despite the reverse yield gap. A reverse yield gap occurs when rates of interest in the capital markets exceed dividend yields. Institutions invest, however, not only for dividends but also for capital gains. Another factor of some importance has been the fact that brokers discourage small investors by minimum commission charges.

A factor of great importance has been the growth in the level of savings particularly of a contractual nature and these savings are ultimately invested in the Stock Exchange.

Extrapolations have been undertaken by a number of researchers to forecast levels of institutional shareholding. For example, Dobbins and Greenwood (1975) have suggested that by 1990 over 70 per cent of the equities will be owned by the institutions. However, there is a danger in all extrapolations since steady growth based on past information does not necessarily mean such a rate will continue.

Other researchers, for example Breakwell (1982), have suggested that the rate of growth in institutional investment has reached its peak and may in fact decline slightly. Evidence put forward includes the fact that since exchange controls were terminated in the UK in 1979 there has been considerable overseas investment by the institutions. Furthermore, with relatively high rates of unemployment there has been a decrease in the inflow of resources to the pension funds and in some cases net withdrawals. Also, with lower levels of salary increases the rate of money inflows received by the institutions has fallen to lower levels as pension contributions are based on gross percentages. Another factor put forward was the Social Security Pensions Act 1975 which permitted companies to contract out and develop their own pension schemes. A substantial inflow of resources to the insurance and pension funds occurred which has now stabilized.

Since 1979, share ownership in Britain has trebled, principally as a result of privatization, according to a Treasury/Stock Exchange survey of share ownership. The survey was carried out by National Opinion Poll Market Research between 22 January and 18 February 1987. A total of 7008 interviews were conducted with adults (defined as individuals aged sixteen and above) in an attempt to be representative of the adult population in Britain. The results of the survey were as follows:

1 Share ownership trebled from 7 per cent of the adult population in 1979 to nearly 20 per cent at the beginning of 1987.
2 6.5 million, or 15 per cent of the adult population, held shares in privatized companies or the Trustee Savings Bank Group.
3 3.5 million, or 8 per cent of the adult population, held shares only in privatized companies or the TSB.
4 1.5 million, or 3.5 per cent of the adult population held shares in the company for which they work.

These changes were attributed to the privatization of businesses previously state-owned and by favourable tax treatment for employee share schemes. The Economic Progress Report (March–April 1987) published by the Treasury makes some international comparisons. It compares the UK level of share ownership (21 per cent) with that of the US, estimated to be between 20 per cent and 27 per cent of the adult population. It adds that the rate of increase in Britain is faster. Comparisons are also made with France (9 per cent) and Japan (5 per cent). In conclusion, the Report states that the 'Treasury/Stock Exchange survey shows a dramatic increase in the proportion of the population owning shares. The government remain committed to encouraging a further spread. The recently introduced personal equity plans scheme, and further privatizations, are expected to help achieve this.'

What can be made of such rhetoric from the Treasury? Perhaps it is best for the student to consider the following issues carefully:

1 Does the transfer of ownership from the state (56 million people) to a selected (based on wealth) group within society represent wider share ownership?
2 If the objective is to make public sector industries more efficient how many thorough investigations into the efficiency of nationalized industries have been undertaken before privatization?
3 Who gains and who loses from privatization? Is it desirable to increase public sector prices to increase returns to make it more attractive to privatize?
4 What experience has the UK government in controlling private monopolies? Can the government ever 'satisfactorily' control a private monopoly?
5 Compared with Sweden, the UK has a lower proportion of its adult population owning shares and yet Sweden has not privatized its public sector businesses. How has this occurred?
6 What will the reaction be of 'new' shareholders in Britain who have invested in privatized companies, to a decrease in their wealth due to the stock market collapse in October/November 1987?
7 Should individuals and companies sell off assets to raise short-term funds?

The public sector is considered in more detail in Chapter 20.

The role of the institutions in influencing corporate management has also been a source of some debate. Some would assign roles to institutions that they themselves are unwilling to accept. For example, the following have been put forward as some of the roles that could be adopted:

1   Protector of the private investor
2   Supervisor of resources to ensure efficiency
3   Auditor of efficiency
4   Investment advisers
5   Enforcer of the firm's social responsibilities
6   Provider of new capital for industry
7   Consultant on corporate planning
8   Protector of the firm's market capitalization

All these roles could be adopted by the institutions but they are generally unwilling to involve themselves so closely because to do so might have a detrimental effect on their investment. Institutions prefer to divest rather than to highlight a company's weaknesses and watch the share price collapse. Furthermore, if they adopt a more active role they could be accused of interference, of insider dealing or even precipitating government action against their involvement. At present, there is little evidence to suggest that the institutions will play a more active role in corporate management.

Summary

There is a considerable range of debt and equity instruments in the UK. Equities offer the greatest risks but also the greatest potential rewards. In a democratic country it seems inequitable that companies are able to issue ordinary shares with reduced or no voting rights. This is not unique to the UK. For example, in Sweden foreign shareholders are not normally allowed to own more than 20 per cent of the shares of a Swedish company and these shares may have voting rights equivalent to 0.001 of the voting rights attached to a share held by a Swedish citizen.

The functions of the Stock Exchange have not changed since the early seventeenth century but the way it undertakes transactions has changed rapidly. Considerable changes occurred in 1986 and 1987. In 1986 a new information source, SEAQ, was introduced which provides information about the market itself and dealings in it. Furthermore, fixed commission charges and single capacity roles were finally abolished in 1986. The abolition of single capacity roles heralded the formation of financial conglomerates. Changes in placement thresholds were introduced at the same time as a result of lobbying from certain parties that suggested that business may be lost to London if they were not raised.

This has had the effect of making offers for sale, other than privatizations, relatively rare. Instead, shares are invariably placed with the institutions to keep costs down. Since most issues in 1986 and 1987 went to premiums the profits have gone to institutions rather than the individual investor. A secondary effect has been that those companies making offers for sale have found their issue being massively oversubscribed. However, the oversubscribing is due to pursuit of premiums rather than the pursuit of the shares since the secondary market in some of these issues has been less than buoyant.

In addition to these major changes, the Financial Services Act 1986 was gradually phased in over 1987. The new regulatory system is described as self-regulation with the full force of the law behind it.

References

Breakwell, B., 'Institutions in Retreat – or is that Heresy', *Accountancy*, April 1982.

Dobbins, R. and Greenwood, D. 'The Future Pattern of UK Share Ownership', *Long Range Planning*, Vol. 8, No. 4, August 1975.

Wolff, C. C. P., 'Pre-emptive Rights Versus Alternative Methods of Raising Equity on the London Stock Exchange?', *The Investment Analyst*, 80, April 1986.

Further reading

Bannock, G., and Doran, A., (1987) *Going Public*, Harper and Row.

Bristow, R. J. and Dobbins, R., 'The Growth and Impact of Institutional Investors' – A Report to the Research Committee of the ICAEW, ICAEW.

Dobbins, R. and McRae, T. W., *Institutional Shareholders and Corporate Management*, M. C. B. Monographs, 1975.

Donaldson, J. A., 'Pre-emption Rights or Obligations?', *The Treasurer*, July/August 1984.

Ingram, D., 'Change in the Stock Exchange and Regulation of the City', *Bank of England Quarterly Bulletin*, December 1987.

Jackson, P. D., 'New Issue Costs and Methods in the UK Equity Market', *Bank of England Quarterly Bulletin*, February 1986.

Midgley, K., 'How Much Control do Shareholders Exercise?', *Lloyds Bank Review*, October 1974.

Midland Bank Review, *Annual Review of UK Capital Markets: 1986*, Spring 1987.

Peasnell, K. V. and Ward, C. W. R., *British Financial Markets and Institutions*, Prentice-Hall, 1985.

Shaw, E. R., *The London Money Market*, Heinemann, 1983.

The Stock Exchange, *The Stock Exchange Survey of Share Ownership*, November 1983.

11 Small firms and their financing

Introduction

In the 1980s there has been increasing interest in the small firms sector in government circles. This interest represents a radical change from the 'big and beautiful' concept that prevailed throughout much of the 1960s. Indeed, the Labour government of 1966 set up the Industrial Reorganization Corporation to encourage rationalization where it was apparent that the market mechanism was moving too slowly to meet the challenges of the day. It did this by promoting mergers in particular sectors of the economy by providing assistance, both financial and otherwise.

Interest by various parties, including the government, in the small firms sector can be attributed to a number of factors. First, concern has been expressed about the high levels of concentration in British industry vis-à-vis our competitors, which may provide monopoly power that could be detrimental to the interests of consumers and detrimental to the interests of our national economy within an international context. National monopolies or oligopolies may not seek efficiency gains that are often sought as a result of competitive pressures. No generalizations can be made since it depends upon the type of industry and freedom of entry into the market. For example, one of the ways of controlling increasing levels of concentration is to adopt a liberal import policy. The UK has adopted such a strategy to protect consumers from increases in prices and reductions in output. Many British industrialists have found that such a policy is difficult to live with, particularly in the short term. Many examples could be cited, for example, in the consumer durables sector. In contrast, a liberal import policy may be inadequate in ensuring that a competitive environment exists. For example, brick manufacturing in a country is effectively protected from imports in the sense that most of the cost of a delivered brick consists of transportation expenses. In the UK, the cost of importing this product would be prohibitively expensive thereby permitting abnormal profits to be earned by oligopoly within a country.

The second reason for interest in small firms is that many large firms have been created as a result of acquisitions and some of the evidence, particularly that based on accounting data, tends to suggest that many mergers do not succeed.

A third factor is that the incidence and duration of strikes tends to increase with the size of firm. This may be because labour in large numbers is more able to unionize and exert influence.

A fourth reason seems to be that some politicians believe that large firms have failed to generate the levels of employment and economic prosperity expected of them. However, no one knows what would have happened if the British economy had had a larger proportion of small firms.

For the above reasons the British government, and also many overseas governments, have tried to encourage small firms and engender an 'enterprise culture'.

Definition of a small firm

So far we have discussed small firms as though it is clear what one is; this is not the case, however. The Bolton Report on small firms, which was published in November 1971, found it impossible to define a small firm in terms of assets, turnover and, indeed, employment. The Committee did identify three main characteristics of small firms. First, a small firm was one which could not influence prices in the market or influence the external environment. Thus, a small firm was one with a small share of a market that could not use its influence to competitive advantage. A second feature was that the proprietors also formed the management team. A third characteristic was that the managers had freedom of action, not enjoyed so readily in large organizations, although this freedom would be curtailed somewhat if the firm borrowed from financial institutions.

While the Bolton Committee identified the economic characteristics of a small firm it tried to be more specific about a definition in the manufacturing sector. The threshold of 200 employees was chosen as an appropriate criterion to conform with the economic characteristics of small firms. The Committee was less specific about the non-manufacturing sector although it did identify some definitions based on number of employees or turnover.

Evidence on concentration

Statistics on concentration within a country need to be treated with caution and this is particularly true when comparing UK concentration

Table 11.1   Distribution of employment by establishment size – 1981

	Establishment size (number employed)			
	Very small (1–19)	Small (20–99)	Medium (100–499)	Large (500+)
Austria[1]	33.6	27.9	23.1	15.4
Belgium[2]	22.2	22.6	26.0	29.2
France[2]	32.1	28.0	23.4	16.5
Italy[3]	43.4	30.4	14.2	12.0
Japan	49.4	27.7	14.6	8.3
Great Britain[4]	26.1	22.6	26.1	25.2
United States	26.1	28.4	24.0	21.5

1   Wage and salary earners
2   1983
3   The first two bands are 1–9, 10–99
4   The first two bands are 1–24, 25–99
Source: OECD Employment Outlook, September 1985

levels with other countries. Based on the work of Prais (1981) it appears that, in terms of employment in large enterprises compared with the total population, the UK is more highly concentrated than other EEC countries and the US. The figures are somewhat dated, being based on data for 1972, and are subject to considerable comparability problems. A likely corollary of a high concentration in large enterprises is that the small-firm sector will be correspondingly small. Of course, it is possible for a country to have a lot of small firms employing a reasonable proportion of the population, few medium-sized firms and a number of very large enterprises.

The Bolton Committee (1971) reported that the post-war decline in employment in the small-firm sector had been more dramatic in the UK than many other countries. An OECD study (1985) on the distribution of employment by establishment size in 1981 is the most recent international comparison (Table 11.1). The OECD survey suggests that the small firms sector is important for each of the countries covered, but particularly important to Japan and Italy. Great Britain and the US had the second lowest proportion in the small-firm sector. Considering firms with an excess of 100 employees, Japan had the lowest proportion (22.9 per cent) whereas Belgium (55.2 per cent) and Great Britain (51.3 per cent) had the highest.

Perhaps the higher proportion of smaller firms in Japan contributes to flexibility in reaction to changes in economic events. For example, as a result of an agreement between the Group of Five in September 1985, there was increasing intervention in the foreign exchange markets to force down the US dollar and force up the value of the yen. In response to the increase in value of the yen some Japanese companies sought to relocate their activities in countries where a vital factor of production is cheap relative to is productivity. For example, Aiwa, the Japanese consumer electronics group, moved most of its productive capacity to Singapore.

Studies on US data, for example Doyle and Gallagher (1986), suggest that small firms have been very important in employment growth in the 1970s and 1980s. Similar conclusions have been made using UK data, see for example Gallagher and Stewart (1984), although the effect has not been as pronounced as in the US.

Another source of information on companies is Companies House. The number of companies on the register at the end of 1967 was 569,820 and this had grown to 744,441 at the end of 1978 and 1,004,106 at the end of 1985. While the number of companies on the register has increased considerably the number of companies struck off the register rose from 17,751 in 1967 to 61,606 in 1985.

The need for finance

Businessmen in small firms must decide on how much finance is required, the nature of that finance, and the risk element involved. How much finance is required depends upon the nature of the business, the rate at which the proprietor wants to grow and the amount the owner reinvests.

In deciding upon the nature of finance proprietors must consider their own aspirations, how much control they are willing to sacrifice and the rate of interest the business is willing to pay.

The risk element in providing finance is an important consideration for a financier. Any financial institution will consider, amongst other things, the proposals prepared by management, the past performance record of the firm, and the likely future performance of the business bearing in mind the individuals who will be responsible for future managerial control. One of the problems is that many small firms have little or no past record to demonstrate good performance to a financier.

Principal sources of finance

The most important source of finance for a small business is the proprietor's own resources. In practice many businesses are started by people investing personal cash, perhaps by realizing investments, and by extending personal credit. Personal credit can be extended by buying goods using credit cards, by obtaining personal loans from banks, or by the deferment of unpaid personal or household bills. If the would-be entrepreneur's spouse has a steady outside job, this is also a useful approach to starting a business as it provides the security of a steady income in the early difficult days.

Proprietors sometimes pledge their own house as security for a loan or take out a second mortgage. Other assets, such as a portfolio of stocks, or life assurance policy, can be used as security for a loan. If a business is already in existence a proprietor will often retain a higher proportion of earnings to finance growth.

The second most important source of finance for small firms comes in the form of bank loans. The Bolton Report found that the reliance on bank overdrafts by small businesses was staggering. Indeed, small firms seemed reluctant to look further than the commercial banks to finance growth. The problem from the banks' perspective is that small firms are often high risk. In fact, about 50 per cent of new businesses go into liquidation within five years of formation. The banks' reaction to high risk is to avoid it, or when embarked upon there will be demands for high returns to reflect above average risk and/or security for the loan. Security may take the form of a charge on the assets of a business or a charge on the personal property of the proprietors. The charge may take the form of a fixed charge on a specific asset or a floating charge on the assets. The banks' approach to lending is dealt with in more depth in Chapter 12.

An alternative source of finance is trade credit. The difficulty for small businesses is that in times of economic recession large customers often delay payment and banks refuse to extend facilities when there is a credit squeeze.

Other sources of finance such as acceptance credits, factoring, invoice discounting, hire purchasing, leasing, mortgages, sales and leaseback are often relatively difficult for a small businessman to arrange and where possible the costs can often prove to be prohibitive.

Are the capital markets deficient in supplying funds to small businesses?

One of the major problems for small businesses is that credit restrictions and ceilings imposed on commercial banks tend to affect small firms more than large firms. This is because small firms rely more heavily on banks when raising external finance and because when credit restrictions are imposed, official restrictions are often interpreted to favour exporters – small firms tend not to be major exporters. A further aspect is that credit restrictions often impose higher standards of creditworthiness for funding, a requirement that small firms have more difficulty in proving. In practice, restricted funds are often allocated according to bargaining power with the inevitability that large firms are favoured to the detriment of small firms.

The Macmillan Committee on Finance and Industry reported in 1931 that there was a gap (the Macmillan gap) in the provision of long-term funds to small and medium-sized companies because they were too small to go to the capital markets. The Radcliffe Committee in 1957 reported that the gap had largely been filled by the Industrial and Commercial Finance Corporation (ICFC), a company owned by the commercial banks and Bank of England. The Radcliffe Committee reported that the commercial banks should offer more term loans, the upper limit on ICFC loans should be raised in the light of inflation, and a new institution should be formed to facilitate the commercial exploitation of technical innovation.

The Wilson Committee in 1980 stated that the banks could be more supportive towards small businesses and recommended the establishment of a Small Firm Investment Company and the formation of a loan guarantee scheme.

Another area that has consistently been identified is the inability of a small firm to raise start-up and venture capital from the capital markets especially the Stock Exchange. Since the costs involved in raising funds on the Stock Exchange are high it is not economical to raise small amounts. A variety of schemes have been advanced including the development of markets specifically designed for smaller businesses and the development of over-the-counter markets.

In the next section recent developments in the financing of small firms will be considered but at this stage it is appropriate to summarize some of the problems that a small business may face:

1 No established reputation.
2 No past personal understanding with a bank manager.
3 Loans often require security and interest rates charged for small businesses are higher than for large firms to reflect the additional risk.
4 Because of a lack of administrative and financial controls it may be difficult to convince a bank manager that the business is viable and that profits generated will be adequate to meet interest and cash payments.
5 In times of recession small firms often do not have the reserves to tide them over e.g. the liquidity crisis of 1974.
6 Institutions may be reluctant to lend money because of the high cost of evaluating proposals for small amounts and the high cost of monitoring.
7 Banks do not like to take high risks.

Recent developments in the financing of small firms

In response to perceived weaknesses in the provision of finance to small businesses a number of initiatives have been undertaken in the 1980s and some changes in attitude have occurred. For example, in 1981 the government introduced a loan guarantee scheme in an attempt to alleviate the 'equity gap'. The scheme was designed to assist small businesses to raise loan capital from thirty financial institutions taking part in the scheme. The government guarantees a proportion of a new loan (originally 80 per cent reduced in 1984 to 75 per cent and reduced to 70 per cent in 1986), not existing loans, up to £75,000 for loans repayable over a period of between two and seven years. A premium is charged on a quarterly basis (originally 3 per cent but raised to 5 per cent in 1984 but reduced to 2.5 per cent in 1986) as compensation for the guarantee cover. The scheme extends to manufacturing, retailing and service sectors although some business activities e.g. agriculture, banking and education, are not eligible. The premium charges have meant that the scheme has had only modest success and failure rates have been high.

In contrast to the loan guarantee scheme, the business expansion scheme has had a more important influence and is likely to continue to do so. The scheme was introduced in 1983 and provided tax relief for equity investment in unquoted independent companies. Investments in eligible companies up to £40,000 per annum may be made provided that the shares are held for a period of at least five years. Tax relief can also be provided on investments in approved funds even where the shareholder is the owner. The scheme has not been without its critics and many property-based transactions were undertaken initially which were eventually outlawed by the Finance Act 1986. The Finance Bill 1987 proposed changes in the business expansion scheme (BES) to enable investors in BES companies to be able to claim for one-half of the relief in respect of investments made before 6 October in a tax year to be set against income of the previous tax year. The maximum carry-back will be £5,000 and is available on investments made after 5 April 1987.

Another area for criticism of the scheme is that the rules are complex for small investments and that this has had a deterrent effect on private investors.

Despite these initiatives, the equity gap still does exist for loans up to £150,000 and particularly for funding less than £50,000. Reluctance to invest at this end of the market occurs because of high assessment and monitoring costs and the reluctance of businessmen to permit equity participation. However, attitudes towards equity participation seem to have changed in the 1980s and there is now less resistance to giving up equity.

Another recent development has been the provision of additional equity markets. Under the Financial Services Act 1986 all share transactions on an open market should be carried out on a Recognized Investment Exchange. The Stock Exchange Recognized Investment Exchange consists of the main market, the Unlisted Securities Market (USM), and the third tier market. The first two markets are covered in Chapter 10 so it is only necessary here to consider the third market.

At its inception in 1980 the USM was aimed at smaller businesses but since Big Bang a small business is often referred to as one with a market capitalization less than £100 million. Many sponsors stipulate a minimum market capitalization figure of £10 million. This changing role of the USM has left a vacuum for small companies. Furthermore, there has also been concern about the lack of demand and level of trading of some USM stocks – illiquidity in the market. In addition, the over-the-counter markets have expanded recently, especially since the introduction of the Business Expansion Scheme. These markets have challenged the growth in the USM.

These factors have led to the formation of the third market, although in January 1987 problems of illiquidity were preventing rapid growth in the number of stocks quoted. By March 1987 there were ten companies quoted on this market and trading is thin.

There is no minimum size criterion for third tier companies. Companies will normally be incorporated in the UK although permission may be given by the Committee on Quotations for foreign companies to enter the market. There is a restriction on the eligibility of companies where more than 10 per cent of a company's turnover, profits, or capital employed are involved in investment, property or other dealing activities. Such companies are disqualified from the market – an effective prohibition on investment companies.

Summary

There has been a substantial increase in interest in small firms in the 1980s by various parties including government. A number of reasons may explain this change, including the alleged inability of large firms to secure adequate efficiency gains, and their inability to generate employment and economic prosperity, despite their large size.

In comparing levels of concentration on an international basis it appears that, in terms of employment, the UK has higher levels than many of its international competitors. It would be rash to draw policy implications from such data alone since, for example, the higher proportion of small firms in Japan may contribute to its flexibility in reaction to changes in economic events but it may also impede its ability to compete internationally in certain sectors, for example in chemicals.

While a number of schemes such as the loan guarantee scheme and the business expansion scheme have been introduced by the government there still remains a problem for small businesses to raise start-up capital. This is unlikely to change, however, because unproven business ventures are notoriously high risk.

References

Bolton Committee Report, HMSO, 1971.

Doyle, J. R. and Gallagher, C., *The Size-distribution, Potential for Growth, and Contribution to Job-generation of Firms in the UK, 1982–84*, Research Report No. 7, Department of Industrial Management, University of Newcastle, July 1986.

Gallagher, C. and Stewart, H., 'Major Share of Job Generation by Small Firms', *British Business*, 13 July 1984.

Prais, S. J., *The Evolution of Giant Firms in Britain*, Cambridge University Press, 1981.

Further reading

Banking Information Service, *The Banks and Small Firms*, 1983.

Bannock, G., *The Economics of Small Firms*, Basil Blackwell, 1981.

Ganguly, P. (edited by G. Bannock), *UK Small Business Statistics and International Comparisons.*, Harper and Row, 1985.

Midland Bank Review (1987) 'Small firms', Spring 1987.

Peasnell, K. V. and Ward, C. W. R., *British Financial Markets and Institutions*, Prentice-Hall, 1985.

Radcliffe Committee Interim Report, *The Financing of Small Firms*, HMSO, 1979.

Robson Rhodes, *A Study of Business Financed under the Small Business Loan Guarantee Scheme*, Department of Trade and Industry, 1984.

Shaw, E. R., *The London Money Market*, Heinemann, 1983.

Wilson Committee Interim Report, *The Financing of Small Firms*, HMSO, 1979.

12 Funding institutions

Corporate sector finances

Since 1981 company profitability has been improving at a steadily increasing rate. For example, in 1981 gross trading profits were 2.9 per cent whereas by 1986 they had risen to nearly 8 per cent. Figure 12.1 shows the change in levels of profitability since 1964 and although the high rates of return of the 1960s have not, and will not, be reached again the current level of corporate profitability is the best since 1973. This recovery has been achieved by higher levels of productivity which have been accomplished by a large reduction in numbers employed. Productivity trends are shown in Table 12.1.

The improvement in profitability and low level of investment has produced large financial surpluses in the corporate sector. Some of this has been used to acquire other companies – direct investment in companies rather than new investment in physical assets.

Despite high levels of corporate liquidity, external funding has continued to provide about 30 per cent of total sources of funds. Table 12.2 shows the proportion of each source of external finance.

It is noticeable that bank borrowing has declined in importance since 1984 at the expense of ordinary share issues and loan stock. This is accounted for by the fact that higher levels of profitability together with optimism in world trade has led to unprecedented increases in share prices in many parts of the world. Consequently it has become more attractive to issue securities rather than borrow from the banks.

Pension funds

Pension or superannuation funds grew very rapidly in the 1970s and early 1980s thereby conferring upon them considerable power, particu-

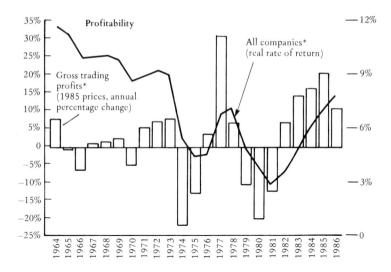

*Industrial and commercial companies
(excluding North Sea operations)

Figure 12.1   Profitability of industrial and commercial companies

Table 12.1   Productivity trends (output per head of the employed labour force)

| Period averages | Annual percentage change | | |
	Manufacturing	Non-manufacturing[1]	Whole economy[2]
1964–73	3.75	3	2.75
1973–79	0.75	0.5	0.5
1979–86	3.5	1.25	1.75
1985*	2.25	1.25	1.25
1986*	6	2.75	2.75

*   End-year-to end-year comparison
1   Excludes public services and North Sea sector
2   Excludes North Sea sector
Source: Barclays Bank Review

larly in UK equity markets. Not surprisingly the use of that power and taxation advantages conferred upon pension funds have become political issues. Indeed, one of the major factors for their growth was the 'approved status' classification, enacted in the Finance Acts of 1970 and 1971, which permitted the contributions of both employer and employee to be deducted against tax. By the end of 1985 total investments

Table 12.2   Industrial and commercial companies' external finance

| Period averages | Constant 1985 prices, £billion (proportion of total external finance in parentheses) | | |
	Bank borrowing	Ordinary share issues	Loan stock*
1964–73	6.0 (62)	0.8 (8)	2.9 (30)
1973–79	6.4 (70)	1.5 (16)	1.2 (13)
1979–86	6.4 (62)	2.3 (22)	1.7 (16)
1984	7.4 (77)	1.2 (13)	1.0 (10)
1985	7.3 (57)	3.4 (26)	2.2 (17)
1986	4.9 (37)	5.0 (38)	3.3 (25)

* Includes debentures and preference shares, capital issues overseas, other loan and mortgages
Source: Barclays Bank Review

controlled by the pension funds exceeded £157 billion compared with some £40 billion in 1981.

A pension scheme may be funded or unfunded. A funded scheme is one in which funds are channelled to the scheme for investment in order to fulfil obligations. These obligations consist primarily of meeting pension payments to its members in accordance with the rules of the scheme. The pension fund invests its resources either directly or through insurance companies. The administration and control of assets is placed in the hands of the trustees of the scheme whose responsibilities are determined by the trust deed and by trust law, in particular the Trustee Act 1925. The office of trustee is a fiduciary one and where it is necessary to make discretionary decisions it is essential that the interests of members are safeguarded by acting prudently.

In contrast to the funded scheme, an unfunded scheme is one in which a separate fund is not established and benefits are paid on a cash basis as they arise. A classic example of an unfunded scheme is the civil servant pension obligation. However, in the nationalized industries separate funds have been established and some of the major funds include the Post Office Staff, National Coal Board, British Rail, Electricity Council and British Steel.

The taxation advantages of an occupational pension scheme are so significant that it is inconceivable for a scheme to be developed without obtaining approval from the Inland Revenue Superannuation Funds Office. If the scheme fulfils the statutory requirements of the Income and Corporation Taxes Act 1970, as subsequently amended, it is granted exempt approved status, which enables it to obtain the following tax advantages:

1   The employer's contributions are allowable against corporation tax.
2   The employer's contribution does not constitute a taxable benefit in the hands of the employee.

Table 12.3   Pension funds inflows compared to wages and salaries

Year	Net acquisition of assets (£m)	Wages and salaries	Asset (%)
1966	533	20,389	2.61
1970	725	26,994	2.72
1975	2511	59,292	4.24
1980	5514	115,103	4.79
1982	7404	136,792	5.41
1983	7912	146,619	5.40
1984	7973	156,245	5.10
1985	9051	169,865	5.33
1986	9185	183,954	4.99

Source: Financial statistics

Table 12.4   Pension funds, net acquisition of assets

| | Local authorities | | Other public sector | | Private sector | | Total |
	£m	%	£m	%	£m	%	£m
1965	75	15	140	29	274	56	489
1975	335	13	1163	47	993	40	2491
1980	963	18	1789	34	2509	48	5261
1985	1333	15	2267	25	5451	60	9051
1986	1136	12	2205	24	5844	64	9185

Source: Financial statistics

3   The employee's contribution is deductible as an allowable expense.
4   The fund is exempt from income tax on investment income, exempt from capital gains tax on the disposal of investments, and any tax deducted at source, such as advance corporation tax, may be reclaimed.

The increasing significance of pensions funds in the UK is shown in Table 12.3 which demonstrates that the net assets acquired during 1986 was in excess of £9 billion. The proportion of wages and salaries invested in this form of contractual savings has risen from 2.61 per cent in 1966 to 5.41 per cent in 1982 with a slight fall in 1986 to 4.99 per cent (Table 12.3). Table 12.4 shows that there was rapid growth in occupational pensions in the public sector between 1965 and 1975. Since 1975 the growth rate in the public sector has been less and private sector schemes have grown rapidly so that by the end of 1986 the private sector schemes exceeded public sector and local authority schemes by a factor of 1.75. As already mentioned the biggest individual schemes are still predominantly in the public sector.

Since the trustees of pension schemes must act prudently it is important that they hold a well-diversified portfolio which includes both risky and relatively riskless assets. Consequently, pension funds hold a range of assets including British government securities, which are relatively riskless, company securities in the UK and overseas, and short-term assets and property. A number of features are apparent from Table 12.5 which shows the distribution of net acquisitions of assets between 1980 and 1986. While investment in government securities was reasonably high between 1980 and 1985 the figure fell sharply in 1986. This was the result of the realization of index-linked investments made for periods up to fifteen years as a hedge against inflation. Second, there was a rapid growth in diversification on an international basis rather than merely in the UK. This prompted the Labour party to bring forward proposals which would limit the taxation concessions to UK investments. Another feature of 1986 was the very high level of assets being held as cash and balances with banks.

Until 1985 pension schemes were controlled only by general trust law – this despite their significance to the UK economy. However, the Social Security Act 1985 introduced a new regulatory framework which came into effect from 1 November 1986. The Act made it compulsory for the following information to be disclosed:

1   All members must receive details on who is eligible to join and whether membership is compulsory.
2   Members must be informed of the contributions they have to pay and how they are to be calculated.
3   Members should be informed of the benefits of the scheme including how they are calculated and the conditions attached to payment.
4   Members must be informed about discretionary payments.
5   Members should be informed about which benefits are funded and which are not, whether any benefits are guaranteed by insurance policies or statute, and to what extent an employer has contracted to pay benefits or meet any underfunding.
6   Members should be aware of provisions to increase pension payments, about their rights when leaving the scheme early and about scheme changes.
7   The right of members to a cash equivalent of accrued benefits.
8   Increases in deferred pensions.
9   An annual report including audited accounts, the latest actuarial statement, an investment report and a trustees' review.
10 The actuarial valuation which must be conducted at least every three and a half years.

Before these regulations were introduced the Accounting Standards Committee issued a Statement of Recommended Practice on pension

Table 12.5   Distribution of net acquisition of assets by pension funds

Year	British government securities (£m)	Company securities (£m)	Overseas securities (£m)	Short-term assets (£m)	Property (£m)	Other investments (£m)	Total (£m)
1980	2083	2180	1459	−303	907	291	6617
1982	1372	2196	2221	360	802	453	7404
1983	2704	1680	1320	1392	569	247	7912
1984	2214	2853	468	1744	678	16	7973
1985	2749	3743	2399	−160	489	169	9051
1986	816	3359	2393	2302	306	−9	9185

Source: Financial statistics

Table 12.6   Net investment by UK insurance companies

	1981 (£m)	1982 (£m)	1983 (£m)	1984 (£m)	1985 (£m)
British government and government guaranteed securities	2,910	1,907	2,380	2,432	1,893
UK local authority securities	(18)	(12)	(67)	(19)	(29)
Company securities (ordinary and preference shares, debentures and unit trusts)	2,190	2,934	2,815	2,894	5,443
Overseas government securities	142	409	579	327	86
Mortgages and loans	247	66	373	383	286
Land, property and ground rent	1,133	1,160	960	873	990
Other invested assets	26	0	0	33	0
Total invested assets	6,629	6,465	7,040	6,923	8,669
Cash and short-term assets, agents' balances, etc.	968	663	861	n/a	n/a
Total	7,597	7,128	7,901	n/a	n/a

n/a = not available
Source: Association of British Insurers

scheme accounts which has, in effect, been given legal recognition by the new Act.

Insurance companies

The role of insurance companies is to pool resources in order to provide for unexpected, yet quantifiable contingencies and to provide for death benefits. The pooled resources are invested to obtain a diversified portfolio of assets similar to that of the pension funds. Indeed, some insurance companies act for pension funds in investing long term to meet its long-term obligations.

A breakdown covering transactions in financial assets by all UK insurance companies and UK branches of overseas companies is provided in Table 12.6. The figures do not include those of overseas subsidiaries of UK companies.

Figures in Table 12.6 in parenthesis denote a net disinvestment and all figures cover both life and general insurance funds. It is noticeable that over the period a higher proportion of total funds has been invested in company securities – the proportion was approximately 33 per cent of total invested assets in 1981 whereas it was 63 per cent by 1985. This

Table 12.7   Total invested assets* of UK insurance companies 1976–85

Year	Total invested assets (£m)	% Growth per annum
1976	2634	–
1977	3487	32
1978	4291	23
1979	5068	18
1980	5639	11
1981	6629	18
1982	6465	(2)
1983	7040	9
1984	6923	(2)
1985	8669	25

* including cash and short-term assets, agents' balances etc.
Source: Association of British Insurers

Table 12.8   Total invested assets 1981–5

Year	Life business (£m)	General business (£m)	Total (£m)
1981	62,499	15,843	78,342
1982	82,047	20,083	102,130
1983	99,302	23,352	122,654
1984	117,977	26,653	144,630
1985	142,596	28,805	171,401

Source: Association of British Insurers

was primarily due to buoyant world stock markets and a policy of international diversification. Indeed in 1983 investment in overseas securities exceeded that in UK company securities. In addition to investing in company securities and British government securities, insurance companies also offer mortgages on property and are interested in sales and leaseback operations, particularly where there are good insurance prospects.

Table 12.7 shows the annual invested assets over the period 1976 to 1985 and the annual growth rate. By 1985 total investments, excluding cash and other short-term assets, stood at £171,401m compared to £78,342m in 1981.

The majority of the total invested assets are in life business and this is shown in Table 12.8.

The two main categories of insurance are the life business, consisting of death and pension benefits, and the general business. Sometimes the former is referred to as long-term business and the latter as short-term business. The net income from investments in life business is accumulated in a life fund which is established to meet the obligations of policyholders. Each life company has an actuary whose responsibility it is to value the liability to policyholders and to decide whether there is a deficit or surplus. If a surplus exists it is apportioned between those holding with-profits policies and the company's shareholders.

The general or non-life business consists of insuring for events such as accidents or fire. Profits from this business are available for distribution to shareholders and losses are the responsibility of its shareholders. Some insurance companies operate as composites which allows them to undertake both life and general business. However, since 1982 no new composites have been approved in compliance with EEC directives. The reason for this is that life funds should be kept quite separate and not used to cross-subsidize other insurance business.

The London insurance market is the largest in the world and all companies and individuals wishing to operate an insurance business may do so only after approval from the Department of Trade and Industry, although there are notable exceptions, for example, friendly societies, trade unions, employers' associations, and members of Lloyds.

The tax position with respect to insurance premiums changed in 1984 so that from 14 March 1984 policies do not qualify for tax relief. In contrast, there have been no major changes in the taxation advantages accruing to pension contributions so that pension funds have become a major source of work for insurance companies in arranging portfolios.

Considerable control over insurance funds now exists in the UK and it is exercised by the Insurance Companies Division of the Department of Trade and Industry. This increase in control resulted from the fact that there were three major insurance scandals in the UK in the 1960s and 1970s, and also as a result of harmonization of European Community Law. The Department of Trade and Industry not only authorizes companies who can carry out insurance business but also regulates the conditions in which they can operate. As part of the regulation process all insurance companies must submit substantial annual returns to the Department within six months of the company's financial year end. As part of the return a solvency calculation must be undertaken to comply with the Insurance Companies Act 1982 and subsequent statutory regulations. The solvency margin calculation is based on the difference between assets and liabilities and the type of company and its classes of insurance cover. However, for all companies there is a minimum margin based on a fixed sum for different types of company and it is referred to as the 'minimum guarantee fund'.

When reporting to shareholders insurance companies are required to prepare financial statements in accordance with the Companies Act 1985 and to prepare annual returns in accordance with the Insurance Companies Act 1982 and to file that return with the Department of Trade. The financial statements are distributed to shareholders and policyholders and the annual return may be obtained by them on request.

Curiously, despite some major insurance scandals in the 1960s and 1970s, companies legislation still permits exemption under the Companies Act. For example, insurance companies do not have to prepare their financial statements in accordance with standard formats and they do not have to disclose movements on reserve.

The Department of Trade does not exercise the same level of control over Lloyds underwriters compared with other insurance companies. This is because Lloyds is a marketplace for general non-life business and for insurance underwriters and liability is unlimited for its members. Wealthy individuals group together to form syndicates rather than companies and as such Lloyds has been left to largely regulate itself. A single return is made on an annual basis to the Department which covers Lloyds as a whole as if it were one entity.

The commercial banks

In 1959 the Radcliffe Report recommended that the commercial banks should offer term loans as an alternative to overdrafts. Such loans represent about 50 per cent (1987) of the banks' non-personal lending. Term loans are contractual by nature, usually for periods of between five and seven years. The contract covers the purpose of the loan, the period of repayment and associated conditions such as fees. The loans are often at variable rates of interest based either on a margin over minimum lending rates or a margin over the offered rate on the London inter-bank market (LIBOR).

The banks will try to ensure that the customer can service the debt and eventually repay the capital. Naturally this involves an assessment of the borrower's creditworthiness.

The banks will be interested in the following:

1   Past performance of the business.
2   An assessment of the current financial position and the likely changes in that position in the future particularly in light of the increased gearing.
3   A review of audited accounts.
4   Further information will be required when there has been significant changes in performance.
5   Detailed budgets and cash flow forecasts.
6   An assessment of the character, and integrity, of the management team.
7   An assessment of the experience of the management team.
8   An assessment of the abilities of the management team.

The above represents some of the items that a bank will be interested in discussing with the borrower. Research undertaken by Berry, Citron

Table 12.9 Use of sources of information available without recourse to the borrower

	Always (%)	Often (%)	Occasionally or never (%)
Audited accounts	83	16	1
Bankers' internal records from previous experience of loans to the company	84	12	4
Interim reports	59	23	18
Memorandum and articles of association	57	13	30
Register of charges	41	17	42
Information published in newspapers, etc. relating to the company or its industry	19	41	40
Comparisons with other companies in like industries	7	30	63
Information published by the banks' own intelligence departments	8	23	69
Reports on company from outside agencies	8	16	76
Published government statistics	1	6	93

Source: CACA's Research Report 7, *The Information Needs of Bankers Dealing with Large and Small Companies*

and Jarvis (1987) for the Chartered Association of Certified Accountants attempted to assess what financial information was important in making lending decisions and the relative importance of accounting information compared with other information. Their results are based on a questionnaire and interview survey of 254 bankers including sixty-two foreign banks and all the five major clearing banks operating in the UK. The survey highlights the importance attached to accounting information and in particular audited information. Table 12.9 shows the use made of available information without recourse to the borrower. Surprisingly, information produced from outside sources such as the banks' own intelligence department or published government statistics are not often consulted. While this might be understandable for small companies it is less so for medium-sized companies.

Considerable attention is attached to the profit and loss account, the balance sheet and the notes to the accounts (Table 12.10). Less attention is paid to the statement of accounting policies which should be scrutinized thoroughly along with the financial statements – accounting policies and changes thereto are fundamental to a thorough understanding of the financial statements. The auditors' report, like the directors' report and chairman's report, is treated as an exception report – scrutinized for problems.

In using sources of information not available to the public the researchers found personal interviews to be most important. The researchers described this feature as 'striking'. Probably it represents the roots of branch banking in the UK. In 1977 one of the commercial banks

Table 12.10   Use of individual sections of audited accounts

	Read thoroughly (%)	Read briefly for interest (%)	Not read at all (%)
Profit and loss account	96	4	–
Notes to the accounts	95	5	–
Balance sheet	96	3	1
Auditors' report	91	9	–
Sources and applications of funds statement	79	21	–
Statement of accounting policies	67	32	1
Directors' report	69	30	1
Chairman's report	64	36	–
5–10 years summary of key figures	37	61	2
Statement of value added	24	61	15

Source: CACA's Research Report 7, *The Information Needs of Bankers Dealing with Large and Small Companies*

undertook some research on the decision-making process of branch managers in deciding on loan applications by small businesses. The bank found that their managers relied far more heavily on personal interviews and contacts than on financial statements. Since then there has been a more rigorous approach to loan applications, particularly in the light of record insolvencies in the early 1980s. Nevertheless it is apparent from the research undertaken by Berry *et al.* that personal interviews with representatives of the company are still very important.

The researchers also found that many businesses were reluctant to supply confidential internal information such as management accounts and it is not surprising, therefore, that the 'gone concern' approach is adopted more often than the going concern approach in such cases.

The general approach in the UK is that a bank will first look at the business as a going concern and then supplement this assessment with a 'liquidation' or 'gone concern' test. The gone concern test represents an assessment of the risk the bank is taking if the assumptions of the going concern approach are incorrect – this test may lead the bank to ask for security.

In evidence to the Wilson Committee, US banks stated that UK banks were unduly concerned with security whereas US banks placed most emphasis on future cash-generating capacity. However, since US bank lending in the UK is largely confined to medium and large British companies their need for security may be somewhat less. This may occur because medium and large companies are better able to employ personnel to develop systems that provide financial projections with reasonable accuracy. Sine many UK banks lend to small firms as well there is often a need for security.

One of the questions often asked of the banks is whether they have failed British industry. For example, there was considerable criticism of the banks in the 1970s from a study group established by Michael Grylls. The main criticism was that funds had been channelled into the personal, rather than the industrial sector. The Wilson Committee, like that of the Macmillan Report (1931) and Radcliffe (1959), found that the problem was not a shortage of funds but a lack of demand for them because of the long-term decline in profitability. However, as Table 12.2 shows the 1986 level of bank borrowing of £4.96 billions was lower than the average for the 1970s of £6.46 billions (both figures are constant 1985 prices), this despite high levels of profitability. The question remains as to why, with higher levels of profitability, investment has been slow to increase particularly in the manufacturing sector. The ratio of fixed investment to profits has fallen from 70 per cent in 1980 to 48 per cent in 1986. A factor of some importance is that higher profitability should permit higher retentions and this in turn can lead to lower borrowings. While the ratio of fixed investment to profits has fallen markedly up to 1986, one factor is the significant use in company profits for investment since 1980 so that the absolute amount of investment would not show the same dramatic fall. It should also be borne in mind that significant changes in the industrial environment have taken place in the 1980s, making comparisons with previous periods very difficult.

Merchant banks

Merchant banks are specialists in corporate finance and most listed companies will appoint at least one to advise it on such matters. The lead authority in controlling merchant banks is the Accepting Houses Committee which reflects the origins of the business as accepting houses. The essential ingredient of the relationship between a merchant bank and a company is trust, since confidential information is disclosed which may be of a price sensitive nature e.g. a takeover bid.

The range of services offered by merchant banks is extensive. The corporate finance department of a merchant bank is involved in:

1 Primary equity issues on the Stock Exchange and unlisted securities market.
2 London listings for overseas clients.
3 Rights and other secondary issues.
4 Advice on mergers and acquisitions.
5 Fixed interest issues.
6 Advice on sources and structure of finance.
7 Advice on profit sharing and share option schemes.
8 Advice on acquisition policy and searches.

In addition to the above, corporate finance departments are normally able to advise on all matters involving banking and finance, international capital markets, public finance and can offer expertise on dealing in foreign exchange, bullion, securities and in the money markets.

The origins of merchant banks can be traced back to their role in the nineteenth century as houses that accepted bills of exchange. However, the Accepting Houses Committee, which represents the interests of its members was not formed until 1914. Members hold bills of exchange and accept them (guarantee them) for a fee. Bills can be discounted on the discount market.

The accepting houses and other merchant banks belong to the Issuing Houses Association and at 31 December 1986 there were fifty-one members. Most issuing houses perform the same functions as accepting houses.

Discount houses

The discount houses have a long history of discounting bills stretching back to the early nineteenth century. In 1987 there were eight major houses who were members of the London Discount Market Association and these, together with discount brokers, are collectively known as the 'money market'. The market deals in discounted bills, overnight lending and inter-bank lending. The largest of the houses is the Union Discount which deals in commercial bills, treasury and corporation bills and gilts and in certificates of deposit.

Bills of exchange will be dealt with in Chapter 14 so it is only certificates of deposit that will be explained here. A sterling certificate of deposit is defined as 'a negotiable receipt issued by a bank or licensed deposit taker in respect of a specified sum of money deposited with that institution at a fixed rate of interest, with an undertaking to repay to the bearer of the certificate, at a specified date, the sum deposited with interest outstanding'. The minimum denomination of a certificate of deposit is £50,000 and in excess of that in multiples of £10,000 up to £1m. The certificates are issued for a minimum period of twenty-eight days and a maximum period of five years and they may be purchased in the market with a minimum life of one day. Deals concluded before midday are usually settled the same day although a transaction may be made for settlement forward, i.e. at a future date. Where a certificate of deposit is issued for a period in excess of one year the interest is paid annually on the anniversary of the date of issue and for any remaining period at maturity. Interest is paid gross and title to a certificate changes on delivery and there is no contingent liability after sale.

The advantages of a certificate of deposit are security, liquidity, and competitiveness in terms of interest rates. The holder of a certificate has the written and signed undertaking of the issuer to repay the deposit with interest at maturity. Security therefore rests in the name of the issuer. A second advantage is one of liquidity in that the certificate is a

Table 12.11   Growth of outstanding credit 1982–6

Year	Outstanding credit (£m)
1982	12,144
1983	14,351
1984	17,429
1985	20,622
1986	23,978

Source: Finance Houses Association

negotiable bearer instrument in an active market. A seller of a certificate wishing to sell before maturity contacts a secondary market dealer and after a rate is agreed delivery is necessary to receive payment. The third advantage is that rates of interest are competitive reflecting the fixed-term deposit market.

Certificates of deposit are issued by most of the major banks in London including the clearing banks, the merchant banks and overseas banks and in addition, licensed deposit takers are also active issuers. The issuance of certificates is referred to as the primary market and where it is sold and bought again the transaction takes place on the secondary market. Discount houses only operate in the secondary market and not in the primary market.

The largest part of the London money market is probably the inter-bank market where deposits are transferred from one bank to another. The rate at which one bank will offer for a deposit from another bank is referred to as the London Inter-bank Offered Rate (LIBOR). Deposits may be in any currency with which there is an active market in London and includes eurocurrency deposits. The deposits range from one year to five years.

Finance Houses Association

The Association was formed in 1945 to represent the interests of its members and to promote standards of conduct for the instalment credit industry. At the end of 1986 there were forty-six finance houses in membership who were primarily involved in providing instalment credit to both industry and the consumer. In the industrial sector, finance is primarily available for the purchase of equipment including office equipment, aircraft, ships and oil refineries. In the consumer sector, finance is available for the purchase of consumer durables, cars, houses, and for personal loans. Credit is also offered in the form of credit cards, deposit accounts, current accounts, and revolving credit.

There has been a considerable growth in outstanding credit over the period 1982 to 1986 and this is shown in Table 12.11.

Table 12.12   Outstanding advances on lending business

	Value of outstanding credit at 31 December 1986 (£m)	Increase through the year	
		in cash (£m)	% increase
To businesses (excluding leasing)	6,098	631	12
Leasing to businesses	8,771	859	11
Total business	14,869	1,490	11
To consumer	9,109	1,866	26
Total – consumers and businesses	23,978	3,356	16

Source: Finance Houses Association

Table 12.12 shows the split between consumer and business lending and the movement during the year. The biggest increase in outstanding credit in percentage terms has been the consumer sector which has resulted from the discontinuance of official controls on the volume of bank lending in 1980, from the ending of terms control on hire purchase lending by finance houses in 1982 and from the abandonment of the building societies' cartel in 1984 which had effectively rationed mortgage credit. This trend in consumer credit is likely to continue as building societies extend their range of financial products. For example, building societies have been able to grant unsecured personal loans since January 1987 as permitted under the Building Societies Act 1986.

The Bank of England has estimated that between 1980 and 1986 total outstanding personal liabilities, including both mortgages and consumer loans, rose from 40 per cent to 70 per cent of annual personal disposable income. Similarly there was rapid growth in personal holdings of liquid assets from 90 per cent to 160 per cent of disposable income. Income gearing, in terms of gross interest payments as a percentage of gross personal income rose from 6 per cent in 1980 to 9 per cent in 1985 but fell to 8 per cent in 1986. A feature of this growth according to the Association has been equity withdrawal from owner-occupied housing as houses have been exchanged. Some estimates suggest that as much as 40 per cent of new mortgage lending has been equity withdrawal to finance consumer spending and the acquisition of financial assets.

One of the dangers of the increase in consumer spending is the increase in possibility of bad debts. The Finance Houses Association reports that there was an increase in the early 1980s but that this has declined somewhat in 1986. The proportion of accounts by value which were more than two months in arrears rose from 4.7 per cent at 31 December 1979 to 8.5 per cent at 31 December 1984 and fell to 7.25 per cent at 30 June 1986. Part of this decrease may be due to an increase in

Table 12.13 Growth in outstanding credit by category

Year	Consumers (£m)	(%)	Business (£m)	(%)	Total (£m)
1982	4,937	(41)	7,207	(59)	12,144
1983	6,250	(44)	8,101	(56)	14,351
1984	7,594	(44)	9,835	(56)	17,429
1985	8,927	(43)	11,695	(57)	20,622
1986	10,592	(44)	13,386	(56)	23,978

Source: Finance Houses Association

use of credit scoring techniques which has enabled a more selective approach to the assessment of credit applications.

Table 12.13 shows the growth of outstanding credit between 1982 and 1986 categorized into consumer and corporate sectors. Consumer spending has been fairly constant around 44 per cent of the total over the period 1983 to 1986. Finance Houses offer a variety of capital financing particularly in the area of asset finance such as hire purchase and leasing. In 1986 lending and leasing to industry and commerce, excluding property loans, represented 21 per cent of all UK fixed investment in plant and machinery. Growth in leasing of motor car fleets was particularly significant in 1986.

Unit trusts

A unit trust involves a large number of investors pooling their money in order to obtain a spread of professionally managed Stock Exchange investments that would be difficult to replicate individually. Since the specific risk of a portfolio is reduced as more securities are added, an investor can take advantage of diversification without having to make direct equity investments. Furthermore, since unit trusts are professionally managed they often have greater and wider expertise than a direct equity investor.

A unit trust is divided into units of equal portions and their price is calculated regularly, often daily, by the managers. Two prices are quoted for each unit representing the price at which investors purchase units, the higher price, and the price at which investors sell units, the lower price. In contrast to a unit trust, an investment trust is a listed company in which an investor buys shares rather than units.

The price of a unit in a trust depends upon the underlying value of securities in the portfolio and therefore is subject to fluctuation. A market in unit trusts may only be made by unit trust managers.

A unit trust is set up by a trust deed which represents an agreement between the trustees and the managers to the fund. Unit trusts are controlled by the Department of Trade and each trust deed must be approved by them. The Department vets both the directors and the shareholders of the management company. The trust deed provides details of the fund including responsibilities of those involved, maximum charges for administering the fund and provision for buying and selling units.

The trust managers own the trust in terms of units whereas the trustee is independent and holds the cash and securities held by the trust. The trustee also ensures that the trust is being administered in accordance with the approved trust deed. A bank or insurance company usually acts as a trustee and a normal requirement is that the trustee should have an issued share capital of at least £0.5m of which £0.25m must be paid up. This type of structure is to safeguard the interests of investors from financial collapse.

The funds of a unit trust may only be invested in companies that are listed on the Stock Exchange or the Unlisted Securities Market but in addition investments may be made in traded options. Direct investments in property may not be made. To ensure an adequate degree of diversification, not more than 5 per cent of the fund may be held in one investment. However, movements in price may mean that such a holding could increase disproportionately so that the limit is exceeded – this is acceptable provided its value does not exceed 7.5 per cent. A further restriction is that a unit trust may not hold more than 10 per cent of the issued share capital of any company.

There are a variety of different types of unit trust. A distribution trust is one that distributes net income at least twice a year whereas an accumulation trust reinvests income. An investor does not avoid taxation by investing in an accumulation trust since a distribution is deemed to have been received on his share of reinvested income. Another type of trust is the exempt trust which can allow tax-exempt organizations, such as pension funds, to avoid capital gains tax.

Managed authorized unit trusts in the UK have a trade association called the Unit Trust Association. The Association protects the interests of its members and undertakes negotiations with City organizations including the self-regulatory organizations. At the end of 1986 the Association had 964 unit trust members compared with only fifty-one in 1960. The growth in the number of unit holders accounts is shown in Table 12.14.

The Unit Trust Association also produces a summary table of the comparative performance of different sectors. The median trust is used and long-term rather than short-term performance is considered by looking at three time horizons, five, ten and fifteen years. In order to demonstrate performance against other savings arrangements the Association also compares the results of £1,000 invested in a bank deposit account, a building society and National Savings Certificates (Table 12.15).

Performance figures can be calculated either on an offer-to-offer basis

Table 12.14 Growth in unit holder accounts

January–December	Net new investment (£m)	Value of funds at end of period (£m)	Unit holder accounts at end of period (m)
1980	107.56	4,968	1.72
1981	527.57	5,902	1.79
1982	509.28	7,768	1.80
1983	1,499.6	11,689	2.03
1984	1,441.5	15,099	2.20
1985	2,537.6	20,307	2.55
1986	5,234.6	32,131	3.41

Source: The Unit Trust Year Book, 1987

Table 12.15 Value of £1,000 (offer to bid, income reinvested) on 1 January 1987

Market sector	Median values and number of trusts in each sector over:					
	5 years		10 years		15 years	
UK general	2,881	(69)	6,951	(60)	6,714	(48)
UK growth	2,748	(72)	6,408	(53)	5,982	(35)
UK equity income	3,263	(66)	6,813	(53)	7,849	(31)
Mixed income	3,159	(10)	5,472	(10)	5,717	(4)
Gilt and FI income	1,728	(29)	2,919	(5)	3,036	(2)
Gilt and FI growth	1,982	(7)	–		–	
International	2,496	(61)	5,113	(42)	5,583	(20)
North America	2,106	(39)	3,518	(17)	3,834	(7)
Europe	4,538	(9)	9,319	(4)	8,009	(1)
Australia	1,343	(6)	2,948	(3)	4,075	(1)
Japan	3,837	(14)	7,278	(5)	12,752	(3)
Far East	2,594	(20)	5,727	(8)	–	
Commodity and energy	1,247	(14)	3,512	(11)	4,581	(8)
Investment trust units	3,126	(5)	7,203	(4)	6,573	(3)
Financial and property shares	2,725	(12)	6,845	(12)	6,231	(10)
Bank deposit accounts	1,305		1,806		2,266	
Building societies	1,422		2,127		2,944	
National savings certificates	1,648		2,545		3,371	
Indices						
FT industrial ordinary	2,920		5,412		4,863	
FT all share	3,147		7,904		7,437	

Source: Unit Trust Association

or an offer-to-bid basis. The former compares differences in the price at which an investor can buy units and is therefore a consistent calculation whereas the latter compares buy to sell prices over a period which reflects more accurately the prices an investor would face in buying and selling over the period.

Table 12.16 Number of members and distribution of assets

31 December	Number of members	UK assets (£m)	UK (%)	Total overseas assets (£m)	Overseas (%)
1985	166	8,620	49.6	8,332	48.0
1984	164	7,127	45.5	8,124	51.9
1983	184	6,094	45.1	7,277	53.8
1980	195	4,470	59.8	2,822	37.7
1979	201	3,897	65.0	1,856	30.9
1975	240	3,201	56.5	2,162	38.1
1960	271	1,396	70.7	559	28.3

Source: Investment Trust Year Book, 1986–7

Investment trust companies

The Association of Investment Trusts was formed in 1932 to protect the interests of its members. Members of the Association are the trust companies themselves and not their management teams and as such they seek to protect institutional investors. At the end of 1985 the Association had 166 members with total assets in excess of £17bn.

Companies may be admitted to membership by the General Committee provided the following conditions are fulfilled:

1 The company must be listed and incorporated either in the UK or in the Channel Islands.
2 The articles of association must prohibit the distribution as a dividend of any profits arising from changes in its investments.
3 The company must be taxed as an investment company.
4 At least 60 per cent of the assets of the company should be invested in listed securities other than those of a subsidiary or an associated company which is not itself an investment trust.

Table 12.16 shows the number of members and distribution of assets from 1960 to 1985. The number of investment trusts has declined steadily since 1960 and a noticeable switch has been from investment primarily in UK assets in 1960 to a somewhat even distribution between UK assets and overseas assets in 1985. Furthermore, the proportion of UK registered equity securities held by investment trusts has also declined from 8.7 per cent in 1974 to 5.0 per cent in 1985 (Table 12.17). The evidence seems to suggest that investment trust companies have become relatively less popular as unit trusts become more popular.

An investment trust is a closed-end fund with a fixed capital structure so that any variation in the demand for shares is reflected in movements in market prices rather than supply movements. In contrast, a

Table 12.17   Growth of the industry

31 December	Market valuation of ordinary and deferred shares of UK investment trusts (£m)	Total market valuation of UK registered equity securities (£m)	Investment trusts as a percentage of total (%)
1985	12,264.6	244,711.0	5.0
1984	10,991.1	204,418.3	5.4
1983	9,670.0	155,692.3	6.2
1982	7,322.3	121,557.6	6.0
1979	3,872.5	66,932.8	5.8
1974	1,509.8	17,270.7	8.7

Source: The Stock Exchange

unit trust is an open-ended fund since its capital can be increased without shareholder approval to satisfy changes in demand and supply. The unit trust fund can repurchase any units that are presented to it for redemption.

In order for an investment trust to qualify as an approved fund a company must satisfy the regulations set out in Section 359 of the Income and Corporation Taxes Act 1970 as amended by Section 93(6) of the Finance Act 1972. Essentially an investment trust must be a resident listed company in the UK, and derive its income substantially from securities. It cannot invest more than 15 per cent of its assets in any one company and it cannot retain in excess of 5 per cent of the income it receives from its investments in shares and securities. Once approved investment trusts are exempt, under the Finance Act 1980, from tax on capital gains. Since capital gains cannot be distributed to shareholders in the form of dividends any gains are therefore reinvested.

An individual investor is liable for tax on the sale of trust shares as he would be for those of any other company. Naturally the capital gains exemption (£6,600 1987–8) applies and the excess is taxed at 30 per cent. Any dividend income received is accompanied by an income tax credit which fulfils the obligation to basic rate tax.

Venture capital

Venture capital is the provision of risk capital to young unquoted companies with high growth potential. Sometimes venture capital is categorized into seed capital, 'grass roots' finance, and development capital. Seed or start-up capital, as its name suggests, is the provision of finance at the earliest stage with the objective of turning ideas into

Table 12.18   Estimated size of international venture capital industry 1986

	Total number of venture capital firms	Total venture capital pool ($m)
US	550	20,000
UK	110	4,500
Canada	44	1,000
Japan	70	850
France	45	750
Netherlands	40	650
West Germany	25	500
Sweden	31	325
Norway	35	185
Denmark	14	120
Ireland	10	100
Australia	11	50

Source: Venture Economics

marketable products or services. The next stage is 'grass roots' finance where commercial production exists but there is a lack of capital to expand production. Third, development capital refers to the provision of finance where there is a consistent profits record and further expansion and funding for higher levels of working capital is required. In almost all cases it is riskier to provide finance the earlier the stage of development and it is not surprising, therefore, that institutions are reluctant to provide start-up capital.

The estimated size of the UK venture capital market compared with other countries is shown in Table 12.18.

The US venture capital market is estimated to be the biggest in the world, some 4.4 times larger than that prevailing in the UK. Since the US population is approximately five times that of the UK it is apparent that the UK has a considerable number of venture capital firms with a substantial capital pool.

Growth in UK venture capital to independent funds has increased substantially since 1979 as shown in Table 12.19. The biggest rise in venture capital funds has been the institutionally backed funds where new capital raised during a year rose from £7.4m in 1979 to £195m in 1986. The rapid increase in venture capital in the UK is beginning to occur in Europe and in fact one of Britain's major venture capital suppliers, 3i, now has offices in Paris, Frankfurt, Holland and Portugal as well as in the US. The UK is the biggest venture capital market in Europe in terms of equity finance for small companies (Table 12.20).

The reasons for the growth in venture capital are numerous. In the UK there seems to have been a change of attitude by both financiers and entrepreneurs. Financiers have become more interested because of opportunities for capital gains and with the enhanced prospects of a

Table 12.19 New capital raised for independent funds in the UK

	Publicly listed (£m)	BSS and BES funds (£m)	Institutionally backed (£m)	Total (£m)
1979	–	–	7.4	7.4
1980	–	–	19.5	19.5
1981	62.2	9.8	42.6	114.6
1982	4.9	4.2	33.7	42.8
1983	51.6	44.6	64.4	160.6
1984	36.7	37.5	147.8	222.0
1985	–	31.3	246.8	278.1
1986	4.0	26.5	195.0	225.5

Source: Venture Economics

Table 12.20 Equity finance for small companies in Europe

Country	Estimate end – 1985 (million ECU)	Increase on 1984–5 (%)	Percentage of total
Belgium	535.1	10.3	8.12
Denmark	127.2	39.3	1.93
Spain/Portugal	404.0	63.8	6.2
France	887.6	30.3	13.47
Greece	19.8	75.4	0.3
Ireland	169.3	35.1	2.57
Italy	90.9	119.8	1.38
Netherlands	1074.2	32.1	16.3
FRG	562.1	57.1	8.53
UK	2715.1	42.6	41.2
Total EEC	6590.0	38.0	100.0

Source: European Venture Capital Association

listing on one of the three tiers of the Stock Exchange. Second, entre-preneurs seem more willing to accept outside shareholders if higher levels of growth can be subsequently achieved thereby enhancing their personal wealth. With relatively low rates of marginal taxes the oppor-tunity to acquire substantial levels of wealth has become a realistic target.

Not only have the venture capital institutions been willing to increase investments in small companies, but also pension funds and insurance companies have increasingly become interested and in 1985 nearly 29 per cent of EEC venture capital came from this source.

One of the main areas where new finance has been channelled is to management buy-outs. This aspect is dealt with in more detail in Chap-ter 17. Another initiative in venture capital has been the Business

Table 12.21   Investment by size range 1985–6

Size range (£000)	Number of financings	Percentage of financings	Amount (£m)	Percentage of amount
0–24	2	1.2	0.0	0.1
25–49	22	12.7	0.8	2.1
50–99	31	17.9	2.2	6.0
100–199	61	35.3	8.5	23.3
200–499	42	24.3	12.8	35.4
500–999	12	6.9	7.5	20.6
1,000–1,999	3	1.7	4.5	12.4

Source: Venture Economics

Expansion Scheme which was launched in 1983. The aim of the scheme was to induce individuals to invest in riskier projects. The new scheme was a follow up to the Business Start-up Scheme and was considered to be experimental although the 1986 Finance Act extended the scheme indefinitely.

The scheme is quite complicated and there is no general clearance procedure for proposals. Generally the scheme offers income tax relief to individuals of up to £40,000 a year provided the investment is for eligible shares. Relief is given at the individual's highest marginal rate of tax in the year in which the shares are issued.

Eligible shares are those in UK unquoted trading or holding companies where not more than half of the net assets consists of land and buildings. The company must undertake a qualifying trade which, in general, means that the business should not be of a financial or passive nature. An investor may not be connected with the company or receive any benefit from it and the investment must be held for a period of at least five years. When the shares are eventually sold no chargeable gain or loss arises and if the Inland Revenue considers that the rules have been broken the relief may be claimed back.

In the first three years of operation the scheme raised £105m, £136m and £147m. The size range of investments and sectors of application are shown respectively in Tables 12.21 and 12.22. Consumer-related industries have been most popular and investments of between £100,000 and £500,000 have been the major area of interest in terms of number and percentage of financings.

One of the most important companies in venture capital in the UK is Investors in Industry (3i) and this organization will be considered in more depth.

Investors in Industry

Investors in Industry (3i) is the name used for one of the world's largest sources of venture capital. Its origins can be traced back to 1945 but its present name resulted from a rationalization and restructuring process

Table 12.22 Investment by industry sector

Industry sector	Percentage of amount invested			Total (£m)	Percentage of amount
	83–4	84–5	85–6		
Consumer-related	32.3	34.2	55.5	50.5	39.7
Technology	25.9	16.0	9.2	22.0	17.3
Industrial/manufacturing	10.2	15.5	15.6	17.6	13.8
Medical/health	5.6	7.1	2.2	6.6	5.2
Construction	7.9	4.6	1.4	6.1	4.7
Other services	8.7	8.6	8.1	10.8	8.5
Other	9.4	14.0	8.0	13.7	10.8
Total	100	100	100	127.3	100

which was completed in July 1983. Part of the reason for the restructuring was to improve public perception of the group as a whole and to highlight its core activities. The group structure is shown in Figure 12.2.

Investors in Industry Group plc acts as a holding company and is the principal borrowing vehicle for the group. Minority investments in companies are owned substantially by 3i which carries on the group's investment activities. In addition to lending money the group offers advisory activities through a number of its subsidiaries and its overseas activities are conducted by subsidiaries in the Channel Islands, US, France, the FRG, Australia and the Irish Republic.

Before April 1985, 3i traded under the name Industrial and Commercial Finance Corporation. Its aim is to provide credit and finance by means of loans or the subscription of loan or share capital to industrial and commercial enterprises in the UK. Generally 3i are willing to provide equity and loan finance of up to £2m. Loan investments are no longer necessarily at a fixed rate of interest and both variable rates and the option to convert a variable rate loan into a fixed rate loan are available. Investments made by 3i are always on a minority interest basis since control is not a goal of this organization. In addition to investments by loans and shares, 3i also offer hire purchase, leasing, guarantees, and business premises services. The latter is conducted through its property division.

In addition to assistance to small and medium-sized businesses, 3i also specializes in meeting the sophisticated and complex financing needs for larger companies. Through its City offices it is willing to provide equity and loan capital for viable projects of amounts up to about £35m. All types of projects are considered including financing for shipping by way of medium and long-term loans and through leases. For large loans syndication with other investors may be undertaken.

3i is also willing to invest in high-technology enterprises and where necessary the company can offer day-to-day advice through its specialized ventures team. Advice is also offered in a number of other areas through its subsidiaries. For example, 3i Portfolio Management Ltd

Figure 12.2   Structure of Investors in Industry

Investors in Industry Group plc

Advisory activities	Other subsidiaries providing services	Investment activities	Fund raising activities	Overseas subsidiaries
3i Portfolio Management Ltd	3i Unit Trust Managers Ltd	Investors in Industry plc (3i)	Investors in Industry Industry International BV (The Netherlands)	In Jersey, Guernsey, Isle of Man, Republic of Ireland, USA, France, FRG and Australia
3i Corporate Finance Ltd	Investors in Industry Trustee Company Ltd	3i Investments plc		
3i Consultants Ltd	Ship Mortgage Finance Co. plc	3i Developments Ltd		
	Gardens Nominees Ltd	3i Commercial Properties Ltd		
	Gardens Pension Trustees Ltd			

Table 12.23 Investors in Industry–amounts outstanding by value

Amounts outstanding at 31 March	1986				1985	
	Number	%	£000	%	Number	£000
0–£10,000	487	10.1	2,348	0.2	481	2,458
£10,001–£20,000	468	9.7	6,961	0.6	395	7,281
£20,001–£50,000	1,162	24.1	38,892	3.3	941	39,786
£50,001–£100,000	893	18.5	66,277	5.6	902	67,851
£100,001–£150,000	465	9.7	57,645	4.8	465	57,465
£150,001–£200,000	261	5.4	46,427	3.9	259	43,763
£200,001–£250,000	203	4.2	46,253	3.9	195	43,139
£250,001–£300,000	118	2.5	32,270	2.7	127	31,572
£300,001–£350,000	92	1.9	30,035	2.5	88	27,168
£350,001–£400,000	87	1.8	32,394	2.7	63	21,885
£400,001–£450,000	59	1.2	25,198	2.1	74	30,839
£450,001–£500,000	67	1.4	30,631	2.6	45	20,171
£500,001–£1,000,000	254	5.3	176,590	14.8	197	138,865
£1,000,001–£2,000,000	117	2.4	164,010	13.8	112	149,274
£2,000,001–£5,000,000	61	1.3	197,073	16.6	52	171,286
£5,000,001 and over	22	0.5	236,728	19.9	27	288,926
Loans and shares	4,816	100	1,189,732	100	4,423	1,141,729
Other assets			498,623			462,053
Total			1,688,355			1,603,782

provides a full range of investment management services and manages the group's listed portfolio. 3i Corporate Finance Ltd offers general financial advice and specialist services in respect of fund raising, mergers and acquisitions and new issues and 3i Consultants Ltd provides consultancy advice to companies in all industrial and commercial sectors.

Investors in Industry raise money from a variety of sources including the gilt-edged market and Eurobond market. The company's borrowings include debenture stocks, unsecured loan stocks, notes, loans, overdrafts, bills discounted and deposits.

An analysis of amounts outstanding by value and by industry is shown in Tables 12.23 and 12.24. The shareholdings in the group is shown in Table 12.25.

Summary

Company profitability and productivity has been improving since 1981 although unemployment remains high and investment sluggish. High levels of corporate liquidity and buoyant stock markets have led to decreases in bank borrowing and increases in ordinary share issues.

Over the last two decades there has been considerable criticism of the City and the role of the banks. The Wilson Committee, like its predecessors, found that there did not appear to be a shortage of funds but

Table 12.24   Investors in Industry – amounts outstanding by industry

Amounts outstanding at 31 March	1986 (£000)	1985 (£000)	1984 (£000)	1983 (£000)	1982 (£000)
Agriculture, forestry and fishing	5,879	5,317	4,680	6,110	6,773
Energy and water	24,504	28,899	18,675	11,164	7,405
Mining and quarrying	7,534	3,519	4,027	2,799	2,568
Metal and other mineral manufacture	78,378	85,929	86,187	86,245	70,393
Chemicals and manmade fibres	59,737	56,790	47,061	27,001	24,336
Mechanical engineering	88,188	84,152	85,844	76,230	68,254
Manufacture – office machinery and data processing	14,913	15,110	12,247	6,798	3,870
Electrical and electronic engineering	78,974	50,195	44,298	30,412	27,949
Vehicles, transport manufacture	19,486	11,062	11,299	11,984	10,881
Instrument engineering	12,024	12,929	13,240	11,676	11,834
Food, drink and tobacco	64,654	75,341	74,652	72,023	80,717
Textiles and leather goods	20,951	17,228	17,023	14,310	11,465
Clothing and footwear	14,101	12,515	10,834	10,527	11,953
Timber and furniture etc.	16,387	17,149	15,575	12,232	11,092
Paper, printing and publishing	55,429	45,129	40,197	45,120	37,586
Other manufacturing and repairs	82,713	101,665	85,767	81,388	85,957
Construction	33,711	36,910	30,619	28,505	26,359
Wholesale distribution	64,399	66,799	51,448	42,004	40,129
Retail distribution	62,868	72,551	48,562	37,703	33,270
Hotel and catering	72,043	85,434	74,553	63,757	54,610
Transport and communication	69,225	71,686	67,187	67,479	39,663
Insurance, banking and leasing	60,902	57,418	40,595	30,934	40,753
Other business services	129,655	94,868	77,961	66,961	56,898
Health education community services	19,935	16,505	14,242	11,824	12,716
Recreational and personal services	33,142	16,629	11,558	10,900	10,345
Loans and shares	1,189.732	1,141,729	988,331	866,086	787,776
Other assets	498,623	462,053	416,366	379,466	344,958
Total	1,688,355	1,603,782	1,404,697	1,245,552	1,132,734

Table 12.25   Investors in Industry – shareholders as at 31 March 1986

		%
Bank of England		15.00
Bank of Scotland		3.11
Barclays Bank plc		18.83
Lloyds Bank plc		13.68
Midland Bank plc		16.16
Clydesdale Bank plc		1.84
The Royal Bank of Scotland plc		7.58
National Westminster Bank plc	22.97	
Coutts & Co.	0.70	23.67
Waterloo Trustee Co., Ltd*		0.13
		100.00

*   The Waterloo Trustee Co. Ltd is trustee for the group's profit sharing plan.

rather a lack of demand for them. However, despite higher levels of profitability the demand for bank loans for investment has been poor. The question remains, therefore, as to why this has been occurring. It is clear that there is a lack of demand at the terms being offered i.e. the cost of borrowing is too high. One factor is that higher profitability permits higher retentions which can lead to lower borrowings. The significant rise in profits since 1980 is an important factor in explaining the decline in the ratio of fixed investment to profits.

Since 1982 there has been a massive increase in outstanding credit particularly to the consumer sector. This can be accounted for by a discontinuance of official controls over bank lending, and an oversupply of credit from institutions and lately building societies. The high propensity to offer credit is normally a symptom of high margins.

The UK venture capital industry has expanded considerably in the 1980s and is now one of the biggest in the world relative to its population. There still remains difficulty in finding money for start-ups but this is to be expected bearing in mind the level of risk attributable. Institutions naturally prefer to invest in companies with a good profits record with potential for further expansion. Not only have the venture capital institutions been willing to invest in smaller companies but also pension funds and insurance companies are increasingly interested in doing so particularly where there are prospects for a quotation on one of the three tiers of the Stock Exchange.

References

Berry, A., Citron, D., and Jarvis, R., *The Information Needs of Bankers Dealing with Large and Small Companies*, CACA Research Report 7.
Bollon Committee Report, HMSO, 1971.
Macmillan Committee Report, HMSO, 1931.
Radcliffe Committee Report, HMSO, 1959.

Further reading

Arnaud, A. A., *Investment Trusts Explained*, Woodhead-Faulkner, 1983.

Carrington, J. C. and Edwards, G. T., *Financing Industrial Investment*, Macmillan, 1979.

Carrington, J. C. and Edwards, G. T., *Reversing Economic Decline*, Macmillan, 1981.

Clay, C. J. J. and Wheble, B. S. (eds), *Modern Merchant Banking*, Woodhead-Faulkner, 1986.

Corner, D. C. and Burton, H., *Investment and Unit Trusts in Britain and America*, Elek, 1986.

Corner, D. C. and Stafford, D. C., *Open-End Investment Trusts in the EEC and Switzerland*, Macmillan, 1977.

Drury, A. C., *Finance Houses*, Waterlow, 1982.

Equipment Leasing Association, Annual Report, 1986.

Finance Houses Association, Annual Report, 1987.

Franklin, P. J. and Woodhead, C., *The UK Life Assurance Industry*, Croom Helm, 1980.

Freear, J., *The Management of Business Finance*, Pitman, 1980.

Grylls, M., *The Grylls Report* (First, Second and Third Report), 1981–3.

Peasnell, K. V. and Ward, C. W. R., *British Financial Markets and Institutions*, Prentice-Hall, 1985.

Plender, J. *That's the Way the Money Goes: The Financial Institutions and the Nation's Savings*, André Deutsch, 1982.

Unit Trust Association, Annual Report, 1986.

Wilson Committee Report, HMSO., 1980.

Wilson, K. W., *British Financial Institutions*, Pitman, 1983.

Young, M. and Buchanan, N., *Accounting for Pensions*, Woodhead-Faulkner, 1981.

13 Currency risk management

Introduction

One of the few certainties in the current economic climate is that exchange rates will remain unstable. The consequence of this, coupled with continuing internationalization of the UK economy, is that companies are more conscious of their vulnerability to losses arising from these movements.

Currency risk as a subject is made more difficult by the extensive use of jargon. Therefore the chapter commences with three important definitions. First, 'currency risk' – this is synonymous with foreign exchange risk and can broadly be defined as the risk that a firm may suffer monetary loss, expressed in a base currency (for UK based companies £ sterling), as a result of changes in foreign exchange rates. Second 'exposure' is synonymous with risk but 'an exposure' refers to a particular amount at risk. Finally 'hedging' can be described as the taking of an action which reduces or eliminates an exposure position. Given this basic terminology we continue.

Currency risk management involves three processes. First the quantification and analysis of the risk in terms of the present situation and various time horizons; second the development and implementation of strategies to deal with exposures and lastly the use of various hedging techniques to eliminate or reduce positions. While this chapter deals with currency risk management in isolation, students should remember that a business is subject to many risks and exposes itself to currency risk for wider strategic reasons (for example, goods might be obtained from an overseas supplier with the objective of diversifying sourcing or factories set up overseas with the intention of circumventing tariff barriers). Therefore currency risk management must be seen in context and strategies adopted integrated within the firm's overall corporate objectives and policies.

Defining the risk

Currency risk has three distinct but inter-related components: transaction, translation and economic exposure.

Transaction exposure refers to the gains or losses which arise whenever a payment or receipt takes place at an exchange rate different to that prevailing when the transaction was initiated. The exposure covers all business cash flows denominated in foreign currency including trade receipts and payments, dividend and interest flows, loan repayments, investments, borrowing movements and inter-company trade accounts. The time period of an exposure may range from several years in the case of overseas borrowing to a relatively short period for payments to overseas creditors. The instant when the transaction risk is initiated may be difficult to identify. Probably it is best thought of as when the contractual obligation to pay, or entitlement to receive arises. However, situations such as the issuing of a foreign currency price list or the tendering for a contract with payments in foreign currency create a potential exposure despite being outside the definition. This 'grey area' must be resolved by organizations when information systems are designed. The death of the exposure occurs either when the payment or receipt is made or when the risk has been hedged.

Translation exposure refers to the possibility that gains or losses may result from the translation upon consolidation of foreign enterprises' financial statements into the currency of the parent. If refers to unrealized gains and losses quantified in accordance with accounting rules, which in the UK are based upon Statement of Standard Accounting Practice 20 (SSAP 20). This requires that the profit and loss account be translated at either the average or closing rate and the balance sheet at the closing rate with resultant gains and losses dealt with through the reserves. (Students should contrast this with transaction exposure in SSAP 20 where realized gains and losses are based upon translation at the conversion date rate and unrealized gains and losses, perhaps a currency loan, are converted at the closing rate with the net effect charged to the profit and loss account.) Translation exposure is born when an enterprise is set up overseas and only ceases when the undertaking is wound up.

Economic exposure is the risk that the value of the business, expressed as the net present value of its future cash flows, will be affected by exchange rate movements. The impact is all pervading and may be classified as either direct or indirect. The direct effect is upon the value of future remittances from overseas enterprises, the cost structure and profit margins of entities within the group and general competitiveness. The indirect consequences relate to the changes in economic climate brought about by exchange rate movements. Therefore, even a firm with no overseas investments, no overseas sales or purchases and no overseas competitors will suffer economic risk to the extent that, say, a devaluation of the currency leads to higher interest rates and inflation with a resultant change in the demand for the business's products.

Table 13.1 Forward and spot rates against the pound

Currency	Spot	One month	Three months
US dollar ($)	1.5130–1.5140	0.44–0.41c pm	1.28–1.23c pm
Japanese yen	239¼–240¼	1⅛–⅞Y pm	3¾–3Y pm
West Germany mark (DM)	3.24¾–3.25¾	1⅝–1⅜ pf pm	4½–4⅛ pf pm
Italian lira	2232–2233	1–6 dis	5–12 dis

Note: pm = premium and dis = discount

It must be stressed that while this analysis into three separate risks is convenient they are closely inter-related. For example, translation risk affects the equity investment in a foreign operation. When profits are remitted translation exposure is reduced and replaced by transaction risk. Further equity is equivalent to net assets, which could include debtors and creditors denominated in other currency and therefore a transaction exposure. Similarly economic exposure, which embraces changes in the value of the foreign operation other than upon consolidation, incorporates the impact of changes which will later be reflected in translation and transaction exposures. (A more discursive definition of exposure is contained in Appendix 13.1.)

Fundamental terminology

The purpose of this section is to introduce the world of foreign exchange calculations. Table 13.1 provides spot and forward rates against the pound sterling for four currencies. The presentation is similar to that which might be expected from banks and the financial press.

Let us now consider how the information above is used in the following buying and selling situations:

1 Spot (for delivery two business days after the date of the deal) based on pounds sterling (for example purchasing US dollars with pounds).
2 Spot between non-sterling currencies (for example converting marks into yen).
3 Forward markets.

Spot – sterling

Table 13.1 shows two exchange rates for each currency. One applies if the currency is being purchased and the other if it is being sold. The trick is to use the correct rate for each situation. There are two approaches to this problem. The first is to utilize the obvious fact that for a bank to make money on currency deals, a company must pay more to acquire a given amount of a foreign currency than it could sell it for. Consider $1000 US – converted at the lower rate of 1.5130 it yields £660.94 while at the higher rate of 1.5140 gives £660.50. From the previous logic it follows that a bank sells currency at the lower rate and buys at the higher rate. Alternatively the choice of rate could be based upon the mnemonic 'buy high, sell low' referring to the action of the bank which means that a company gets the low rate when buying and the high rate when selling. As a further example, suppose a company wished to buy 100,000 yen – using the mnemonic that a bank 'sells low' the lower rate would be applicable giving a sterling cost of £417.97. If it had wished to sell 100,000 yen – using the mnemonic that a bank 'buys high' the sterling proceeds would be £416.23. This outcome agrees with the logical approach that buying costs more than the proceeds of selling.

Spot – other currencies

Suppose a company wishes to change one million lire into German marks. In effect this could be achieved by converting the lire into pounds sterling and using these to buy marks, however this incurs extra conversion costs and therefore a lira/Deutschmark (DM) cross rate must be calculated. Since we know from Table 13.1 that one pound buys 2232 lire or 3.2475 DM, one lira must buy 3.2475/2232 lire – 0.0014549 DM or perhaps better expressed as 1000 lire buys 1.4549 DM. In the general case, a cross rate is achieved by division hence:

$$\text{Lira/DM} \quad \frac{3.2475}{2232} - \frac{3.2575}{2233} = 1.4549 - 1.4587 \text{ DM per 1000 lire}$$

Alternatively for $/yen as £1 = $1.5130 or 239¼ yen
$1.5130 = 239¼ yen and therefore $1 = 239¼/1.5130 yen so:

$$\text{\$/yen}: \frac{239\frac{1}{4}}{1.5130} - \frac{240\frac{1}{4}}{1.5140} = 158.13 - 158.68 \text{ yen}$$

At this point readers might like to attempt to calculate lira/yen and $/DM rates.

(lira/yen 0.1072 – 0.1076 or 107.2 – 107.6 yen per 1000 lira)
($/DM 2.1464 – 2.1516).

Cross rates are important as in practice exchange rates, apart from the £/$, are quoted in dollars and therefore calculating £/DM involves cross rate calculations of the £/$ and $/DM – suppose $/DM rate 2.1464 – 2.1516 as above:

£1 : 1.5130 – 1.5140 $ (Table 13.1)

$$\$1 : \frac{1}{1.5130} - \frac{1}{1.5140} \quad 0.6609385 - 0.660502 \; £$$

from $/DM £0.6609385 = 2.1464 DM
  and   £0.660502 = 2.1516 DM

$$£/DM \quad \frac{2.1464}{0.6609385} - \frac{2.1516}{0.660502}$$

which is 3.2475 – 3.2575 DM conforming with Table 13.1.

Forward rates

In the forward market companies have the opportunity of fixing an exchange rate now for a future foreign exchange transaction. Table 13.1 shows forward rates as quoted in the financial press with no information on actual rates but merely in terms of an adjustment to the spot rate. The rule for the adjustment is that a premium is subtracted from the spot rate and a discount is added to it. The table indicates whether a currency is at a premium or discount to the £ sterling but banks' quotations do not. However a simple rule determines this:

Adjustment falling – a premium
Adjustment rising – a discount

Another feature of Table 13.1 is that the currency of the adjustments is given, for example c for cents, Y for yen and pf for pfennigs. Whereas bank quotations are in terms of points (for example dollars 44 to 41 points and lira 1 to 6 points based on one month forward) with the addition and subtraction of points being right hand justified against the quoted spot rate.

To summarize, there is a threefold translation process to find the forward rate from a bank's quotation in terms of points:

1 Are the points rising or falling.
2 Addition of discounts/subtraction of premium.
3 Use the full spot rate moving points to the right.

For example buying 10,000 dollars forward one month, points 44–41 and selling 1,000,000 lire forward three months, points 5–12 with spot as per Table 13.1.

	Dollars		*Lire*
Spot	1.5130	Spot	2233
Subtract premium – 44		Add discount + 12	
Forward rate 1.5086		Forward rate 2245	

Cost $\dfrac{10,000}{1.5086} = £6628.66$ Proceeds $\dfrac{1,000,000}{2245} = £445.43$

As well as fixed term forward contracts it is possible to enter into forward option contracts where maturity is specified as occurring at the discretion of the firm at any time between two dates (readers must not confuse these forward contracts with currency options, which will be discussed later in this chapter). Forward option contracts are used when there is uncertainty as to the precise date of a currency payment or receipt, with the possibility of extra currency transactions being required to honour the fixed contract. For example if one million Deutschmarks are sold forward for delivery on 1 March based upon a due receipt which does not in fact occur until 2 March the company will be forced to buy the Deutschmarks to fulfil the contract at the rate ruling on 1 March and hence incur additional transaction costs. A forward option contract would overcome this difficulty by specifying delivery of the money between say 1 and 31 March enabling a considerable delay to occur without adverse consequences. The disadvantage of forward option contracts is that they are expensive since banks quote the most costly rate within the option period. Option contracts typically are in monthly units to correspond with the normal forward rate quotations. The rate giving the most costly option will depend upon whether the currency is at a premium or discount. Consider one to three month options on one million lira and ten thousand Deutschmarks with a UK company buying and selling. The cost if they were ordinary forward contracts of one month and three months can be calculated thus:

		One month	*Three months*
Lire –	buy spot	2,232	2,232
	points	+1	+5
		2,233	2,237
	sell spot	2,233	2,233
	points	+6	+12
		2,239	2,245
DM –	buy spot	3.24¾	3.24¾
	points	− 1⅝	− 4½
		3.23⅛	3.20¼
	sell spot	3.25¾	3.25¾
	points	− 1⅜	− 4⅛
		3.24⅜	3.21⅝

One million lira	£	£	*Working*	
Cost of buying	**447.83**	447.03	1,000,000/2,233	1,000,000/2,237
Proceeds of selling	446.63	**445.43**	1,000,000/2,239	1,000,000/2,245

Ten thousand DMs				
Cost of buying	3094.78	**3122.56**	10,000/3.23⅛	10,000/3.20¼
Proceeds of selling	**3082.85**	3109.21	10,000/3.24⅜	10,000/3.21⅝

The figures in bold indicate the most favourable outcomes for the bank. Therefore it follows that when a currency is at a premium, as with Deutschmarks, the rate received from the bank when buying will be that applicable on the last day of the option period; whereas, for sales of currency it will be the rate on the first day of the option period; and vice versa when a currency is at a discount (lire). The rate applicable to a company on a forward option contract rule is:

Currency	Buying	Selling
Premium	Last day	First day
Discount	First day	Last day

Since this always gives the bank the most advantageous terms. After a pause for reflection readers should realize that choosing the rate for a forward option contract only requires the rule of the bank taking the most advantageous rate. Readers by now should appreciate whether a rate of 2,233 or 2,237 is more advantageous to the bank when buying lira and therefore the choice follows logically without memorizing the rule table.

Forward contracts are legally binding and must be complied with irrespective of whether delays, disputes or other circumstances alter projected currency cash flows. This means that where an agreement has been made to sell currency, which has not arrived, the company must buy the currency just to fulfil this obligation. Similarly when currency has been bought forward, the purchase must take place, even though the money is not required, and the unwanted currency sold. The company will incur a loss on the spread of rates each time and be liable to costs and commission charges from the bank. The harshness of this situation can be alleviated by extending the contract at the first indication of problems or rolling the contract forward. In the former situation there would be a settlement of the original contract and the taking out of a new forward contract while in the latter instance the existing rate is adjusted to take account of rate movements. In practice banks discourage rolling the contract forward unless both the amount involved and the time difference are small.

It is often thought that forward rates represent a forecast of the exchange rate upon a future date. However, in reality, forward rates are derived from the interaction of spot and interest rate differentials. Conceptually when a bank provides forward cover it enters into an arrangement to remove any risk. Suppose, therefore, that a company agreed with a bank to sell one million French francs forward three months. When the contract is agreed the bank borrows a sum of French francs which with interest will amount, by the due date, to one million French francs. At the same time the French francs are converted at the spot rate into sterling and invested. After three months the company hands over the one million French francs, which the bank uses to pay off the borrowings, and receives the sterling investment plus interest less costs and the bank's margin. This final sterling amount equates with the French francs converted at the three months forward rate. Forward rates are therefore a matter of calculation using the spot rate and the interest rates applicable to deposits in each of the currencies with discounts arising when interest rates in the base currency are lower and premiums when they are higher than the foreign currency. From Table 13.1 it can be seen that interest rates in the UK are lower than in Italy but higher than in the US, West Germany and Japan.

Finally in examining the costs and proceeds derived from exchanging foreign currency, it must be borne in mind that banks, in addition to making profit on the spread of rates between buying and selling, usually charge commission on each transaction's sterling value expressed as 'per mille' – effectively one thousandth part (contrast with per cent).

Strategies

An organization may adopt one of a number of strategies to deal with foreign exchange exposure. The simplest is avoidance. The firm decides to invoice only in the base currency, buy goods only from suppliers who quote prices in the base currency, borrow only in the base currency and undertake no overseas investments. This approach is successful in eliminating transaction and translation exposures but cannot remove all economic risk. As the value of the base currency changes relative to other currencies there will be effects upon the economic environment of the organization and the position of competitors which will have an impact upon the business's cash flows. An avoidance strategy has a high cost in terms of restrained growth and reduced competitive strength and is not a viable alternative for any but the smallest firms. Another approach is to deliberately ignore foreign exchange exposure. The wisdom of this depends upon the composition of a firm's foreign exchange involvement. Few problems arise if the currency risk is confined to receivables in a currency strong relative to the base currency or to payables in a weak currency. Further, when the time-scale of exposure is short and margins are high there should be few difficulties. However, where foreign exchange exposure is significant in terms of major overseas transactions or investments it would be imprudent for an organization to follow this strategy. Finally organizations acknowledging the inevitability of involvement will undertake an exposure management strategy. Options for an exposure management strategy are best considered by reference to the risk involved. However it is important at the outset to distinguish between exposure management and speculation. The former is concerned with the management of exposure positions arising from the activities of the organization in an efficient and effective manner whereas the latter involves the opening of positions in order to make profits from exchange rate changes.

With respect to transaction risk the strategy of the firm may range from a position of covering all exposures to covering no exposures. A risk averse organization will prefer to hedge exposures on the grounds that this removes uncertainty over the base currency equivalents of foreign exchange cash flows. This has the disadvantage of removing any opportunity for additional profit and is therefore not totally riskless. Alternatively less risk averse companies will take a decision upon whether to expose or close out a transaction exposure with the aim of identifying the optimum point for converting the transaction. In essence this involves exposing receivables and investments and hedging payables and borrowing denominated in strong currencies (which will appreciate against the base currency) and vice versa for weak currencies. Another approach would be to adopt a 'stop loss' where cover would be effected once an adverse variation of a certain percentage had occurred (for example if the rate for an exposed currency deteriorates by more than 5 per cent since inception). Obviously the success of this strategy will depend upon accurate forecasting of currencies' movements and requires the organization to accept the risk of losses as compared with automatic forward cover.

In contrast to transaction risk, translation exposure does not have any direct cash flow or profit and loss account impact (both SSAP 20 in the UK and FASB 52 in the US require translation gains and losses to be accounted for through reserve movements). Nevertheless changing foreign exchange rates, with their consequent impact upon the net worth of overseas subsidiaries, may have adverse effects upon target corporate gearing ratios, performance ratios and loan covenants. For these reasons consideration must be given to translation risk management. Strategies available involve the manipulation of the net worth exposed. This can be achieved by matching net worth exposed with currency borrowings thereby aiming to eliminate the exposure by setting up an equal and opposite liability, actively managing the risk to expose strong currency net worth and hedge weak currency net worth, coordinating borrowing strategy by matching wherever it was deemed sensible and manipulating capital transfers, dividends and pricing in order to minimize the net worth exposed. The scope for management may well be limited by government legislation in various countries leading to monitoring of thin capitalization (funding a business purely on local borrowings without any direct investment), controlling the level of remittances and preventing transfer pricing abuses. The decision on whether to manage translation exposure depends upon the circumstances of individual organizations. There are, however, strong arguments against fully covering translation exposure – first, transaction costs and conceivably real losses will be incurred to avoid paper losses; second, investors may view a share as being a portfolio of different currency investments and that it would be a mistake to hedge and destroy the mix; and finally, within net worth are a number of transaction exposures already subject to management.

Economic exposure management will principally be carried out at the stage when the strategic plans for the whole organization are developed. The impact of changing exchange rates upon the expected cash flows from present investments in the home and overseas markets and assessment of the likely result of future investments involves an implicit management of the economic exposure through the planning decisions made. There are, though, some circumstances which give rise to economic exposure with a finite life (for example issuing price lists denominated in a foreign currency, tendering for overseas contracts and fixed term joint ventures). In these circumstances it would be possible to sensibly cover the economic risk and therefore suitable strategies may be developed in the same manner as for transaction and translation exposures.

Strategies have been discussed in isolation in this section. However the approach to risk management must integrate taxation, foreign legal requirements and exchange control regulations into the strategic framework.

Hedging techniques

The techniques for hedging currency risk are many and varied. Further, the financial markets have the flexibility to create new instruments in response to market demands. This section covers the major techniques in use at the end of 1986. However, readers should expect changes in such a dynamic environment and are therefore advised to consult the accountancy and financial press to keep abreast of developments.

It is usual to divide techniques between those relating to internal organizational and policy adjustments and those involving resort to external markets or bodies.

Internal

Netting
Netting is a technique whereby inter-company indebtedness is settled on a net basis using a common currency. The simple situation is bilateral netting, which occurs when pairs of subsidiaries enter into an arrangement to offset inter-company indebtedness. Multilateral netting, a more complex situation occurs where group companies report their indebtedness to a central treasury, which contrasts overlapping positions and informs subsidiaries of the net payment or receipt required to settle their foreign exchange inter-company positions. In both instances indebtedness needs to be expressed in a base currency for those in the system, usually the US dollar or pound sterling. Figure 13.1 shows diagrammatic representations of netting situations. Table 13.2 shows the same information in tabular form.

The netting system greatly reduces currency flows. In the bilateral example currency flows equivalent to $3 million are settled by one payment of $1 million; while for multilateral netting $7.5 million equivalent flows are cleared by payments of $2 million by one subsidiary. In consequence transaction costs are reduced and inter-company exposure minimized. The disadvantages of the approach are that multi-

Bilateral

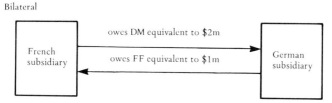

Settlement of $1 million paid from the French to the German subsidiary

Multilateral

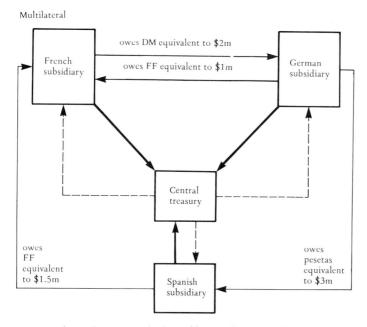

Settlement by German subsidiary of $2m, paid $1.5m to the Spanish
and $0.5m to the French subsidiary

Note: $ = US dollars, m = million, ──────▶ direction of indebtedness,
─────▶ information flows and ── ──▶ payment instructions.

Figure 13.1 Netting situations

Table 13.2   Netting situations

Subsidiary	Owes ($ millions)	Owed ($ millions)	Net ($ millions)
French	(2)	2.5[1]	0.5
German	(4)[2]	2	(2)
Spanish	(1.5)	3	1.5
Total	(7.5)	(7.5)	0

Notes:
1   1.5 (Spanish subsidiary) + 1.0 (German subsidiary)
2   3.0 (Spanish subsidiary) + 1.0 (French subsidiary)

lateral netting requires a centralized treasury infrastructure with associated cost implications; settlements may have taxation and occasionally legal effects, which hinder the process; and it is possible that exchange losses tend to recur in particular subsidiaries with adverse consequences for its performance.

Matching
Matching occurs when receipts in a foreign currency are used to meet payments in the same currency. The system is workable whenever there are receipts and payments denominated in the same foreign currency within one company or companies in a group. The benefits of matching arise from the saving of transaction costs, both in buying and selling and hedging instruments, and the provision of cover for transaction exposure. The success of matching depends upon the coordination of currency flow forecasts by a central treasury and the speed of transfer of funds to where they are needed. Given uncertainty with respect to the timing of flows, matching systems usually operate with currency bank accounts and overdraft facilities to enable obligations to be met. (For example, if there was a delay on a payment of DM 2 million receivable on 1 January and intended for use in paying loan interest of DM 1 million due on the same day; the central treasury could use a Deutschmark overdraft facility to pay the loan interest and settle this when payment was received.) As well as matching to reduce transaction exposure, currency assets and liabilities can be matched to lessen translation exposure and provide cover for the balance sheet.

Leading and lagging
Leading and lagging refers to adjustment of the payment terms between firms in order to benefit from favourable, and protect against adverse, currency movements. Suppose a company was expecting an order worth $100,000. If the expectation was for the dollar to appreciate against the pound sterling, a UK company would be prepared to offer lengthy credit terms (lagging); whereas if the dollar was weakening a

UK company would press for immediate payment or a very short credit period (leading). In either case the technique requires confidence in exchange rate forecasts and an appreciation of non-currency factors (for example interest foregone when lagging in this situation, price discount to encourage leading and the overall state of the negotiations). Within groups of companies central treasury departments apply leading and lagging on inter-company payments and in practice this is probably the commonest application area. Again legal and tax constraints may prevent the operation of the technique in certain countries.

Invoicing
The currency of invoicing is likely to be determined by reference to a number of factors – for example competitive pressures allowing the purchaser to fix trade practices (oil price denominated in US $), legal constraints and taxation implications. Nevertheless in certain situations negotiating a favourable invoicing currency may be a viable option, or failing this a currency protection clause, operable if rates move beyond a certain level, might be inserted to protect prices. Third, in rare circumstances companies dealing in overseas currency may attempt to gain higher margins to act as a cushion against adverse currency movements.

Finally, consideration may be given in large deals to barter arrangements. US organizations, such as Univex, arrange the initial exchange of goods and the disposal of the bartered goods in one package without foreign currency changing hands (part of the 1986 British Aerospace/ Saudi Arabian arms deal was paid for in oil).

External

Forward contracts
As has already been mentioned earlier in this chapter forward contracts represent agreements to buy or sell specified amounts of a currency on an agreed future date at an exchange rate fixed when the contract is entered into. As well as fixed forward contracts there are forward option contracts where, instead of delivery on an agreed date, delivery may take place between a range of specified dates and on a piecemeal basis if so desired. Both types of forward contracts have a long history and provide certainty as to the value of a future currency receipt. There is a forward market available for most of the world's major currencies for periods of up to twelve months. Longer durations and more exotic currencies may only have a very thin market or even no market at all.

Short-term borrowing/currency bridging accounts
These are used as alternatives to, or in conjunction with, forward contracts to cover transaction and translation exposure. In essence the company creates its own forward contract. For receivables it borrows a

currency sum, which with interest will, on the due date, equal the receipt, and converts it into sterling. Similarly for payables sterling borrowings are converted into the desired currency immediately and invested for the currency plus interest to the due date to be equivalent to the payable. In each case the cost of currency is fixed in terms of sterling provided due dates are kept and interest rates remain constant. The main advantage of this approach is that facilities can usually be renegotiated in the event of delays to transactions. Indeed the most satisfactory way to deal with a delayed forward contract is through bridging with overdrafts or similar facilities.

Options
Options must be distinguished from forward option contracts, which provide latitude as to the timing of the transactions, but must be fulfilled whereas with option contracts, as with share options, there is no obligation to fulfil the contract. In brief an option is a right, but not an obligation, to buy or sell currency at an agreed exchange rate for a specified time period. The advantage of options is that they provide the opportunity for profit while limiting losses to the premium paid for the option. In practice options are used to cover indeterminate exposures such as long-term contract tenders where receivables are in a foreign currency or there are conditional currency purchases. Consider for example a company tendering for a contract in dollars, which requires specialist equipment obtainable only from Germany and payable in Deutschmarks. An economic receivable and payable exposure exist and both can be covered using options. Let us examine the dollar position – suppose the proceeds are $2 million and that if the contract were awarded these would be received in six months time. Given a spot rate of $1.50, a six months forward quote of $1.51 and an option for the period at $1.51 with a premium of £10,000. Consider the difference in situations if the rate six months hence is (a) $1.40* and (b) $1.60.*

Forward contract (m = million)

	£
Contract awarded ($2m/1.51)	1,324,500
(against either £1,428,600 or £1,250,000 if spot taken in six months time)	
Contract not awarded rate $1.60 purchase of $2m costs	1,250,000
therefore profit	74,500
rate $1.40 purchase of $2m costs	1,428,600
therefore loss	104,100

---

* The use of single rates is purely a simplification. In reality there would be buying and selling rates for a currency transaction.

Options

	£
Contract awarded – option to sell at $1.51	1,324,500
Premium	10,000
Minimum net proceeds	1,314,500
If rate $1.60 exercise the option	
If rate $1.40 do not exercise the option but sell for	1,428,600
spot yielding	
Premium	(10,000)
Net proceeds	1,418,600
Contract not awarded	1,250,000
If rate $1.60 buy $2m	1,324,500
and sell using the option	74,500
Premium	(10,000)
Net profit	64,500

If the rate is $1.40 do not exercise the option and the loss is limited to the premium. (Transaction costs other than the premium ignored.) Options are new hedging instruments originating on the Philadelphia Stock Exchange in late 1982. Currently they are available for only a relatively few currencies and are obtained either direct from exchanges (Philadelphia, Montreal, London, Chicago and other leading centres) or 'over the counter' from banks. Option contracts from exchanges are for standard units and durations whereas 'over the counter' options can be tailored to meet a company's requirements.

Futures
Futures offer the opportunity to buy or sell foreign currency in agreed units against dollars on a specific future date with the exchange rate fixed at the start of the contract. Quotations are in currency per dollar and cover is typically available in Deutschmarks, sterling, Swiss francs and yen from centres such as Chicago and the London International Financial Futures Exchange (LIFFE). Units are quite small (for instance £25,000 for £/$ on LIFFE) and maturity dates are the third Wednesdays in March, June, September and December although the majority are closed out in advance. Futures provide cover because there is a strong link between spot prices at any point in time and futures quotations. Therefore if a loss arises on exchange rate it will be offset by profits on the futures contract. For example, suppose a UK company owes $70,000 payable in one month's time. The company sells £50,000 of futures contracts as the rate is $1.40 and when the payment is due and the rate is $1.35 closes out the futures contract with a profit of £1,852 which exactly offsets the increased cost of the payment in sterling terms. (The calculation works as follows: the futures contracts gives the right to $70,000 dollars for £50,000. When payment is due $70,000 cost £51,852. However, because the futures contract is an asset and its rates closely follow spot, there is a counterbalancing increase in its value of £1,852.) While this is a perfect match, in practice, spot and

future rates vary. The advantages of futures are that the initial security to obtain them is low, they are available in relatively small units and commission charges are below forward contracts. The main disadvantage relates to the payment system. Futures are covered by an initial margin for each contract unit, typically $1,000, with the company agreeing to meet daily variations in the value of the future once this initial margin is breached (or receive money in the case of appreciation). Therefore currency risk is matched at the expense of exposing cash flows to future exchange rate movements and additional administrative work.

Currency exchange agreements
Currency exchange agreements relate to parallel loans and swaps. Parallel loans are the more traditional form. Under parallel loan agreements two companies have a requirement to raise similar amounts of finance in each other's currency contract to provide the other's need. Suppose A, a UK holding company had a subsidiary in the US which required dollar finance while X, a US holding company had a UK subsidiary which required sterling. Under the parallel loan system A lends sterling to the US subsidiary in the UK and X lends dollars to the UK subsidiary in the US. Currently more popular is the swap whereby the organizations agree to exchange funds directly. In a similar situation to that described for parallel loans, A would sell sterling spot to X in exchange for dollars at the current exchange rate. Simultaneously A and X contract to sell back the currency at an agreed future date and rate (usually that initially used). The currency thus raised is used by A and X to fund their subsidiaries. Figure 13.2 gives a diagrammatic representation of the processes involved.

Currency exchange agreements provide long-term exchange cover and avoid substantial transaction costs. Parallel loans are principally used to avoid exchange controls as no currency crosses international boundaries; while swaps avoid credit risk difficulties inherent in parallel loans.

Discounting
Bills of exchange denominated in a foreign currency may be discounted and converted at the current rate into sterling, the exchange risk being eliminated for the cost of the discount.

Factoring
As with domestic indebtedness, receivables factoring is available but only at considerable cost since the factoring company must price its services to cover the exchange risk. (See Chapter 14 for a detailed discussion of factoring.)

Government guarantees
In the UK a government body, the Export Credit Guarantee Department (ECGD), offers insurance against exchange risks. Policies, based upon payment of a premium, cover either exposure from a submitted tender

Parallel loan

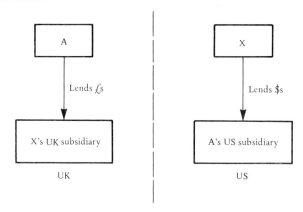

Swap

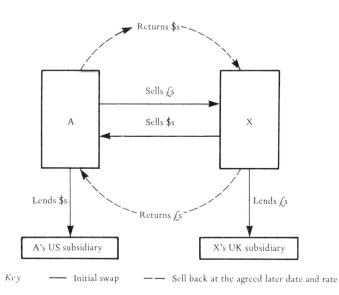

Key   —— Initial swap   – – Sell back at the agreed later date and rate

Figure 13.2 **Parallel loans and swaps**

to the award of a contract or the currency cash flows from a particular project. The advantage of using the government scheme is that cover is available for longer periods than with the normal forward markets and in the case of the tender to contract situation the firm avoids taking out a forward position which would be unmatched if the bid were unsuccessful.

Organizational considerations

The organizational structure developed by firms exposed to significant currency risk must reflect information and control requirements. Systems of data gathering aim at the provision of three levels of reporting. At the highest level there are strategic reports. They provide information upon the natural currency positions of the organization with a view to monitoring changes in circumstances impacting upon them, assessing the vulnerability of the organization to these positions and developing strategic responses. Examples of possible natural positions might be 'long in dollars' for a UK oil company, whose income is in dollars and expenses in a variety of currencies, or for a UK importer of Japanese cars, 'short in yen', unless the Japanese firm bills in sterling. Below this corporate planning level are tactical reports. These report transaction, liquidity, balance sheet and income statement exposure on a regular basis. The transaction report would cover known and anticipated receipts and payments for a given period ahead together with information upon existing cover against these cash flows. Liquidity reports would compare liquid assets against borrowings on a forecast basis. While the income statement and balance sheet exposure reports would analyse items by currency distinguishing between items translated at the current exchange rate and the historic rate due to their different treatments under current accounting standards. Examples of all four types of report are included in Tables 13.3–13.5.

Finally there are operating reports with information provided daily/ hourly on balances, currency movements and cover positions. These reports enable appropriate decisions to be made and positions entered into.

With respect to control, the crucial question in the area of currency risk management is the degree of centralization of the function. In the extremes either the group centre can deal with all situations involving currency risk or subsidiaries and operating units can be given complete autonomy. Between, central control could be exercised through issuing specific directives on the action to be taken when exposure arises or general guidelines on approaches with the centre offering an advisory service. The arguments for and against a centralized approach are little different to those for any other function. In brief centralization provides economies of scale in dealing since some deals will be unnecessary due to netting and matching and the centre will have access to the largest markets with the finest margins; whereas individual subsidiaries will

Table 13.3   Proforma tactical reports

Transaction exposure report	Periods					
Currency						
Line Date	1	2	3	4	5	6
1 Receipts – known	x	x	x	x	x	x
2 – estimated	x	x	x	x	x	x
3 Receipts exposure (1 + 2)	x	x	x	x	x	x
4 Existing cover	(x)	(x)	(x)	(x)	(x)	(x)
5 Net receipts exposure (3 – 4)	x	x	x	x	x	x
6 Payments – known	x	x	x	x	x	x
7 – estimated	x	x	x	x	x	x
8 Payments exposure (6 + 7)	x	x	x	x	x	x
9 Existing cover	(x)	(x)	(x)	(x)	(x)	(x)
10 Net payments exposure (8 – 9)	x	x	x	x	x	x
11 Netted exposure (5 – 10)	x	x	x	x	x	x

Liquidity exposure report	Periods					
Currency						
Line Date	1	2	3	4	5	6
Liquidity – cash	x	x	x	x	x	x
– short-term deposits	x	x	x	x	x	x
– long-term deposits	x	x	x	x	x	x
1 Total liquid resources	x	x	x	x	x	x
Borrowings – overdrafts	x	x	x	x	x	x
– bills/acceptance credits	x	x	x	x	x	x
– short-term loans	x	x	x	x	x	x
2 Total short-term borrowings	x	x	x	x	x	x
3 Net borrowing/liquidity (1 – 2)	x	x	x	x	x	x
4 Existing cover	(x)	(x)	(x)	(x)	(x)	(x)
Net liquidity exposure (3 – 4)	x	x	x	x	x	x

deal in small amounts in their markets and at poor margins. Further the centre can concentrate expertise and exclude the currency variable in the measurement of subsidiary performance. Against this the centre will lack local knowledge and will be removing from local management control of a key variable, which could have a disincentive effect. In practice where exposure is significant there is some form of central-ization with subsidiaries reporting all exposures above a set limit to the centre. Several different organizational systems can achieve this. At a partial level of centralization subsidiaries inform head office of expo-sures and their actions if any to cover them. Head office then takes the decision as to whether to cover any uncovered position or not. This gives the subsidiary local responsibility but leaves the group position under the centre. Because this system does not give dealing economies, some groups set up currency clearing centres to manage the risks. These are bodies through which subsidiaries in each clearing centre's sphere

Table 13.4 Balance sheet report

Balance sheet account	Items translated at current exchange rates				Items translated at historic exchange rates				Total exposure
	Local currency (amount)	Foreign currency (amount)	Conversion rate	Local equivalent rate	Local currency (amount)	Foreign currency (amount)	Conversion rate	Local equivalent rate	
Current assets (by category)									
Fixed assets (by category)									
Total assets									
Current liabilities (by category)									
Long-term liabilities (by category)									
Total liabilities									
Shareholder funding (by category)									
Total equity									
Total liabilities and equity									
Net exposed assets/liabilities									
Net covered assets/liabilities									
Uncovered net position									

Reproduced with permission from *Foreign Currency Exposure and Risk Management*, International Federation of Accountants, February 1987, Appendix 116, p. 18.

Table 13.5 Income statement report

Income statement category	Items translated at current exchange rates				Items translated at historic exchange rates				Total exposure
	Local currency (amount)	Foreign currency (amount)	Conversion rate	Local equivalent rate	Local currency (amount)	Foreign currency (amount)	Conversion rate	Local equivalent rate	
Revenues (by category)									
Less: Cost of sales (by category)									
Gross profit									
Less: Expenses (by category)									
Earnings before interest and tax interest									
Earnings before tax									
Tax									
Net income									
Net exposed position									
Net covered position									
Net uncovered position									

Reproduced with permission from *Foreign Currency Exposure and Risk Management*, International Federation of Accountants, February 1987, Appendix 116, p. 18.

of influence are expected to route foreign exchange denominated purchases and sales. The most sophisticated centralization systems involve reinvoicing centres, which centralize control of a group's exposure and liquidity systems. Reinvoicing centres are sited to tax and exchange control advantage and encompass inter-group and third party transactions. Unlike currency clearing centres, reinvoicing centres become legal owners of the goods. Essentially the reinvoicing centre buys products when the invoicing currency differs between the parties and ensures that each side of the transaction is in the appropriate currency of the buyer or seller. Thus if a UK subsidiary sells goods to a French counterpart, it invoices the goods to the reinvoicing centre in sterling and the centre bills the French unit in francs. Further if a UK subsidiary sells to a third party for any currency other than sterling a similar transaction takes place with the reinvoicing centre buying for sterling and selling on in the appropriate currency. As well as purchase and sale transactions reinvoicing centres can also move liquidity around the group with the centre absorbing the exchange risk. The administrative complexities involved limit reinvoicing centres to large multi-national organizations. In all these arrangements there is, of course, the trade off to be considered between possible additional expense and the added operational efficiency of centralized or partially centralized international currency management systems.

Taxation principles

Taxation and currency risk management is a lengthy and complex subject, perhaps involving the interaction of different countries' taxation systems. In practice tax advisers would be closely involved in the group's currency risk management strategy especially when major deals, for example swaps, are proposed. This section merely emphasizes that tax considerations are important and superficially discusses the UK taxation rules relating to exchange gains and losses, some of which are not recognized at all for taxation purposes; while others are categorized between trading and capital gains and losses. The effect of this is that there is a possibility that cover may not be effective if the two sides of the transaction are subject to different tax treatments.

The distinction between trading and capital gains and losses depends upon whether transactions are of a revenue or capital nature. Revenue transactions relate to the day-to-day trading activities of the business. They are assessed under Schedule D Case I as part of trading income and are subject to corporation tax at the current rate (year ended 31 March 1987 – 35 per cent). Capital transactions are best defined as those that relate to the financial structure or fixed asset base of the company. These are assessable to capital gains tax at the current rate (year ended 31 March 1987 – 30 per cent). Capital gains tax, however, has disadvantages. First losses can only be offset against capital gains of the same or future periods and second it only applies to assets. Therefore no relief is available for capital losses or liabilities. Thus, if a foreign currency borrowing is taken out to match an investment in the same currency and sterling weakens, the realization of the asset will give rise to a gain subject to capital gains tax whereas the loss on repayment of the loan will find no tax relief. The only exception to this rule is loans on security where the security is negotiable. For debts under this classification, losses are relievable and gains taxable under capital gains tax. Therefore a treasurer will attempt to make borrowings secured where they are expected to yield a loss but where gains are anticipated to make the debt unsecured in order that no capital gains tax is payable. Of course in practice, tax will only be one of several factors to be considered in decision making. Obviously a revenue/capital split is open to interpretation difficulties in certain cases and the third tax situation is for currency involvement to give rise to items of a revenue nature which are not associated with normal trading. These are charged under Schedule D Case VI, which restricts offset for losses to other Case VI income.

The treatment of hedging techniques depends upon the revenue capital classification but typically forward contracts, currency futures and options are treated as revenue unless circumstances dictate otherwise. Greater complexity arises with currency swaps since the sale back leg of the swap gives rise to a gain or loss, which for tax purposes is treated as arising at the date of the agreement. Therefore tax returns may have to be left open with potential liabilities for interest on overdue tax.

Forecasting

Forecasts of foreign exchange rates have an important role in treasury strategy and the active management of currency risk. Major forecasting approaches can be classified into intuitive, econometric and technical analysis systems.

The intuitive approach relies upon human expertise. Over a period of time a person involved in studying foreign exchange movements acquires a bank of knowledge from past situations, which is converted into a series of intuitive rules. The expert has the advantage of filtering information from formal approaches and external forecasting services into a coherent whole. The advantage of the intuitive approach is that responses to market changes can be virtually instantaneous.

Econometric approaches attempt to predict future exchange rates from underlying economic factors. A variety of hypotheses exist to link exchange rate variations with economic causation. Foremost amongst these is the 'Four Way Equivalence Model', which states that given open markets there is an equilibrium exchange rate for a currency determined by interest rate, inflation and spot to forward differentials. The four relationships in equilibrium are given by:

1   The interest parity theorem which holds that the difference between
    spot and forward rates equals the difference in interest rates be-
    tween the currencies.
2   The Fisher relation, which states that interest rate differentials
    reflect and are equal to differences in inflation rates.
3   The purchasing power parity theorem, which puts forward that
    currencies are valued according to purchasing power and therefore
    movements in spot rates will equal inflation differentials.
4   The forward parity theory, which contends that forward exchange
    rates are equivalent to future spot exchange rates.

Overall the 'Four Way Equivalence Model' is arguing that if real
interest rates and purchasing power between the domestic and foreign
economy are equal, then forward exchange rates will match future spot
rates. Other variables included in econometric exchange rate forecasts
relate to the balance of payments and money supply. An adverse balance of payments situation means that the supply of home currency on
world markets increases, pushing up the demand for foreign currency to
bridge the deficit with a consequent fall in home currency value (subject always to compensating capital movements). Similar monetary
growth ahead of output in an economy will have an impact upon
interest and inflation rates and weaken the value of the currency in
comparison with more strongly disciplined economies. Econometric
models incorporating some or all of the variables discussed have, in
practice, a mixed record of success in predicting exchange rate changes
over a variety of time periods.

   The technical analysis approach or chartism emphasizes not economic variables, on the grounds that investors are rarely wholly rational,
but the importance of market psychology and the repetitive nature of a
market's behaviour. The raison d'être is that patterns of price movements become familiar to a market and will be repeated. Therefore if
the nature of these patterns can clearly be established future exchange
rates will follow them and may accordingly be predicted. Patterns are
established by using and comparing trends calculated from a variety of
techniques and deriving rules based on discerned dependencies. Suppose that it is noted that usually after the strengthening of a currency
there is a fall; a company selling forward after the last strengthening
will make abnormal returns as against forward rates which will merely
reflect interest rate differentials.

   Given a series of forecasts generated by these different techniques,
how is a treasurer to decide upon likely future rates and act accordingly. In practice experience of past performance will enable the treasurer
to exercise judgement based on advice from a number of quarters and
this may be formalized into an opinion weighting system as shown in
Table 13.6.

   Table 13.6 shows, given weightings based on past experience, the
collected wisdom of a number of sources. In particular by looking at the
percentage of average deviation to expected value an idea of volatility

Table 13.6 Currency forecast analysis

Period forward: 3 months			Currency	
Source		$/£	Yen/£	FF/£
Econometric model	(1)	1.50	225.00	11.40
Chartists	(2)	1.48	230.00	10.20
Advisers	(3)	1.52	232.00	11.00
Market forward rate	(4)	1.50	230.00	11.60
Weighting	(1)	0.25	0.50	0.25
	(2)	0.25	0.20	0.25
	(3)	0.30	0.20	0.25
	(4)	0.20	0.10	0.25
Weighted average value		1.50	227.90	11.05
Average deviation*		0.01	2.8	0.45

* Deviations from weighted average value ignoring the sign divided by number of sources

can be obtained in this case the French franc is the most volatile at 4 per cent and the US dollar the least at 0.7 per cent.

Despite great effort from the worldwide financial community no foolproof forecasting system exists. The treasurer must therefore accept this uncertainty and attempt to make his decisions in the light of his own experience and information from a variety of forecasting models and sources.

Other matters

Two closely allied topics are now covered – the financing of overseas subsidiaries and exports. Financing any business requires balancing equity and debt sources, long and short-term components, and secured against unsecured positions within a framework of providing funds at a reasonable cost. Financing overseas subsidiaries has some additional problems in terms of country and currency risks.

Four main sources of funding are available: equity or loan finance from the parent; local borrowings; international borrowings; and intercompany credit. Investment by the parent in equity or loans issued by the subsidiary leads to both country and currency exposures. Country risk covers changes in political, economic and other environmental factors which impact upon the value of the funds committed. At the political level, the concern is with government action which devalues the investment including: confiscation, with or without compensation, of the business; nationalization through a majority government shareholding again with or without compensation; insistence upon its own nationals on the board and at manager level; high taxes; discriminating against 'foreign-owned' business when awarding contracts; and exchange controls preventing the realization of the funds committed or the remittance of interest and dividend income to the parent. Economic exposures, in country risk, refer to underlying economic situations within the country and cover factors like the rate of growth within the economy, inflation, availability of skilled labour and world debt problems. Obviously outside very stable countries, such as Switzerland and West Germany, these risks act as a disincentive to long-run parental funding. However, countries in their quest for foreign exchange injections into the economy will often legislate to prevent 'thin capitalization' and insist upon a minimum element of parental funding. At the currency risk level, parental funding opens transaction, translation and economic exposures. Funds cross borders and require conversion when the investment is made. Similarly during the investment period, there is a balance sheet exposure at each year end and transaction and economic exposure arise from the dividend, interest and repayment flows. Local borrowings circumvent most of the exposures mentioned to a greater or lesser extent. With respect to country risk, first, if funds do not cross borders, they cannot be blocked; second, assets that might be confiscated are matched by local liabilities, which would usually also be adopted and at an economic level the funds would reflect local conditions and interest rates. For currency risk no transaction risk arises since borrowings in the local currency are spent in the country; similarly translation risk can be managed by matching local assets with the borrowings to minimize net worth exposed. Problems may, however, arise when local borrowings are backed by parent company guarantees, which effectively undertake that the lender will be reimbursed by the parent in the event of the subsidiary defaulting. Further it could be argued that local borrowings, as the automatic choice for finance, leads to borrowing policy being dominated by the avoidance of country and currency risks. International borrowings may be resorted to as a first choice or when parental or local sources are insufficient. This option has no obvious benefits in avoiding country or currency risks but within the group context it may optimize group borrowing and currency risk situations. Inter-company credit covers short-run problems and is in essence akin to parental funding. On the inter-company accounts, subsidiaries owing money to the one being funded pay promptly and those owed money accept longer payment intervals. As the funding is essentially short run it presents a lower risk profile than equity or loan input by the parent.

While it may appear, in as far as it coincides with overall group borrowing strategy, that local borrowings are the best option; the decision must be taken in the light of the circumstances of each case and a knowledge of the tax and legal positions involved.

It might be thought that exports would be financed from the same sources as other elements of working capital. However, certain problems involved in the order to payment cycles are more acute in the case of exports. First, the length of the cycle is normally longer than for domestic sales and second the establishment of a customer's creditworthiness is more problematic. To counter these problems financing methods specific to exports have been developed.

Before addressing different forms of finance it is worth considering the steps which may be taken to gain assurance on the creditworthiness of the customer. The minimum approach is to investigate this through reference to credit agencies (for example Dun & Bradstreet), the British Overseas Trade Board or reports from the international banking system. The scrutiny of accounts obtained through specialist agencies, such as Extel or direct may also be attempted but there should be caution about the quality of the information. In many cases a business will resort to credit insurance provided by either ECGD or private insurers. ECGD is most widely used and offers three main types of policy.

1 Comprehensive – appropriate to continuous and repetitive export business. It covers, subject to certain specified exclusions, a company for either 90 per cent or 95 per cent, depending upon the reason for default, of the loss due to non-payment. The loss being based on incurred costs up to shipment and shipment value thereafter. The cover relates to all a company's exports of goods and services, unless specifically excluded, for a predetermined period.
2 Services – covers companies carrying out services for organizations overseas and includes payments for licences, royalties and patents as well as maintenance and consultancy work. Terms are similar to comprehensive cover.
3 Specific   intended to cover projects which are too large to be included in comprehensive policies. The extent and terms of cover are subject to negotiation and often linked to the finance method.

The main sources of export finance are: bills of exchange; secured bank lending; documentary letters of credit; acceptance credits; and export factoring. Let us consider each in turn.

Bills of exchange

A supplier may arrange for the overseas customer to accept a bill of exchange drawn on him for the value of the goods and services to be supplied. The bill may either be payable on acceptance (sight bill) or at a future date (term bill). Bills are usually executed through banks and it is common to give the banks the shipping and title transfer documents for release only on payment or acceptance. The principal advantage for the supplier is that the bill of exchange can be negotiated with the bank for immediate cash, less the discount and service charge. However, the system does not remove credit risk, and should the customer default the bank has recourse to the supplier for the face value of the bill. Where an exporter sells regularly abroad through bills of exchange, the bank may agree to a line of credit whereby it is prepared to negotiate any bills up to an overall limit.

Secured bank lending

As well as negotiating bills, banks can provide secured finance for exports. For instance, instead of being negotiated an accepted bill of exchange may be used as security for an advance of usually 80–90 per cent of its face value with the loans repayable from the proceeds of the bill. Another source of security for a bank loan on exports is an ECGD banker's guarantee, which may either be indirect or direct. Indirect guarantees relate to the exporter assigning his rights under an ECGD credit insurance policy to the bank when seeking to borrow on the security of bills or promissory notes. Obviously the bank will only advance the portion covered but in the event of a customer default the bank has recourse to ECGD. The problems with this as security is that the default may be for a reason not covered by the ECGD policy or the fault may lie with the supplier. To overcome this ECGD offers a range of direct guarantees covering short to medium-time periods. Direct guarantees cover supplier credits under which ECGD guarantees to support a loan from the bank to the exporter, and buyer credits whereby ECGD guarantees loans by UK banks to the customer to enable him to pay the exporter. In either case, as ECGD is meant to cover its costs and losses, a premium is payable for this security.

Documentary letters of credit

Documentary letters of credit are agreed as a payment method when the contract is signed. The buyer agrees with his nominated bank (the issuing bank) that a credit should be set up to be drawn off in accordance with a detailed schedule analysing the contract into its constituent parts. For each part there is a detailed description of the goods, their quality and price, and the range of dates when documents proving shipment may be presented for payment. The sum of the parts adds up to the credit negotiated by the buyer and the availability of the finance is guaranteed by the issuing bank to an advising bank which acts on behalf of the exporter. When the exporter despatches goods he presents the agreed documents (bills of lading, insurance certificates, inspection reports, invoices etc.) to the advising bank who provides payment under the method agreed, which could be cash or acceptance of a bill of exchange. The advising bank sends the documents to the issuing bank which pays the advising bank before passing on the documents to the importer to enable him to take delivery. If the advising bank also enters into guaranteeing the credit it is termed the confirming bank. The system requires close cooperation from banks and firms must be careful to ensure that documents presented conform with the original credit line terms. Procedures adopted by banks are formulated by the International Chamber of Commerce.

Acceptance credits

Large companies have access through merchant banks to acceptance credits – also known as accommodation finance. The merchant bank accepts bills, up to an agreed limit, drawn on it by the exporter in exchange for security in the form of the bill drawn on the overseas customer. The exporter has a more readily discountable bill, which will attract a lower discount rate, with which to obtain finance; while the merchant bank has a trade bill as security. As the security is imperfect the creditworthiness of the exporter must be excellent.

Export Factoring

As in the domestic market, factoring may be available for export business. The services available can include a combination of finance secured on invoices, credit insurance, and assistance with documentation and sales accounting. Typically the service is expensive with appeal mainly to smaller businesses.

Summary

Currency risk management is a major responsibility for the treasurer. This chapter has analysed the risk into its component parts and discussed the strategies appropriate to managing each category of a risk. Further the chapter has examined the techniques available to the treasurer and considered the organizational and information system consequences of the risks faced. Finally discussion has covered specific topics regarding the financing of overseas subsidiaries and exports.

In conclusion it is worth reiterating that currency risk is but one of many risks faced by the treasurer and the business. Therefore it should be viewed in context and readers should refrain from the idea that currency risk strategies are ends in themselves and no merely an element in the formulation of overall corporate objectives and policies.

Appendix 13.1: Exposure*

Definition

Foreign currency exposure is the extent to which transactions, assets and liabilities of an enterprise are denominated in currencies other than the reporting currency of the enterprise itself. The results and financial position of the enterprise are, therefore, susceptible to variations in foreign currency exchange rates. It is a neutral concept involving the identification of existing and/or future currency relationships which arise from the activities of an enterprise and is, therefore, a statement of fact.

---

* Reproduced with permission from *Foreign Currency Exposure and Risk Management*, International Federation of Accountants, February 1987

Types of exposure

Transaction exposure

This is also referred to as conversion exposure or cash flow exposure. It concerns the actual cash flows involved in settling transactions denominated in a foreign currency. The existence of an exposure alerts one to the fact that any change in currency rates, between the time the transaction is initiated and the time it is settled, will most likely alter the originally perceived financial result of the transaction. It is, for example, important to commence tracking the exposure from the time an order is initiated, not merely when delivery takes place. The financial or conversion gain or loss is the difference between the actual cash flow in the domestic currency and the cash flow as calculated at the time the transaction was initiated.

Translation exposure

This is also referred to as accounting exposure or balance sheet exposure. The restatement of foreign financial statements in terms of a reporting currency is termed translation and the exposure arises from the periodic need to report consolidated worldwide operations of a group in one reporting currency.

It is measured at the time of translating foreign financial statements for reporting purposes and indicates or exposes the possibility that the foreign currency denominated financial statement elements can change and give rise to further translation gains or losses, depending on the movement that takes place in the currencies concerned after the reporting date. Such translation gains and losses do not represent realized cash flows unless, or until, the assets or liabilities are settled or liquidated in whole or in part.

Economic exposure

Economic exposure is concerned with the strategic evaluation of foreign transactions and relationships. On the one hand it concerns the expected change in future cash flows which may arise because of changes in exchange rates, and on the other, its operating position. Its determination requires an understanding of the structure of the markets in which an enterprise and its competitors obtain capital, labour, materials, services and customers. Identification of this exposure focuses attention on that component of an enterprise's value that is dependent on, or vulnerable to, future exchange rate movements. This has bearing on a corporation's commitment, competitiveness and viability in its involvement in foreign markets and its susceptibility to foreign competition in its domestic markets. Thus, economic exposure refers to the possibility that the value of the enterprise, defined as the net present value of future after tax cash flows, will change when exchange rates change.

Economic exposure can have more important significance than transaction or translation exposure to the long term well-being of the enterprise. By its very nature, it is subjective and variable, due to the need to estimate future cash flows in foreign currencies. Once a foreign investment is made or a foreign transaction entered into, the enterprise cannot do very much except respond in the best way possible as economic conditions change.

Further reading

OVERVIEW ARTICLES:

The Treasurer, September 1985, a collection of seven articles on foreign exchange exposure management covering transaction exposure management, translation exposure management, economic exposure, futures and swaps, options, taxation and a systematic approach to hedging.

Willingham, D., 'Fluctuating Exchange Rates and International Business', *Management Accounting*, September 1982.

RELEVANT ARTICLES:

Aylward, J., 'Keeping your Options Open against Currency Risk', *Accountancy*, June 1985.

Bailie, R. and McMahan, P., 'Forecasting Foreign Exchange Rates', *The Accountant*, 20 November 1985.

Collier, P. and Davis, E. W., 'Currency Risk Management in UK Multinationals', *Accounting and Business Research*, Autumn 1985.

Dare, P., 'Getting a Good Foreign Exchange Deal', *Accountancy*, August 1981.

Furse, C., 'Chartists Fly the Flag', *The Accountant*, 7 August 1985.

Gillet, P., 'Managing Foreign Exchange Exposure', *Accountancy*, May 1985.

Hughes, S. and Redhead, K., 'Liability Management with Swaps', *Management Accounting*, January 1987.

Martin, I., 'Foreign Exchange: An Old Game With New Players', *Accountancy*, July 1985.

RELEVANT BOOKS:

Buckley, A., *Multinational Finance*, Philip Allan, 1986.

Donaldson, J., 'Corporate Currency Risk', *The Financial Times*, 1981.

International Federation of Accountants, *Foreign Currency Exposure and Risk Management*, IFAC, 1987.

McRae, T. W. and Walker, D. P., *Foreign Exchange Management*, Prentice-Hall, 1980.

Rodrigues, R. M. and Carter, E. E., *International Financial Management* (3rd edition), Prentice-Hall, 1981.

Shapiro, A. C., *Multinational Financial Management* (2nd edition), Allyn & Bacon, 1986.

14 Short-term funding

A distinction is often made between the money markets, which deal with short-term loans, and the capital markets, which exist for the raising of long-term funds. This chapter deals specifically with the main methods of raising short-term funds, particularly to enhance a company's working capital position. The institutions involved have already been covered in Chapter 12. The main sources of short-term finance are covered here together with a discussion of international money and capital markets and the management of a debt portfolio.

Bank borrowing – overdrafts

Traditionally, raising finance in the form of an overdraft from a bank has been one of the most important external sources of short-term finance, particularly for small businesses. The Bolton Report (1971) found that the level of reliance by small firms on bank overdrafts was staggering. Indeed, up until the mid-1970s small firms were reluctant to look further than the commercial banks for finance. However, since the mid-1970s the banks have had to face increasing competition in this area and the consequence is that there are a number of alternative sources of finance. Nevertheless a bank overdraft still remains popular.

The popularity of an overdraft is due to a number of reasons. The loan is flexible in that a bank agrees a limit (facility amount) and the client can call off money up to that amount when funds are required. Arrangements are normally informal and applications for extensions of the overdraft can be quickly dealt with. Legal documentation is kept to a minimum and typically amounts to a letter from the bank advising on the facility, the interest to be charged, when the bank will review the facility and any security that may be required. The banks prefer self-liquidating loans, i.e. an overdraft used for a specific short-term project that will generate sufficient cash to repay both interest and principal. Often an overdraft will be used to even out cash flow where the business is subject to seasonal fluctuations, e.g. farming.

The rate of interest that the bank will charge will depend upon the creditworthiness of the client and the purpose for which the loan is to be applied. Typically the rate will vary between 1 and 4 per cent above base rate and is charged on the outstanding balance only. In cases where the business continually has an overdraft the bank may deem part of the overdraft to constitute term-lending and charge a higher rate of interest on the hardcore element.

The main disadvantage of an overdraft is that the overdrawn balance is repayable on demand and the facility can be withdrawn at any time. It is not usual for a bank to withdraw the facility without good reason or prior notification although the banks are subject to their own pressures of limitations on lending and an obligation to meet all cash withdrawals. Banks have limits on their lending which depend upon the maturity structure of their assets and liabilities, cash and liquidity ratios, and an obligation to comply with official monetary and credit controls.

Another characteristic of an overdraft is that due to the fact that it is repayable on demand, funds should be used to finance short-term fluctuations and short-term projects and should not be used for long-term projects, or to fund dividend payments as occurred in the late 1970s.

Trade credit

Trade credit is a valuable source of short-term finance because it is convenient and readily available – goods are received and payment becomes due at a later date. No formal credit application is required although a prudent seller should always assess the creditworthiness of new customers. The terms of a sale are those negotiated by seller and buyer but typically payment becomes due thirty days after invoice with an incentive, in the form of a discount, being offered for early payment. For example, a 2 per cent discount may be offered for payment within ten days or net thirty days ($2/10$ net 30). As a result of incentives being offered for early payment there is an opportunity cost involved in not taking the discount. The annualized cost for a £100 invoice can be determined as follows:

$$\frac{(\text{invoice value} \times \text{discount offered})}{\text{invoice value} - \text{discount on invoice}} \times \frac{\text{number of days in the year}}{\text{period between payment dates}}$$

$$\frac{(100 \times 2\%)}{(100 - 2)} \times \frac{365}{(30 - 10)} = 37.2\% \text{ p.a.}$$

For a £500 invoice with identical terms of sale of $2/10$ net 30 the annualized cost is the same:

$$\frac{(500 \times 2\%)}{(500 - 10)} \times \frac{365}{(30 - 10)} = 37.2\% \text{ p.a.}$$

Since the opportunity cost is expressed as an annualized percentage it is possible to generalize the formula for all invoice values to:

$$\frac{\text{discount percentage}}{100 - \text{discount percentage}} \times \frac{\text{number of days in the year}}{\text{period between payment dates}}$$

Whether a discount is sufficient to warrant early payment depends on the relationship between the rate of return that can be obtained by investing the money elsewhere between day ten and day thirty and the implied cost of interest as calculated above. If the return on investing the funds elsewhere is less than 37.2 per cent per annum it will be profitable to accept the discount whereas if the return elsewhere is greater than 37.2 per cent per annum it will be beneficial not to make the early payment but to invest in the more profitable alternative.

The terms of trade credit vary from industry to industry and depend upon a number of other factors. For example, the type of product influences terms because high turnover goods are sold on short credit, e.g. groceries, whereas low turnover goods, e.g. furniture, have longer periods of credit. As well as the economic nature of the product the financial circumstances of seller and buyer are also important. Obviously if a seller is in a weak financial position he would prefer early settlement or not to offer credit at all. However, pressures will usually force the seller to offer terms similar to those of its competitors. In contrast, a weak buyer would prefer to take a long time before final settlement is made in which case the seller may offer a higher cash discount in order to encourage early settlement.

In addition to the factors discussed above, trade credit varies from industry to industry for other reasons. For example, companies involved in long-term contracts will not be willing to accept settlement once the project is completed but will require stage payments as the work progresses. Furthermore, special features of trade credit exist in certain industries. For example, brewers often provide loans for the fitting out of licensed properties, and petrol companies sometimes provide funds for fitting out garage forecourts. The terms of such loans are normally more favourable than bank loans although conditions may be imposed that will reduce the proprietor's independence of operation.

While trade credit is convenient, flexible and useful, especially to small firms that may not be able to borrow from financial institutions, disadvantages do exist. Since trade credit generates a degree of loyalty between buyer and seller, failure to pay on time can lead to a loss of goodwill and the accumulation of debt. Furthermore, trade credit has a double-edged significance. For example:

Purchases each day on average £50,000
If average creditors payments extend to 25 days
    then average creditors will be: £1,250,000

Sales each day on average £80,000
If average debtors' payments extend to 30 days
  then average debtors will be: £2,400,000
The company is extending net credit continuously of   £1,150,000

(This represents approximately £75,000 interest per annum at an after tax rate of interest of 6.5 per cent.)

Until the late 1970s and particularly during the liquidity crisis of 1973–4 large firms tended to be net suppliers of trade credit to the advantage of smaller and less well capitalized companies. However, recession in world trade in the late 1970s and early 1980s coupled with an increasing tendency for businesses to fail has changed that position. Indeed, some large companies are now net takers of trade credit.

Factoring

Factoring involves raising funds on the strength of a company's debts in order to release working capital tied up in credit to customers for more profitable use. There are two types of factoring: sales ledger factors and confidential invoice factoring (invoice discounting).

Sales ledger factoring is commonly referred to merely as factoring. The factor is responsible for the whole of the sales ledger administration and credit protection. In addition, the factor may offer a non-recourse service whereby full credit protection is provided on all approved sales, thereby guaranteeing payment in the event of a bad debt. In contrast, the recourse factor will not offer credit protection as part of the service, and in the event of customer default the factor has recourse to his client. The company itself must make the decision on the type of factoring it requires after considering the relative costs and benefits presented by the alternatives and by assessing which system best suits the company's needs.

The essence of factoring is that the seller receives early payment of its debts by receiving an advance from the factor against invoices accepted for factoring. Up to 80 per cent of the invoice value can be made available immediately with the balance being paid when the customers pay the factor or after an agreed period. The advantage of this operation is that funds are released more quickly enabling the company to make accurate cash-flow planning a reality. These funds can then be used to pay suppliers more promptly, thereby improving its credit reputation and enabling it to obtain quantity and financial discounts offered by suppliers. Another way in which factoring can facilitate budgeting is by smoothing out seasonal fluctuations in demands for cash. A further advantage of factoring is that as sales increase factored debts automatically increase and advances increase. A more dubious advantage is that factoring represents a form of off-balance sheet finance.

While factoring may save costs of running a sales ledger and generates cash more quickly the factor undertakes these services at a cost.

Costs consist of a fee for the services rendered and a separate charge for the finance made available against sales. The service fee is determined for each client and depends upon the volume of sales, the type of industry in which the client operates, the average value of invoices and the number of customers and whether credit protection is provided. These charges vary between about 0.5 per cent and 2.5 per cent of gross annual turnover. The charge for finance, as and when it is taken, is geared to current base rates and is commensurate with bank overdraft rates of about 1 to 2 per cent over base.

The disadvantage of factoring, other than its costs, is that factors are usually not interested in companies with a large number of accounts consisting mainly of small value transactions since administrative costs become excessive. Factors are typically looking for companies that are soundly managed and growing profitably with a turnover in excess of £100,000 per annum. Sales should consist of products or services on short-term credit to trade customers in the UK or abroad.

The second type of factoring is called invoice discounting and involves a factor providing a cash advance on either all sales invoices or those on selected accounts. The service is normally provided on a recourse basis although non-recourse invoice discounting can be arranged in some circumstances. This form of factoring is sometimes referred to as confidential invoice factoring as the client remains responsible for its own accounts' collection and credit administration. Invoice discounting is a form of off-balance sheet finance that is available to businesses with good accounts administration and low bad debt risk.

The main charge for invoice discounting is a discount charge linked to base rates. As with full factoring, the charge is calculated on a day-to-day basis on funds actually used. In addition, a commission on sales is levied to cover the administration of the arrangement.

An Association of British Factors was formed in 1976 which has eight members. Companies and associations like to show growth in their business over time and this is easier to do if historical figures are used – every Christmas heralds record sales! However, if the historical figures are adjusted for the effects of inflation, here defined as changes in the retail price index, then a better picture of the overall trend is revealed. Table 14.1 demonstrates the historical and inflation-adjusted trend. Whereas the historical figures demonstrate almost uninterrupted growth it is noticeable that the inflation-adjusted figures demonstrate lower levels of factoring business in 1980 and 1981 followed by growth.

The factoring figures can be disaggregated into domestic, non-recourse and recourse, and international business and this is shown in Table 14.2. A noticeable feature is that recourse factoring has become more important over the period although non-recourse factoring still accounts for two-thirds of the domestic business. In 1976 non-recourse factoring accounted for 84 per cent of the domestic business but by 1986 this had fallen to 66 per cent.

Table 14.3 shows that there were increases in numbers in all categories of turnover although in percentage terms, clients with turnovers

Table 14.1 Growth in factoring business

Year	£m	RPI average for the year	Inflation adjusted figures	Growth rate (%)
1976	629	100	629	–
1977	703	115.85	607	(3)
1978	1,021	125.46	814	34
1979	1,325	142.27	931	14
1980	1,463	167.86	871	(6)
1981	1,454	187.78	774	(11)
1982	1,674	203.95	821	6
1983	1,998	213.30	937	14
1984	2,590	223.93	1157	23
1985	2,931	237.56	1234	7
1986	3,358	245.64	1367	11

Source: Association of British Factors

Table 14.2 Domestic and international factoring

Year	Domestic Non-recourse (£m)	Recourse (£m)	Total (£m)	International (£m)	Total (£m)
1976	441	83	524	105	629
1977	446	122	568	135	703
1978	691	153	844	177	1021
1979	891	220	1111	214	1325
1980	941	283	1224	239	1463
1981	917	283	1200	254	1454
1982	1056	364	1420	254	1674
1983	1185	563	1748	250	1998
1984	1502	771	2273	317	2590
1985	1710	861	2571	360	2931
1986	1922	1008	2930	428	3358

Source: Association of British Factors

Table 14.3 Analysis of clients by size

Size of client's turnover (£000)	1985 Number	Percent	1986 Number	Percent
0–250	1165	31.8	1313	31.7
251–500	829	22.7	840	20.3
501–1000	751	20.5	830	20.0
1001–2000	508	13.9	618	14.9
2001–5000	284	7.8	396	9.6
5001 +	121	3.3	148	3.5
	3658	100.0	4145	100.0

Source: Association of British Factors

Table 14.4   Analysis of clients by type of business

| | 1985 | | 1986 | |
	Number	Percent	Number	Percent
Manufacturing				
Textiles	164	4.5	110	2.7
Furniture/timber processing	205	5.6	167	4.0
Rubber and plastics	141	3.9	140	3.4
Metal goods	623	17.0	461	11.1
Clothing and footwear	182	5.0	120	2.9
Other	372	10.1	623	15.0
	1687	46.1	1621	39.1
Distribution				
Metals	178	4.9	249	6.0
Building materials	108	3.0	152	3.7
Textiles, toys, luxury goods	355	9.7	336	8.1
Other industrial materials	434	11.8	695	16.8
	1075	29.4	1432	34.8
Services				
Printing and publishing	300	8.2	354	8.5
Business services	349	9.5	409	9.9
Catering and other	247	6.8	329	7.9
	896	24.5	1092	26.3
Total	3658	100.0	4145	100.0

Source: Association of British Factors

of up to £0.5 fell between 1985 and 1986 from 55 per cent to 52 per cent. Clients with turnovers in excess of £1m accounted for 28 per cent in 1986 compared with 25 per cent in 1985. Table 14.4 provides an analysis of clients by type of business and shows increases in the distribution and services sectors and a decline in the manufacturing sector.

Bills of exchange

A bill of exchange is defined in Section 3 of the Bills of Exchange Act 1882 as: 'An unconditional order in writing, addressed by one person to another, signed by the person giving it, requiring the person to whom it is addressed to pay on demand, or at a fixed or determinable future time, a sum certain in money to, or to the order of, a specified person, or to bearer.'

A trade bill is a bill of exchange as defined under the above Act and is characterized by the fact that it is not endorsed by a bank. A trade bill is drawn by the seller and forwarded to the buyer for goods purchased. The terms of the bill include the amount to be paid, and in what currency, and the due date for payment. The date for payment may be an actual date or it may be a certain period after sight or after a specific event. A bill can be drawn for any period of time although only one, two, three or six month bills are usually prepared. In practice a ninety day bill is the most common.

A bill that is drawn and is payable in the UK is referred to as an inland bill and all other bills are called foreign bills. The distinction is only important in the case of default.

When the buyer receives the goods and the bill of exchange he signs the latter to confirm that he accepts the liability for the transaction. The bill is returned to the seller who either holds it until it matures or sells it to a bank for a sum less than the face value which reflects the cost of finance. A bank will only be willing to purchase the bill if the credit-worthiness of the buyer and seller is good although the bank does have recourse to both parties.

The advantage of such an operation as far as the seller is concerned is that it can receive most of the invoice value before maturity of the bill thereby providing a source of finance. The seller does have a contingent liability for the bill since the bank has recourse against it.

From the buyer's point of view a bill of exchange often provides an extended period of credit and thereby is an effective source of funds to itself. The advantage from the bank's perspective is that it is a profitable source of business and in the case of default it has recourse to the buyer who accepted it. The fact that the buyer accepted the bill is sufficient proof that the debt is good. Furthermore, if the buyer cannot meet its obligation the bank has recourse to the seller. A trade bill with a good credit risk is referred to as a fine trade bill. Where there is concern about a particular transaction or the parties involved, it is sometimes possible for a credit insurance company to provide a guarantee for a premium which will enable the bill to be discounted at a reasonable rate.

The Radcliffe Committee 1959 noted an irreversible decline in bill financing due in particular to a series of credit squeezes. There has been a revival in the late 1970s and early 1980s in their use although trade bills do not provide a major source of finance for many companies. One of the problems of a trade bill is that although it is a useful source of short-term finance it is linked to transactions which increase administrative costs. An alternative is for a bill of exchange to be used as a source of short-term finance without the need to link it with a transaction. This type of funding is referred to as an acceptance credit.

The use of acceptance credits has grown considerably in the late 1970s and 1980s, particularly by large and medium-sized companies. This source of finance is the next most important external source of finance after bank borrowing and effectively provides an overdraft facility for short-term requirements that is not recorded in the balance sheet. A bill is drawn by a company and accepted by an accepting house which pays a cash advance to the drawer. The accepting house can either hold the bill until maturity or rediscount it through bill brokers.

The setting up of the facility is similar to negotiating any other bank line. The accepting house offers an agreed line at a certain commission rate depending upon the purpose for which finance is required and the financial structure of the company. The normal minimum level for a facility is £100,000 with the maximum level being about £500,000 and since it is normally undertaken on an unsecured basis the company must be one of financial standing that can easily support the loan. While acceptance credits have often been used to finance international trade they are also used for financing working capital. The purchase of fixed assets by acceptance credits is not appropriate since the credits are concerned with self-liquidating short-term transactions.

Acceptance credits are categorized into eligible and ineligible bills depending upon their status with the Bank of England. A bill that is accepted by an eligible bank (the major banks and accepting houses only) and has a clause stating the transactions the funds are to be used for, constitutes an eligible bill. An eligible bill can be discounted at finer rates than an ineligible bill.

Acceptance credits range from thirty days to 180 days with the most common being for ninety days. Costs consist of an acceptance commission and the discount based on prevailing discount rates which depend on market conditions. An acceptance commission is paid at the time of acceptance of up to 0.5 per cent per annum on the amount of the bill and not on the discounted proceeds. In addition to acceptance commission and discount charges a fee may be levied to cover the facility. Whether there is an interest rate advantage in favour of acceptance credits depends upon the rate of discount, which is known at the time of acceptance, and current money market rates. Where money market rates are rising over the period there may be an advantage to have an acceptance credit facility and vice versa.

Hire purchase (instalment credit)

Hire purchase is a convenient source of finance for buying plant and equipment since it releases funds for other uses. The large capital outlay is not required to purchase the equipment, so that for a small outlay the asset can be used to generate cash flow. The hiree company obtains the writing down allowances against tax as if the firm had purchased the asset although strictly speaking, from a legal point of view, the hirer remains the legal owner until the final payment is made. An additional advantage of hire purchase is that 'skip arrangements' can sometimes be made whereby instalments may be omitted at certain times during the year, usually when seasonal trade is low.

A feature of the agreement is that the equipment must be readily identifiable and its effective life should exceed the period of the agreement so that in the case of default a valuable asset can be taken and disposed of. In practice, hire purchase agreements do not usually extend beyond five years. The main advantage is that the cost of finance is expensive, typically between 20 per cent and 40 per cent.

Hire purchase is the best known form of instalment credit but other forms include credit sales, conditional sales and equipment leasing. A credit sale has already been dealt with in this chapter. A conditional sale is one in which the seller retains ownership of a good until the final payment is made. Equipment leasing is of sufficient importance to be dealt with separately.

Equipment leasing

In 1971 the Equipment Leasing Association (ELA) was formed to represent the interests of its seventy-two member companies and to provide a framework within which business should be conducted. The ELA has defined a lease as 'a contract between lessor and lessee for hire of a specific asset selected from a manufacturer or vendor of such assets by the lessee. The lessor retains ownership of the asset. The lessee has possession and use of the asset on payment of specified rentals over a period.'

Legally a lease is a contract of bailment in which there is a contract between owner and user for the letting of a specific asset. The lessee has the right to use the asset for a fixed period of time, unless there is a breach of the agreement, for a specified rental. The rental sometimes consists of a primary period, the period over which the lessor recoups its investment and makes its profit, and a secondary period in which the lessee may continue to use the asset for a nominal or peppercorn rent. A feature of a lease contract is that the lessor retains legal ownership of the leased contract and the lessee has no right or obligation to acquire the asset when the lease term expires.

Leases may be classified into operating and finance leases. This distinction depends upon the role of the lessor – does the lessor regard himself as lending money to obtain interest, or does the lessor regard himself as operating an asset in order to make a profit from it?

A lessor is normally responsible for maintenance and insurance in an operating lease whereas a finance lease normally requires the lessee to be liable for these costs. Under an operating lease the lessee may be able to return the asset prematurely without incurring a major penalty whereas penalty clauses are often inserted in a finance lease for premature termination of the lease. A key distinction between the two types of lease is that the lessee contracts to use an asset for only part of its useful life in an operating lease whereas the lessee will contract for the whole, or essentially all, of the expected life of the asset in a finance lease. In summary, an operating lease is one in which the risks and long-term benefits of the asset are retained substantially by the lessor and the emerging profit depends to a great extent on the asset value at the end of the lease. In contrast, a finance lease or full-payout lease is one in

Table 14.5   Growth in leasing business

Year	£million	RPI average for the year	Inflation-adjusted figures	Growth rate (%)
1976	421	100	421	–
1977	675	115.85	583	38
1978	1,214	125.46	968	66
1979	1,802	142.27	1,267	31
1980	2,359	167.86	1,405	11
1981	2,674	187.78	1,424	1
1982	2,834	203.95	1,390	(2)
1983	2,894	213.30	1,357	(2)
1984	4,012	223.93	1,792	32
1985	5,757	237.56	2,423	35
1986	5,182	245.64	2,110	(13)

which the risks and benefits of the asset are conveyed substantially to the lessee and the emerging profit depends, not on the terminal value of the asset, but rather on the finance charges levied.

The growth in leasing business since 1976 is shown in Table 14.5. Until 1986 the ELA has described each year as another record performance and for 1986 the Association described performance as 'only slightly less than the £5,757m of assets leased in 1985, the last full year before the new corporate tax system was finally phased in'. However, by adjusting the figures for the retail price index there appears to have been a surge in activity between 1977 and 1979, followed by a relative plateau and then considerable growth in 1984 and 1985.

Leasing developed rapidly between 1977 and 1979 because much of industry was in a non-taxpaying position. This arose because of generous 100 per cent first-year allowances on the purchase of plant and machinery and other concessions such as stock relief. As a result many companies had carried forward taxable losses so that if additional plant and equipment was purchased capital allowances could not be relieved until the company made taxable profits. In contrast, financial institutions such as banks always seem to have taxable profits regardless of recession or boom. As such, additional capital allowances to relieve their tax burden are always welcomed by them. Due to the lack of symmetry between the taxation position of different companies, leasing schemes became popular in which the lessor, usually a financial institution, purchased plant and equipment and obtained the first year allowances. These allowances could be offset quickly against taxable profits. If a contract is then written which passes substantially all the risks and rewards of that asset to another company (the lessee), it is possible for the lessor to pass on some of the taxation benefits to the non-tax paying lessee in the form of reduced rentals. Thus, taxation has been an important factor in the growth of leasing.

Growth in real terms in leased assets was curtailed in the period 1981–3 and was followed by an upsurge in 1984–5. This upsurge in activity can be explained, to a large extent, by the Finance Act 1984. This Act started the process of reducing the corporation tax rate from 50 per cent in 1983 to 35 per cent in 1986 coupled with the abandonment of 100 per cent first-year allowances on plant and machinery, to be replaced by 25 per cent annual writing down allowances. The upsurge in activity can be accounted for as a rush to write contracts before the final implementation of the Act, although improvements in the economy also led to an increase in industrial investment. The fall in leasing business in 1986 reflects the start of the post-implementation period of the new tax regime. It represents the first fall in activity.

What happens in the future depends upon the ability of lessors to convince companies that leasing is worthwhile for other reasons. Other reasons for leasing include the flexibility of such an operation, particularly where high technology goods are involved. In areas such as computer equipment a company may wish to renew after a short period of time. However, finance companies are aware of such strategies and will ensure that the lease payments reflect anticipated obsolescence. The following other advantages may also ensue:

1 Rentals are tax deductible.
2 An asset can be used efficiently without actually owning it.
3 By leasing instead of outright purchase, funds are released for other more profitable uses.
4 It is easier and quicker to arrange than many other sources of finance.
5 Maintenance normally obtained under an operating lease agreement may be better than could be provided oneself.
6 There is flexibility through the matching of rental payments to the lessee's cash flows.
7 Medium to long-term finance is provided at fixed or variable rates to match the lessee's needs.
8 Finance is guaranteed for the period of the contract.
9 In the past the advantage as a source of off-balance sheet financing has also been important.

While the above advantages will undoubtedly be emphasized by the ELA two key issues that will affect business will be taxation and the financial accounting aspect of leased assets. Concern about the 1984 Finance Act led the ELA to sponsor two independent studies of different aspects of the tax changes. One study by Lewis and Morgan (1985) used both economic analysis, through computer simulations using a macroeconomic model and a corporate sector database and fieldwork interviews with a sample of lessee companies. The main finding of the report was that by 1991 the level of industrial and commercial investment in the UK could be 4 per cent lower than would otherwise be the case, as a result of the tax changes. The effect of these tax changes was considered equivalent to that of a sustained 4.5 per cent increase in interest rates. Furthermore, the findings assumed a 5 per cent average future inflation rate whereas the situation might be considerably worse if the inflation rate rose above that level.

A second report prepared by Ernst and Whinney found that the reduction in incentives to leasing would lead to a fall in the attractiveness of the UK from fourth to seventh place among the nine major OECD countries.

Concern about the medium-term effects of the tax changes prompted the ELA's Chairman to issue a press release in 1987 stating that '25 per cent writing down allowances are inadequate to match the true depreciation cycle of many types of equipment. We remain concerned at the longer term outlook for UK fixed investment under the new tax systems, particularly in the light of the incentives available for fixed investment in competing countries overseas.'

A second important development has been the implementation of SSAP 21, accounting for leases and hire purchase agreements, which was introduced in 1984. The standard requires lessees to capitalize assets subject to a finance lease in the same way that assets purchased on hire purchase are treated as if bought outright. The essence of this is that economic substance should take precedence over legal form. The ELA was opposed to the standard for two reasons. First, by enforcing capitalization it eliminates it as a source of off-balance sheet financing. Second, there was concern that the Inland Revenue may change the practice of giving writing down allowances to the lessor and instead give them to the lessee. The Revenue has stated that the change in financial reporting does not imply a change in taxation treatment. However, the Revenue has been concerned about the possibility of duplicated claims for capital allowances. In response the ELA has advised member companies that leasing agreements written after 1 September 1986 that involve the lessor claiming capital allowances, should contain a clause drawing attention to that fact and warning that the lessee is not itself entitled to claim such allowances.

Table 14.6 shows the types of assets being leased in 1985 and 1986. Most of the changes over the year are due to changes in the national economy or international environment. For example, depression in shipping and the oil market led to a downturn in leasing activity in both of these sectors. In contrast, the technological revolution and Big Bang in particular led to an increase in computer and office equipment being leased by banking, finance, insurance and business services for their own use. The length of primary periods is shown in Table 14.7. The cumulative percentage figures show that over the period an increasing proportion of short-term leases are being written. For example, in 1985 59 per cent of all leases were for periods up to five years whereas in 1986 the figure had risen to 68 per cent. The reason for this is probably related to taxation. The ELA was concerned about depooling arrangements for short-life assets introduced in the 1984 Finance Act and lobbied the government accordingly. As a result the Finance Act

Table 14.6 Type of assets leased

| | 1985 | | 1986 | | % + |
Type of asset	£m	%	£m	%	(−)
Plant and machinery	1,858	32	1,406	27	(24)
Computer and office equipment	1,305	23	1,597	31	22
Oil exploration and extraction equipment	152	3	88	2	(42)
Aircraft	561	10	329	6	(41)
Ships	247	4	81	2	(67)
Commercial vehicles	609	11	579	11	(5)
Cars	583	10	814	16	40
Property	145	2	128	2	(12)
Other	297	5	160	3	(46)
Total	5,757	100	5,182	100	

Table 14.7 Length of primary periods

| | 1985 | | | 1986 | | |
| | | | Cumulative | | | Cumulative |
Primary period	£m	%	%	£m	%	%
Up to 2 years	238	4	4	363	7	7
Over 2 and up to 3 years	775	13	17	1,072	21	28
3–4 years	750	13	30	750	14	42
4–5 years	1,643	29	59	1,340	26	68
5–7 years	688	12	71	625	12	80
7–10 years	767	13	84	393	8	88
10–12 years	491	9	93	183	4	92
12–15 years	234	4	97	316	6	98
Over 15 years	171	3	100	140	2	100
Total	5,757	100		5,182	100	

1985 contained a new concession in which owners, including lessors, could elect to have short-life assets excluded from the general pool of equipment. The advantage of such an arrangement is that balancing taxation allowances can be claimed on disposal if it arises within a four-year period from the end of the year of acquisition. The ELA tried without success to get the period extended to five years. As a result it is not surprising that more short-life contracts are being written.

Sale and leaseback

A sale and leaseback operation involves the sale of a valuable asset, usually property, to an insurance company or other financial institution followed by an immediate leaseback to the vendor at a negotiated rental. Such operations have proved very popular during periods of rapid increases in property values as the vendor is able to turn a fixed asset into cash. Naturally it will only be profitable if the cash proceeds can be used more profitably elsewhere.

There are, of course, a number of disadvantages of a sale and lease-back operation. By selling a valuable asset the firm loses the possible benefits of future property appreciation. Furthermore, the relinquishing of title means that the asset cannot be used as security for future capital raising. The act of selling property may bring forward the tax liability as the excess in value over the tax written down value will be subject to capital gains tax. Other disadvantages include the imposition of restrictions on the future use of the property, and the fact that while rents may be reasonable to start with rental contracts often have rent review clauses. In addition, a rental agreement normally extends for a considerable period of time and the costs involved may well exceed those of a mortgage.

Mortgages can normally be arranged with insurance companies, investment companies, and pension funds, where a valuable asset can be used as security. The initial costs will probably be higher than in a sale and leaseback operation although rent review clauses will ensure that rentals move in line with the market. Consequently, the long-term costs of a mortgage may well be less than a sale and leaseback.

Commercial paper

Commercial paper is a form of short-term promissory note that is sold by a company direct to investors. Traditionally the market has been centred in New York and by the end of 1985 the market totalled approximately $300bn. In May 1986 the UK developed a market of its own that was hailed by some as the most important new financial market in the UK since the Unlisted Securities Market began in 1981.

The development of a commercial paper market is one stage in the development of securitization, a process in which banks are not involved in the issue. Securitization is loose US terminology since the process of eliminating banks from the mediation process is more accurately referred to as 'disintermediation'. In the UK, securitization refers to a phenomenon whereby debt instruments such as mortgages or car loans are repackaged and used as collateral for securities which are issued to investors.

The minimum UK denomination for commercial paper is £500,000 and the borrower promises to repay the money after so many weeks or days. Under Bank of England rules commercial paper may only be given with maturities of less than one year, although in practice maturities are usually only for one to two months. Transactions will normally involve an industrial or service company of high commercial standing borrowing from cash-rich companies such as insurance companies and pension funds. The Bank of England has tried to ensure that only well-known public companies with a good financial record will be able to use the market since the provider of funds stands to risk the entire amount of the loan in the case of default. The first two borrowers were Hawley, the cleaning and maintenance services group, and Redland, the building materials company.

The default record in the US has been good ever since Penn Central railroad company failed with outstanding commercial paper amounting to $100m. In the US it is a requirement for the borrower to have both a bank guarantee and a good credit rating.

The advantage to the borrower is that the cost of finance should be cheaper as a result of the elimination of an intermediary and this source of finance is flexible. For the lender it represents an alternative to placing short-term money in a bank.

International money and capital markets

One of the major changes in international capital markets over the last twenty years has been the growth of eurocurrency. Eurocurrency is any currency owned by a firm or individual resident outside the country where the currency was issued, and lent to another non-resident. The eurocurrency market has grown from $27 billions in 1967 to $4073 billions in 1986. It is also noticeable that the majority of all eurocurrencies are denominated in US dollars. The growth in international money markets has resulted from major economic changes in the world economy.

In 1957 there was a crisis in confidence in the use of sterling as a major international currency. As a result the British government placed restrictions on its use for financing foreign trade. In particular, the use of sterling acceptance credits was banned to finance trade between non-residents which led to demands for an alternative currency. Furthermore, banks located in Western Europe encouraged dollar deposits.

A further economic factor was the development of multinationals. As multinationals diversified their product ranges and diversified regionally, banks reacted by diversifying the work they undertook to meet customers' needs. Furthermore, growth in the size of multinationals increased demands for substantial amounts of capital.

A number of other factors were important in precipitating the development of the eurocurrency market. Rigidities in the US banking system in the early 1960s led to difficulties in access to US capital markets. For example, regulation 'Q' fixed the maximum rate of interest US banks could offer on time deposits and these rates were lower than those prevalent in many parts of the world. Furthermore, in 1963 an interest equalization tax was imposed which represented a penal tax on US residents who bought foreign securities which had the effect of stopping foreign companies issuing securities in the US market.

In the 1960s and 1970s East European countries decided to transfer their dollar balances away from the US and deposit them in Europe.

The reason for this was the fear that if a dispute arose between an east European country and the US it would be possible for the US to freeze the dollar balances of an overseas country. The shift of dollar balances to Europe represented a hedge against this political possibility.

Another important point was the growth of dollar balances accruing to European residents as a result of the US balance of payments deficit. This deficit arose due to the financing of the Vietnam war, a vast aid programme, and because US companies and commercial banks holding dollars outside the US wanted to invest in eurodollars because of the higher rates of interest.

A eurocurrency deposit is a certificate of deposit with a life usually of between three months and five years, although it is possible to place minimum deposits of $50,000 on an overnight basis. The certificate of deposit is a negotiable instrument, a bearer bond, with a variable rate of interest, and which may be sold on secondary markets before its maturity.

The eurobond market is an international market without regulations in which bonds are issued on behalf of a multinational company, state or other borrower. The market is virtually uncontrolled since a manager can bring an issue forward to the market without having the consent of a central bank, a credit rating agency or indeed approval from any other source. A typical eurobond issue would involve a lead manager, co-managers, underwriters and a large selling group. The lead manager prepares the documents of issue, is responsible for keeping the books of account and, together with senior underwriters, prices the issue. The choice of lead manager, one with considerable standing in this area, is important since it is damaging to a company's reputation if the offer is withdrawn. If adverse conditions prevail a company will need a leading bank which can absorb a substantial proportion of the issue itself. The leading bank will also be responsible for encouraging the rest of the management team to absorb a proportion of the issue likewise. In addition to the ability to absorb an issue another factor is the adeptness of a lead manager to price appropriately so that the issue is successfully absorbed by the primary market. Inappropriate pricing will lead to the management team having to release issues through the secondary market at discount prices. Thus, factors other than obtaining the finest terms are important in establishing a management team.

Where a eurobond issue is placed rather than issued to the public, the management team consists only of a lead manager and co-managers. Placement is simpler and less formal and can be completed in a shorter period of time. The ability to move quickly is often important to take advantage of market opportunities.

Since a eurobond issue is normally unsecured the company must have a first-class reputation. A number of documents must be sent out with allotment letters which include:

1 The trust deed which provides an agreement between the borrower and the trustee.

2 The prospectus.
3 A certified copy of the minutes of the borrowing company's board approving the borrowing.
4 Legal opinion that the loan contract is binding and enforceable.
5 A copy of the prospectus signed by the directors accepting responsibility for its contents, if the issue is quoted in London. Bonds can be publicly quoted such as in London, Zurich and Luxembourg.
6 Any powers of attorney for individuals who are required to sign relevant documents.
7 A letter of comfort giving consent to the publication of the borrowing company's audited published accounts.

The requirements of a prospectus will be determined by the stock exchange on which it is to be listed but the contents will usually include details about the borrower, the bonds, and the guarantor, if one is used. The details about the bonds will include information on interest and redemption. Interest is usually calculated on a 360 day year of twelve months of thirty days each and is paid on an annual basis. Redemption may be a simple repayment or be a complex sinking fund depending upon the maturity of the loan. For example, where a eurobond is issued for a period of less than five years it is usual for repayment in one tranche rather than by a sinking fund arrangement. Under a sinking fund arrangement the borrower will redeem bonds over a period of the last few interest payment dates.

While most of the bond transactions are in US dollars there are also eurosterling, eurodeutschmarks, Swiss francs, Dutch guilder bonds and composite or 'cocktail' currencies. A composite currency unit includes a European Unit of Account (EUA), a European Currency Unit (ECU) or a European Composite Unit (EURCO). For example, an ECU bond is one which is denominated in any one of the currencies of the six original members of the EEC and which is repayable in any currency determined at the outset by a fixed exchange rate.

There are a number of types of eurocurrency loans. For example, there are fixed interest loans with a maturity up to five years and there are floating rate notes in which the interest rates are adjusted every three to six months to reflect changes in inter-bank rates in the international market.

Managing a debt portfolio

One of the responsibilities of a corporate treasurer is to balance a debt portfolio which depends upon maturity, currency and interest rate changes. For instance, a treasurer will seek to have loans with varying maturities since the portfolio's asset structure is normally composed of variable life elements. Consequently short-term borrowing should not represent too high a proportion of company finances – long-term assets should be financed by long-term funds.

While funding requirements are often categorized into short term or long term the real choice for the treasurer is between medium and long-term financing.

The phrase 'medium-term funding' is often referred to in connection with the syndicated credit market through which a number of banks supply funds at variable interest rates over periods of from three to seven years. In contrast, long-term funds usually refer to maturities in excess of ten years. Maturity refers to the maximum period for which the funds may be borrowed.

In choosing between medium and long-term funds the treasurer must make a decision about his objectives. Some treasurers take the view that long-term funding offers stability, security and confidence in the company whereas others take the view that funding is for specific requirements and that borrowing in excess of that required represents speculation on future interest rates. However, funding for any reasonable period is based on a view of future interest rates in the sense that a normal-shaped yield represents the fact that higher rates are offered for longer maturities. The treasurer is responsible for balancing these risks with the need for security for a reasonable period and thereby to avoid repetitive borrowing and repayment obligations.

Once a treasurer has decided on the maturity structure of the company's debt portfolio the next choice is that of the currency in which the borrowing is to be denominated. It is normal for a treasurer to minimize the company's exposure to foreign exchange risk by borrowing in the currency required when the funds are to be invested. For example, a company would borrow US dollars to invest in assets in the US. A classic example of not following this policy was Laker Airways which called in the receiver on 5 February 1982. One of the many problems of Laker Airways was that the company borrowed $228 million in 1980 to be repaid in nine years in order to help purchase five McDonnell Douglas DC-10 aircraft. The dollar borrowing was to be repaid at a rate of $2.25 to the pound and no forward contracts were taken to cover the risk. Provided the pound sterling did not fall relative to the US dollar there would not have been any exchange losses. Indeed the pound strengthened against the dollar initially providing exchange profits of £1.5 million out of its profits of £2.2 million for the year ended 31 March 1981. However, by August 1981 the pound had fallen 18 per cent and Laker Airways began to seek a debt rescheduling programme. Ignoring the naivety of no forward contracts, the company's revenues were primarily in sterling but its borrowings were in dollars.

The matching of borrowings with asset investments is, however, not without its problems. For instance, if a UK company purchased a US company for $17.5 million when the exchange rate is $1.75 to the pound it would borrow the funds in dollars. In sterling terms the UK company has acquired assets worth £10 million. Let us assume that when the loan is due to be repaid the pound has fallen and the exchange rate is now $1.5 to the pound. If nothing else has changed the UK company has to repay £11.67m which is matched by the increase in value of the assets. However, the company will not liquidate its assets in order to repay its loan so that while its profit position has been protected its cash position has not.

A second problem is that in large companies it is not possible to match investments with funds. This is the same for a domestic company which views its funding as a pool from which investments can be made. The practicable way of dealing with this problem is to look at the currency structure of the group balance sheet. One approach is to maintain a reasonable level of currency exposure through the forward foreign exchange markets. A more common method in the UK is to adopt a broad approach by generally matching fixed assets with medium and long-term borrowings.

The third important area in managing a debt portfolio is to manage interest rates. This involves balancing fixed interest borrowings with variable interest borrowings (floating rate debts), and a consideration of the likely trend of interest rates. It is normally appropriate to have a mix of fixed interest and variable interest borrowings since reliance solely on the latter can leave the company exposed during periods of high interest rates. Since high interest rates may be more prolonged during a recession the company may suffer from both a reduction in cash flow from a downturn in business activity and high interest rates. In contrast, if interest rates are expected to fall a high proportion of fixed interest rate loans leads to unnecessary interest charges. The type of business a company is in is also important since capital intensive industries usually have high fixed costs so that profitability is sensitive to volume. Consequently, a lower proportion of variable interest borrowings is appropriate for a capital intensive industry as compared to a labour intensive industry.

In managing interest rates the treasurer will need to take a view of trends in rates over borrowing periods and take appropriate action to minimize risks. This may be achieved by interest rate swaps, forward rate interest agreements, interest rate futures and interest rate guarantees.

An interest rate swap may develop where there is a mismatch between a company's need for funds and its ability to raise the right type of funds. For example, Company A may require a fixed interest loan but be able to obtain much better terms by raising a variable rate loan. Company B may wish to obtain variable rate funding but only be able to obtain a fixed interest loan. Thus there is a mismatch between the two companies that can be resolved by a swap. Each company borrows according to its most favourable terms and then swaps with the other company to fulfil their objectives. Thus one set of financial obligations is substituted for another set of obligations.

A forward interest rate agreement is a hedge against unfavourable future changes in rates. An agreement may be entered into with a bank that fixes a rate of interest at a particular time for a future loan. If the actual rate of interest at the time of the borrowing is higher than the fixed rate the bank compensates the company for the difference. If the actual rate of interest at the time of the borrowing is lower than the fixed rate the company is obliged to compensate the bank for the difference. An interest rate future is similar except that the terms and conditions of the loan are standardized and are traded on the London International Financial Futures Exchange.

A further variation of the forward interest rate agreement is an interest rate guarantee, sometimes referred to as interest rate option or cap, in which the maximum rate of interest on the borrowing is guaranteed by the banks. If the actual rate exceeds the maximum the bank compensates the company for the difference. However, the company has the option not to utilize the guarantee by abandoning it and borrowing at a lower market rate if available. The additional risk to the bank is reflected in higher bank charges.

Summary

A financial manager needs to consider all debt instruments in relation to capital structure. Generally short-term debt is less costly than long-term debt but in many respects it is more risky. For example, bank overdrafts are a traditional source of finance for the small or medium-sized company and yet they are repayable on demand. The interest rate charged depends upon the cost of funds to the bank, minimum lending rate, the creditworthiness of the borrower, and the relationship with the bank.

Trade credit is a significant source of short-term funds for all businesses. It is flexible and depends upon the terms offered by the seller and its ability to collect debts as they fall due. Cash discounts which are offered and not taken are normally costly means of extended credit. Deliberate slowness in paying debts can lead to friction between customer and seller and can lead to a deterioration in a firm's credit rating.

Factoring involves raising funds on the strength of a company's debts. The seller receives early payment by receiving an advance from the factor against invoices accepted for factoring. While there are obvious attractions to such schemes the disadvantages include cost and also that factors are not normally interested in companies with a large number of accounts consisting mainly of small value transactions.

Other sources of short-term finance include bills of exchange, hire purchase, leasing, sales and leaseback and commercial paper. There has been considerable growth in leasing business over the period 1976 to 1986. The upsurge in activity occurred in 1984–5 which to a large extent can be explained by the Finance Act of 1984. The Act started the process of reducing corporation tax from 50 per cent in 1983 to 35 per cent in 1986 together with an abandonment of 100 per cent first year allowances. In order to take advantage of the higher capital allowances there was a considerable increase in the number of leases written before the new tax regime was fully implemented. A fall or levelling off in activity is expected in the future.

International capital markets have developed considerably over the last twenty years, not least because of a lack of control of the markets. The eurobond market is an example of an international market without any controls. Eurocurrency deposits normally have a life span ranging from a few months up to five years.

References

Bolton Committee, Report, HMSO, 1971.

Further reading

Clark, T., *Leasing*, McGraw-Hill, 1978.
Davis, B., *Business Finance and the City of London*, Heinemann, 1982.
Goddard, S. and Jay, S., 'Credit Management', *Management Survey Report* No. 52, BIM, 1981.
Lewis, M. and Morgan, E. J., *The 1984 Budget: Effects on Corporate Tax and Investment*, Bath University Discussion Paper No. 67, November 1985.
Office of Fair Trading, *Credit Scoring: A Consultative Document*, 1983.
Peasnell, K. V. and Ward, C. W. R., *British Financial Markets and Institutions*, Prentice-Hall, 1985.
Penneck, S. and Woods, R., 'Effects of Leasing on Statistics of Manufacturing Capital Expenditure', *Economic Trends*, HMSO, 1982.
Taylor, T. W., *The Financing of Industry and Commerce*, Heinemann, 1985.
Tomkins, C., Lowe, J. and Morgan, E., *An Economic Analysis of the Finance Leasing Industry*, Saxon House, 1979.
Wilson Committee, *Survey of Investment Attitudes and Financing of Medium-Sized Companies*, Research Report No. 1, HMSO, 1978.
Wood, A., 'Financial Evaluation – Reducing the Lending Risk in Corporate Credit Assessment', *Credit Quarterly Review*, Finance Houses Association, 1983.

15 Working capital management

Introduction

In some texts the term 'working capital' refers to current assets and is distinguished from 'net working capital', which is defined as current assets less current liabilities. For the purposes of this chapter, 'working capital' refers to net current assets or net current liabilities, where current liabilities exceed current assets. It therefore encompasses short-term resources (inventory, debtors, investments and cash) and short-term funding (creditors and other borrowings). Since short-term funding is covered in Chapter 14 and investment management is the subject of Chapter 16, the emphasis of this chapter, after a discussion on the overall management of working capital, will be on the financial management aspects of cash, inventory, debtors and creditors.

The importance attached to working capital management by treasurers can be attributed to several factors. First, working capital presents a continuous set of decision-making alternatives, which respond speedily to policy changes. In contrast fixed assets and long-term funding management involve discrete decisions often with long lead times before results are apparent. Second, although the individual transactions involved in working capital flows are relatively small in comparison with fixed assets and longer term funding, current assets and liabilities are significant in balance sheet terms. Typically in a manufacturing concern current assets would exceed half the value of total assets; and current liabilities might be expected to surpass half of the debt from outside sources. Finally surveys of treasurers, such as Davis and Collier (1983), suggest that working capital occupies the greatest percentage of treasurer's time in terms of the day-to-day operations of the finance function.

From the viewpoint of financial management theory, working capital needs to be split into its current asset and current liability components.

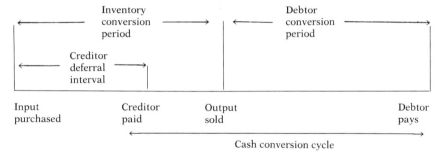

Figure 15.1 Working Capital Cycle

Based on the theoretical arguments in previous chapters the principles involved are twofold:

1 Current assets should be increased provided their return is greater than the cost of the firm's capital – that is to the point where the marginal revenue from extra current assets equals the marginal cost of financing them.
2 Current liabilities should be substituted for longer term debt provided the weighted average cost of capital is reduced.

Working capital cycles

The dynamic aspects of working capital can best be appreciated through the cash conversion cycle approach of Richards and Laughlin (1980). The entire working capital cycle can be viewed as extending from the acquisition of inputs to the payment for the output produced from them. As can be seen from Figure 15.1, this process can be analysed into the inventory and debtors conversion periods. By introducing the idea of the creditor deferral interval, as the period between inputs being received and paid for, the cash conversion cycle can be derived as in Figure 15.1.

In the form of an equation, it can be stated that:

cash conversion cycle	=	inventory conversion period	+	debtor conversion period	–	creditor deferral interval

Since the length of conversion and deferral periods is directly related to the level of current assets and liabilities (for example if the inventory conversion period doubles, inventories must double), the level of a firm's working capital is dependent upon the length of the cash conversion cycle. Later sections of this chapter will address how the cycle can be reduced through management action aimed at reducing debtor and inventory conversion periods and increasing the creditor deferral interval.

The cycle approach can be extended, with information about the value of input and output flows over time, to show the impact of changes in the level of activity upon the investment of the organization in working capital. Suppose a company with annual sales of £12,000 has an inventory conversion period of one and a half months, a debtors conversion period of two months and a creditor deferral interval of one month. If input costs were 50 per cent of sales value, working capital would be £2,250 calculated thus:

		£
Inventory	50% × £12,000 × 1½/12	750
Debtors	£12,000 × 2/12	2,000
Creditors	50% × £12,000 × 1/12	(500)
		£2,250

Now let us consider the effect of increases in activity measured by sales volume on the working capital requirement. Three scenarios may be surmised:

1 Conversion periods are unchanged.
2 Conversion periods for inventory and debtors lengthen with or without an increase in the creditor interval. This arises because debtor periods are lengthened to attract customers. Parts and work in progress increase to meet higher production levels and finished goods stock increases to enable salesmen to offer speedy delivery.
3 Extra sales volume leads to a more efficient use of working capital with a reduction in the cash conversion period.

These situations can be illustrated with our simple example. For scenario two assume that inventory and debtor periods increase by a quarter of a month; while for scenario three they decrease by a similar amount. In both cases the creditors interval is unchanged. The impact of a 25 per cent increase in volume is shown in Table 15.1.

The message from Table 15.1 is that even if the efficiency of working capital management improves it is almost certain that as the level of activity in an organization rises, the requirement for working capital will also increase. If careful consideration is not given to how this increase in working capital should be financed, it is possible that the company, although trading at a profit, will find that it cannot obtain cash to pay its day-to-day bills. This situation is known as overtrading.

Indications that overtrading is taking place are as follows:

1 Sharp increases in sales volume.
2 Falling margins through higher sales discounts being offered to keep sales increasing and rising unit costs due to overtime working, production bottlenecks and other diseconomies of scale.
3 Deteriorating debtor, inventory and creditor turnover ratios. Typically debtors and inventory grow faster than sales (scenario 2 of

Table 15.1 Impact of a 25 per cent sales increase on working capital levels

	Scenario 1 constant £		Scenario 2 increasing £		Scenario 3 decreasing £
Conversion period					
Inventory 50% × £15,000 × 1½/12	937.5	50% × £15,000 × 1¾/12	1,093.75	50% × £15,000 × 1¼/12	781.25
Debtors £15,000 × 2/12	2,500	£15,000 × 2¼/-2	2,812.5	£15,000 × 1¾/12	2,187.5
Creditors 50% × £15,000 × 1/12	(625)		(625)		(625)
Working capital required	2,812.5		3,281.25		2,343.75
Increase over the £12,000 volume	562.5		1,031.25		93.75
Increase % over the £12,000 volume	25%		46%		4%

Table 15.1) while creditors may also be paid less promptly to compensate.

4   Reliance upon short-term funding, particularly bank overdrafts with limits frequently being renegotiated.

These problems are exacerbated by a large bad debt or a series of defaults, the purchase of new fixed assets without matched funding, the need to repay borrowings and overgenerous distributions to the owners; until the bank refuses to advance further funds. Ironically it is normal at this stage for the businessman to blame the financiers for his failure rather than appreciate that it is the failure of the organization to plan and arrange finance for the expansion which has led to difficulties.

Overtrading type problems also occur during periods of high inflation. The business results may reflect profits but after distributions, the funds retained in the business may be insufficient to fund the increased replacement cost of fixed assets or the greater level of working capital needed as prices and therefore sales rise. It is thus possible to run into a shortage of cash without sales volume growth. Obviously any company expanding in inflationary periods is doubly at risk.

The impression should not be given that overtrading is necessarily bad, indeed many companies have grown through 'controlled overtrading' but it is not a practice to indulge in without adequate planning and the full support of those providing the necessary finance. At the other end of the spectrum from overtrading is the problem of overcapitalization. This occurs when working capital exceeds that required by the business and arises from a failure to manage this investment effectively. Overcapitalization is characterized by a low turnover of working capital, high liquidity with high current and quick asset ratios, long stock and debtor turnover periods and a low level of creditors relative to activity. The policies required to correct this problem will be the subject of later sections of this chapter.

Working capital policies

Working capital policy is a function of two decisions:

1   What is the appropriate investment in, and mix of, current assets at any given level of activity.
2   How should this investment be financed?

The desirable level of current assets for a firm depends upon the trade off between the risk of insolvency through having insufficient cash to meet debts as they fall due and the returns foregone from the decision to invest in current assets rather than another project. These risks and returns will be unique to each firm. The risk will depend upon levels of uncertainty in the environment; while returns will vary in accordance with investment opportunities. Figure 15.2 shows three possible policy stances.

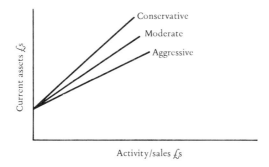

Figure 15.2 Current asset policy stances

An aggressive stance will be appropriate if there is little uncertainty as to future flows and is characterized by a minimum holding of cash, other liquid assets, debtors and inventory. At the other extreme in business areas where there is little environmental stability, a firm will adopt a conservative approach with significant cash and near cash balances, higher debtors through laxer credit control policies and greater inventories with safety stocks of parts and finished goods – the former safety stocks to prevent production delays and the latter to prevent sales being lost from an inability to deliver. The moderate policy may be seen as points between these two approaches.

The second working capital policy decision is part of the wider question of how the funding of the total assets of a business, fixed and current, should be split between long and short-term sources, equity and debt and current liabilities respectively. To consider this policy it is necessary to take into account that in practice asset levels are rarely constant. In particular the level of current assets will fluctuate in response to business and seasonal cycles. However current assets will never fall below a certain level and current assets up to this level are often referred to as permanent current assets and recognized as similar in nature to fixed assets. At any point in time:

Total assets = fixed assets + permanent current assets +
                fluctuating current assets

Again three possible financing positions can be used to illustrate the range of policies available to the treasurer. These are shown in Figure 15.3. The first is the moderate approach which follows the principle of maturity matching. This is based upon the idea that the net cash flows from the asset should be used to repay the debt and therefore the life of the asset and the debt financing it should match. This gives rise to the policy that fixed assets and permanent current assets should be financed from long-term debt, while fluctuating current assets should be funded by short-term debt as in Figure 15.3(a). An aggressive financ-

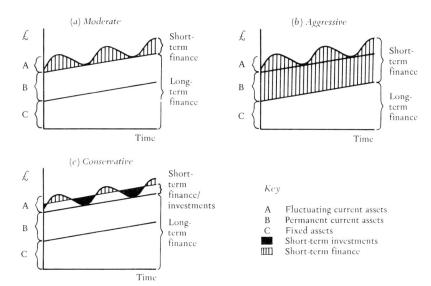

Figure 15.3   Financing policy stances

ing approach would result in an increased use of short-term debt, which is more volatile. In Figure 15.3(b) it is shown as being used to finance permanent and fluctuating current assets but any move from the moderate stance towards greater short-term funding would be described as aggressive. The alternative to the aggressive approach is to increase the funding of total assets by long-term debt as compared with the moderate position so that part of the fluctuating current assets are funded by these funds as in Figure 15.3(c). Peaks are met by short-term finance while during troughs excess funds are placed in short-term investments and realized as required.

In examining financing it is worth briefly comparing long-term and short-term sources of finance and their advantages and disadvantages. With respect to cost, the term structure of interest rates follows the curve in Figure 15.4 which can be derived by plotting the yield from government securities of various maturities at any point in time.

Therefore longer term debt is more expensive than short-term borrowing and an aggressive financing approach lowers interest costs. Further finance from trade creditors, accruals and other current liabilities may be costless or only represent discounts foregone. The penalty for lower cost is increased risk. First, short-term borrowing is vulnerable to interest rate volatility, whereas with long-term debt interest rates are certain and second, there is the need to continually refund short-term debt whereas long-term debt refunding is only an intermittent problem. Since generally poor trading conditions, high interest rates and a disinclination to provide funds are connected, firms reliant upon high levels of short-term funding are especially at risk during periods of recession.

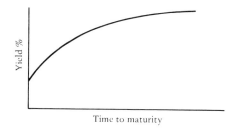

Figure 15.4   The term structure of interest rates

In contrast long-term debt has disadvantages with respect to flexibility. For example, short-term debt can be raised more quickly and with fewer formalities than an issue of long-term debt. Further long-term debt often involves the pledging of assets as securities and provisions restricting the future actions of management. Finally early repayment of long-term debt will often be more difficult than in the case of borrowings with a shorter duration.

In practice the working capital financing decision is reflected in target gearing ratios set within the overall corporate planning process.

Objectives of cash management

Cash management is concerned with ensuring that a company's cash resources are employed efficiently. There are three main aspects to this. First, the planning and control of liquidity over the medium and longer term time horizons. This involves forecasting cash flows for the annual master budget and indicating the impact upon cash flows of the firm's corporate strategies for periods of three to five years and beyond. Based upon the forecasts, plans can be developed to provide funds in times of deficiencies and to make effective use of surpluses. The second element relates to banking strategy. This involves deciding upon the firm's relationships with bankers and a consideration of the flow of funds between entities within the firm with respect to the degree of centralization of banking and the most efficient arrangements for the flow of funds. Finally there is the day-to-day tracking and control of cash within the firm aimed at minimizing the opportunity cost associated with maintaining cash balances in order to pay creditors and other commitments as they fall due. This chapter principally concentrates upon this last area.

The treasury cycle and cash management

Figure 15.5 shows the stages in the process leading to receipts and payments. Responsibility for the entire cycle is usually divided but the cash manager will have an influence upon all stages with a view to

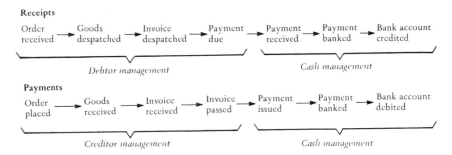

Figure 15.5   Stages in the processes leading to receipts and payments

minimizing the receipts intervals and maximizing the payments intervals within the context of other business objectives.

In the narrowest sense cash management concentrates upon four elements:

1   Available cash balances – the bank balance recorded in the bank's books at any point in time includes amounts credited against the account which have not been cleared through the bank clearance system. Available cash balances are the recorded bank balance less these uncleared items as these should not be drawn against before they are cleared, unless this has been arranged by prior agreement.
2   Receipts float – comprises receipts recorded in the company's books, which have either not been credited in the bank account or although credited remain uncleared.
3   Payments float – consists of cheques written and entered in the books of the firm but which have not yet been cleared and debited to the bank account by the bank. The extent of the payments float will depend upon the time taken for cheques to reach the payee and for them to be banked and cleared.
4   Unbilled and outstanding debtors – covers invoices not raised, invoices in process and uncollected debts.

The four together are often referred to as the 'cash pool'. Management aims to maximize the available cash balances through manipulating the other factors. Of particular usefulness in this respect are ways of circumventing the delay between a cheque being paid into a company's account and value being received. In the UK, the bank into which a cheque is paid sends the cheque to the payer's bank. Normally notification that the cheque has been passed is not given, the arrangement being that defaulting cheques must be returned by first class post on the day they are presented. Therefore in general, unless both accounts are in the same branch, a period of two to four days elapses, before value is received by the payee.

Various systems exist to give a cash manager same-day value. The three most important within the UK are:

1 Town clearing – this method, soon to be replaced by the Clearing House Automated Payments System (CHAPS), requires the payer and payee to have accounts at one of the 100 or so 'town' branches of major banks, all situated within the City of London. Cheques processed in the system must be in excess of £10,000 and drawn on, and paid into, town branches. The main disadvantage of this system is that companies outside the City have logistic problems in getting cheques to town branches and therefore CHAPS has been developed.

2 CHAPS – launched in 1984, the system is based upon payment messages being transferred through a British Telecom packet switching service. Direct links into CHAPS are restricted to settlement banks but other organizations can access CHAPS through a terminal or computer link into these institutions. Although CHAPS will eventually operate without a lower limit, at present £10,000 is the minimum transaction size. The big advantage of CHAPS is that payment is notified to the company paying in and funds guaranteed upon notification.

3 Bankers Automated Clearing Services (BACS) – this provides a regular money transfer system based upon a central computer facility. The paying company provides a computer tape in a set format to BACS two days in advance of the clearing date. The service covers bank account to bank account transfers and is used for standing orders, bank giro credits, payroll credits, direct debits and the payment of creditors.

Internationally the receipts float can be speeded up by a number of devices. For instance in the US, long clearing times have led to lockbox systems whereby cheques are directed to a post office box for daily collection by the bank rather than to the organization. The bank provides a daily statement of amounts credited and the clearing process begins without the delay of the cheque being passed through the firm. Also there are international electronic systems like SWIFT (Society for Worldwide Interbank Financial Telecommunications), which is a means of conveying money transfer instructions around the world (but not the actual transfer of funds). Its contribution to cash management is therefore to reduce the delay in transfer instructions being notified. An example of an automated money transfer system on an international scale would be the Clearing House Interbank Payment System (CHIPS), which processes over 90 per cent of US dollar denominated international transactions giving same day value.

Overall these automated systems provide two benefits to treasurers. First they provide greater certainty as to when value is given and received, and second they minimize the time funds are in the banking system and available to neither the payer or the payee.

More specifically cash management concentrates upon use of the float. As far as the bank is concerned the available cash balance at bank is the actual bank balance less deposits credited but not yet collected. On the other hand, ignoring items in transit, the company's book ba-

Table 15.2   Float management

	Bank's records (£000s)		Company's records (£000s)
Statement balance	500		500
Receipts credited but not cleared (receipts float)	200	Cheques drawn not presented (payments float)	400
Funds available to the company per the bank	300	Funds available per company's books	100

Note: £200,000 difference is the payments float less the receipts float.

lance will be the actual bank balance less the payments float. Since the bank is unaware of the payments float until the cheques are presented, provided the payments float exceeds the receipts float, the bank balance available to the company is greater than that recorded in the company's books by the net of these floats (and less if the receipts float exceeds the payments float). The situation is shown in Table 15.2.

To summarize, if experience shows that the payments float consistently exceeds the receipts float, the funds available to the company are increased above the level shown in the company's books by the net of the payments and receipts float so at any time:

$$\text{Funds available to the company} = \text{Company's book bank balance} + \text{Payments float} - \text{Receipts float}$$

Failure to realize this leads to idle funds which have an opportunity cost in terms of interest foregone. Float management presents a significant opportunity for corporate treasurers to improve their cash flow. However in the UK the widespread existence of overdraft finance has reduced the opportunities for corporate treasurers to use these methods.

Critical to successful float management is a sophisticated system for forecasting. Here the emphasis is on the accurate prediction of available balances, as distinct from book balances, and involves the assessment of float and clearance times for the transactions occurring within the time horizon covered, usually eight to twelve weeks divided into daily periods.

Two methodologies exist – distribution and scheduling. Distribution is appropriate to businesses where cash flows are regular and is implemented by spreading a forecast of the total monthly flows over the days of the month with adjustments for known intra-month cash flow patterns. Scheduling refers to the construction of a forecast from primitive data covering receipts and payments. Most sophisticated cash forecasting approaches combine these two techniques.

Within domestically and internationally complex groups, there exists considerable scope for the use of computer-based cash management systems to aggregate bank balances by currency and manage group

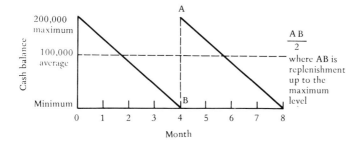

Figure 15.6 Cash balance behaviour under the Baumol assumptions

balances for the centre as a single multicurrency entity. Details of this are included in Chapter 9 covering the organization of the treasury function and Chapter 13 on netting systems.

Set against all these opportunities for benefits from active cash management must be set the costs of the cash management team and of money transmission and banking. Banks typically charge businesses on the basis of a turnover charge; Kirkman (1987) quotes 3p to £1 per £100 of debit turnover, the rate being dependent upon the cash flow patterns of individual customers. In addition banks charge standing fees for access to additional services often with a usage fee in addition. For instance with BACS there is a fixed charge to cover branch costs plus a negotiated charge per transaction.

Cash management models

Assistance with cash management decisions has been provided by the development of theoretical models, which give valuable insights to problems. Perhaps the best known cash model is Baumol (1952). This drew an analogy between cash and inventory and applied the economic order quantity model (Figure 15.6) to enable the firm to determine the cash input which would minimize the total costs of holding funds. The assumptions made were of a steady state environment where cash flows are certain and constant; cash outflows are in advance of receipts and continuous; and cash inflows are regular and periodic. Consider a firm planning to expand whose outflows exceed inflows by £50,000 per month. Consider a commencing cash balance of £200,000. The position would be as in Figure 15.6.

The maximum balance takes four months to deplete. If the firm held a maximum cash balance of £100,000 instead it would need to inject cash twice as frequently but would only have an average cash balance of £50,000 (100,000/2). This implies high transaction costs since there are twice as many transactions in a given period but half the opportunity cost from holding cash and therefore not being able to invest it or use it to reduce borrowings. An optimum cash injection to minimize these

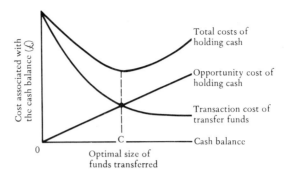

Figure 15.7   Cost functions associated with cash balances

combined costs, which move in opposite directions, is as shown at point C in Figure 15.7.

The optimal point can be found from the equation:

$$C = \sqrt{\frac{2bt}{i}}$$

where C = cash injection and therefore the maximum balance
      b = brokers fees
      t = net cash flow over the period
      i = opportunity cost from return foregone or cost of borrowing to provide funds

Therefore, if for the example discussed we incorporate brokers' fees of £5,000 per withdrawal and an opportunity cost of 12 per cent over a one year period, we could state:

1   Cash injection and maximum balance was £223,607 from

$$C = \sqrt{\frac{2 \times 5,000 \times (12 \times 50,000)}{0.12}} = £223,607 \, ;$$

a year will consist of a cummulative build up of twelve average outflow balances of £50,000.

2   2.7 transactions per year or every four and a half months from (12 × 50,000)/223,607.

3   As flows occur evenly the average cash balance would be C/2 which gives 223,607/2 = £111,803.50.

The model has two major drawbacks. First its assumption that a steady state exists is unrealistic and second it is inapplicable where funding is provided from an overdraft.

The Miller–Orr model (1966) overcomes the first objection, by substituting the assumption that net cash flows occur in a random pattern,

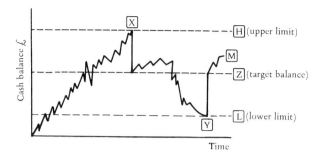

Figure 15.8 Miller–Orr model

and extends the basic inventory model to incorporate a simple control limit function as is shown in Figure 15.8.

The line M on Figure 15.8 is the hypothetical path of a cash balance generated by a stationary random walk. If the line touches or breaks the control limits as at X or Y an amount is invested in short-term investments or injected to return to the target Z.

The model assumes that transfers can take place at any time and are instantaneous with a fixed transfer cost. The lower limit (L) is set by management, dependent upon the precautionary balance desired, and the model calculates Z, H and the average cash balance (W) from:

$$Z = \left[\frac{3F\sigma^2}{4K}\right]^{1/3} + L$$
$$H = 3Z - 2L$$
$$W = (4Z - L)/3$$

where F = transaction cost
          K = daily opportunity cost of cash balances
          σ^2 = variance of net daily cash flows

To illustrate their application, suppose that for one thirty day month management decides upon a lower limit of £5,000. If the standard deviation of daily cash flows is £1,000, the transaction cost is £500 and the opportunity cost for the period is 1 per cent monthly – the calculation of Z and H would be as follows:

Daily opportunity cost (K) from $(1 + K)^{30} - 1.0 = 0.1$
                                        $K = 0.00034$

Variance of daily cash flows (σ^2) from $(1,000)^2$
                               σ^2 =   £1 million

Therefore from the formulae:

$$Z = \left[\frac{3 \times 500 \times 1,000,000}{4 \times 0.00034}\right]^{1/3} + 5000 = £15,332$$

and

$$H = 3 \times 15{,}332 - 2 \times 5{,}000 = £35{,}996$$

also

$$W = \frac{4 \times 15{,}332 - 5{,}000}{3} = £18{,}776$$

It is worth noting that the target cash balance is not midpoint between the higher and lower limits. This reflects the trade off between the opportunity cost of holding cash are transaction elements. In the example opportunity costs of holding cash and dominant and therefore the target balance is well below the midpoint balance of £20,498 [(35,996 + 5,000)/2]. Stone (1972) refined this Miller–Orr model for application with an independent forecast of net cash flows, an estimate of the uncertainty associated with the forecast and a schedule of investment maturities. Instead of automatically realizing investments or borrowing when limits are reached, Stone incorporates a heuristic rule based on examining forthcoming cash flows with a view to avoiding unnecessary transactions.

Another genre of models attempts to build up to cash requirements. For example Archer (1966) analysed requirements into transaction and precautionary balances and determined needs to cover each motive (transaction and precautionary) from an examination of historic and forecast data. Other models in a similar vein have applied Monte Carlo simulation techniques to assumed probability levels for sales activity and other key elements in a cash budget with a view to establishing the most likely cash balances and their variability. Finally approaches like Beehler (1978) have concentrated upon time series decomposition to identify seasonal, trend, cyclical and random patterns in a firm's cash flows in order to establish the cash balance needed.

Looking at surveys like Smith and Sells (1980), which showed only 5 per cent of the Fortune Top 1000 corporations using these techniques, it is easy to dismiss these models as irrelevant and argue that they are based upon restrictive assumptions. However, the Miller–Orr model when tested, has outperformed intuitive cash management and in any case much of a model's value arises from its contribution to management's understanding of the behaviour of the variables involved in cash management decisions.

Inventory management and the financial manager

Inventory is a major asset for many firms, especially those involved in the manufacturing, construction and retail business sectors. The nature of inventory varies widely and depends upon context. It can best be considered as elements involved in the transformation process towards a saleable entity. Therefore for a manufacturer, inventory comprises raw materials, bought and made-in components, work in progress and finished goods together with tangentially related items such as consumable stores (for example paints and lubricants), scrap awaiting disposal, maintenance materials and office stocks (for example stationery, diskettes and typewriter ribbons). In contrast, inventory for a construction firm would be site or project costs less progress payments, for a retailer it is goods purchased for resale and in the service sector, for example advertising, inventory is unbilled time and other costs.

Inventory management is concerned with defining objectives and formulating policies with respect to the levels, types and location of inventory. Further it covers the development and implementation of the organizational structure, systems and controls to ensure that strategies aimed at achieving the objectives are effective. The financial manager will not be responsible for physical aspects of inventory management for instance inventory movements, security and location but will focus his attention on determining the optimal level of inventory for the organization through an appraisal of the trade offs involved between holding stocks and releasing the funds tied up. Therefore, while production views inventory as the provider of inputs to ensure the continuation of the transformation process and marketing considers inventory in terms of supplying customer needs; the financial manager approaches it as an investment which must earn an adequate return for the funds committed.

Inventory analysis

The quantity of inventory held by a firm will be a function of a number of variables including the levels and volatility of sales and production; the duration of the production process; and the nature of inventory items with respect to factors like susceptibility to deterioration, ease of storage and risk of obsolescence. Thus machine tool manufacturers have high stocks due to the long production cycle whereas food retailers have relatively low inventories because the goods are perishable.

In analysing the trade off problems outlined earlier, it is usual to consider the cost of inventories under the headings of holding and ordering expenditure. The former covers not only the opportunity cost from the funds tied up but also other costs associated with holding inventory. These include: losses from obsolescence, deterioration and damage; insurance charges for the stock and storage premises; labour and equipment costs for handling, recording and controlling the inventories; and rent, rates, lighting and other overheads. The other overheads contain: purchasing department costs associated with placing an order; the expenses of handling goods and related paperwork within other departments; transport and insurance charges; and discounts foregone. Obviously there are difficulties in establishing figures for these costs when it comes to relating them to a particular inventory line since the majority of the cost, outside the opportunity cost of funds, is fixed in nature. The normal approach is to use an average absorption-based full cost and this should be borne in mind when interpreting the

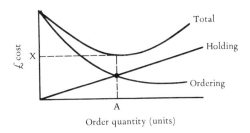

Figure 15.9 Optimal cost of inventory

results of analyses as it is unlikely that the actual cost changes associated with any one line equate with the average.

Holding and ordering costs move in opposite directions. High stocks imply infrequent orders. This means that holding costs will be high and ordering costs low and vice versa. Management should determine the economic order quantity (EOQ) which minimizes these combined costs. In Figure 15.9 this occurs where the EOQ is A and the total of holding and ordering costs is £X.

This concept can be extended to inventory levels by assuming that for a period: ordering and holding costs are constant; the usage of inventory is fairly even; and there are no buffer stocks. Figure 15.10 shows the inventory balance behaviour with Z being the maximum inventory, Y the average inventory and XZ the EOQ.

Assuming that inventory balances behave in this way, the total cost curve can be expressed as the sum of the average inventory multiplied by the holding cost per unit for the period plus the number of orders in the period multiplied by the cost per order. Therefore total cost (TC) is given by the equation:

$$TC = \frac{H.EOQ}{2} + \frac{O.U}{EOQ}$$

where   H = holding cost per unit of inventory for the period
        O = cost per order for the period
        U = period usage in units

If this total cost equation is differentiated with respect to EOQ and the derivative set equal to zero the equation for the EOQ associated with minimum total costs can be stated as:

$$EOQ = \sqrt{\frac{2\ U.O}{H}}$$

To illustrate this suppose a firm has a component W. It uses 10,000 units per year and has calculated that orders cost £16 each and the holding costs per unit amount to £2. From the formula:

$$EOQ = \sqrt{\frac{2 \times 10,000 \times 16}{2}} = 400 \text{ units}$$

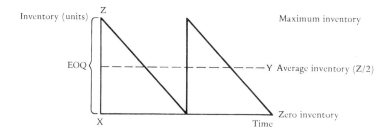

Figure 15.10 Inventory balance behaviour

total costs associated with this EOQ are

$$\frac{2 \times 400}{2} + 16 \times \frac{10,000}{400} = £800$$

and the orders are placed twenty-five times per year (10,000/400) from U/EOQ.

Further from Figure 15.10 it can be stated that maximum inventory being the same as EOQ is 400 units and average inventory is 200 units (400/2).

The analysis to date has ignored the uncertainties associated with inventories. Two main areas of risk are identifiable – usage rates and lead time. Uncertainty connected with usage applies particularly to finished goods inventories because customer demand is notoriously unpredictable. In the case of raw materials, components and work in progress, production planning provides reasonable estimates of usage and therefore the associated uncertainty is lower. The lead time problem relates to uncertainty with respect to the duration of the order to delivery cycle. Its impact is greater for raw materials, components and work in progress than for finished goods, since the latter are directly controlled by management whereas the former are often dependent upon the performance of parties over whom the firm has little control. The solution to uncertainty problems is for the organization to hold buffer (also known as safety) stocks – but at what level? A sophisticated approach is to determine the buffer stock which would minimize associated costs. The costs involved are holding costs, as discussed previously, and the costs of a stock out. A stock out occurs when stock is required but is not held. Its cost implications are twofold. In the case of finished goods, there will be financial consequences from lost orders; and for other inventories, there will be costs from production disruptions. The typical method adopted is to define probability distributions for the uncertainties involved and explore the cost implications of holding safety stocks at various levels using a Monte Carlo simulation technique. The safety stock with the lowest combined cost from the exercise would be chosen.

In practice a more pragmatic approach is adopted with the reorder

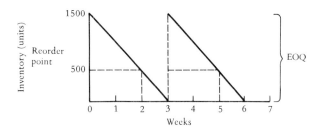

Figure 15.11   Reorder level illustration

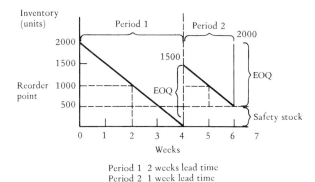

Period 1 2 weeks lead time
Period 2 1 week lead time

Figure 15.12   Safety stock illustration

level being modified to reflect subjective uncertainty. The reorder level may be defined as the inventory level at which an order must be placed to prevent a stock out occurring. To illustrate this consider a component where usage is 500 units per week, the EOQ 1500 units and the lead time one week. To avoid having no stock a new order must be placed when the inventory falls to 500 units – that is where the stock equates with the usage in the interval between the order and delivery. This situation is shown in Figure 15.11 where new orders are placed at Week 2 and Week 5.

An extension of this for safety stocks again requires an appraisal of the impact of uncertainty. Suppose it was felt that the lead time could be as high as two weeks. In this situation a stock out would occur unless adjustments are made to the reorder level and the stock level to compensate for the 500 unit usage in the period of uncertainty. The solution is to set up a safety stock of 500 units. This increases the reorder level to 1000 units and the maximum inventory holding to 2000 units as is shown in Figure 15.12.

In Period 1 the lead time deteriorates to two weeks. However as there is a safety stock, the EOQ delivery of 1500 units at the end of Week 4 prevents a stock out. In Period 2 the lead time reverts to one week and

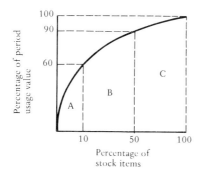

Figure 15.13 Pareto relationship

therefore by the end of Week 6 inventory returns to the maximum level of 2000 units.

As well as protecting against delays in lead time, a buffer stock provides cover in the event of usage exceeding the anticipated rate provided that the lead time does not simultaneously deteriorate. For instance, if the usage increased to 750 units per week, the reorder point would be reached after one and one-third weeks and new supplies received after two and one-third weeks when stock at this rate of usage would have fallen to 250 units.

The application of inventory analysis in practice

The techniques described in the previous section are extremely time consuming to operate, except in the simplest situation, unless the control systems are computer-based. Even if computers remove the drudgery of the calculations there are risks due to two factors. First, an inability of the user to cope with the level of information produced by the system and second a failure by users to update the information in the computer to reflect dynamics in the environment. For example the purchasing department may renegotiate a supply agreement with new lead times but fail to inform the inventory department to have this reflected in reorder level and EOQ computations. It is therefore crucial that management focuses control on critical inventory lines as defined in terms of value or the implications of a stock out.

One approach is to analyse inventory by reference to the usage value of each line over a period (usage value = usage times cost per unit). For many firms inventory will exhibit the Pareto relationship shown in Figure 15.13. This suggests that 60 per cent of the stock usage value for a period is represented by 10 per cent of the stock lines, a further 30 per cent of usage value by the next 30 per cent of lines and remaining 10 per cent usage value by the final 60 per cent of stock lines. These are often referred to as classes A, B and C respectively.

The implication of this analysis is that management's control efforts must concentrate on class A items. An extension of this is the management importance value which takes account of the lead time and importance of a stock out through the formula:

$$\text{Management importance value} = \text{usage value} \times (\text{lead time multiplier} + \text{stock out multiplier})$$

where the lead time multiplier and stock out multiplier are subjectively assessed in order to reflect the relevance of these factors.

Therefore an item with a short lead time and no stock out consequences might have a value of one $(1 + 0)$ for these whereas another with a long lead time and dire consequences if a stock out occurred might have a value of fifty $(10 + 40)$. As well as divisions on a value basis, inventory management must distinguish between the various categories of stock and develop control systems to deal with the special problems relevant to raw materials and components, work in progress and finished goods. Finally stock control systems should direct management's attention to slow moving and static items in order that corrective action can be taken.

While the treasurer's main concern with inventory relates to the impact upon liquidity of the investment in it, it is essentially physical in nature. Therefore the efficient management of the investment depends upon the establishment of effective physical controls to ensure that the inventory required for production and marketing purposes is at an optimum level with regard to the opportunity cost of the funds tied up.

Debtor management

Figure 15.5 on the treasury cycle shows debtor management as ranging from the receipt of the order up to payment being received. As with other elements of current assets, the objective of debtor management is not merely to minimize the investment but to optimize the level of debtors by examining the costs and benefits involved.

The crux of debtor management, as with the management of any resource, is for the board or senior management to lay down policy guidelines and delegate responsibility and authority for them to be carried out. The policy formulated will probably be unique to an individual organization and involve balancing a number of factors including:

1 *The ability of the firm to finance the investment in debtors:* Funds are a scarce resource for most firms and therefore there is a limit to the level of debtors which may be carried. In examining this maximum level, consideration must be given to seasonal or cyclical fluctuations in order that cash crises are not caused by a failure to provide finance at peak periods. If finance is seriously constrained the firm may seek to use invoice discounting or factoring whereby debtors partly fund themselves.

2 *Trade practice and the nature of the product:* There may be credit norms for the market sector within which the firm competes. Failure

to match the terms of competitors will lead to a serious loss of business. Again typical credit terms are often influenced by the life of the product. Short-life products, especially services, are often sold in short credit periods, while long-life items, for example consumer durables, are offered on more generous credit terms since there is a possibility of recovering the good.

3 *Pricing strategy of the firm:* Credit may be viewed as part of the overall price package offered. One pricing strategy may be to keep prices and margins high but offer generous credit terms with a view to attracting buyers who would have difficulty in purchasing without credit. While another may be to not offer credit and consequently to be able to undercut competitors' prices.

4 *The competitive situation in the market:* A monopoly supplier may set credit terms in isolation with the intention of maximizing profits. However, in a highly competitive situation the firm has ·little alternative but to match or better competitors' terms.

5 *The acceptable level of bad debts:* In general as credit periods extend and credit becomes more accessible, bad debts increase in terms of the number of accounts who are unable to pay. The crucial factor in this is the profile of a firm's portfolio of accounts. If debtors comprise a large number of small value accounts, a number may go bad without any great impact upon the results of the company. However, if there are a number of significant accounts, there is a chance that bad debts might lead to insolvency. In the latter instance bad debts are not acceptable while in the former a certain level can be tolerated.

6 *The cost benefit trade off:* The decision to offer credit can only be justified by the benefits it yields in terms of the additional contribution from the extra business generated. Against these benefits must be set the costs associated with the provision of credit. These can be classified into administrative and finance categories. Administrative costs arise from the recording, monitoring and collecting of debts. Broadly these costs are fixed, however significant variations in the number of accounts or the amount outstanding may lead to changes in the level of expenditure. In particular costs related to bad debt collection, both legal and other, and credit insurance premiums will reflect the level of activity; while other administrative costs will change as the scale of operations increases or decreases. Finance expenditure refers to the cost of finance for the investment in debtors and losses arising from bad debts. These cost sources are largely variable and will move in direct relationship to the value of total debtor balances. Therefore decisions to relax or tighten credit policies are dependent upon balancing the impact on margins from changes in sales with the decreases or increases in administrative and finance costs. Beyond this trade off, debtor management is also concerned with whether or not it is worthwhile to offer a discount to obtain earlier payment. The factors involved in the decision are the cost of the discount and the saving in finance costs from earlier receipt of the money.

For the policy guidelines to operate, systems and procedures need to be set up to cover the areas of credit analysis, credit control and debt collection.

Credit analysis may be defined as the collection and analysis of relevant information on an organization in order to determine whether credit should be granted. Credit analysis should not only be applied for new customers but be used on existing accounts on a regular basis as well as when requests are received to raise credit limits. The information sought will come from several sources. An obvious start is to obtain and analyse a set of the company's latest accounts. In addition to this it is normal practice to take up references from the customer's banker and one or more suppliers already granting credit. In both cases the references should establish the length of the relationship between the referee and the customer and be written in the knowledge of the amount of credit required. If additional comfort is wanted a credit agency (for example Dun & Bradstreet) may be approached to obtain information from wider sources and finally trade gossip and the press may provide further evidence (see Chapter 18 for details of more scientific approaches to predicting insolvency).

Credit analysis and the overall debtor management guidelines provide the two central statistics for credit control: credit limit and credit terms. The former applies to the maximum amount which may be outstanding at any point in time and the latter refers to the interval between the invoice and payment becoming due. It is important that these terms are incorporated in the supplier-to-customer contract by being notified in writing. Further it is common for the credit limit and due date to appear on every invoice sent. The credit limit is normally operated either at the order receipt or despatch stage. If the goods are specific to the customer, it is essential that credit limits are checked at the order point since beyond this point resources are irretrievably committed. However, this does present practical problems since at this instant the debtor balance will not reflect orders in process or future payments up to the point of despatch of the new order. Computer power can be used to provide forecasts of the balance at despatch based on information about orders in process, process times and cash receipt patterns or the decision can be left to the judgement of a senior official on a case by case basis. The credit terms, set in accordance with policy guidelines, rely upon prompt recording and regular monitoring for enforcement. The sooner the invoice is sent to the customer the earlier it can be recorded in his accounts and the more likely it is that payment will be made within the credit terms. Therefore invoicing, if possible, occurs simultaneously with despatch. Further the interval between the invoice being raised and recorded in the organization's books should be minimized in order that the customer indebtedness is as current as is possible. In computerized systems if invoices are batch processed delays will inevitably occur but with the more online systems this problem should be less common. In either event care must be taken to ensure that all relevant transactions (invoices, credit notes, cash received and adjustments) have been processed before monitoring reports are produced. The main monitoring report is an ageing of debtors' balances analysing each customer's balance into current and overdue portions with the overdue being further analysed into time categories such as one month, two months and over two months overdue. As well as the analysis for individual accounts, summary age analysis reports for all debtors will be provided for comparison with previous periods in total and through ratio analysis. The interval between age analysis reports will depend upon the nature of the business but weekly, four-weekly and monthly intervals are typical.

Debt collection is not an activity for the finance function to carry out in isolation. It is important that marketing is involved and it is common for ageing reports to be sent to this department. Collection procedures should be systematic. The usual pattern is that the first approach is made by phone hopefully exploiting any rapport which has built up over time. In the event of this failing a reminder letter followed by a final demand are sent at specified intervals. As a last resort legal action can be taken for recovery of the debt or the account handed over to a debt collection agency.

A final consideration for the financial manager is the possibility of insuring against bad debts. Credit insurance is available in a range of forms and from a variety of sources. Policies available include:

1 Whole turnover, which provides cover against any insolvencies.
2 Datum line, which only covers above a certain level for each account. For example if £10,000 was owed by company Y, which had become insolvent, and the datum line was £2,000, the cover would only be for the £8,000 over the datum line.
3 Specific account, which is limited to accounts selected by the policy holder.
4 Insolvency policies, which operate only on legal insolvency of the debtor.

In general it is prudent for organizations to have specific account or datum line insurance for any accounts where a failure might lead to the insolvency of the firm. Insurance is also a feature of certain invoice discounting and factoring schemes.

Debtor analysis

Decisions in debtor management focus on the impact of changing credit policies and the use of discounts. Central to these two types of decisions is the quantification of the investment represented by a debtor. Three bases can be argued as representing the investment in goods or services supplied on credit: marginal cost; full absorption cost; and selling price.

Given the usual rules on relevant costs for decision making full absorption can be rejected as incorporating fixed costs which are not affected by the credit decision. Between the remaining two bases, marginal cost represents the outflow which corresponds with the future

Table 15.3   Impact of credit policy alternatives

	Existing policy	*Option 1*	*Option 2*
Credit terms (days)	30	14	60
Sales (£000s)	1,000	960	1,200
Bad debts (% of sales)	5	3⅓	6
Credit administration cost (£000s)	20	12	25
Average collection period (months)	1½	¾	2½

Note: The credit terms differ from the average collection period as not all debtors adhere to the conditions

inflow from the debtor but only selling price reflects the opportunity cost of the decision since changes in policy lead to an acceleration or deferral of this amount.

Consider a company operating a standard credit period of thirty days and whose contribution on sales is 40 per cent. It is choosing between two alternative credit policies – one is to reduce the credit period to fourteen days and the other is to extend the interval to sixty days. The firm requires a rate of return of 20 per cent per annum upon investments. The finance manager has prepared forecasts of the impact of these policies on key variables. They are as stated in Table 15.3.

An analysis of this decision follows in Table 15.4.

Overall it appears that there is little to choose between the policy options although both are an improvement upon the existing situation. The most volatile assumption would appear to be the change in sales volume and if the forecast in this area understates the decrease or overstates the increase, a change in policy may not be viable. In general terms the example illustrates the trade offs involved in formulating credit policy.

Another trade off arises from the decision on whether, and at what level, to offer trade discounts. The main purpose behind discounts is to tempt early payment and therefore initially it seems a question of balancing the cost of the discount with the savings from shorter average collection period and lower debtors' balances. However, in some situations discounts might also stimulate demand from cash-rich firms, which seek attractive discounts, and reduce bad debts.

The simplest approach is to annualize the discount cost and compare this with the firm's required return on investments. For example a 2 per cent discount for cash instead of the usual thirty days can be seen as the equivalent of borrowing for one month at a monthly rate of 2 per cent. In annual terms this is a compound rate of approximately 27 per cent $((1 + 0.02)^{12})$.

An alternative where more involved trade offs exist is to compare costs and benefits. Suppose a company has credit sales of £1 million and an average collection period of three months. As borrowing currently costs 16 per cent, consideration is being given to offering a 5 per cent discount for payment within thirty days. It is estimated that half the

Table 15.4 Analysis of the credit policy options

	Existing situation (£000s)	Option 1 (£000s)	Option 2 (£000s)	Effect of change to: Option 1 (£000s)	Effect of change to: Option 2 (£000s)
Sales	1,000	960	1,200	(40)	200
A Contribution (loss)/gain @ 40%				(16)	80
Average debtors (average collection period × sales) ÷ 12	125	60	250	(65)	125
B Interest (cost)/saving on average debtors at 20%				13	(25)
Bad debts (sales × bad debt %)	50	32	72		
C (Increase)/decrease in bad debts				18	(22)
D Administration cost (increase)/decreases				8	(5)
Net profit/loss against the existing policy (A + B + C + D)				23	28

Table 15.5   Analysis of discount decision

Savings (£000s)			Costs (£000s)	
Sales before discounts	1000		Cost of discount	
Sales after discounts (1000 × 1.05)	1050		(½ × 1050 × .05)	26.25
Additional sales	50			
Contribution @20%		10		
Investment in debtors:				
before discounts 1000 × ³⁄₁₂	250			
after discounts 1050 × ²⁄₁₂	175			
Reduction in investment	75			
Interest saving @16%		12		
Bad debt saving		10		
Total savings		32		
less Total costs		26.25		
Net benefit		5.75		

customers will accept these terms and that sales will rise by 5 per cent due to the attraction of the discount. The current contribution margin on sales is 20 per cent and it is anticipated that bad debts will be £10,000 lower if discounts are offered. The decision is analysed in Table 15.5.

Therefore the analysis shows that the company would be £5,750 per annum better off if it adopted the policy of offering a discount in order to reduce the investment in debtors. However, it might have been possible to achieve some of the benefits without the cost of discounts through tighter credit controls and better collection procedures.

Creditor management

The major component of creditors in manufacturing and many other concerns is trade creditors. Typically trade credit is seen as a free source of funds. Therefore the policy adopted, after an assessment of whether discounts are advantageous, is to pay creditors only when pressed and use delaying payments to creditors as a first resort when there are temporary cash shortages.

This approach is somewhat shortsighted since it may lead to retaliation from existing suppliers and difficulties with obtaining credit from new suppliers, that are aware of the firm's reputation for slow payment. Typical steps taken by firms, which are not paid on time, include reducing the credit period allowed, insisting upon cash with order and raising prices. A more enlighted policy appreciates that credit terms are an integral part of the overall price negotiations. The firm should seek to obtain the lowest overall cost bearing in mind the opportunity benefit provided by longer credit. Once credit terms have been set the firm should pay in accordance with them or after a period which does not adversely affect the relationship between supplier and customer.

Another aspect of creditor management is the need to monitor the financial health of key suppliers. Key suppliers being those whose failure would have adverse financial and other consequences for the firm. Such an analysis should be carried out whenever significant new suppliers are taken on, and on a regular basis for existing creditors. In certain cases the financial reliability of a particular trader may be crucial in deciding where business should be placed especially in the case of long-run contracts.

Overall, trade creditor management reflects debtor management since one company's creditor is another's debtor. With regard to non-trade creditors, for example accruals, dividends and tax, the scope for management is reduced since the date of payment of the obligation is effectively fixed. In conclusion the financial management of creditors must seek to establish policies which negotiate optimal credit terms, reduce the risk of the failure of a key supplier and effect payment with sufficient timeliness to prevent any adverse consequences.

Summary

The management of working capital, defined as current assets less current liabilities, is a central part of the treasurer's work. Mismanagement can have serious consequences either through overtrading and an inability to pay debts as they fall due, or as a result of losing profitable opportunities due to a shortage of funds when there is an excessive level of working capital.

At a global level, the emphasis has been upon two decisions. First, establishing an appropriate level of current assets for the business and second, determining the extent to which current liabilities should be used to finance total assets. At a theoretical level the answers are clear. For the former decision, current assets should be increased provided the return generated exceeds the minimum required and that available from alternative projects. While for the latter it can be stated that current liabilities should be substituted for longer term debt provided the effect reduces the overall cost of capital. However, in more practical terms, the levels of current assets and liabilities are the result of numerous trade offs and environmental influences.

After this overview the chapter analyses the nature of the financial decisions concerned with determining an optimum level for each element of working capital. The factors involved in this are examined from both a practical and theoretical viewpoint in order that the multitude of factors involved in determining and operating policies in these areas can be appreciated.

References

Archer, S. H., 'A Model of the Determination of Firm Cash Balances', *Journal of Financial and Quantitative Analysis*, March 1966.

Baumol, W. J., 'The Transactions Demand for Cash: An Inventory Theoretic Approach', *Quarterly Journal of Economics*, November 1952.

Beehler, P. J., *Contemporary Cash Management, Principles, Practices, Perspectives*, J. Wiley & Sons, New York, 1978.

Davis, E. W. and Collier, P. A., *Treasury Management in the UK*, Association of Corporate Treasurers, 1982.

Kirkman, P. R. A., *Electronic Funds Transfer Systems*, Basil Blackwell, 1987.

Miller, M. H. and Orr, D., 'A Model for the Demand for Money by Firms', *Quarterly Journal of Economics*, August 1966.

Richards, V. D. and Laughlin, E. J., 'A Cash Conversion Cycle Approach to Liquidity Analysis', *Financial Management*, Spring 1980.

Smith, K. V., and Sells, S. B., 'Working Capital Management in Practice', from *Readings on the Management of Working Capital* (2nd edition), West Publishing Co., 1980.

Stone, B. K., 'The Use of Forecasts and Smoothing in Control-Limit Models for Cash Management', *Financial Management*, Spring 1972.

Further reading

Daellenbach, H. G., 'Are Cash Management Optimisation Models Worthwhile?', *Journal of Financial and Quantitative Analysis*, September 1974.

Sentry, J. A., 'Integrating Working Capital and Capital Investment Processes', from Smith, K. V. (ed.), *Leadership on the Management of Working Capital*, West Publishing Co., 1980.

Smith, K. V., 'On Working Capital as an Investment by the Firm', from Smith, K. V. (ed.), *Readings on the Management of Working Capital*, West Publishing Co., 1980.

RELEVANT ARTICLES

Cane, A., 'The EFT Revolution', *The Banker*, February 1982.

Kearney, K. J., 'The New Payment Technology', *Journal of Bank Research*, 1981.

Richards, J. and Flook, J., 'Cash Flow: Recipe for Success' *The Treasurer*, May 1984.

Williamson, J. M., 'Pricing Money Transfer Services', *Journal of Bank Research*, 1981.

RELEVANT BOOKS

Bass, R. M. V., *Credit Management*, Business Books, 1979.

Kirkman, P. R. A., 'Working Capital Management', from Firth, M. and Keane, S. M. (eds), *Issues in Financial Management*, Philip Allan, 1986.

Lewis, C. D., *Scientific Inventory Control* (2nd edition), Butterworths 1981.

Smith, K. V., *Guide to Working Capital Management*, McGraw-Hill, 1979.

16 Investment management

Introduction

Investments undertaken by companies may be classified, by reference to their duration, into long-run and short-run categories. Long-run investments typically cover investments in property, shares, loan stock and other assets where the funds are committed on a relatively permanent basis and the motivation for the investment was strategic; that is closely tied to the achievement of corporate long-run objectives, for example, land and property acquired for future expansion or shares in a competitor held to provide a base for a takeover bid. In contrast short-run investments are intended to optimize the use of cash surpluses.

Cash surpluses arise for many reasons and last for varying time periods. Examples might include a seasonal or cyclical trade pattern, asset sales, a failure to apply borrowed money, accumulations to pay tax or dividends and improved working capital management. In principle where there is no foreseeable use for these balances the cash should be distributed in dividends or used to repay debt. However, as well as holding cash to meet transaction needs companies also retain funds from precautionary and speculative motives. In the former instance money is retained against unexpected losses, while in the latter case cash is held to enable advantage to be taken of unforeseen investment opportunities. Therefore, although companies with an aggressive working capital policy may plan to minimize surplus funds preferring to borrow whenever cash is needed, more defensively inclined companies would set aside surplus cash in an investment portfolio to provide liquid funds as and when needed.

This chapter concentrates upon the practical aspects of the management of a portfolio of short-run investments with the treasurer as fund manager. Longer run investment decisions are dealt with in Chapters 6 and 8.

Objectives

The primary objective of the treasurer is, in principle, to maximize the after tax returns from the portfolio. However, the situation is more complex than this. Surplus funds are invested within the wider context of an organization's working capital policy and therefore the portfolio must be able to provide liquid funds as required. There must be a synchronization of the liquidity profile of the investments with forecast cash requirements, plus any buffer against unforeseen claims. Since, typically the longer the maturity the greater the return, the liquidity constraint directly contradicts the primary objective. The treasurer is therefore required to balance the increased returns from committing funds for definite periods against the costs associated with borrowing when liquid funds are not available.

Another constraint on the maximization of after tax returns is the need for the portfolio to have an acceptable risk profile. There are two major risks involved in short-run investment – default risk and valuation risk. Default risk is the chance that the borrower may fail to pay interest or repay the capital sum as it falls due. Default risk will be negligible for UK government securities but might be considerable with shares and unsecured loans or overseas government securities. Valuation risk may be defined as the possibility that, upon the realization of a security, the sum received is lower than the original investment. This can arise either because of a discount (or penalty) for realization other than at a specified time or because interest rates in the economy have changed. As interest rates rise the value of fixed interest securities will fall and vice versa.

Therefore the objective of investment management must be to maximize the after tax return earned by the portfolio, subject to the constraints imposed by liquidity and risk considerations.

Policy

The objectives of maintaining a portfolio should be translated into a formal document covering the company's investment policy. The board of the company should pass a resolution authorizing the treasurer and his subordinates to invest surplus funds in accordance with this policy. The matters referred to would include:

1 *Objectives* – a statement of the broad aim of the portfolio management team.
2 *Funds* – a definition of the funds to be placed at the treasurer's disposal. This may be complex in the group situation if attempts to develop a central portfolio are undertaken, since subsidiaries will require their own working cash surpluses and therefore rules on the maximum size of these balances before transfer to the group portfolio will have to be decided upon. Further it will be necessary to lay

down procedures for the transfer of funds to and from the subsidiaries to ensure that their liquidity requirements are still met.

3 *Types of investments* – the universe of investment opportunities, each with its own return, liquidity and risk characteristics is extremely large, covering UK and overseas government and private securities as well as the more exotic alternatives, e.g. options, futures and swaps. In authorizing the treasurer to manage the portfolio, limits on this universe of investment opportunities should be set provided they are compatible with the portfolio objectives. For instance, overseas investments may be excluded because of their additional exchange risks, shares and unsecured loans may be vetoed as having too high a valuation risk and limits may be set on maturity dates to avoid realization problems.

4 *Maximum holdings* – even with approved instruments it may be prudent to limit, either in monetary terms or by proportion, the funds in any one particular security. For example it might be stated that no more than one million pounds be held in bank deposits or not more than 20 per cent of funds may be in overseas investments.

5 *Intermediaries* – the names of approved institutions should be defined both for reputable dealers, through whom securities may be bought and sold, and banking institutions with whom deposits may be placed.

6 *Staff* – a list of staff authorized to deal in portfolio securities specifying whether they are permitted to buy only, sell only or do both, and setting limits on the value of individual transactions and the types of securities in which they may deal.

This policy document should obviously be subject to regular review but it does provide a framework within which the treasurer can act.

Investment selection

Potentially the treasurer faces a bewildering range of investment opportunities but in practice matters are somewhat simpler. First, the treasurer's actions are limited by the company's policy. In most companies there will be an emphasis upon ensuring that liquidity requirements can be met and that investments represent a store of value with minimal valuation risk. Second, the funds available may themselves limit the options; for instance, inter-bank deposits require £1 million and certificates of deposit £50,000 as a minimum investment. Finally the treasurer will concentrate investment in instruments where the department has appropriate expertise.

Such constraints mean that portfolios of short-run investments will be concentrated in the short-term money markets. In these markets the opportunity for above average returns with acceptable risk are extremely limited and therefore the treasurer's attention will focus on the

Table 16.1   Interest rate structure

| | Maturity | | | |
Instrument	One month	Three months	Six months	One year
Treasury bills (buy)	$9\frac{13}{16}$	$9\frac{9}{32}$		
Sterling certificates of deposit	$10\frac{1}{16}$	$9\frac{21}{32}$	$9\frac{7}{16}$	$9\frac{7}{16}$
Bank deposits	$10\frac{3}{32}$	$9\frac{27}{32}$	$9\frac{21}{32}$	$9\frac{21}{32}$
Local authority bonds	$10\frac{7}{16}$	$10\frac{3}{16}$	10	10

Note:
1. At this time interest rates fall as maturities lengthen. However the opposite is equally likely as is demonstrated by the *Financial* Times London Money Rates' shown in Appendix 16.1.
2. The term 'bank deposit' used in Table 16.1 covers a range of investment opportunities with the following characteristics:
   1   Fixed money value.
   2   Risk associated with them is negligible especially with the major clearing banks.
   3   Repayable on demand or after a prearranged interval.
   4   Usually interest bearing (the best example of a deposit without interest is the funds in a current account at a clearing bank).
   One of the main functions of banks is to take deposits, however there are two distinct markets. First, the retail sector, which takes deposits through a network of branches on standard terms. Second, there is a wholesale market centred on the head offices of banks where deposits are taken through brokers or direct contacts for periods varying from overnight to over a year. The rates of interest obtained by depositors are negotiated individually. The term bank deposit in this chapter refers to the wholesale market.

structure of interest rates, tax efficiency and administrative ease when investments are selected. Table 16.1 shows the relationship between maturity and interest rates for a variety of instruments at 1 July 1986.

There are three main reasons for differences in the interest rates over time and between different instruments. First as security falls, interest rates rise, hence treasury bills with UK government backing have a lower yield than bank deposits, which are not quite so securely backed. Second there is a premium for marketability; bank deposits and certificates of deposit are both secured with a bank. However certificates of deposit are negotiable whereas bank deposits are not. The interest rate premium on bank deposits reflects this lack of liquidity. Finally there is the maturity factor. In Table 16.1 as the term of the investment increases the interest rates fall. This is a reverse of the expectation that the longer the funds are tied up the higher will be the interest paid. The situation reflects a market expectation that rates will fall and therefore an investor in certificates of deposit for one year at 9.44 per cent is better off than one who places for three months at 9.65 per cent by which time rates have fallen to say 9 per cent and can thus only achieve 9.32 per cent for the year. The treasurer with funds available for one year could choose between twelve one month, four three month, two six month, a one year or any acceptable combination of these maturities. In selecting a strategy the treasurer would normally resort to computerized financial modelling using a range of interest rate forecasts. Success in this environment depends upon being in short maturities as interest rates rise and in long maturities as they fall.

As well as studying the structure of interest rates, the treasurer can improve portfolio performance by selecting portfolio investments by reference to their relative taxation advantages. In the past strategies have concentrated upon the gilts market and the practice of 'bond-washing'. Under this system gilts were purchased ex-dividend and sold cum-dividend in order to convert income into a capital gain. Further if the gilts were held for more than one year they would be exempt from tax. However, since February 1986 this practice has been prevented by a scheme which requires accrued interest to be accounted for and treated as income for tax purposes. To prevent making the gilts market unattractive to investors, from the same date any capital gains on gilts and other qualifying bonds will be exempt from capital gains tax. This concession frees treasurers to realize capital profits without consideration of time constraints or tax consequences and gives an incentive to investment in these securities.

Where the portfolio includes overseas investments or investments held overseas the taxation situation will be more complex and pose problems regarding double taxation agreements and remittability. In these situations the investments will need to fit in with corporate strategies.

Finally the difficulty of obtaining above-normal returns suggests that the factor of administrative simplicity should be considered when selecting investments. The time, and consequently money, involved in forecasting rates, switching funds and monitoring the situation daily may well not be justified unless very large portfolios are involved.

Performance comparisons

Another complexity facing the treasurer investing in the short-term money market is the different ways in which returns are stated. There are three ways:

1 Discount
2 Coupon
3 Redemption yield

Investments issued at discount include treasury, trade and bank bills. Under discounting an instrument is issued at one price and redeemed on the maturity date at a higher price, the price difference effectively being the interest element. It is therefore not immediately clear how to compare a discount with a rate of interest. Suppose a three month (ninety-one day) treasury bill was issued at 97.5 per 100, a discount of 2.5. The annualized interest rate is calculated thus:

Return (interest)   2.5
Investment period   91 days
Return $(2.5/97.5) \times 100 = 2.56$ per cent
Annualized return $2.56 \times (365/91) = 10.27$ per cent

This methodology can be generalized in the expression:

$i = (M - I)/I.n$

where   i = annualized interest as a decimal
        M = maturity value
        I = the investment
        n = number of years or part of year

e.g. $(100 - 97.5)/(97.5 \times 91/365) = 0.1027$ or as a percentage 10.27 per cent.

The formula can be modified to enable an interest rate to be converted into a discount rate:

$d = (M - I)/M.n$

where   d = the discount rate as a decimal and others as before

Coupon instruments include certificates of deposit, bank deposits and inter-bank deposits. Interest is based upon the quoted rate being applied for the whole year with the amount subject to adjustment for the investment's duration. For example, £100,000 is deposited for six months (182 days) at a quoted rate of 10 per cent. The interest earned would be calculated as:

Annual interest $0.1 \times £100,000 = £10,000$

Interest for period $\frac{182}{365} \times 10,000 \quad = £\ 4,986$

In comparing interest rates, it is apparent that for the examples used treasury bills provide the slightly higher interest rate (10.27 per cent against 10 per cent). If the discount rate were to be compared for the treasury bill the rate is:

$d = (100 - 97.5)/(100 \times 91/365) = 0.1003$ or 10.03 per cent

and for the deposit:

$d = (104,986 - 100,000)/(104,986 \times 182/365) = 0.0952$ or 9.52 per cent

As would be expected both interest rate and discount rate methods provide a similar ranking.

Redemption yield covers short and longer dated securities, such as gilts, where the return is a combination of discount or premium and interest payments. The return earned on these instruments can be obtained by solving an equation to discover the interest rate which equates the current price of the security with the future flows generated. Therefore solve for r:

$$I = \sum_{t=1}^{n} \frac{i}{(1+r)^t} + \frac{M}{(1+r)^n}$$

where I = investment   i = interest received   t = time periods
       M = maturity value   n = time to maturity

This may be carried out either using specially constructed bond tables or by arithmetic interpolation (exactly as for redeemable debentures – see Chapter 7).

Suppose a company purchases 10 per cent treasury stock, redeemable June 1987, in January 1986 for £99 per £100, with interest payable twice yearly in June and December. The future cash flows associated with this investment are three interest payments (June 1986, December 1986 and June 1987) plus the redemption value. To find the redemption yield (r) we must solve:

$$99 = \frac{5}{1+r} + \frac{5}{(1+r)^2} + \frac{5}{(1+r)^3} + \frac{100}{(1+r)^3}$$

This gives a six-months redemption yield (r) of 5.36 per cent. To convert this to the annual redemption yield $1 + r$ is squared, to allow for reinvestment of the interest after six months, giving 1.11, i.e. 11 per cent annual redemption yield. (The *Financial Times* redemption yield statistics are based on doubling the six-month yield.)

While these calculations enable the performance of different instruments to be compared from a relatively common base, they do not remove the selection difficulties caused by instruments maturing at different points in time, when interest rate structures, and hence the ranking of investments by the treasurer may be very different. It is of little consolation to place funds on bank deposit for six months at 12 per cent, the best obtainable, if one month later similar deposits attract a 13 per cent coupon.

Short-term money markets and instruments

The securities in which a treasurer invests arise from three main short-term money markets:

1 Discount market
2 Parallel money markets
3 International money markets

The discount market has a crucial role in effecting government monetary policy. This is achieved by discount houses and other approved intermediaries acting as buffers between the Bank of England and the commercial banks in influencing interest rates. The market handles the sale of treasury bills by weekly tender as well as dealing in government stock maturing in less than five years, bank bills and local authority bills. Alongside the discount market are the parallel money markets including the inter-bank, local authority deposit and financial futures markets. The most important of these is the inter-bank market which involves a large number of banks and commercial lenders dealing in non-negotiable bank deposits and negotiable certificates of deposit of various durations. The international money markets refer principally to the eurocurrency market that encompasses international loans and deposits in US dollars, Deutschmarks, Swiss francs, Dutch guilders and other widely traded currencies, where the loan or deposit is held outside the country of the currency. Thus eurodollars are US dollars held outside the US; for example, US dollars deposited in London by international investors to finance a project in Italy would be eurodollars. The instruments traded include eurobonds issued for periods of over five years, eurocurrency certificates of deposit, inter-bank eurodeposits, euronotes and eurodeposits.

While the instruments in which the treasurer invests are traded in these markets, normally the treasurer will deal in a secondary market, the market for old issues, through financial intermediaries (banks, stockbrokers, discount houses and others). The remainder of this section details some of the more important instruments available to the treasurer. It must be borne in mind that the list is not comprehensive and that the markets are highly inventive with the ability to develop new securities as conditions change.

Sterling instruments

1 *Treasury bills* – bearer documents issued weekly by the Bank of England with a standard maturity of three months. Applications in the primary market are by tender with the minimum tender being £50,000. It is normal for applications to greatly exceed bills on offer. There is a large secondary market in maturities from three months downwards. The instrument is highly secure and liquid – it therefore yields the lowest return.

2 *Bank bills and acceptance credits* – bills of exchange, in the case of the bank bill, drawn by a creditor upon a debtor company and guaranteed by a bank or discount house, while for acceptance credits the debtor draws the bill which is similarly guaranteed. The maturity of these instruments varies from three to twelve months and their acceptance by the banks or discount houses means that

there is minimal risk for the investor. Returns are marginally better than treasury bills.

3 *Deposits* – time deposits available from a number of sources, banks, local authorities and building societies. They are non-negotiable and cover a wide range of durations from five years to overnight. They represent the largest short-term market for funds, however the lack of negotiability is a drawback and their yield therefore exceeds that of bills.

4 *Certificates of deposit* – negotiable deposits issued by banks and building societies. The depositor receives a bearer certificate with a coupon. Maturity periods are usually less than one year and liquidity, especially for short maturities, is excellent. Interest is payable upon maturity or annually but the yield is slightly below deposits due to negotiability.

5 *Gilts* – gilt-edged securities are government backed, registered and quoted on the Stock Exchange. They are available in a large range of maturities, including undated; however the treasurer will concentrate upon maturities of less than five years. Rates offered are tied to money market rates but the return may be improved by capital gains tax advantages.

6 *Bonds* – registered securities quoted on the Stock Exchange and issued by local authorities. Rates are tied closely with the money market and liquidity is good.

7 *Certificates of tax deposit* – deposits with the Inland Revenue which may be surrendered for cash (but with an interest rate penalty) or used in settlement of a wide range of tax liabilities. The certificates offer a convenient investment for short-term surpluses retained for this purpose.

8 *Floating rate notes* – bearer certificates with variable interest rates and longer maturities (over five years) issued by a range of financial institutions. The yield is relatively high but marketability may not always be easy.

9 *Sterling eurobonds, debentures and loan stock* – fixed interest instruments in bearer and registered form issued by the corporate sector. A wide range of longer maturities with yields which take account of the long-run interest rate risks and varying marketability.

Non-sterling instruments

The investment portfolio might also contain non-sterling instruments either because surplus finds have arisen in other currencies or because international exchange rate movements offer above average returns. The majority of sterling instruments described have currency counterparts. Examples might include eurocurrency certificates of deposit issued by banks in countries such as Canada, US and Japan, eurocurrency deposits from overnight to the medium term, eurobonds for the longer run, euronotes and a range of overseas government securities, for example US treasury bills.

Administration

The implementation of an organization's investment policy needs a suitable administrative framework. The management of an investment portfolio will require a minimum of two people to provide back up and internal control.

The basic administrative steps associated with a decision to invest are as follows:

1 *Quotation* – invitations to quote should be sought in accordance with the formal policy document. The number of quotations required will depend on the instrument and the company's access to current rates through Reuters or Telerate systems. For instruments such as treasury bills and gilts, where market rates vary little, few quotes are required. However for bank deposits, where rates depend upon a bank's circumstances, more quotations may be appropriate. Overall the regular following of rates through an online terminal service will reduce the number of quotes required.
2 *Documentation* – once a quotation has been accepted, the investment management section must raise appropriate documentation notifying the bank to transfer or receive funds and specifying the movement of certificates.
3 *Accounting* – for internal control reasons this activity will be separate from the documentation. The accounts department will check that correct amounts are paid and received and ensure that the transaction is reflected in the portfolio records, which include:
   (a) Transaction details – full information of each contract, the contract date, number of units, purchase or sale, cost or proceeds, interest and maturity.
   (b) Movements – records of the flow of funds into and out of the portfolio.

These records should enable a full portfolio listing to be extracted; however often it is felt simpler to maintain a continuously updated list. For large portfolios the use of a computer and suitable software will simplify the record keeping.

Apart from the day-to-day aspects of administration within the department liquidity guidelines, maturity rules and other aspects of the formal policy document need to be kept constantly under review together with the performance of the function.

Performance evaluation

The decision to actively manage surplus cash resources within an investment portfolio has cost implications. Personnel involved will expend time in routine trading and keeping abreast of market trends and developments. As well as these salary costs, there will be associated overheads from departmental administration and other services plus

Table 16.2 Proforma portfolio reconciliation

	£000	£000
Opening valuation		xxxxx
Add:		
Cash inflows	xxxx	
Interest received	xxxx	xxxx
Less:		
Cash outflows		(xxxxx)
Add/less:		
Investment value changes		xxx
Closing valuation		£xxxxx

the opportunity cost in diverting people with specialist skills from other areas.

Given that the increased returns from active management may be small, for example perhaps only 1 per cent in the short-term money market, it is vital that the performance of the treasurer is regularly assessed to ensure that policy guidelines are complied with, and to demonstrate that the activity is a proper use of resources.

Central to an appraisal system is regular valuation of the portfolio. This, together with a reconciliation of the movements since the last valuation, provides a clear indication of management's performance. Table 16.2 shows a proforma for this reconciliation.

With large portfolios the valuation procedures will be tedious unless the system is computerized. The value of marketable securities, for example gilts, treasury bills or certificates of deposit can be obtained from brokers or dealers. More difficult is valuing non-negotiable instruments, for instance bank time deposits, since initial value plus accrued interest does not reflect performance regarding the interest rate obtained. Possibly the best solution is to treat such investments as negotiable and impute a market price using certificates of deposit as a guide. Longer term investments (property and unquoted shares) may be separated from the portfolio for the purpose of the regular valuation and assessed separately.

The choice of a benchmark against which to establish the excess returns obtained from active management is problematical. Solutions must fit the circumstances of each company but appropriate measures could include:

1 The use of overnight deposit interest rates.
2 The analysis of the portfolio into broad liquidity bands. For the highly liquid band use overnight rates with appropriate time deposit rates for the other bands.
3 The establishment of a representative portfolio based upon the policy guidelines.

Appendix 16.1   *London Money Rates*

The *Financial Times* Money Lates Table shows the rates quoted for a number of different instruments with maturities ranging from overnight to one year. In contrast to Table 16.1, the rates rise as maturities increase

October 20	Overnight	7 days notice	One month	Three months	Six months	One year
Inter-bank[1]	11.5	$9\frac{11}{16}$–$9\frac{9}{16}$	$9\frac{7}{8}$–$9\frac{3}{4}$	$10\frac{1}{4}$–$10\frac{1}{8}$	$10\frac{1}{2}$–$10\frac{3}{8}$	$10\frac{3}{8}$–$10\frac{1}{2}$
Sterling CDs	–	–	$9\frac{27}{32}$–$9\frac{23}{32}$	$10\frac{3}{16}$–$10\frac{1}{16}$	$10\frac{3}{8}$–$10\frac{1}{4}$	$10\frac{3}{8}$–$10\frac{1}{4}$
Local authority departments	$9\frac{1}{8}$	$9\frac{1}{2}$	$9\frac{3}{4}$	$10\frac{1}{4}$	$10\frac{3}{8}$	$10\frac{1}{2}$
Local authority bonds	–	–	10	$10\frac{3}{16}$	$10\frac{7}{16}$	$10\frac{5}{8}$
Discount market deposits	10.9	$9\frac{5}{8}$–$9\frac{1}{2}$	$9\frac{1}{2}$	$9\frac{3}{4}$	–	–
Company deposits	$9\frac{1}{2}$–$9\frac{1}{4}$	$9\frac{3}{4}$–$9\frac{5}{8}$	$9\frac{13}{16}$–$9\frac{7}{8}$	$10\frac{5}{16}$	$10\frac{7}{16}$	$10\frac{3}{14}$
Finance house deposits	–	–	$9\frac{7}{8}$	$10\frac{3}{8}$	$10\frac{5}{8}$	$10\frac{7}{8}$
Treasury bills (buy)	–	–	$9\frac{11}{16}$	$9\frac{3}{4}$	–	–
Bank bills (buy)	–	–	$9\frac{23}{32}$	$9\frac{7}{8}$	$10\frac{1}{16}$	–
Fine trade bills (buy)	–	–	$10\frac{11}{32}$	$10\frac{1}{2}$	$10\frac{11}{16}$	–
Dollar CDs[2]	–	–	8.00–7.95	8.40–8.35	8.50–8.45	9.95–9.90
SDR linked deposits[3]	–	–	$6\frac{7}{8}$–$6\frac{3}{4}$	$7\frac{11}{16}$–$7\frac{7}{8}$	$7\frac{13}{16}$–$7\frac{11}{16}$	8–$7\frac{7}{8}$
ECU linked deposits[3]	–	–	7–$6\frac{7}{8}$	8–$7\frac{7}{8}$	$8\frac{3}{16}$–$8\frac{1}{16}$	$8\frac{1}{4}$

Notes:
1   The inter-bank rates are those for lending and borrowing in substantial amounts between the banks.
2   Dollar CDs (Certificates of Deposit) relate to the rates for eurodollar CDs.
3   SDR (Special Drawing Right) and ECU (European Currency Unit) linked deposits relate to rates for deposits calculated in these international currency substitutes. As SDRs and ECUs represent a composite of several currencies (five in the case of SDRs and all EEC currencies except the drachma for the ECU), they are less volatile than deposits denominated in one currency.
Reproduced with permission from the *Financial Times*, Thursday 21 October 1987.

Whatever approach is adopted, the evaluation process is important in demonstrating that the active management of surplus funds is justified.

Summary

From 1980 onwards net cash flows for the UK corporate and commercial sectors have been strongly positive. Simultaneously the money markets have become more sophisticated and increased the opportunities for portfolio managers. These two factors have led to investment management becoming an increasingly important part of the treasurer's role.

The investment management function requires a clearly stated policy to enable sensible choices to be made from the infinite variety of investment opportunities. The policy objectives must reach a compromise between the maximization of after-tax returns from the portfolio and the counterbalancing factors of liquidity requirements and acceptable risk. The balancing of return, liquidity and risk requires accurate forecasting both of cash flows within the company and of the future of interest rates within the economy.

For these reasons it is important to realize that investment management is not an isolated activity but is an integral part of the financial management of the company with implications for cash and working capital management and risk management.

Further reading

RELEVANT ARTICLES

Grey, G., 'Short Term Investments – Choices for the Treasurer', *The Treasurer*, May 1986.

Smail, B. C., 'Surplus Funds Management and Corporate Strategy', *The Treasurer*, May 1986.

Comer, G., 'Practical Surplus Funds Management – a Treasurer's View', *The Treasurer*, May 1986.

RELEVANT BOOKS

Rutherford, J., *Introduction to Stock Exchange Investments*, Macmillan, 1985, Chapters 4 and 6.

Hodson, D., *Corporate Finance and Treasury Management*, Gee & Co., 1984, Sections D1 and D2.

Part Five

Company Valuations and Reorganizations

17 Mergers and acquisitions

Introduction

For many years mergers and acquisitions have been a popular form of corporate reorganization. Over the period 1982–6 there has been a massive increase in the average value of transactions, a trend that has occurred not only in the UK but also in the US. While mergers often come in waves depending upon the level of corporate liquidity, the availability of outside funds, and share price levels on the stock market, there is no reason to believe that will go out of fashion.

This chapter considers some of the more important issues relevant to UK acquisitions although a more comprehensive review is provided in Cooke (1986). Many other countries have experienced increases in the level of takeover activity and there is now considerable interest in cross-border transactions. Such transactions are highly complex and some of the major issues are considered in Cooke (1988).

Throughout this chapter the terms 'merger' and 'acquisition' are used synonymously since in virtually every transaction it is possible to deduce the acquirer and acquiree (the victim). In fact a genuine merger, the coming together of two similar-sized organizations for mutual benefit, is very rare indeed despite protestations to the contrary by the Accounting Standards Committee.

The following types of transaction are undertaken in the UK:

1 A privately negotiated agreement with members of the company being taken over.
2 The purchase of new shares by private treaty.
3 The acquisition of the assets of the target company.
4 The purchase of shares on the Stock Exchange.
5 An offer to all shareholders for all or part of the offeree's share capital.

Control of the behaviour of participants in takeovers in public and some private companies is largely vested in the City Code. The Code, that is administered by the Panel on Takeovers and Mergers, stipulates that where a company acquires 30 per cent of the shares of another company it must make an offer for the rest of the share capital. Thus the Code views 30 per cent as effective control even though a company must acquire over 50 per cent to achieve legal control. Partial bids that result in the acquisition of between 30 per cent and 50 per cent are not normally permitted and require approval from the Panel.

Takeover trends

Concentration in UK industry has increased considerably this century and a significant part of this increase has resulted from takeover activity (Prais, 1981). Indeed, in terms of employment in large enterprises the UK and US are more highly concentrated when compared with most European countries. Prais has estimated that approximately 50 per cent of the change in concentration in the UK is directly attributable to merger activity.

Statistics on acquisitions and mergers are compiled by the government from information published in newspapers, information supplied directly to them and sometimes from requisitions to companies. The figures are published on a quarterly basis in *Business Monitor MQ7* and Table 17.1 summarizes the information for the period 1969 to 1986. In

Table 17.1   Mergers and acquisitions within the UK

Year	Number acquired	Percentage change	Value (£m)	Percentage change	Average value (£m)
1969	846		1069		1.26
1970	793	−6.3	1122	+5.0	1.41
1971	884	+11.5	911	−18.8	1.03
1972	1210	+36.9	2532	+178.0	2.09
1973	1205	−0.4	1304	−48.5	1.08
1974	504	−58.2	508	−61.0	1.01
1975	315	−37.5	291	−42.7	0.92
1976	353	+12.1	448	+54.0	1.27
1977	481	+36.3	824	+83.9	1.71
1978	567	+17.9	1140	+38.3	2.01
1979	534	−5.8	1656	+45.3	3.10
1980	469	−12.2	1475	−10.9	3.14
1981	452	−3.6	1144	−22.4	2.53
1982	463	+2.4	2206	+92.8	4.76
1983	447	−3.5	2343	+6.2	5.24
1984	568	+27.1	5474	+133.6	9.64
1985	474	−16.6	7090	+29.5	14.96
1986	695	+46.6	13535	+90.9	19.47

Source: Numbers acquired and value from *Business Monitor MQ7*

terms of numbers of acquisitions the level of activity was at its highest in 1972 and 1973. Furthermore, despite high rates of inflation in the 1970s the average value of transactions occurring in 1972 was not exceeded until 1979. The period 1982–6 was characterized by high-valued acquisitions, a trend that also occurred in the US. The average value of transactions in 1981 was £2.53m and this had risen to a dramatic £14.96m in 1985 despite low levels of inflation. A list of the UK's fifteen largest transactions is provided in Table 17.2 – the table excludes takeovers involving foreigners.

A further feature of acquisition activity is that equity as a percentage of total expenditure on UK acquisitions exceeded cash payments in 1983, this being the first time since 1972, when industry was suffering a cash crisis. However, equity was more important than cash in 1985 and 1986 reflecting the fact that many of the high-valued transactions were conducted on the basis of a share-for-share exchange. Table 17.3 shows acquisition currency as a percentage of total expenditure over the period 1969 to 1985.

Motives for mergers

Steiner (1975) has emphasized the multivariate nature of motives for mergers and argues that mergers are contingent upon actors, climates, motives and participants. He summarizes motives for and against mergers as follows:

1   Profit increasing for the firm, achieving real efficiencies, increasing market power, tax and accounting opportunities.

Table 17.2   Major UK acquisitions up to 31 December 1986

Year	Bidder	Target	Consideration (£m)
1986	Hanson Trust	Imperial Group	2660
1986	Guinness	Distillers	2531
1986	Habitat Mothercare	British Home Stores	1520
1983	BAT	Eagle Star	968
1986	Vantona Viyella	Coats Paton	690
1986	Dee Corporation	Fine Fare/Shoppers Paradise	686
1984	BAT	Hambro Life	664
1983	BTR	Thomas Tilling	660
1985	ASDA	MFI	569
1985	Burtons	Debenhams	566
1986	P & O	Stock Conversion	402
1984	Sun Alliance	Phoenix Assurance	396
1984	BP	Selection Trust	390
1984	Unilever	Brooke Bond	389
1973	Grand Metropolitan	Watney Mann	376

Table 17.3 UK acquisition currency (percentages of total expenditure)

Year	Cash	Equity	Fixed-interest securities
1969	27.7	51.6	20.7
1970	22.4	53.1	24.5
1971	31.3	48.0	20.7
1972	19.5	57.6	22.9
1973	53.0	35.7	11.3
1974	68.3	22.4	9.3
1975	59.4	32.0	8.6
1976	71.7	26.8	1.5
1977	62.1	36.9	1.0
1978	57.4	40.6	2.0
1979	56.3	31.1	12.6
1980	51.5	45.4	3.1
1981	67.7	29.6	2.7
1982	58.1	31.8	10.1
1983	43.8	53.8	2.4
1984	53.8	33.6	12.6
1985	40.3	52.3	7.4
1986	17.9	63.8	18.3

Source: Business Monitor MQ7

2 Growth as a goal.
3 General (external) speculative goals.
4 Insider opportunities: to stockholders; to acquiring managements; to financial groups.
5 Deterrents: antitrust law enforcement; securities law and enforcement; transactions cost; public and congressional opinion.

The above summary demonstrates that motives for mergers are complex and change over time and some of these motives will be considered further.

Synergy

Synergy refers to the concept by which two firms combine and increase their value i.e. $2 + 2 = 5$. The basis of synergy is operating economies of scale that may result from combining existing firms currently producing at sub-optimal levels. Indivisibilities can occur with individuals, overheads or equipment. For example, indivisibilities may often occur in industries with heavy equipment such as the highly competitive steel industry, where it is essential for optimum levels of production to be achieved.

Another source of operating economies of scale may arise from economies of increased dimensions as lower unit costs are achieved at higher levels of capacity. In addition, specialization and learning effects are another source of cost savings. Transaction costs involved in raising funds are also reduced as larger sums of money are raised – financial economies of sale.

Diversification

Diversification is a motivation adopted by many companies wishing to acquire different product ranges in an attempt to smooth earnings and reduce risk. The applicability of the product life-cycle to most products means that the ultimate outcome for a one-product firm is normally liquidation. Consequently companies try to be multi-product based and for some companies this means expanding overseas. For example, strategies adopted by Volkswagen and Volvo were designed to reduce their vulnerability to the cyclical fluctuations of the car industry.

Acquisition of growth

In order to improve its growth prospects some companies adopt a strategy of acquiring related firms. Bearing in mind that the market capitalization of a firm is often less than the replacement cost of its assets it is frequently cheaper to buy companies rather than to adopt a building strategy by buying assets. An example of an acquisitive company adopting such a strategy is C. H. Beazer (Holdings), a housebuilding and property developing company. Its profits for the year ended June 1986 increased by nearly 97 per cent from £15.81m to £31.12m on an increased turnover to over £50.7m. During the year the acquisitions of French Kier from Trafalgar House and Wallis and Sons were integrated into the group and two other takeovers were completed.

Acquiring assets

The motive here may be to obtain the right to a particular asset such as a good management team or good research and development facilities but also with a view to acquiring assets at a discount. Assets acquired at a discount may be retained or sold off piecemeal – an approach more common with tangible rather than intangible assets.

Acquiring market share

There is a high correlation between increased market share and increased profitability and this fact has led to the advice that in making acquisitions a sizeable slice of the market should be obtained (see for example Kitching (1974) and Biggadike (1979)).

Taxation and accounting reasons

A number of taxation advantages may accure to the acquisition of a particular company. For example, the acquisition of tax losses may be useful if they can be relieved within the group, certain capital gains advantages may be achieved and relief for existing unrelieved advance corporation tax may be obtained.

The method of financing a takeover may be influenced by accounting methods. For example, a company may wish to acquire another using its shares as consideration in order to account for the transaction as a merger rather than an acquisition. Using merger rather than acquisition accounting will lead to distributable profits being higher and asset values being lower.

Managerial motives

Managers may wish to pursue an acquisitive strategy because growth in profits and assets may enhance their own salaries, perquisites and status. Alternative theories of the firms have been suggested to explain managerial behaviour and include Marris's (1964) theory which suggests that managers pursue growth-maximization policy out of self-interest. Newbould (1970) established that managers' motives for merger were often to increase the acquirer's dominant position in the market and to defend existing market positions.

Merger control

Control over mergers in the UK may be divided into legal aspects, and self-regulatory controls administered by the Stock Exchange through the Panel on Takeovers and Mergers. Additional controls are exercised by the EEC in Articles 85 and 86 of the Treaty of Rome.

Legal controls

Fair Trading Act 1973
The Secretary of State for Trade and Industry is empowered by Section 1 of the Fair Trading Act to appoint a Director General of Fair Trading whose duty it is to constantly review the commercial activities relating to goods and services. One of the responsibilities of the Director General is to ensure that circumstances do not occur that adversely affect the economic interests of consumers.

The Director General reviews all takeovers, other than those involving newspapers, that meet the following criteria as laid down by the Act:

1   Where at least one-quarter of all goods of a particular description are supplied by an enterprise.
2   Where the value of the assets taken over exceeds £30m.

Section 64(7) of the Act provides authority for the Secretary of State to raise the asset threshold by order of a statutory instrument. The threshold originally laid down was £5m and this was increased to £15m in April 1980 and increased to its present level in July 1984.

All mergers meeting the criteria laid down in the Act are reviewed by the mergers secretariat of the Office of Fair Trading to establish whether there are any public interest considerations. Information on mergers is collected from the financial press and from companies although there is no prenotification requirement. Relevant parties are consulted and where there are questions of public interest the Director General may recommend that the takeover should be investigated by the Monopolies Commission. The Secretary of State is not obliged to accept the recommendation of the Director General although in nearly all cases he does.

A feature of the UK system is that companies may seek confidential advice from the Office of Fair Trading as to the possibility of a referral, often before a bid is made.

Another feature is that the criteria provided for a review do not apply to newspaper mergers. The Act specifies that all newspaper transfers with a circulation of 500,000 or more are illegal, unless consent for the transaction is given by the Secretary of State. Section 58(2) of the Fair Trading Act states that an opinion is only normally given after a report from the Monopolies Commission. It is a pity that a succession of Secretaries of State have regularly flouted Parliament's intention by using get-out clauses in the Act. For example, *The Times* and *The Sunday Times* takeovers by Rupert Murdoch were given consent, without a reference, on the grounds that neither newspaper was economic as a going concern as a separate newspaper and that the case was one of urgency.

The Fair Trading Act specifies the matters that should be considered in determining the public interest and these include:

1 The maintenance or promotion of effective competition.
2 The promotion of the interests of consumers, purchasers and users of goods and services in the UK in respect of prices, quality and variety.
3 The desirability of promoting the reduction of costs, the development and use of new techniques and new products and the entry of new competitors.
4 The maintenance and promotion of a balanced distribution of industry and employment in the UK.
5 The maintenance and promotion of competitive activity in markets outside the UK on the part of the UK producers of goods and suppliers of goods and services.

Over the period 1973 to 1985 there were 2527 mergers which met the criteria laid down in the Act and only seventy-six cases were referred to the Monopolies Commission. Of the referrals twenty-two were abandoned and a further twenty-two were found against. Thus only 3 per cent of cases meeting the criteria were referred to the Monopolies Commission and these had a good chance of being cleared.

On the face of it it may be concluded that the probability of a referral is so remote that the Act has had a minimal impact on UK industry. However, the existence of the Act may signal to companies that the acquisition of a company with a large market share may be challenged and as such it may have been a deterrent to some takeovers.

Competition Act 1980

The Competition Act is complementary to the Fair Trading Act in that the former relates to individual firms that restrict, distort or prevent competition whereas the latter applies to all firms in a complete market sector supplying goods or services referred. The Competition Act empowers the Director General of the Office of Fair Trading to undertake a preliminary investigation to establish whether an anti-competitive practice exists. Where an anti-competitive practice exists an undertaking from the company concerned may be accepted or the matter may be referred to the Monopolies Commission. Where the Commission finds against a practice the Secretary of State has the power to prohibit it or to ask the Director General to obtain an undertaking.

In June 1986 the Secretary of State for Trade and Industry announced a review of competition policy covering the Fair Trading Act 1973 and Restrictive Trade Practice Act 1976 but not the Competition Act 1980. The Competition Act was excluded on the grounds that it was too soon to undertake an evaluation of the effectiveness of the legislation. The committee is being chaired by Mr Hans Liesner and is expected to report on its findings in 1988.

The Financial Services Act 1986

This Act is important to investors and relevant to takeovers and was covered in Chapter 10.

Self-regulatory controls

Control over the securities markets is undertaken by a self-regulatory body, the Council of the Stock Exchange which in turn is responsible to the Securities and Investments Board whose authority derives from the Financial Services Act 1986. The Stock Exchange imposes self-regulatory controls over its members and places a continuing obligation on listed companies to keep shareholders adequately informed.

The Council for the Securities Industry issues a City Code which represents good business practice in the field of mergers and acquisitions. The Code is administered by the Panel on Takeovers and Mergers and is applicable to public companies, both listed and unlisted, but not private companies, unless they were involved publicly within ten years prior to an offer. The Code does not have statutory backing but if it is not observed the facilities of the securities market in the UK may be withdrawn.

The Code is divided into ten general principles of conduct some of which are based on the concept of equity between one shareholder and another. While equity between shareholders is enshrined in the City Code it is not a feature of takeover activity in the US. In addition to general principles, there are thirty-seven rules representing the practical application of these principles to specific areas.

Prior to Big Bang it is reasonable to conclude that the City Code was very successful in achieving its aim of regulating behaviour in bid situations. In the majority of cases the rules were observed and the Code had the flexibility to react quickly to changes in market conditions. This flexibility and speed of action is very important in an area where deals are often completed within three months of the first bid. However, the existence of multi-service financial organizations after Big Bang poses new challenges to the Panel. Indeed, a few weeks before the changes in market trading conditions in the City, which were introduced on 27 October 1986, it was necessary to start amending some of the rules with respect to concert parties (persons acting together). With the integration of share purchasing and market making activities it was necessary to relax the concert party rules on condition that exemption to the rules was applicable only to financial groups that would satisfy the Panel that their portfolio management business and their market making activities were kept entirely separate. These so-called 'Chinese walls' pose considerable challenges to control over the City.

The Takeover Panel tried to assert its authority by a judgement made on 27 October 1986, the day of Big Bang, that was highly critical of Hill Samuel, Cazenove, and Midland Bank. The judgement criticized these three companies for failing to disclose share dealings which enabled AE, the Midlands engineering group, to escape a takeover bid by Turner and Newall. The Panel will need to impose its authority at more regular intervals than before Big Bang if it is to ensure that its Code is adhered to.

Valuation of companies

Valuation is an art rather than a science. The agreed value placed on a company is a result of negotiation between buyer and seller. Such a valuation may be completely different for another buyer and depends upon what the purchaser intends to do with the target company. For example, an acquirer wishing to dismember a target company with valuable assets may place a different value on the company than an acquirer wishing to retain its assets with a view to exploiting its earnings potential.

Valuation depends upon the type of company to be acquired and the proportion of share capital it wishes to obtain. In its investigation of the target company the major characteristics of the business should be ascertained and the key features of the industry established. Checklists are often useful in ensuring that all salient features are established and examples of comprehensive lists are contained in Cooke (1986) and Cooke (1988).

As well as undertaking a thorough investigation into the company an acquirer will need to collect information on the industry in which the target operates. For example, it is important to ascertain whether the industry is a 'fashionable' high-growth sector or whether it is facing severe structural problems. That is not to say that the former are desirable targets and the latter not, since what is crucial is the ability of the acquirer's management team. For example, BTR has a habit of turning round unprofitable companies whereas Hanson Trust acquires growth by acquisition and often dismembers the target company to recoup its initial investment. In establishing information on an industry and its prospects, government statistics and stockbrokers' reports are useful sources. Of particular importance is the nature of the industry, particularly with respect to its seasonal volatility or cyclical downturns.

In addition to an assessment of the target company and a consideration of the characteristics of the industry, an evaluation of major competitors should be undertaken with a view to establishing respective market shares. Market share is important because profitability tends to increase the greater the share of the market. Furthermore, an analysis should be undertaken of key sales customers and key suppliers to the target company, as another company may be crucial to its own survival.

The proportion of share capital to be acquired is also important since restrictions on the transfer of shares are often incorporated in the Articles of Association of a private, but not a public company. Due to the lack of marketability of the shares of a private company a discount is normally incorporated that depends on restrictions placed on the transfer of shares. The degree of discount applied in practice seems to vary from 0 per cent, where no restrictions apply, to 50 per cent, where marketability is severely restricted. The key levels of shareholding are summarized in Table 17.4.

If 100 per cent of the voting rights are acquired, there does not appear to be good reason for applying a discount. At the other extreme, the acquisition of a small minority shareholding may necessitate a substantial discount to reflect the lack of marketability and its inability to influence management. In between these extreme positions the greater the percentage of voting rights being acquired the lower the required discount although it is important to note that the range is discrete rather than continuous.

Valuing a listed company for which there is an active secondary market may seem straightforward since there is already a market capitalization. However, the market price reflects trading in small quantities only. For example, if a seller wished to dispose of a large block of

Table 17.4 Key level of shareholdings

Percentage of voting rights held	Powers
90+	If an offer is accepted by more than 90 per cent the offeror can compulsorily acquire the rest on the same terms
75+	Can change the Articles or place the company in voluntary liquidation
50+	Control of management and dividend policy
30+	For public companies control is deemed to exist and it is required to make a takeover offer
25+	Minority influence management and dividend policy and can block changes to the Articles and prevent liquidation
20+	Presumed to be a related company under Companies Act 1981
15+	If more than 15 per cent of the voting rights is acquired for cash in the twelve months before an offer, then there must be a cash offer
10+	Can prevent a complete takeover
5+	An investor in a public company must notify where more than 5 per cent is acquired

shares the demand–supply equilibrium may be disturbed and reflected in a new lower price. However, in a takeover situation it is usual for a premium to be paid for control – a reflection of the disturbance in the demand–supply equation for small parcels of shares.

A number of approaches to valuation will now be outlined followed by a consideration of their relevance to particular situations.

The earnings approach

The approach laid down in Statement of Standard Accounting Practice 3 (SSAP 3) on earnings per share (EPS) is that published in the *Financial Times* i.e. the last declared earnings figure before extraordinary items, but after deducting tax, minority interests and preference dividends, to obtain the earnings attributable to ordinary shareholders from normal activities. The yield figure is the gross equivalent, calculated as follows:

$$\frac{(\text{EPS} \times 100)}{(\text{Price})} \times \frac{(100)}{(1 - \text{standard rate of tax})}$$

The reciprocal of the earnings yield figure is the price-earnings (P/E) ratio and is calculated by dividing the current price of the share by the

Table 17.5 A takeover analysed in terms of P/E ratios

	Company A	Company B
Total earnings (£ thousand)	2000	1000
EPS	10p	10p
Share price	£1.00	£0.80
P/E ratio	10:1	8:1
Number of shares (thousand)	20000	10000

Table 17.6 Post-merger details

	Company (A+B)
Total earnings (£ thousand)	3000
Number of shares in issue (thousand)	28000
EPS	10.71p

company's earnings per share. (For further details on the calculation of EPS see Chapter 4.) The P/E ratio of the acquiree in a takeover situation is referred to as its exit P/E and the higher the ratio an acquirer is willing to pay reflects the extent to which it is prepared to go to achieve its aim.

Traditionally, acquisition analysis has been based on P/E ratios and EPS although such approaches are somewhat myopic. Since there are many problems involved in establishing earnings and calculating EPS and there are many factors affecting share prices, P/E ratios must be viewed with an element of caution. However, the fact remains that if a company acquires another with a P/E ratio lower than its own, EPS will increase and market capitalization will be enhanced provided the earnings of the victim are capitalized at a rate above that prevailing before the bid. An example should clarify this notion.

Assume Company A wishes to acquire Company B. The relevant financial data is summarized in Table 17.5. If Company A acquires Company B at market price in a share-for-share exchange deal, the shareholders in B will receive 8 million shares in A. This is readily obtained, since B has 10 million shares in issue with a market price of £0.80 each giving a market capitalization of £8m. Thus B's shareholders will receive £8m worth of shares at £1.00 per share, which equals 8 million shares.

The situation after the merger is shown in Table 17.6. The EPS in the new group is higher than that prevailing in either Company A or Company B. However, the market price needs to be determined to establish who gains or who loses. It is not possible to say how the market will react but investors will evaluate the new situation and make a judgement as to whether the merger will yield benefits or not. From a logical point of view one might argue that the post-merger P/E ratio should be a weighted average of the earnings of companies A and B, that is:

$$\frac{(10 \times 2000)}{3000} + \frac{(8 \times 1000)}{3000} = 9.33$$

This would give a market value in company (A+B) of 10.71p (EPS) × 9.33 (P/E) = £1.00. There would, therefore, be no gain to A's shareholders or in fact to B's shareholders since in the latter case each share has a value of £1.00 but the market exchange ratio was only 0.80 (£0.80 divided by £1.00), giving a real value of 0.80 × £1 = £0.80.

In practice, the market does not react in this manner since the facts of the new grouping are assessed and the potential for synergy evaluated. Usually the post-merger P/E ratio is somewhere between the logical approach outlined above and the extreme position where the earnings of the acquiree are capitalized at the P/E ratio of the acquirer. In our example let us evaluate the merger by assuming a mid-way point. Based on a weighted average of earnings the post-merger P/E ratio has already been established as 9.33. The P/E ratio of A before the bid was 10 so that a mid-way point is 9.67. In this case the market price of company (A+B) would be 10.71p × 9.67p = £1.04 – a gain of 4p per share to shareholders in A. The impact on B's shareholders is that the effective EPS is 10.71p × 0.80p (the market exchange ratio) = 8.57p capitalized at 9.67 is 83p, i.e. a gain of 3p per share. Thus the immediate effect of the merger is to improve the wealth of all shareholders and occurs because the exit P/E ratio of the acquiree is less than that of the acquirer.

One of the inherent problems of this type of analysis is that it utilizes P/E multiples immediately before the bid as if the market did not anticipate the bid before it was made. In practice, work by Firth (1976) and Franks, Broyles and Hecht (1977) has suggested that the market often begins to adjust to a bid any time up to six months before it is made. Whether this is the reaction of a highly efficient market, the purchasing of shares on the market by the acquirer, or the result of insider dealing is open to dispute.

A second inherent problem is that the approach assesses the immediate benefits and ignores the long-run effects. Since the P/E ratio of Company A reflects its better growth prospects compared with Company B there will be a time, in the long run, when the EPS of A would have exceeded the EPS of the new group.

There are a number of other problems in utilizing this approach which are based on the vagaries of financial accounting. Earnings figures should not be assessed in isolation but must be considered in relation to a company's accounting policies. Problems arise in key areas such as extraordinary items, the treatment of taxation including deferred taxation and problems with establishing inflation-adjusted figures. Such problems must be borne in mind in any final evaluation.

Probably the most important criticism of this approach is that long-run earnings are not considered and the time-value of money is ignored. Two approaches are now reviewed, one based on the future earnings of a company and incorporating sensitivity analysis and a second approach based on discounted cash flows.

Future earnings basis of valuation

In practice, it is more common to forecast net maintainable earnings and capitalize them at a suitable rate. This may involve estimating future maintainable earnings for each division or subsidiary so that an appropriate P/E ratio may be applied to each sector. Maintainable earnings are calculated on the basis of assets that will be retained and the resale value of surplus assets must be added to the capitalized earnings.

It is notoriously difficult to forecast profit levels with any degree of accuracy, particularly for small companies where the necessary skills and adequate systems are often found wanting. In addition to forecasting earnings, it will be necessary also to forecast levels of gearing and taxation. If a return (earnings yield) of 12.5 per cent after tax is required, the value of the investment will be eight times the net earnings. For example:

	£000s
Net maintainable earnings	900,000
Less: loan interest £1.25m × 10%	125,000
Profit before taxation	775,000
Taxation (35%)	271,250
Net earnings after taxation	503,750
Price/earnings ratio	8
Earnings yield required	12.5%
Capitalized value of the company	£4,030,000

Where management has undertaken similar acquisition transactions on previous occasions some information will be available on an appropriate capitalization rate to use. Where there is no past practice, a comparison with transactions undertaken by competitors may prove to be useful. Alternatively, published data on P/E ratios of similar companies may be used and adjusted in the light of the information obtained on the target company.

If an acquisition of an unlisted company is contemplated it may be necessary to use a P/E ratio of a similar quoted company and adjust it for lack of marketability. While this approach is useful in providing guidelines to valuation it is sometimes difficult, in practice, to find a similar company with a quotation, and where one is available all the problems of differing accounting policies must be faced.

It is quite common in practice for sensitivity analysis to be undertaken by identifying a range of P/E ratios and a range of maintainable earnings. Such an approach is illustrated in Table 17.7.

As can be seen from Table 17.7 the range of valuation is from £3.6m to just over £6m. Sometimes the highest P/E ratio might be applied to

Table 17.7 The sensitivity of valuation to changes in P/E ratios and forecasts of net maintainable earnings

Forecast of net maintainable earnings (£000)	Price/earnings ratios					
	8.0	8.5	9.0	9.5	10.0	10.5
450	3600	3825	4050	4275	4500	4725
475	3800	4038	4275	4513	4750	4988
500	4000	4250	4500	4750	5000	5250
525	4200	4463	4725	4988	5250	5513
550	4400	4675	4950	5225	5500	5775
575	4600	4888	5175	5463	5750	6038

the lowest forecast of net maintainable earnings and the lowest P/E ratio to the highest forecast of net maintainable earnings. If such an approach is adopted the valuation range is £4.6m to £4.725m.

Discounted cash flow

A more advanced approach to valuation, but less common in practice, is to find the net present value of the future incremental cash flows. The cost of the investment includes all costs involved in negotiating and completing the transaction and any compensation paid to shareholders of the acquired company. The expected gain to the acquirer's share-holders is the difference between the cost of the investment and the present value of the shares of the acquiree and that being offered by the acquiree.

The discounted cash flow approach has a number of variants. One approach is to use dividends and another is to use earnings. The case against using dividends is that acquisitions are concerned with gaining control which includes control over dividend policy. As such, a di-vidends approach is relevant to evaluating a minority shareholding but not a majority shareholding. Further, as was highlighted in Chapter 7 Miller and Modigliani (1961), view dividends as a residual activity.

An alternative approach to finding the present value of dividends is to establish the present value of earnings. Provided all earnings are distributed in the long run there is no difference between the two approaches.

The net present value calculations may be treated like any other investment project. An example is shown below.

Brian plc wishes to acquire 100 per cent of the voting shares of Cloughie plc. The average cost of capital of Brian plc is 14 per cent and Cloughie plc maintains a constant payout ratio with a current dividend of 20p per share. Cloughie's earnings are expected to grow annually at a rate of 12 per cent into perpetuity and the existing share price is £10.50. The theoretical market price is calculated as follows:

$$P_0 = \frac{D_0(1 + g)}{r - g}$$

where P_0 = the theoretical market price per share
   D_0 = the current dividend
   g = the growth rate
   r = average cost of capital

$$P_0 = \frac{0.20\ (1 + 0.12)}{0.14 - 0.12}$$

$$= £11.20$$

Since the theoretical share price is greater than the current price there will be a positive net present value per share of £0.70. Thus the merger appears worthwhile to both parties if the bid price is somewhere between £10.50 and £11.20 per share.

The net present value approach has the advantage that it considers both forecasted earnings and the time value of money and the investment is treated like any other capital budgeting project. However, use of this approach suffers from all the problems inherent in establishing cash flows and determining respective costs of capital. This method may be made more sophisticated by incorporating sensitivity analysis and probability distributions to try to take such uncertainties into consideration. However, other problems still remain such as the impact of synergy, the covariance of acquired cash flows with existing cash flows, and the stationarity (the extent to which it remains constant over time) of the cost of capital. Furthermore, if we accept the empirical evidence that the market begins to anticipate a merger well before a bid is made problems are created when comparing the theoretical share price with the existing price. One approach to take such factors into consideration might be to use the market model.

The market model
The market model is based on a linear relationship between the return on an individual security and that of the market. Fluctuations in the return of security (R_i) depend upon:

1   The market factor, which depends, amongst other things, on the market model.
2   A firm specific factor, where the residual u_{it} is assumed to be uncorrelated with the return on the market.

The return of a share i is a linear function of the form:

$$R_{it} = \alpha_i + \beta_i\ R_{mt} + u_{it}$$

Where R_{it} represents the return of a share i in period t; R_{mt} the return on a general market index, e.g. the FT All-Share Index in period t; u the degree to which the share varies other than with the market; and α_i, β_i the intercept and slope of the linear relationship between R_{it} and R_{mt}.

The model may be used to establish the theoretical price of the share without anticipation of merger benefits, so that the maximum premium that can be paid above the market price is the present value of the unanticipated benefits. The first step is to establish the theoretical share price, excluding any anticipation of merger benefits. If the market index has increased by 15 per cent over the four months prior to the bid and the security has a beta factor of 1.25, the share price would be expected to increase by 18.75 per cent (1.25 × 15 per cent), if we assume that alpha is zero. If the share price has increased by 25 per cent, then the market has anticipated the merger benefits by (25 − 18.75 per cent) = 6.25 per cent. If the present value of the unanticipated future benefits of the merger is 12 pence per share, then the maximum price that can be paid, and still be worthwhile, is the current price of the victim, say 100 pence, plus the merger benefits (12 pence) less the extent to which the market has already anticipated the benefits. For example:

Share price four months ago (100/1.25)	= 80p
Theoretical increase in share over last four months, excluding anticipation of benefits (80 × 18.75%)	= 15p
Theoretical price at time of the bid	95p
Actual price at time of the bid	= 100p
Merger benefits already anticipated by the market	5p
Maximum price to pay = 100 + (12 − 5)	= 107p

An implicit assumption in the above analysis is that the abnormal return over the four-month period prior to the bid is the result of anticipation of the merger. However, there may be other reasons such as better than anticipated earnings forecasts or dividends announcements.

The assets approach to valuation

This approach values a business on the basis of the fair value or open-market value of the net assets of the business rather than the historical cost of the assets. Fair value is defined in SSAP 22 on accounting for goodwill as the amount for which an asset (or liability) could be exchanged in an arm's length transaction. Alternatively open-market value should be based on existing use and is the price which might be realized by private treaty on the day of the valuation.

Some would argue that the assets approach is irrelevant to a takeover since the method ignores earnings and its future prospects. However, since a shareholder with 75 per cent or more of the voting shares can put the company into liquidation, the break-up value of the assets will be relevant. Furthermore, some acquisitive companies such as Hanson Trust actually sell parts of an acquired business that are not considered useful in an attempt to recoup much of their initial investment.

Fundamental differences arise when using the assets approach to value listed companies as compared to unlisted companies. With a quoted company the asset value of the company may be considerably in excess of its market capitalization reflecting the inability of any individual shareholder to realize those assets. In contrast, a private company has a limited number of shareholders, many of whom have sizeable shareholdings and therefore a few shareholders could liquidate the assets. Consequently, the assets approach may be of more relevance to unlisted companies and, in practice, is often used in conjunction with the earnings basis.

In addition to the above circumstances the assets approach will be relevant where the valuation of a company may be independent of its profitability such as where a company's expected earnings are unsatisfactory.

The appropriate basis for valuation

Approaches to valuation discussed in this section are not mutually exclusive and in practice a number of methods are used in order to compare their results. In practice, an approach based on forecasted maintainable earnings is used and compared with at least one other approach depending upon the particular circumstances. Earnings approaches and more sophisticated methods such as those based on the market model are appropriate to listed companies but not to unlisted companies where a well-organized secondary market does not exist. Furthermore, when valuing unlisted companies restrictions on voting rights and on the ability of the directors to issue new shares must be considered. In addition, the directors may have special powers with respect to the disposal of profits, their emoluments and pensions, and also on options to directors and senior staff to purchase shares at discounted prices.

A different approach to comparing valuations based on alternative methods may be to weight valuations based on earnings, dividends and assets. Where a substantial minority shareholding is to be acquired (in smaller companies only) in a company where no one shareholder owns more than 50 per cent of the voting rights, the earnings approach should carry the majority of the weights. The earnings approach will also be appropriate where an acquisition of a majority shareholding is undertaken with a view to exploiting the company's earnings potential.

Where a shareholding of over 75 per cent is envisaged the assets approach may be used in conjunction with the earnings basis. The dividend approach is more relevant where a small minority shareholding is to be acquired so that in the context of takeovers it is not of great importance.

Evidence on the performance of mergers

Two types of approach have been adopted by empirical researchers concerned with assessing the economic impact of mergers and acquisitions. First, studies have been undertaken using share price data in order to establish the distribution of gains and losses to shareholders. This type of empirical research has implications for capital market theory. Second, managerial performance measures of profitability have also been undertaken by comparing the combined pre-merger profitability with the post-merger rate of return adjusted for the effects of type of industry.

The conclusions of these types of study are sometimes conflicting. For example, work undertaken by Firth (1980), Franks, Broyles and Hecht (1977) and Franks (1986) have all concluded that the acquiree's shareholders gain as a result of a takeover. However, whether the shareholders of the acquirer company gain seems open to dispute. For example, Firth (1980) found that the acquirer's shareholders lost an aggregate amount equivalent to the gain made by the acquiree shareholders, so that in aggregate the economic impact on the economy was neutral. In contrast Franks, Broyles and Hecht (1977) found that the acquirer's shareholders made marginal gains and Franks and Harris (1986) found that they made substantial gains.

Studies undertaken using accounting data as the measure of profitability have all concluded that mergers were unprofitable. See, for example, the work by Singh (1971), Utton (1974), and Meeks (1977). That these studies are at odds with research undertaken on share prices may merely confirm the widely held belief that a considerable amount of information, other than accounting data, is reflected in the share price of a company.

Defences against takeovers

A share price determined by the market represents an equilibrium price between buyers and sellers for transactions in small parcels of shares. However, when large parcels of shares are transacted this equilibrium is disturbed and a new equilibrium determined. Unless a target company is suffering financial difficulties it is very likely that a premium will be paid to take over another company. On this basis existing shareholders of the target company will make a profit on the pre-bid price. If the offer is unacceptable to the directors it is their duty to convince shareholders that it is not in their best interest to accept. The directors of the target company usually try to convince its shareholders that the offer price is too low in relation to earnings and assets.

A typical defence practice is to issue a profit forecast demonstrating an improved future performance. Since the behaviour of participants in a takeover is governed by the rules of the City Code extravagant claims should not be made. Consequently, the City Code emphasizes that profit forecasts should be of the 'highest standards of accuracy and fair presentation'. The sole responsibility for compiling a profit forecast rests with the directors although the accounting policies and calculations must be examined and reported on by the auditors or consultant accountants.

Another typical defence strategy is to revalue assets to demonstrate that their values stated in the balance sheet understate the true worth of the company. Substantial differences between book value and actual value did exist in the 1970s but many companies try to reflect changes in the value of their fixed assets by periodic revaluations. Nevertheless, this strategy was adopted by London Brick in its defence against a takeover by Hanson Trust and by Currys in its defence against Dixons – the defence strategies of both companies failed!

A third defence strategy is to convince shareholders that the offeror is unsuitable and incapable of managing the business more effectively than existing management. Such a strategy normally involves disputes, often vitriolic, involving profits, dividends and past performance, as well as management style.

Another weapon is to reveal new commercial developments that the bidder may be aware of but which are not generally known. For example, a new product perhaps involving a scientific breakthrough or the culmination of considerable research and development expenditure, new businesses, or new-look management that will enhance future growth prospects.

Tactical defence strategies that are prevalent in the US are severely curtailed in the UK during the bid period. For example, a 'crown jewel' strategy involving the sale of a key asset or business is not an available option in the UK during the bid period. However, a 'white knight' strategy which involves encouraging an acceptable suitor to make a bid to avert a hostile takeover is possible. For example, in 1983 Eagle Star was pleased to attract the interest of BAT as an alternative to a takeover by the German company, Allianz Versicherung.

More recently there has been a tendency for beleaguered management teams to encourage the Office of Fair Trading to refer a bid to the Monopolies Commission with the object of at least delaying the takeover and gaining time. However, this strategy has its drawbacks as London Brick quickly found out. London Brick prepared a substantial submission in anticipation of a referral of the bid by Hanson Trust to the Monopolies Commission. However, the Secretary of State for Trade and Industry quickly indicated that a reference would not be made – an outcome that encouraged the predator to complete the transaction.

Capital reconstruction schemes

Procedures under sections 425 and 427 Companies Act 1985 (respectively sections 206 and 208 Companies Act 1948) may be utilized to acquire a company provided the acquiree's shareholders agree. Such an approach may be of value where the long-term prospects are good despite short-term difficulties. These difficulties may arise from past losses so that it may be in the interests of creditors and members to argue for a reconstruction and scheme of arrangement rather than liquidate the company immediately.

Where a compromise or arrangement is proposed by either shareholders or creditors the court can, on application, summon the respective
parties to further discussions. Provided that 75 per cent in value of the
creditors or members vote to accept a compromise the court can make
it binding on the rest. One way of undertaking such an approach is
for all shares in the offeree company, not held by the bidder, to be
cancelled. The bidder then issues its own shares to compensate the
shareholders of the offeree company. Where such a procedure is contemplated the court may make provision for the following (section 427
(3) Companies Act 1985):

1 The transfer to the transferee company of the whole or any part of
   the undertaking and of the property or liabilities of any transferor
   company.
2 The allotting or appropriation by the transferee company of any
   shares, debentures, policies or other interests in that company which
   under the compromise or arrangement are to be allotted or
   appropriated by that company to or for any person.
3 The continuation by or against the transferee company of any legal
   proceedings pending by or against any transferor company.
4 The dissolution, without winding up, of any transferor company.
5 The provision to be made for any persons who, within such time and
   in such manner as the court directs, dissent from the compromise or
   arrangement.
6 Such incidental, consequential and supplemental matters as are
   necessary to secure that the reconstruction or amalgamation is fully
   and effectively carried out.

The court will ensure that any scheme of arrangement is fair to all
parties and as such a solution may be very complex as a balance is
achieved between the competing rights of preference and ordinary
shareholders and debtholders. An alternative approach to a reconstruction is under Section 582 Companies Act 1985 (Section 287 Companies
Act 1948) which permits a liquidator to accept shares as consideration
for the sale of company property when a company is being wound up
voluntarily. As part of the scheme the whole or part of the business or
property is transferred or sold to another company. The liquidator may,
with the sanction of a special resolution, accept shares or an arrangement can be made whereby members of the transferor company participate in profits.

Divestment

For every buyer there must be a seller for a transaction to be completed.
A number of reasons might be put forward to explain divestment and
these depend upon whether the company is a private or public company
or part of a group of companies.

Highly acquisitive companies such as Hanson Trust and BTR view companies as a portfolio of assets and acquire and dispose of companies as risks and returns change. For example, while BTR has acquired a number of companies over the last few years, including Thomas Tilling for £700m, it has also indulged in the divestments of Cornhill Insurance for £305m and Heinemann for £100m. Similarly, Hanson Trust frequently acquires companies with a view to retaining some aspects of the business and selling the remainder in order to recoup much of its initial investment.

One reason why a company might wish to dispose of a division or subsidiary is to improve its liquidity position, particularly when a good offer is forthcoming. Often a division or subsidiary that is found to be unprofitable or incompatible with the other activities of the group is sold to enable the group to concentrate on activities in which it is more successful. A classic example of such an approach was Fisons which sold its fertilizer division in 1982 to Norsk Hydro, the Norwegian oil and gas company. For many years the fertilizer division had been a cash absorber mainly because of cost disadvantages relative to ICI. Norsk Hydro, a producer of cheap feedstocks, did not suffer the same cost disadvantages encountered by Fisons so it agreed to the acquisition for £50m. The immediate effect on Fisons was for its share price to increase as a result of divestment. BOC and Arthur Guinness have also adopted successful divestment strategies. Other examples are provided in Coyne and Wright (1986).

Management buyouts

Management buyouts have become increasingly popular particularly since 1980 and available figures are provided in Table 17.8. Part of the reason for this trend is that private companies, not public ones, are able to provide financial assistance for the acquisition of their shares. Section 54 of Companies Act 1948 prohibited the giving of any financial assistance either directly or indirectly with a view to buying shares in the company. However, Companies Act 1981 rescinded these provisions.

Another reason for the growth in management buyouts is that financial institutions are more willing to finance such ventures and indeed a number of specialist companies have developed to take advantage of such opportunities.

In the UK, management buyouts usually occur where a division or a subsidiary of a group is unprofitable and the owner cannot find an alternative buyer at a satisfactory price. However, in a highly competitive environment it may be in the interest of a parent company to sell to its management rather than allow a competitor to make the acquisition. Further advantages can accrue to the vendor in that the cost of buying out expensive directors' service contracts is minimized and redundancy payments are not required. A reputation of being a good employer can be generated in this way and the provision of a loan or

Table 17.8 Estimates of total number and volume of lending to management buyouts 1967–85

	Number	*Value (£m)*	*Average value (£m)*
1967–76	43	n.a.	n.a.
1977	13	n.a.	n.a.
1978	23	n.a.	n.a.
1979	52	26	0.5
1980	107	50	0.467
1981	124	114	0.919
1982	170	265	1.558
1983	205	315	1.536
1984	210	255	1.214
1985	220	900	4.090

Source: Coyne and Wright (1986)

deferred consideration dependent upon future profits can also lead to goodwill.

The disadvantages to a vendor can accrue where a low price is expected for the sale and if one is agreed, management of other group companies may see the terms of the offer as over-generous and be detrimental to their long-term performance. Furthermore, competition on existing product lines may also increase.

An advantage to the management proposing the buyout is that their jobs are retained and their independence provided by a slice of the equity which may prove to be valuable in the future if the company is successful.

Institutional investors are likely to have mixed feelings about management buyouts. It will be necessary for the management buyers to convince the institutions that prospects are better because of their high personal stake in the business. The institutions will need to be convinced that profitability will improve with the same or similar management team and they will be particularly concerned if a quoted company becomes a private company, because of the danger of being locked into their investment.

Since it is unlikely that there will be radical changes in management it will be necessary for the buyers to demonstrate a strong personal financial commitment and the determination to succeed. Since sizeable sums of money are often involved it will probably be necessary for managers to become personally highly geared by borrowing against the security of a second mortgage and life assurance policies.

A number of variations involving different terminology have also developed. For example, buyouts involving substantial funding are referred to in the US as leveraged buyouts. An employee buyout is a variation because it is the workforce, rather than just the management, that do the buying. An alternative is a spin-out which involves the parent company selling a subsidiary but retaining a minority stake and may occur where a considerable amount of research and development has been involved or a new innovation developed. Another variation is a buyin whereby a management group from outside the company raise funds to acquire the company.

Summary

Motives for merger are complex and multivariate. They may be classified into efficiency, inefficiency, strategic and monopoly. Efficiency is presumed to occur if value is increased to shareholders and includes synergy, market share acquisitions, and the acquisition of assets at a discount. In contrast, inefficiency may be a reason for acquisition as the rewards to management are highly correlated with asset size rather than profitability. Consequently management may pursue policies that are consistent with their own utility maximization but may not be consistent with profit maximization.

Strategic reasons are also important and include the acquisition of growth, the reduction in capacity and opportunities for accounting manipulations. Finally, domination of a market is also a reason although controls over the abuse of such positions is encompassed in UK and EEC legislation.

The Fair Trading Act 1973 places an obligation on the Director General of the Office of Fair Trading to review commercial activities relating to goods and services. The Competition Act 1980 extends the Director General's role by placing an obligation on him to review anti-competitive practices. In addition, the EEC has the power to prohibit all agreements that prevent, restrict or distort competition within the Community.

In addition to legislative controls the City Code has been successful in regulating the behaviour of participants in bid situations but it faces increasing problems after Big Bang.

Valuation is a complex area. In practice a number of approaches to valuation are undertaken and their results compared in order to provide a framework for negotiation. No one method is correct and depends upon the particular transaction and particular circumstances.

The empirical evidence on mergers is somewhat confusing. Studies using accounting data suggest that most are failures whereas share price data suggest otherwise. Further evidence is required although such information is unlikely to change the propensity to acquire. There has also been an increase in interest by researchers in divestments and management buyouts as they have become more popular and newsworthy.

References

Biggadike, R., 'The Risky Business of Diversification', *Harvard Business Review*, May–June 1979.

Cooke, T. E., *Mergers and Acquisitions*, Basil Blackwell, 1986.

Cooke, T. E. (ed.), *International Mergers and Acquisitions*, Basil Blackwell, 1988.

Coyne, J. and Wright, M. (eds), *Divestment and Strategic Change*, Philip Allan, 1986.

Franks, J. R., Broyles, J. E. and Hecht, M. J., 'An Industry Study of the Profitability of Mergers in the United Kingdom', *Journal of Finance*, No. 5, December 1977.

Franks, J. R. and Harris, R. S., 'Shareholder Wealth Effects of Corporate Takeovers', the UK Experience 1955–85', *L. B. S. Working Paper*, June 1986.

Kitching, J., 'Why Acquisitions are Abortive', *Management Today*, November 1974.

Marris, R., *The Economic Theory of Managerial Capitalism*, Macmillan, 1964.

Meeks, G., *Disappointing Marriage: A Study of the Gains from Merger*, CUP, 1977.

Newbould, G. D., *Management and Merger Activity*, Guthstead, 1970.

Prais, S. J., *The Evolution of Giant Firms in Britain* (revised edition), CUP, 1981.

Singh, A., *Takeovers: Their Relevance to the Stock Market and the Theory of the Firm*, CUP, 1971.

Steiner, P. O., *Mergers: Motives, Effects, Control*, Ann Arbor: University of Michigan Press, 1975.

Utton, M. A., 'On Measuring the Effects of Industrial Mergers', *Scottish Journal of Political Economy*, February 1974.

Further reading

Barnes, P., 'The Effect of a Merger on the Share Price of the Attacker', *Accounting and Business Research*, Summer 1978.

Buckley, A., 'A Profile of Industrial Acquisitions in 1971', *Accounting and Business Research*, Autumn 1972.

Chiplin, B. and Wright, M., 'The Logic of Mergers', *Hobart Paper* No. 107, IEA 1987.

Coffee, J., Lowenstein, L. and Rose-Ackerman, S. (eds), *Takeovers and Contests for Corporate Control*, OUP, 1987.

Cooke, T. E. and Whittaker, J., 'Extraordinary Items, Deferred Taxation and Earnings Per Share', *Investment Analyst*, July 1984.

Cowling, K. *et al.*, *Mergers and Economic Performance*, CUP, 1980.

Dodd, P., 'Company Takeovers and the Australian Equity Market', *Australian Journal of Management*, July 1980.

Firth, M., *Share Prices and Mergers*, Gower, 1976.

Firth, M., 'Takeovers, Shareholder Returns and the Theory of the Firm', *Quarterly Journal of Economics*, No. 2, March 1980.

Jensen, M. C. and Ruback, R. S., 'The Market for Corporate Control: The Evidence', *Journal of Financial Economics*, No. 11, 1983.

Keown, A. J. and Pinkerton, J. M., 'Merger Announcements and Insider Trading Activity: An Empirical Investigation', *Journal of Finance*, September 1981.

Kitching, J., 'Why Do Mergers Miscarry?' *Harvard Business Review*, November–December 1967.

Knoeber, C. R., 'Golden Parachutes, Shark Repellants and Hostile Tender Offers', *American Economic Review*, March 1986.

Wright, M. and Coyne, J., *Management Buy-outs*, Philip Allan, 1986.

18 Insolvency

Introduction

Business failure is of concern to both successful and unsuccessful companies. On the one hand, successful companies should consider business failure carefully since firms should know their legal rights and alternative methods of recourse in the case of a debtor failing to pay for the goods or services it has received. On the other hand, unsuccessful companies need to consider how best to cushion the financial loss to investors, suppliers and employees.

Until the 1960s, there was a general feeling that business failure only affected smaller companies. However, the collapse or near collapse of such famous names as Rolls Royce, British Leyland, Ferranti, Alfred Herbert, Burmah Oil, De Lorean and Laker Airways have all served to dispel this myth.

Failure may be defined in a number of ways. Economic failure might mean that the rate of return on investment is less than the cost of capital, that costs exceed revenues or that actual returns are less than expected returns. In contrast, financial failure may be categorized into two elements – technical insolvency and legal insolvency. Technical insolvency occurs when a business cannot meet its current debts as they fall due even though its total assets may exceed its total liabilities. Such a situation is not normally sufficient to warrant the winding up of a business. In contrast legal insolvency arises when a firm cannot meet its current and contingent liabilities or if its total liabilities exceed its total assets. It is a serious offence for directors to continue to trade knowing that the company is insolvent.

Dun and Bradstreet have estimated that over 90 per cent of business failures are the direct result of managerial incompetence. Argenti (1976), has identified five key characteristics of managerial incompetence:

1 One-man rule (this does not necessarily mean a one-man business).
2 A non-participating board of directors.
3 An unbalanced team of managers in terms of functions and personality.
4 A weak finance function.
5 Where the chief executive and chairman are the same.

These features of bad management are likely to lead to a deficient accounting information system; to an inability to respond quickly to change; and to the likelihood of making one of three cardinal mistakes. These mistakes are: taking on a project which is so large that the outcome of the company is dependent on the success of the project; overtrading; and reaching a level of gearing not sustainable by the underlying cash flows.

In England and Wales during 1985 there were 5761 winding-up orders made by the courts – an increase of nearly 10 per cent on 1984 and 34 per cent on 1983. Official receivers remained the liquidators of 4486 of the companies concerned in 1985. In respect of 201 of the 1985 liquidations, official receivers had previously been appointed provisional liquidators of the companies concerned pending hearings of the petitions. Official receivers were also appointed provisional liquidators of twenty-one other companies in respect of which winding-up orders had not been made by the end of 1985. Official receivers submitted 278 reports to the Department of Trade and Industry relating to companies in which they considered criminal offences under the Companies Acts and other Acts had been committed and enquiries were made, or are proceeding, either by the Department or by the police on behalf of the Director of Public Prosecutions.

The remainder of this chapter is in three sections. We first review recent changes in legislation (with the recent coming into force of the Insolvency Act 1986) in so far as they relate to companies. The next section reviews the work of some of those who have attempted to develop techniques for the prediction of corporate bankruptcy. We round off discussion of this topic, in the final section, by considering a simple case study on the alternative to bankruptcy – a company reconstruction. This may be possible if it can be shown that if the business continues albeit in a modified form, its value may be more to creditors and investors than if it is wound up.

Insolvency legislation 1986

In 1986 Parliament produced two Acts consolidating the insolvency provisions in the Companies Acts 1985 and the Insolvency Act 1985. These new Acts are the Insolvency Act 1986 and the Company Directors Disqualification Act 1986. These two Acts came into force on 29 December 1986, when many of the provisions in the Companies Act 1985, and practically the whole of the Insolvency Act 1985, were repealed.

The passage of recent insolvency legislation has not been without incident (see Cooke and Glynn, 1985). In part this was due to the speed at which the government attempted to enact its proposals. In 1977, the Insolvency Law Review Committee was set up under the chairmanship of Sir Kenneth Cork. The objectives set for this committee were to provide proposals that would simplify the (then) present insolvency procedures which were generally agreed to be cumbersome, complex, archaic and over-technical. Their brief was also, where possible, to present proposals for harmonizing bankruptcy and liquidation procedures. The final report of the Cork Committee was published in June 1982. Some twenty-one months later, in February 1984, the government published a White Paper, 'A revised Framework for Insolvency Law'. Little time was provided for interested parties to submit comments before the process of drafting the Insolvency Bill began.

McQueen (1986) states, 'the result has been to create an atmosphere of controversy and confusion'. At this stage it is too early to tell. McQueen provides examples of changes in the law on personal bankruptcy that appear quite draconian in nature. He cites the example of a trader who not being registered for VAT is not required by law to keep business books. Yet should this trader become bankrupt having failed to keep such books he commits an offence. It is up to the trader to prove that he had no fraudulent intent to defraud his creditors in transactions arising before he was made bankrupt. McQueen's contentions might well be partially true but it has to be remembered that this legislation was enacted because of the considerable disquiet felt by the public and Members of Parliament that both sole traders and directors had been, in the past, treated far too leniently. The new legislation is an important advance for two reasons. First, it will make the administration of insolvency matters more efficient although there will be no startling difference for the average secured or unsecured creditor. Second, the new provisions will reduce the risk to the business community and the public at large from the activities of dishonest and incompetent businessmen.

The remainder of this section reviews those changes in so far as they appertain to companies and the duties of directors. It is not possible to discuss individual insolvency further.

Insolvency practitioners (s. 388, 389)

Under the provisions of the Insolvency Act 1986, the administration of estates is restricted to licensed insolvency experts. In addition to the Secretary of State for Trade and Industry, professional bodies can also grant practising certificates to those of their members that are deemed suitably qualified. An Insolvency Practitioners Tribunal deals with appeals from persons who have either been refused a licence or have had one withdrawn. A person acts as an insolvency practitioner in relation to a company by acting as its liquidator; administrator; administrative receiver; or supervisor of a composition or scheme. For individuals and partnerships, a person acts as an insolvency practitioner by acting as: trustee in bankruptcy or interim receiver of the property; trustee under a deed of arrangement; supervisor of a composition or scheme of arrangement; or administrator of the insolvent estate of a deceased person.

Company voluntary arrangements (s. 1–7, 386, 387)

Proposals for a composition in satisfaction of its debts or a scheme of arrangement may be made by a company to a suitably qualified insolvency practitioner who is initially known as the nominee. The office holder of a company in liquidation or subject to an administration order, or by the directors in any other case, must submit to the nominee fully documented terms of the composition or scheme together with a statement of affairs. The nominee then has twenty-eight days to submit a report to the courts stating whether in his opinion meetings of the company and its creditors should be summoned to consider the proposal. At such a meeting modifications to the proposal can be made. It is possible, for example, to substitute the proposed nominee but it is not permissible to so alter the proposal that it ceases to be a composition or scheme. No proposal may, without the consent of a secured creditor, alter his rights to enforce his security. The proposal shall not deprive a preferential creditor, without his consent, of his right to be paid in priority nor cause him to be paid at a lesser rate than other preferential creditors. The relevant date for determining the preferential debt shall be the date of the administration order or the date of the approval of the scheme of arrangement by creditors.

The chairman of both shareholders' and creditors' meetings will report the result of the meeting to the court. A composition or scheme will have effect from the time of the creditors' meeting and will bind every person who had notice of, and was entitled to vote, at the meeting, whether or not he was present or represented, as though he were a party to the composition or scheme. If a company is being wound up or is subject to an administration order, the court may give directions with regard to the conduct of the company including staying all proceedings in the liquidation or discharging the administration order. Those entitled have twenty-eight days, from the date of the creditors' meeting, to appeal to the court on the grounds that the approved proposal unfairly prejudices the interests of the creditor, member or contributory of the company or that there has been some material irregularity at, or in, relation to the meetings.

The person who has to carry out the approved proposal is called the supervisor.

The administration procedure (s. 8–27, 123)

The administrator has two tasks. He can try and rehabilitate the company or he may realize its assets by seeking to achieve a sale of the business. The most obvious example of the latter is when the company is facing insolvency but there is no floating charge and the insolvency practitioner appointed believes that the business could be sold as a going concern. In the former situation the administrator is appointed to continue the business and to trade it out of its difficulties.

Petitions to the court for the appointment of an administrator may be made by the company, its directors, its supervisor or its creditors. An administrative order is likely to be made by the court if it is satisfied that the company is, or is likely to be, unable to pay its debts and that the making of the order is likely to secure either one or more of the following purposes:

1 The survival of the company and the whole or any part of its under-taking as a going concern.
2 The approval of a composition in satisfaction of the company's debts or a scheme of arrangement of its affairs.
3 The sanctioning under s. 425 of the Companies Act 1985 of a com-promise or arrangement between the company and its creditors and members.
4 A more advantageous realization of the company's assets than would be effected in a winding up.

No order will be made if the company is already in liquidation, is an insurance company within the meaning of the Insurance Companies Act 1982 or is a recognized bank or licensed institution within the meaning of the Banking Act 1979.

During the period from the presentation of the petition to its accep-tance or rejection, the company may not be wound up, nor may any steps be taken to enforce any security over the company's property or to repossess goods subject to hire purchase, leasing, conditional sale, or retention of title agreements, except by leave of the court. On the making of an administrative order, any petition for the winding up of the company shall be dismissed, any administrative receiver of the company's property will vacate office, and any receiver of part of the company's property shall vacate office on being required to do so by the administrator. The administrator is appointed by the court on the making of an administrative order. Upon appointment he shall take into his custody, or under his control, all the property to which the company is, or appears to be, entitled. While the order is in force, the directors may not exercise, without the administrator's consent, any powers which would interfere with the exercise of the administrator's powers.

When the administrative order is discharged, the administrator ap-plies to the court to be discharged. Provisions also exist whereby the administrator can apply for variation or discharge of the administrative order. Upon appointment the administrator requests key persons in the company to prepare a statement of affairs. This statement has to be verified by affidavit and submitted to the administrator, normally within twenty-one days.

From the time of his appointment, the administrator has three months (or such longer period as the court may allow) in which to send to the Registrar of Companies, and to all known creditors, a statement of his proposals for achieving the purposes specified in the order. A copy of the statement will also be laid before a meeting of the creditors summoned for the purpose at not less than fourteen days' notice. The administrator will also send a copy of the statement to all members whose addresses are known or publish in the prescribed manner a notice giving the address to which members should write for a free copy of the statement.

The creditors' meeting may either approve or modify the proposals with the administrator's consent who, in turn, reports back on the result of the meeting to the court and the Registrar of Companies. If the meeting rejects the proposals the court may discharge the administration order and make such provisions as it considers necessary. The administrator has fourteen days in which to file any order of discharge with the Registrar of Companies. Any member or creditor of the company may petition the court for an order controlling the administrator or even discharging the administration order if he feels the proposal unfairly prejudices his interest.

The administrative receiver (s. 28–9, 33–4, 42–9, 175; schedules 1 and 6)

An administrative receiver is defined in the Act as receiver or manager of the whole or substantially the whole of the company's property, who has been appointed by a debenture holder secured by a floating charge. Schedule 1 of the Act contains certain statutory powers which an administrative receiver, appointed under a debenture, is deemed to have except that they are incompatible with any provisions of the debenture. The Act enables the administrative receiver to obtain the court's authority to seize property subject to a charge ranking before that under which he has been appointed. The net proceeds of disposal must be that which would be realized on a sale in the open market by a willing vendor. The administrative receiver shall be deemed to be the agent of the company until it goes into liquidation and is, normally, personally liable for any contracts entered into by him. The administrative receiver may only be removed from office by order of the court and may resign his office by giving notice of his resignation in the prescribed manner. Similar provisions apply for the provision of a statement of affairs and presentation by him of a report as for administrators reviewed above. In his report the administrative receiver must detail:

1   The events leading up to his appointment.
2   His proposals for dealing with the company's property and business.
3   The amounts of principal and interest payable to the debenture holders who appointed him.

4   The amounts due to preferential creditors.
5   The amount, if any, likely to be available for other creditors.
6   A summary of the statement of affairs and his comments on it.

Winding up by the court (s. 131–4, 136–7, 139–41, 146, 172, 174, 202–3, 205, 212)

The official receiver has a duty to investigate the causes of failure of the company and its affairs generally, and to make a report to the court if he thinks fit. The report will be prima facie evidence of the stated facts therein. Any past or present officer, liquidator, administrator, receiver or manager or other person concerned in the formation or management of the company may, on the application of the official receiver, be publicly examined in court. The official receiver shall so act if requested by a majority in value of the creditors or three-quarters in value of the contributories. Any creditor or contributory may ask questions at such an examination, as well as the official receiver, liquidator or special manager. Failure to attend the court may be regarded as contempt, and the court may issue a warrant for arrest and for the seizure of any relevant documents, money or goods in that person's possession.

Following the making up of a winding up order the official receiver is liquidator until another person is appointed. He may at any time summon meetings of creditors and contributories to consider appointing another person as liquidator, or to apply to the Secretary of State to appoint a liquidator. Where a winding up order is made upon the discharge of an administration order, the former administrator may be appointed liquidator, and if made where there is a supervisor of a composition or scheme, the court may appoint him liquidator. The official receiver may apply to the Registrar of Companies for early dissolution of any company of which he is liquidator if it appears to him that there are no, or negligible, assets to cover costs; and the affairs of the company do not require further investigation. He must give twenty-eight days notice of such action.

When a liquidator, other than the official receiver, considers an administration is for all practical purposes complete, he must convene a final meeting of creditors to receive his final report and to consider whether he should be released from office. The meeting may be convened at the same time as giving final notice of a final distribution of funds. The Registrar of Companies will dissolve the company three months after the receipt of either a notice from the official receiver that his administration is complete, or a notice from the liquidator that the final general meeting of creditors has been held. The Secretary of State may defer the release, subject to a right of appeal to the court.

Voluntary winding up

The Act stipulates that a director's powers are suspended, subject to the court's sanction, from the moment the company resolves to be wound up. A liquidator in a members' voluntary liquidation is required to summon a meeting of the company's creditors when the company is found to be insolvent. He is required to do so within twenty-eight days of forming the opinion that the company will be unable to pay its debts in full with interest within the period stated in the directors' declaration of solvency. The powers of a liquidator appointed by the shareholders is restricted prior to the creditors' meeting to husbanding the company's assets.

In a members' liquidation the liquidator is released when he vacates office after the final meeting of the company. In a creditors' liquidation he is released unless the final meeting objects, when he vacates office. If a meeting resolves against release, he is released when the Secretary of State shall determine.

The Company Directors Disqualification Act

This Act introduced a new civil offence of wrongful trading, in addition to fraudulent trading, and has greatly strengthened the disqualification provisions. The provisions of this Act, and indeed also those of the Insolvency Act 1986, apply equally to shadow directors. A 'shadow director' is a person in accordance with whose directions or instructions the directors act. In most situations it should be clear whether or not a person is a shadow director. Someone for whom the named directors are mere puppets is obviously a shadow director. On the other hand, the company solicitor will not be regarded as such, provided that he does nothing more than his normal duties in such a capacity.

The official receiver, liquidator, administrator or administrative receiver must make a report to the Secretary of State if it appears that the conduct of a director or any past director of a company makes him unfit to be concerned with the management of a company (s. 12). In his turn, if the Secretary of State considers it expedient in the public interest that a disqualification order should be made, he may apply to the court or direct the official receiver to do so in the case of a court winding up. Such disqualification shall not be for a period of less than two years.

A liquidator has power to apply to the court to make any person who was a director or a shadow director of a company which has entered insolvent liquidation liable to contribute to the company's assets (s. 15–16). The new concept of wrongful trading makes this a most important provision since it is designed to provide a more effective means of making responsible those who abuse the privilege of limited liability. It is not sufficient for a director to state that he was unaware that his company was heading for insolent liquidation. The view of the court will be that he ought to have known. A director will have a defence if he can demonstrate to the court that he took every step he ought to have taken in order to minimize the loss to the creditors.

Except with leave of the court, a person who was a director or shadow director within one year prior to a company entering insolvency liquidation is prohibited from being a director or concerned in the management of any company with the same or similar name for a period of five years from the commencement of the liquidation (s. 17). There are penalties including imprisonment for contravention.

Predicting corporate bankruptcy

Argenti (1983, p. 24) states that:

> ... failure does not occur suddenly, is not a lightning flash, is not an Act of God, is not a stroke of bad luck. Failure takes years. Very often it starts at the top and an increasing number of signs and symptoms become visible over the years. Towards the latter half of this process, in say, the final two years, these signs and symptoms of distress become increasingly financial in nature and may be clearly seen in the deterioration of certain well-known and time-honoured ratios.

Readers should already be aware, having read Chapter 4 and Chapter 5 of the benefits of ratio analysis when investigating the 'health' of companies. Liquidity, profitability and gearing ratios can provide important information on a company despite the fact that, being based on accounting conventions, they are probably only indicative rather than being of any direct economic significance. Beaver (1960) found that the best single predictor of failure was provided by the longer-term ratio:

$$\text{Cash flow to total debt} = \frac{\text{cash flow}}{\text{total debt}}$$

In a later paper (Beaver, 1968) he reported on further research which supported his view that longer-term ratios were better predictors than short-term ratios such as the current ratio. To his previous ratio he added:

$$\text{Net profit to total assets} \quad \frac{\text{net profit}}{\text{total assets}}$$

and

$$\text{Total liabilities to total assets} \quad \frac{\text{total liabilities}}{\text{total assets}}$$

A development, pioneered by Altman (1968, 1971), was the use of a multivariate approach called the Z-score. Rather than relying on certain key variables, all independent of each other, the Z-score is calculated by adding together a number of ratios, each ratio having been weighted according to its usefulness. Altman's Z-score is expressed as:

$$Z = 1.2X_1 + 1.4X_2 + 3.3X_3 + 0.6X_4 + 1.0X_5, \text{ where}$$

$$X_1 = \frac{\text{working capital}}{\text{total assets}}$$

$$X_2 = \frac{\text{retained earnings}}{\text{total assets}}$$

$$X_3 = \frac{\text{profit before interest and tax}}{\text{total assets}}$$

$$X_4 = \frac{\text{market capitalization}}{\text{book value of debts}}$$

$$X_5 = \frac{\text{sales}}{\text{total assets}}$$

All of these terms are to be found in the balance sheet and profit and loss account except for the term 'market capitalization' which is simply the number of equity shares on issue multiplied by their current market price. In the case of a non-quoted company market capitalization can be substituted by the sum of the book value of equity, reservers and preference shares. The relevant benchmark for Altman's Z-score is 3.0. Companies scoring above that level should be safe while companies scoring below 1.8 will be classified as potential failures. Altman found this equation to have a predictive accuracy of 95 per cent within one year of failure, 72 per cent within two years but only 48 per cent within three years. Thereafter the predictive ability decreased to less than a third.

Taffler (1983) has also developed a Z-score technique although he has not, in contrast to Altman, published a detailed mathematical equation of his model. He has, however, stated that:

1   A 53 per cent contribution to the model is made by the *profitability measure*:

$$\frac{\text{profits before tax}}{\text{average current liabilities}}$$

2   A 13 per cent contribution is made by the *working capital measure*:

$$\frac{\text{current assets}}{\text{total liabilities}}$$

3   An 18 per cent contribution comes from the *financial risk measure*:

$$\frac{\text{current liabilities}}{\text{total assets}}$$

4   A 16 per cent contribution comes from the *liquidity measure* or 'no credit interval'. This latter term is defined as the number of days a company can finance its operations from its immediate assets if it can no longer generate revenue.

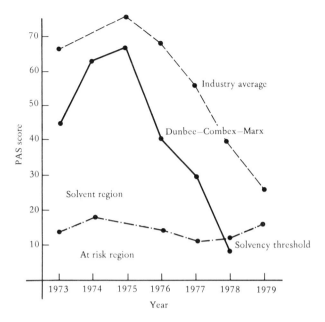

Figure 18.1 Dunbee-Combex-Marx and toy industry PAS trajectories

Taffler's model is of interest as it was initially developed in 1977 explicitly for the analysis of UK quoted manufacturing and construction enterprises. Additionally he has refined his model to eliminate general fluctuations in the economy (for example, a rise in interest rates would cause a deterioration in all companies' income gearing). This he has done by means of a *performance analysis score* (PAS-score) whereby an individual company's Z-score is ranked with the Z-scores of all the companies in its own sector of industry. This approach means that the movement of a company (judged by its Z-score) up or down through the ranks of its own industry may be followed. As Taffler (1983) states:

A company's PAS (performance analysis score) in a particular year is arrived at by ranking the Z-scores of all firms for that year in ascending sequence and observing the percentile in which the Z-score of the concern of interest lies – its PAS. Different calculations are carried out for each year of data for each company so that the company's PAS trajectory indicates its relative performance over time.

Figure 18.1 illustrates Taffler's approach. Dunbee-Combex-Marx (DCM) went into receivership in February 1980 following a strategy of acquisition of large ailing companies overseas. Its PAS declined from sixty-seven (i.e. only 33 per cent of companies performing better) on the basis of 1975 accounts, to seven (i.e. only 7 per cent of companies doing worse) on the basis of its last accounts prior to failure.

An alternative approach to forecasting failure is to study a concern's non-financial features. This highly subjective approach is usually referred to as the A-score technique. As Argenti (1983, p. 21) states:

> The A-score has been designed to systematise and to introduce a measure of qualification into the second main method of failure prediction – that of listing the causes and symptoms associated with failure. It thus provides a further, and quite different, tool to place alongside the ratio and A-scores.

The A-score approach is highly subjective. It relies on an observer/analyst visiting the suspect company, meetings its directors, analysing its products and their marketability and forming his/her views. Proponents of the A-score approach believe that companies fail for broadly the same reasons and that this process takes many years, typically five or more. Typically, companies at risk have autocratic chief executives, weak directors and poor budgetary control (often with no cash flow plan). Such companies fail to respond to changing business environments and find that one of three mistakes lead to their demise – being too highly geared, overtrading or undertaking too big a project. Added to these problems one can usually notice various symptoms that a company is in difficulties for example, the use of creative accounting. Argenti (1983) outlines a table of items that are weighted in accordance with their importance in the failure process (see Table 18.1). Companies scoring above twenty-five marks are deemed to be seriously at risk.

Capital reconstruction as an alternative to bankruptcy

We conclude this chapter by considering an alternative to bankruptcy – a capital reconstruction. Situations can exist when bankruptcy is not necessarily inevitable and, indeed, it could be more preferable to all parties that the company trade out of its economic difficulties. Clearly such decisions depend very much on individual circumstances and the particular alternatives offered to both creditors and shareholders. It may be that if a company is wound up creditors may not receive any, or all, of the monies owing to them. A capital reconstruction may be able to protect all, or part, of their interests even if, for example, there is a delay in the company meeting its obligations. The equity shareholders might also wish for the company to continue and provide some return rather than nothing at all. To illustrate this alternative we consider the (mythical) case of Nova Electronics plc.

Nova Electronics received its stock market listing in the early 1970s. Initially it had been a successful company but its present troubles began in 1982 when it took over a rival company at what, with hindsight, proved too high a price. The company had encountered severe problems with product development and its cash flow position is perilous. Nova's most recent balance sheet is as follows:

Table 18.1 Argenti's A-score table

Defects	
Autocrat	8
Chairman and Chief Executive	4
Passive board	2
Unbalanced skills	2
Weak Finance Director	2
Poor management depth	1
No budgetary control	3
No cash flow plans	3
No costing system	3
Poor response to change	15
Total for defects	43
Pass mark for defects	10

Mistakes	
High gearing/leverage	15
Overtrading	15
Big project	15
Total for mistakes	45
Pass mark for mistakes	15

Symptoms	
Financial signs	4
Creative accounting	4
Non-financial signs	3
Terminal signs	1
Total overall maximum possible	100
Pass mark	25

Source: Argenti, 1983

Nova Electronics plc as at 31 December 1987

	£000	£000		£000	£000
Capital			*Fixed assets*		
Ordinary shares of 25p each		1,800	Goodwill (at cost)	475	
			Premises (at cost)	890	
Long-term liabilities			Plant, machinery and		
9% Debentures		1,010	motor vehicles (net)	745	2,110
Current liabilities			*Current assets*		
Bank overdraft	215		Stock	705	
Creditors	275	490	Debtors	375	1,080
		3,300	Accumulated losses		110
					3,300

The Managing Director of Nova is aware that the bank and debenture holders are very concerned at his company's prospects and that they are considering their respective positions. The following additional information is available on the company:

1   The current value of the premises is estimated to be in the range of £1,125 million and the plant, machinery and vehicles are considered to be worth £690,000.
2   The stock figure is overstated, with many obsolete items, and worth about £30,000 less than stated in the balance sheet.
3   It is considered that an additional £25,000 be provided as a provision for bad debts.
4   The bank overdraft limit has been reached.
5   Debenture holders have a fixed charge on the premises.
6   Although shareholders have not received a dividend for the last three years, certain institutional shareholders may be prepared to bring in an additional £310,000 of equity capital if a satisfactory scheme can be found.
7   Product development problems have been sorted out and future orders look promising.
8   It is considered that a proposed reorganization of the business should result in net profit after tax of £175,000 in 1988 and £240,000 in the following year.
9   It is estimated that additional losses of £220,000 would be incurred if the business was wound up at this time.

Any reconstruction must provide better terms than if the company is wound up. With the above information we can finally consider the likely consequences of being declared bankrupt. The probable position on liquidation would be:

	£000	£000
Proceeds of assets:		
Premises		1,125
Plant, machinery and vehicles		690
Stock		675
Debtors		350
		2,840
Less: Debentures	1,010	
Creditors	275	
Bank overdraft	215	1,500
		1,340
Less: Liquidation expenses		220
Amount available to ordinary shareholders		1,120

The result of liquidation would be that shareholders would receive about 15.5p for every share held, or about 62 per cent of their original investment. However, Nova does not appear to be in a disastrous position. Debenture holders, the bank and creditors will all be repaid but, presumably, could be persuaded to allow the company to continue trading because of (a) its good future prospects and (b) the promise of a further injection of equity capital. Such a proposal would have to write off losses and eliminate the debit balance on the profit and loss account so that the company could once again recommend paying dividends.

Let us suppose the present equity investment is reduced in value by 25 per cent and that the additional share capital is forthcoming. The revised balance sheet of Nova Electronics would appear as follows:

Nova Electronics plc post-reconstruction balance sheet

	£000	£000		£000	£000
Capital			*Fixed assets*		
Ordinary shares at			Premises	1,125	
18.75p each		1,660	Plant, machinery and		
Long-term liabilities			motor vehicles	690	1,815
9% Debentures		1,010	*Current assets*		
			Stock	675	
Current liabilities			Debtors	360	
Creditors		275	Bank	95	1,130
		2,945			2,945

This revised balance sheet places Nova Electronics in a much 'healthier' position. Various assumptions have been made which could be altered if deemed appropriate. For example, the bank overdraft has been totally eliminated but it might have been more prudent only to have reduced it to improve liquid funds. The capital consists of the original investors' capital reduced by 75 per cent (£1.35 million) plus the additional capital injection of £310,000. In the first year of operation the firm would be able to declare a dividend of, say, 5 per cent net which would still leave £92,000 available for transfer to reserve, that is, £175,000 less (£1.66 million × 5 per cent).

Under this somewhat simplified, scenario present shareholders are better off as they will once again receive future dividends, and more of their capital has been saved. Hopefully, as the firm continues to prosper the rise in market value of the shares will compensate for the initial reduction in value. Providing that all parties agree with the Managing Director's calculations and predictions of future prospects, the future of the company seems assured. This example has appeared reasonably clear-cut. Often situations can arise where creditors may not be so secure and, indeed, equity investors could lose all, or most, of their investment. As stated above, each individual situation must be considered on its merits.

Summary

This chapter has considered various aspects of bankruptcy. New legislation has been introduced to encourage directors to take a much more active interest in their companies than they may have previously done and to take corrective action at as early a stage as is practicable. Consideration has also been given to ways in which companies and others can monitor their performance by use of ratio analysis, Z-scores and A-scores. We concluded by considering the possibility of capital reconstruction as an alternative to bankruptcy. Such arrangements can be voluntary or could indeed be proposed by an administrator trying to rehabilitate the company. While most of this text is written with a view to running and operating successful companies, it is a sad fact of life that not all businesses are so fortunate. Clearly if a company is in financial difficulties the ideal situation would be some form of voluntary reconstruction. If this proves impossible then, regrettably, formal liquidation procedures should be entered into.

References

Altman, E. I., 'Financial Ratios, Discriminant Analysis and the Prediction of Corporate Bankruptcy', *Journal of Finance*, 23(4), 1968.

Altman, E. I., *Corporate Bankruptcy in 'America*, Lexington Books, Lexington, Mass., 1971.

Argenti, J., *Corporate Collapse – The Causes and Symptoms*, McGraw-Hill, 1976.

Argenti, J., 'Predicting Corporate Failure', *Accountants Digest* No. 138, 1983, ICAEW.

Cooke, T. E. and Glynn, J. J., 'Different Ways of Going Down', *The Accountant*, 1985.

McQueen, J., Bankruptcy is a Disaster of Titanic Proportions', *Accountancy*, December 1986.

Taffler, R. J., 'The Assessment of Company Solvency and Performance Using a Statistical Model', *Accounting and Business Research*, Autumn 1983.

Part Six

Public Sector

19 The impact of government on the economy

Introduction

In line with other western democracies, the British economy is termed a 'mixed economy' because a large proportion of its gross national product (GNP) originates in the public sector. A mixed economy is a half-way house between a purely market economy and a centrally planned, eastern-bloc style, economy. It reflects the fact that many socio-economic functions, such as health and education, are directly funded and controlled by government. This penultimate chapter is in two parts. By way of introduction to readers not too familiar with the public sector, we first consider the public sector expenditure cycle – the impact of government spending has both direct and indirect effects on the private sector economy. The second half of this chapter examines the influence of government on private sector investment.

The public expenditure cycle

Each year, the Chancellor of the Exchequer presents to the House of Commons his Autumn Statement. This statement brings together a number of economic announcements which very much foreshadow the Expenditure White Paper which is presented to the House of Commons in the spring of the following year. This statement is usually of particular interest to the business community since it provides, as required under the 1975 Industry Act, an economic forecast for the succeeding year. At about the same time the Treasury writes to each central government department requesting their estimates (cash requirements) for the forthcoming financial year, beginning in the following April. After much discussion between individual departments and Treasury officials, these estimates are prepared and submitted by December. Once approved by the government they are presented to Parliament before the budget, which is introduced in March or April each year.

At the time of writing, the most recent Expenditure White Paper is that issued in January 1987 (Cm. 56–I, II) whereas the autumn statement, published in November 1986, gave the broad results of the annual public spending review, this White Paper fills in the details of the plans for the next three years, and provides the basis for supply estimates, cash limits and other spending controls for 1987–8. The Annual Expenditure White Paper is published in two sections. Volume I gives a summary of the new plans, while Volume II goes into more detail by providing further analysis of historical trends in public spending, and detailed accounts of the spending plans, outputs and performance of all parts of the public sector.

Table 19.1 shows that government expenditure has been falling steadily as a percentage of gross domestic product (GDP). Between 1982–3 and 1986–7, a three year period, GDP declined by 2.5 per cent when the proceeds of privatization are excluded (see Chapter 20). Current plans would seem to indicate a further decline of 2 per cent by 1989–90. The three year planning totals in Cm. 56–I are shown in Table 19.2.

Statutory authority for the supply of funds to meet expenditure is provided by means of annual Consolidated Fund Acts and by an annual Appropriation Act. The Appropriation Act, normally in July, authorizes the issue of the consolidated fund of monies sought in the main estimates and summer supplementaries. This act is so titled because it not only grants approval for the total sums requested but also prescribes how the overall sum is to be apportioned to particular votes in order to finance specific services. The Winter Consolidation Fund Act authorizes the issue out of the consolidation fund of the total sum required by the Winter Supplementaries for the current year and for the votes on account for the following year. These votes on account are necessary in order to fund government activity during the transition of the forthcoming Expenditure White Paper. Finally, the Spring Consolidated Fund Act authorizes the issue of the amount required in the spring supplementaries for the current year and also the total sum required to meet any excess votes in the prior year. For further analysis of the process see Glynn (1987, Chapter 7).

Supply estimates are based on a cash accounting system for payments and receipts. The provision for expenditure is intended to reflect actual monies expected to be paid during the financial year. No provision is made in votes for commitments entered into but not yet matured, nor for supporting services for which the receiving department is not required to make a cash payment.

In addition to this year on year process of requesting Parliament to sanction public expenditure, there are also the on-going series of public expenditure surveys which predict the level of public expenditure over the medium term. These forecasts, which are made by Treasury economists, are published twice a year, under Schedule 5 of the 1975

Table 19.1 General government expenditure as a percentage of GDP – plans and outturns

	1983–4 (%)	1984–5 (%)	1985–6 (%)	1986–7 (%)	1987–8 (%)	1988–9 (%)	1989–90 (%)
March 1984 FSBR		44½	43½	42½			
March 1985 FSBR			43	43½	42¼		
January 1986 White Paper				42¾	41¾	41	
This White Paper				42¾	42¾	41¾	41¼

Source: Cm. 56–I (Table 1.10)

Table 19.2 Three year planning totals

	Real terms* (£ billion)	Total planned (£ billion)	Sub-division				
			Central government	Local authorities	Nationalized industries	Public corporations	Reserves balances and adjustments
1987–8	139.3	148.6	108.3	40.2	0.7	1.0	–1.6
1988–9	139.7	154.6	111.2	41.1	0.3	1.0	0.6
1989–90	142.1	161.5	115.7	42.4	–0.1	1.1	2.4

* adjusted to 1985–6 price levels when the planning total was £133.6 billion.
Note: These totals include substantial reserves not specifically allocated to departmental programmes.

Industry Act. One is usually published with the Budget in the *Financial Statement and Budget Report* (FSBR or 'Red Book'). The other is contained in the 'Autumn Statement'. This annual survey for planning public expenditure has now been in use for over twenty years. Its basis followed on from the Plowden Committee's recommendation (Cmnd 1932, 1961) that:

> Previously, the 'volume' plans – that is, plans at constant prices – were regarded by spending managers as entitlements carried forward from year to year regardless of what was happening to costs. This meant that programme managers had little incentive to adapt their expenditures in response to increasing relative costs, except in short-term response to the annual cash limits. For example, if a programme successfully absorbed a cash limit squeeze in one year by increased efficiency, this expenditure saving was not carried forward into future plans. The presumption now shifts in favour of maintaining planned cash expenditure, rather than a given 'volume' of provision regardless of cost.

Cash planning, together with cash limits are just part of the government's strategy to improve efficiency and limit waste in the public sector. Other developments, including management reform, will be discussed in Chapter 20. Currently 40 per cent of public expenditure is directly cash-limited. This includes the external financing limits imposed on nationalized industries. Another 40 per cent consists of 'demand-determined' services where, once policy and rates of payment have been determined, expenditure in the short term depends on the number of qualifying applicants; for example, social security benefits. The remaining 20 per cent represents local authority current expenditure; the rate support grant, the government's main contribution to financing such expenditure.

Having briefly outlined the control procedure for determining the level of public expenditure, brief mention should also be made of the roles played by the Comptroller and Auditor General (C and AG) and the various select committees of the House of Commons. The C and AG's full title is 'The Comptroller General of the Receipt and Issue of Her Majesty's Exchequer and Auditor General of Public Accounts'. As a direct Crown appointee he can only be removed from office by an address from both Houses of Parliament. As his title suggests, he has two functions. As Comptroller General he is responsible for authorizing the amounts paid out to spending departments by the Paymaster General, in accordance with the votes specified in the Appropriation Act. As Auditor General he audits, on behalf of the House of Commons, accounts of the transactions of the Consolidated Fund and the National Loan fund and every Appropriation Account. He submits reports on these and other accounts to Parliament. The National Audit Act 1983 has also enlarged his audit mandate to include aspects of the value for money obtained from public expenditure. Rather surprisingly Schedule 7 of this Act precludes value for money investigations into the activities of some twenty nationalized industries and other public bodies.

Table 19.3 Select Committee in the House of Commons

• Agriculture	• Home Affairs
• Defence	• Industry and Trade
• Education, Science and the Arts	• Scottish Affairs
• Employment	• Social Services
• Energy	• Transport
• Environment	• Treasury and Civil Service
• Foreign Affairs	• Welsh Affairs

Source: Steel, D. R. and Stanyer, J. (1980, p. 400)

The (all party) Public Accounts Committee considers the accounts of each government department together with the reports on them by the C and AG. The Committee has become a powerful instrument for the exposure of waste and inefficiency. It submits to Parliament reports which carry considerable weight, and its recommendations are taken very seriously by the departments and organizations that it examines. The government's formal reply to these reports is presented to Parliament by means of a Treasury minute. A major criticism of this procedure is the time taken before the Public Accounts Committee reports on the Appropriation Accounts. The cycle of events commences with the Permanent Secretary of each department. This person is designated the 'Accounting Officer' and it is his/her responsibility to prepare the accounts of the department by the November following the year end. The Committee usually makes an interim report to the House in the following July and their final report appears about fifteen months after the financial year end.

Public expenditure is also examined by Select Committees of the House of Commons. The system of Select Committees was reformed in 1979 following recommendations contained in the 1978 Report of the Select Committee Procedure; Table 19.3 lists these committees.

The basic framework for controlling public expenditure at the central Government level is one, therefore, that presents very summarized information on a cash accounting basis and relies heavily on the investigatory abilities of both the staff of the C and AG and the various Select Committees. Political scientists such as Heclo and Wildavsky (1981, p. 6) provide an illuminating insight to the political intrigue that underlies the operations of this bureaucratic machine. In their words '... the political administrative culture of British Central Government is a shadowy realm usually left to the chance observations of politicians' memoirs and civil servants' valedictions'. It is usually extremely difficult for politicians and the general public to know what expenditure is spent on what programme. All too often there are expression of great concern when yet another government programme seems almost inexplicably to be overspent. Likierman and Vass (1984, p. 9) state:

There is no easy guide to government financial information, explanations are in some cases in different documents to the text to which they refer, and unless the reader is an MP and can call upon the services of the House of Commons staff, there are few identifiable sources of advice. In short, this is an area plagued by obscurity.

In the last few years government has recognized that there is a need to improve information. Output measures – in terms of manpower figures, activity/achievement indicators and comparative performance indicators – are now included in a variety of government documents. At present, over three-quarters of the measures produced fall within the second category and there is a need for the number of indicators falling within the third category to be greatly increased. Cmnd 9702 (published in January 1986) marked a departure from previous Expenditure White Papers by setting out the spending plans mainly by department, rather than by programme in accordance with the way decisions on funding are actually taken. In the words of Cmnd 9702 (paragraphs 14–15):

> This White Paper is organised by department – *Who plans it*. This covers all spending for which the relevant Secretary of State is responsible, whether it is carried out by central government, local authorities or public corporations ... figures are also given for these differing authorities – *Who spends it* – and for economic activities – *What it is spent on* ...
>
> The programme classification used in previous White Papers analysed spending in part by department and in part by function. In most cases the two approaches are the same, but some departments spend money on a range of different functions. To complement the purely departmental approach, spending can also be analysed on a purely functional basis – for example law and order spending by all relevant departments ... information on *Where it goes*.

This format of analysis in the current White Paper (Cm. 56–I, II) is reproduced here as Figure 19.1. Compared with the previous White Paper (Cmnd 9702), substantial extra provision has been made available for: education (+ £2.2 billion); health and personal social services (+ £0.7 billion); pensions and other social services (+ £1.0 billion). An extra provision of £1 billion of capital spending has also been made, including increases for schools, housing and roads. Reasonably comprehensive notes are provided on each major expenditure heading. We learn, for example under defence, that 80,000 civilian personnel have been transferred to the Royal Ordnance plc (now part of British Aerospace) as part of the government's privatization programme. Whereas ten years ago there were seventy-nine UK-based civilians for every 100 personnel in the regular forces, today the figure is around fifty-two. Each separate heading contains a brief statement of government policy together with supporting commentary.

About 70 per cent of central government spending within the planning total is voted by Parliament through the annual supply estimates. The balance is mainly composed of those social security payments which are paid out of the National Insurance Fund. In total about 40

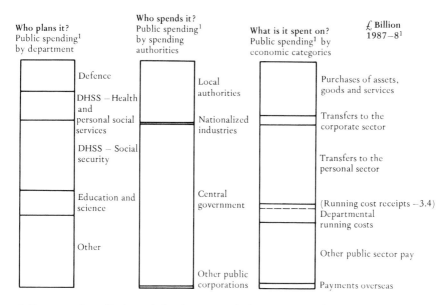

Who plans it?
Public spending[1]
by department

Who spends it?
Public spending[1]
by spending
authorities

What is it spent on?
Public spending[1] by
economic categories

£ Billion
1987–8[1]

Defence

DHSS – Health and personal social services

DHSS – Social security

Education and science

Other

Local authorities

Nationalized industries

Central government

Other public corporations

Purchases of assets, goods and services

Transfers to the corporate sector

Transfers to the personal sector

(Running cost receipts −3.4)
Departmental running costs

Other public sector pay

Payments overseas

1 Departmental spending i.e. excluding the reserve and privatization proceeds

Figure 19.1 Analysis of public spending
Source: Cm. 56–I, Chart 1.3

per cent of central government spending goes on social security. Defence and health rank second and third. Local authorities account for about a quarter of all public spending, with about three-quarters of current expenditure spent on manpower. Education spending is over a third of the total, with most of the rest spent on law and order, housing and other environmental services, personal social services and transport. Cm. 56–I (p. 23) points out that:

> The Audit Commission has estimated that efficiency gains approaching £2 billion are possible in local authorities in England and Wales. Value for money studies are also underway in Scotland. The government continues to look to authorities to improve their efficiency and economy and it is therefore introducing legislation to expose a wider range of their services to competition.

The Audit Commission for local authorities in England and Wales was established by Section II of the Local Government Finance Act 1982. As present the majority of audit appointments remain with the District Audit Service, previously under the control of the Department of the Environment; however, an increasing proportion of audit appointments are being made to private sector accounting firms. In

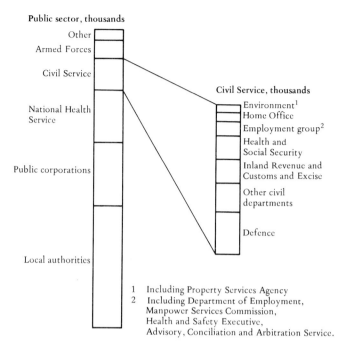

Figure 19.2   Public sector manpower in 1985–6
Source: Cm. 56–I, Chart 1.16

Scotland, a similar body was established by the Local Government (Scotland) Act 1983, and is called the Accounts Commission.

Figure 19.2 shows public sector manpower by employing authority in 1985–6, with a separate breakdown of Civil Service manpower. Of the total of 5,686,000, 41 per cent is accounted for by local authorities, 22 per cent by public corporations, 17 per cent by the NHS, 10 per cent by the Civil Service and 6 per cent by the Armed Forces.

Definitions of public expenditure

Cm. 56–II points out that a number of terms are often used to describe public expenditure and that it is not always clear from the context which definition is being used. The government uses three definitions of public expenditure:

- General government expenditure.
- The public expenditure planning total.
- The supply expenditure.

General government expenditure is the expenditure of central and local government excluding transfers between them such as central government grants to local authorities. For international comparison this measure is generally regarded as the most appropriate since it is less affected by international differences between countries. The public expenditure planning total is the aggregate used by the government for control purposes. The planning total excludes general government gross debt interest, which is not susceptible to the same degree of control as other forms of expenditure, but excludes all the external finance of most public corporations, not just the grants and loans they receive from central government. The determination of the planning total from central government expenditure is quite complex, requiring some twenty-three adjustments. Cm. 56–II (pp. 40–1) provides this detail.

Supply expenditure is that expenditure directly voted by Parliament in the supply estimates. It in turn finances the bulk of central government public expenditure; the biggest exception, as previously stated, being expenditure from the National Insurance Fund which accounts for well over half of social security spending. Other supply expenditure is also not directly reflected in public expenditure because it represents finance provided by central government to one of the other spending authorities. As an example, the estimates include the Rate Support Grant to local authorities which is not direct public expenditure. The relationship between supply expenditure and the planning total is equally as complicated. The *Summary and Guide, Supply Estimates 1986–87* (Cmnd 9742) provides a detailed explanation.

Government incentives to business

Such is the concern of government to regenerate investment in private sector manufacturing industry that it designated 1986 as 'Industry Year'. Jackson (1987, p. 9) has stated:

> The main thrust of the Industry Year movement was to change people's attitudes towards manufacturing industry, and to reverse the view of it as inferior to the professions or the service sector .... Industry year was also a reaction against the long-run decline in the performance of UK manufacturing relative to other parts of the British economy (especially the private services sector), and relative to overseas competitors. Productivity in UK manufacturing remains comparatively low, and since 1983, the country had had a deficit in manufactured goods on current account of the balance of payments. This amounted to £4.9 bn. in 1983 compared to a surplus of £3 bn. in 1980. By 1985, the deficit had increased to £5.8 bn.

The great danger perceived by Jackson and other economists is that growth based on consumer spending, due to recent tax cutting Budgets, is not sustainable in the long run. It would be much more advantageous if economic growth was investment – or export led. Their outlook for

Table 19.4   Manufacturing output by sector (1980 = 100)

	1979	1985	1986 (October)
Total	109.5	103.9	104
Engineering vehicles	107.5	104.2	105
Food, drink and tobacco	100.7	100.9	102
Other manufacturing[1]	111.9	98.8	105
Chemicals	111.3	119.0	122
Clothing	117.9	102.0	102
Metals	131.8	115.0	111
Other			
Minerals[2]	111.0	94.4	98

1   Includes paper, printing and publishing, timber and furniture, rubber and plastic, toys.
2   Mainly building materials.

Source: Central Statistical Office

Table 19.5   Capital investment in UK manufacturing industry (at 1980 prices)

	New investment (£m)	Capital consumption (£m)	New investment (£m)
1979	7,500	6,100	1,400
1980	6,480	6,240	240
1981	4,800	6,310	− 1,450
1982	4,700	6,330	− 1,630
1983	4,780	6,340	− 1,560
1984	5,760	6,360	− 600
1985	5,850	6,380	− 520

Source: National Income and Expenditure, 1986 (HMSO), Table 11.4

1987 is one of a continued growth in consumer spending, with a growth in exports but not at a rate fast enough to exceed the growth in imports. Tables 19.4 and 19.5 consider manufacturing output by industry sector and capital investment in UK manufacturing industry. Output in the manufacturing sector, though continuing to rise slowly throughout 1986, remains lower than its previous peak of 1979. Table 19.4 shows that the metals and textile clothing sectors have suffered most severely since 1979 with falls of 16 per cent and 13.5 per cent respectively. The engineering industry (including vehicles) remains 2.5 per cent below its 1979 level, while chemicals was nearly 10 per cent up. Table 19.5 illustrates that, in net terms, the capital stock of the UK's manufacturing base has been eroded. Jackson (1987, p. 12) considers why this is so. He states:

> One important point may be that decision makers in manufacturing are taking a far too short-term view. The growth in takeovers is an indicator

that individual investors are obsessed with the short-term performance of dividends and share prices rather than with the long-term investment in training, research and development. Too much is spent on pay in the short-run and not enough is allocated to investment. This theme of 'short-termism' (as the Chancellor, Nigel Lawson, called it in his 1986 Mansion House speech) has also been picked up by Sir Gordon Borrie, Director General of Fair Trading. He has suggested that companies making takeover bids ought to be required to show that a merger would produce positive benefits, rather than merely not working against the public interest. The same view has been expressed by the TUC and by Sir Terence Beckett, retiring Director General of the CBI, who blamed financial institutions in the City of London for looking for short-term results, whereas industry should look at the long-term.

The purpose of this chapter is to remain apolitical. It is clear that the political ideologies of the party in government are reflected in the forms of assistance that it provides within its overall expenditure plans to manufacturing industry. Certain governments and recent strategies are now discussed without discussion as to their merits or demerits. Such views are for the individual reader to decide as they are beyond the scope of this text. As there are numerous sources of government finance it is recommended that those interested should contact the Department of Trade and Industry direct. Their booklet *Help for Growing Businesses* in a useful guide.

Regional and local aid programmes

Under the Industry Act 1972 and related legislation, assistance is available for projects which will benefit the economy and are in the national interest. The following are the main types of assistance:

Specific industry schemes
Under Section 8 of the 1972 Act selective financial assistance may be available for particular sections of industry. Included are schemes for micro-electronics; computer-aided design and manufacture; the deployment of industrial robots; tourism; fibre optics; biotechnology and the Small Engineering Firms Investment Scheme. To qualify for assistance, a project must demonstrate the potential to produce a substantial net contribution to UK output or introduce a significant degree of innovation. Typically a cash grant of one-third of costs is available.

Enterprise zones
The government has established twenty-five enterprise zones (see Table 19.6) with the aim of encouraging industrial activity in the private sector by offering tax incentives and reducing, or streamlining, certain reporting and administrative requirements. The major attractions of enterprise zones are that for a period of ten years following designation:

Table 19.6   Enterprise zones

Location	Date effective
Lower Swansea Valley (extended 6/3/85)	11/6/81
Corby	22/6/81
Dudley (extended (3/10/84)	10/7/81
Wakefield (extended 23/9/83)	31/7/81
Clydebank/City of Glasgow	3/8, 8/8/81
Salford/Trafford Park	12/8/81
Gateshead/Newcastle	25/8/81
Speke	25/8/81
Belfast	21/10/81
Hartlepool	23/10/81
Isle of Dogs	26/4/82
Delyn	21/7/83
Wellingborough	26/7/83
Rotherham	16/8/83
Derry	13/9/83
Scunthorpe	23/9/83
Workington	4/10/83
Invergordon	7/10/83
North-West Kent	31/10/83
Middlesborough	8/11/83
North East Lancashire	7/12/83
Tayside	9/1/84
Telford	31/1/84
Glanford	13/4/84
Milford Haven	24/4/84

1 Industrial and commercial property is exempt from rates.
2 One hundred per cent capital allowances are available on industrial, commercial and office property and hotels.
3 There is a reduction in planning controls.

Regional selective assistance
Under Section 7 of the Industrial Development Act 1982 regional selective assistance can be made available to encourage industrial projects which are deemed viable and are expected to increase employment in designated assisted areas. Three main forms of assistance are offered:

1 Grants towards the fixed and working capital costs of projects in mining, manufacturing and construction industries.
2 Office and service industries grants – available to employers and their employees to encourage projects to locate in the assisted areas provided that the project has, in most cases, a 'genuine choice of location' and would not proceed as proposed without assistance.
3 In-plant training grants area – available for manufacturing projects providing a minimum of twenty-five jobs.

The British Technology Group (BTG)
BTG (incorporating the National Enterprise Board and the National Research Development Corporation) can provide equity and loan finance for eligible companies as part of a financial package negotiated with private sector financial sources. BTG provides finance for technical innovation in any technology field. It offers three types of schemes:

1 Joint venture finance – covering 50 per cent of the project and including plant, equipment, working capital and marketing costs. BTG recovers its costs by way of a levy on sales.
2 Recirculating loans are offered for large, unit-based productions like equipment and machinery. When an offer is received for a unit or units BTG can lend the cost of manufacture and delivery. Commercial rates are charged on the loan, which is repayable when the unit has been paid for.
3 Equity and loan finance may be given when the development of new technology is a major part of the business. BTG may subscribe for up to 49 per cent of the share capital.

BTG came into existence in 1981 and also operates the Small Company Innovation Fund (SCIF) and Oakwood Loan Finance. Both of these latter organizations offer funds to small firms. SCIF offers a package which can include any combination of equity, preference shares and loans. It also takes a minority holding in the companies it funds. Oakwood offers loans of up to £50,000 to small companies. These companies should have the potential to produce rapid growth and be unable to provide the security required by traditional sources of finance. The loan is for five years, with a capital repayment holiday for three years. Interest is charged at 2 per cent above base rate.

Investors in Industry (3i)
Investors in Industry – formerly, Finance for Industry – is a holding company owned by the Bank of England and the major banks in England and Scotland. It provides various types of finance, ranging from leasing and line purchase to equity interests.

Industrial and Commercial Finance Corporation (ICFC)
ICFC is a division of 3i which provides long-term finance for small/medium sized firms. It provides finance in the form of loans and subscribes for a minority of equity shares. Loans are repayable between seven and twenty years. The funds provided may be for as little as £5,000 with no specified upper limit.

Loan Guarantee Scheme
This scheme is designed to make commercial finance more readily available to small businesses which have been unsuccessful in obtaining finance on normal commercial terms. Under this scheme the government provides the bank with a guarantee for 70 per cent of the loan, on

amounts of up to £75,000, and the lending bank bears the risk of loss on the outstanding balance. Such loans are repayable over periods between two and seven years. A 5 per cent premium is charged on the guaranteed portion of the loan to cover the cost of the guarantee.

The Business Expansion Scheme
The Business Expansion Scheme, introduced by the Finance Act 1983, superseded the unsuccessful Business Start-up Scheme by removing a number of restrictions of the formal scheme and considerably widening the range of unquoted companies to which this relief applies. Relief is given at the highest rate of tax to an investor who subscribes for equity in qualifying companies for tax years 1983–4 up to 1986–7. Certain complex conditions apply but broadly funds must be kept at risk for at least five years. There is a maximum relief of £40,000 per annum, and a minimum subscription of £500, applying jointly to husband and wife. Subject to conditions, tax relief is available on the whole investment at the investor's marginal rate of tax, giving a substantial potential tax saving for top rate taxpayers (that is, 60 per cent of £40,000 = £24,000 per annum). The full amount invested qualifies as allowable expenditure for capital gains if the shares are sold, but any capital loss is disallowed to the extent of any tax relief given.

Training and labour re-deployment schemes
The Department of Employment and the Manpower Services Commission provide a range of schemes and services for the training and re-deployment of labour, and the development of work opportunities and experience for both school leavers and the long-term unemployed.

Local authorities
The powers granted to local authorities to provide assistance varies from providing an advisory scheme to making finance available. Certain local authorities have special powers under the Inner Urban Areas Act 1978, as follows:

1 Loans may be given of up to 90 per cent of the cost of the acquisition of land and carrying out buildings and site work. The loan can be for up to thirty years but must be at commercial rates of interest.
2 Loans or grants up to 100 per cent of the cost of setting up a cooperative or common ownership enterprise; to a maximum of £1,000.
3 In improvement areas within local authority areas, loans and grants may be available for environmental improvement or the conversion, improvement and modification of industrial or commercial buildings.

Liverpool, Manchester/Salford, Newcastle/Gateshead and certain inner London areas qualify as special areas and these local authorities are permitted to provide limited further assistance. Assistance is unlikely to be given under the Inner Urban Areas Act 1978 if a proposal can be financed adequately from more usual sources and only the minimum will be provided to ensure the proposal will proceed.

Export aid

A variety of government support is available. The British Overseas Trade Board (BOTB) provides information and advice on overseas markets including a series of more than one hundred booklets on overseas markets that deal with currency, exchange regulations, methods of carrying on business and so on. The BOTB also organizes export market research and overseas trade fairs and missions.

The BOTB also operates the Market Entry Guarantee Scheme (MEGS) to assist small and medium-sized business to become involved with new overseas markets. The scheme provides 50 per cent of eligible overhead costs associated with a new project. The BOTB makes a 3 per cent flat rate charge based on the amount provided, and takes a levy on receipts. If the project is unsuccessful, MEGS shares the loss and no further levy payments are required. There is a minimum contribution of £20,000 and a maximum of £150,000. The investment period cannot exceed five years.

The Export Credits Guarantee Department (ECGD) is a government department providing insurance for UK exporters. It insures the exporters against the non-payment of overseas sales and provides guarantees to banks who lend against this insurance at favourable rates of interest. Cover is arranged through the banks but the ECGD may not necessarily misuse all of the debt. The ECGD expects the exporter to pursue any debt, when overdue until such time as it agrees that there is no value in continuing to pursue the debt. The ECGD grades countries according to its view of the risk, and will not insure exports to certain countries. It is estimated that the ECGD underwrites between 30 and 40 per cent of all UK exports. The ECGD guarantee is normally for variable amounts up to 85 per cent of contract value, at a charge of between one-half to three-quarters of 1 per cent of the amount guaranteed. Samuels and Wilkes (1986, pp. 440–2) outline other more specialized financing arrangements in which the ECGD will become involved.

European Economic Community (EEC) assistance

Limited assistance is also available to firms from the EEC. The European Social Fund may provide up to 40 per cent of the cost of in-plant training schemes. This is in addition to any relevant UK grants applicable in assistance areas. The European Coal and Steel Community provides a loan at favourable rates of interest for projects creating new jobs in areas affected by the decline in the coal and steel industries. Loans are from £5,000 up to £1 million through the ICFC. Loans are also available for projects which contribute to increased production, reduced costs or facilitate the marketing of coal and steel products. The European Investment Bank provides loans to businesses at concessionary rates. Loans for up to half the cost of raw capital investment can be obtained for periods of up to eight years. The interest rate is fixed but usually below the prevailing market rate for such loans. Applicants should apply through ICFC, the Midland and National Westminster Banks. The European Investment Bank also makes loans available to businesses in assisted areas.

Summary

Economic Progress Report No. 192 (p. 10), published by the Treasury states that:

> The government want to encourage efficient, flexible markets, capable of responding quickly and effectively to changing economic conditions. With a better performance on the supply side, we can have growth and jobs without inflation.

The present government's assistance to business is part of a general programme to increase the supply side of the economy. On the unemployment front the Youth Training Scheme (YTS) has been expanded to provide two-year courses for sixteen-year-olds, and one-year courses for seventeen-year-olds. Unemployed school leavers under eighteen are now guaranteed a place. About two-thirds of YTS trainees find work or go on to further study and training. Other schemes include: Jobclubs which offer practical help and encouragement to people looking for jobs; the 'Restart' programme for the long-term unemployed; and, more recently, the Job Training Scheme which offers practical work experience and training.

The government has also provided a variety of measures to assist small firms, some of them discussed in the previous section. Similarly too, the government has removed a large number of controls on financial markets, notably on foreign exchange transactions, dividends, hire purchase and bank lending. Investment income surcharge has been abolished. Building societies have been given new powers allowing them to compete more effectively with banks, and other financial enterprises. Following an agreement with the government, the Stock Exchange has: abandoned fixed commissions; allowed outside ownership of members; removed the separation between broking and jobbing functions; and introduced new dealing systems for all types of stock. The more important of these developments have been discussed in earlier chapters. Figure 19.3 summarizes the various measures introduced by government, during 1986 and 1987, to help markets work better.

References

Cm. 56, *Public Expenditure White Paper*, HMSO, 1987.
Cmnd 9702, *Public Expenditure White Paper*, HMSO, 1986.
Glynn, J. J., *Public Sector Financial Control and Accounting*, Basil Blackwell, 1987.

Figure 19.3

Measures to help markets work better – 1986 and 1987

1986 Budget

Basic rate of income tax reduced from 30 per cent to 29 per cent, also small companies' rate of corporation tax.

Main personal allowances raised in line with inflation.

Capital transfer tax (now inheritance tax) reformed to encourage lifetime gifts.

Improvements in tax incentives for employee share schemes.

Restart programme extended nationwide.

Enterprise Allowance Scheme expanded.

Stamp duty on share transactions reduced from 1 per cent to ½ per cent.

Personal Equity Plan scheme announced.

Business Expansion Scheme's life extended indefinitely.

Life of Loan Guarantee Scheme extended and premium reduced.

1987 Budget

Basic rate of income tax reduced from 29 per cent to 27 per cent.

Small companies corporation tax rate reduced to 27 per cent.

Main personal allowances raised in line with inflation.

New tax regime for personal pensions to give greater freedom of choice.

Tax relief for retraining employees changing jobs.

Profit-related pay encouraged by tax relief.

Business Expansion Scheme altered to ease equity raising throughout the year.

VAT arrangements changed to reduce the burden on small businesses.

Other measures

Social Security Act 1986 introduced greater flexibility into pension arrangements and will help to alleviate the 'employment trap'.

1986 Housing and Planning Act encouraged more home purchases by public sector tenants.

Green Paper *Trade unions and their members*, Cm. 95, issued in February 1987, HMSO, contained further proposals to improve democracy and members' rights in trades unions.

White Paper *Building businesses … not barriers* Cmnd. 9794 HMSO, issued in May 1986, listed some 80 proposals for lifting administrative and legal burdens on businesses.

Wages Act 1986 reduced the scope of the Wages Councils' activities.

Technical and Vocational Education Initiative extended nationwide.

City Technology Colleges proposed.

Further employment measures introduced, including expansion of the Community Programme, the Restart Programme, increased number of Jobclubs, and a new Job Training Scheme.

Building Societies Act 1986 allowed building societies to diversify.

Financial Services Act 1986 introduced new system of regulation for financial services industry.

Banking Act 1987 will strengthen framework for banking supervision.

LINK initiative to provide financial support for collaborative research and development.

Local Enterprise Agency Grant Scheme introduced.

Review of law and policy on mergers and restrictive trade practices set up.

Privatization programme continuing: notably British Airports Authority, Rolls Royce, British Airways, British Gas.

White Paper *Housing, the Government's proposals*, Cm. 214 HMSO, issued in September 1987, outlines the reform of the rented housing sector.

Source: Economic Progress Report No. 192 (HM Treasury).

Heclo, H. and Wildavsky, A., *The Private Government of Public Money*, (2nd edition), Macmillan, 1981.

HM Treasury, *Economic Progress Report*, No. 1389, 1981.

Jackson, P., Chapter 2, *Public Domain 1987*, edited by Jackson P. and Tony F., Public Finance Foundation, 1987.

Likierman, A. and Vass, P., *Structure and Form of Government Expenditure Reports – Proposals for Reform*, Certified Accountants Publications Limited, 1984.

Plowden, Lord E. (Chairman), *Control of Public Expenditure*, Cmnd 1432, HMSO, 1961.

Steel, D. R. and Stanyer, J., 'Administrative Developments in 1979: A Survey', *Public Administration*, Winter 1980.

20 Financial management control in the public sector

Introduction

Having outlined, in Chapter 19 the supply procedure and various of the government's assistance programmes to industry, we now consider the process of financial management within the public sector. As Chapter 19, this chapter is in two halves. First, we consider project appraisal. Even though the level of expenditure on a particular year may be limited by a cash limit or capital expenditure ceiling, such constraints do not reduce the importance of appraisal. On the contrary, the necessity for a soundly based system of project appraisal is all the more important. Since the 1960s government's major preoccupation has been with the practices of investment appraisal adopted by the nationalized industries. Only more recently have there been moves to improve the quality of investment appraisal undertaken by government non-trading and service sectors.

The second half of this chapter considers recent efforts to improve the quality of financial control and accountability (broadly defined) to improve the value for money obtained from a wide range of government programmes. These developments are considered under four subdivisions: central government; the National Health Service; local government and the nationalized industries.

Project appraisal

In recent years total government capital expenditure has been of the order of £20 billion per year. However, Brown and Jackson (1983, p. 138) point out that this represents a real reduction of approximately 50 per cent over the last two decades. Stabilized at 1970 prices, Brown and Jackson (1983) calculated public sector capital expenditure at 5.1 per cent of Gross National Product (GNP) in 1966 but only 3.0 per cent in 1980. Over this period total public expenditure on goods and services (at 1970 prices) as a share of GNP remained relatively stable, what happened was that rises in current expenditure were offset against provisions for capital expenditure.

Government policy on project appraisal is to promote the use of the net present value (NPV) approach to discounted cash flows. The rationale behind the use of the NPV approach in the private sector is accepted by government as being exactly analogous to the public sector. To quote HM Treasury (1984, p. 14), 'jam today is worth more than jam tomorrow' because, just as in the private sector, 'more weight is given to earlier than to later costs and benefits'. Some have argued that investment appraisal is inappropriate for those public sector investments which do not produce commercial outputs. This is quite wrong. Outputs can sometimes be valued even when they are not sold commercially; appraisals where such values are regarded as very important (such as with the siting of an airport/hospital or the routing of a bypass) are called 'cost-benefit analysis' (CBA). Even if outputs cannot be satisfactorily valued, investment appraisal can still show the cheapest way of providing a given level of output – this is called 'cost-effectiveness analysis' (CEA). The argument presented in favour of the NPV approach in the private sector in Chapter 6 is equally applicable to the public sector. Government trading organizations will wish to undertake trading opportunities that provide surplus benefits to fund a better long-term provision of service as well as providing funds for government to reapply in other areas. Non-trading and service organizations will wish to value alternative strategies either in terms of CBA or CEA. Only with the use of the NPV technique can there be a rational approach to valuing costs and benefits over time.

As the basic techniques of investment appraisal are broadly the same for both private and public sector investments, this section considers two important aspects – the choice of an appropriate discount rate and the valuation of social costs and benefits.

Test discount rate (TDR)

Government terminology tends to refer to the use of TDR rather than an opportunity cost of capital, although in practice the concept is the same. The difference between the private and public sector is that, whereas in theory there is only one view on the appropriate discount rate to use for private sector evaluations, in the public sector there are many views that prevail.

The basic rate for public sector expenditure (TDR) has been assessed at 5 per cent per year in *real terms* (HM Treasury, 1984). The background to current government policy in this area is provided by two 1978 publications: Cmnd 7131, *The Nationalised Industries*, a White Paper; and *The Test Discount Rate and the Required Rate of Return on Investment*, HM Treasury Working Paper No. 9.

The TDR was originally introduced in the early 1960s as a means of promoting consistent investment appraisal by nationalized industries. Since that time its use has spread to other public sector analyses involving the comparison of costs and benefits over time. The rate is expressed in real terms; that is, it is used to discount costs and benefits expressed in terms of constant prices. Initially the TDR was set at 8 per cent in the mid-1960s and raised to 10 per cent in 1969. The rate was reviewed in 1972 but not changed. Since 1978, as stated above, the TDR was fixed at 5 per cent in real terms (Cmnd 7131, paragraphs 58–65). As Treasury Working Paper No. 9 states (p. 4):

> The view was taken that in order to get the best allocation of investible resources between public and private industries the discount rate used in the public sector should be similar to the return which private firms would consider acceptable on new investment ... it seemed sensible to set a rate for public enterprises which corresponds broadly with that sought by large private firms of good standing engaged in low-risk business.

Since the publication of Cmnd 7131 the discount rate to be used by nationalized industries has not been specified centrally. Each industry, in consultation with its sponsor department, has determined its own discount rate for appraisal purposes, choosing a rate believed to be consistent with earning an overall 5 per cent *required rate of return* in real terms before tax on its overall portfolio of investments.

Public finance economists would term this a *social opportunity cost rate*. A rate whereby government projects should generate a return at least equal to the private sector projects displaced by the government applying the funds to the investment. The argument, currently accepted by government, is that funds should not be diverted to the public sector if they can be applied by a more productive use in the private sector.

Alternate views exist on the use of TDR based on a social opportunity cost rate. Criticism has been made about the validity of basing the TDR on the profitability of the private sector, particularly when used for non-commercial public sector evaluations. Two other, commonly suggested, discount rates are the *long-term government bond rate* and the *social time preference rate*. The long-term government bond rate is the rate paid by government in order to acquire financial resources from sources other than taxation. The problem with this rate is that it is more a reflection of overall government macro-economic policy that bears little relationship to the opportunity cost of individual projects. The social time preference rate can be defined as the rate of return required by the community at large to forego current consumption for future consumption. It stresses that government projects should only be undertaken which produce a favourable trade-off, in the collective judgement of the community, of current for future expenditure. This latter term is clearly the more theoretical of our three definitions.

In theory, with the absence of market imperfections, the social opportunity cost and the social time preference rate should be equal. However, the existence of market imperfections results in the social opportunity rate exceeding the social time preference rate. This has led some authors to suggest a synthetic rate somewhere between these two rates. Baumol (1968) has suggested that the choice between these two rates is 'indeterminate' in the sense that the institutional barriers and the existence of risk will perpetually inhibit any tendency for these two rates to come into equilibrium. For further discussion on this complex debate see Layard (1972).

Social costs and benefits

The second major area of concern of public sector investment appraisal centres around what constitutes the relevant costs and benefits of projects, particularly when there is the absence of a clearly definable end product. For very many investment decisions, the cost criteria will be exactly the same as in the private sector. For example, the replacement of equipment is simply a matter of determining the relevant economic life cycles of each alternative and selecting on the basis of least cost. However, for a wide range of products there are wider considerations than capital costs and operating costs; all too often social costs and benefits have also to be considered. Consider the building of a hospital and a dam. With respect to the hospital social benefits could arise in terms of the time saved in travelling by out-patients, in-patients (particularly emergency cases) and visitors. Conversely social costs can arise in addition to the direct cash outlays associated with the construction of the project. The location of a dam could have important environmental consequences as it may well displace land that would otherwise have been available to farmers, wildlife, outdoor enthusiasts and so on. As Glynn (1987, p. 88) states:

> The accountant engaged in a CBA of a project is not, in essence then, asking a different sort of question from that being asked by the accountant of a private firm. Rather, the same sort of question is being asked about a wider group of people – who comprise society – and is being asked more searchingly. Instead of asking whether the owners of the enterprise will become better off as a result of the firm undertaking productive opportunities, the accountant asks whether society as a whole will become better off by undertaking this project rather than not undertaking it, or by undertaking instead any of a number of alternative projects.
>
> Broadly speaking, for a more precise concept of revenue to the private sector firm, the accountant substitutes the less precise but more meaningful, concept of social opportunity cost – the social value foregone when the resources in question are moved away from alternative economic activities into the specific project. For the profit of the firm, the accountant substitutes the excess benefit over cost, or some related concept used in an investment criterion. Social benefits amount to a potential *pareto* improvement. The project under review, to be economically feasible, must be capable of producing an excess of benefits such that everyone in society could, by a costless re-distribution of the gains, be made better off.

When considering costs and benefits particular attention must be paid to *externalities* and *secondary benefits*. Externalities cover a wide range of costs and benefits which accrue to organizations and individuals other than those responsible for sponsoring a particular project. The question that is of interest therefore is: How far should the project's promoters take these costs and benefits into account? Prest and Turvey (1965) draw the distinction between technological and pecuniary spillovers. Promoters of public sector projects should take into account the external effects of their actions in so far as they alter the physical production possibilities of other producers or the satisfaction that consumers get from given resources. No account should be taken of those side-effects accommodated in the price of other products or factors. Two examples illustrate these points. First, if the construction of a flood barrier necessitates dredging downstream then this cost should be included as part of the overall package of costs. Second, the greater profitability of restaurants and garages adjacent to the M25 motorway should not be included as this simply reflects a transfer of business from less well located establishments.

Secondary benefits and costs need only be considered to the extent that market-determined prices fail to reflect marginal costs and benefits. Glynn (1987, p. 89) cites the example of an irrigation scheme which increases farm production. In such a situation only the costs of providing the water should be considered and not any value arising from increased crop yields. The reason is that a properly functioning price mechanism performs the function of imputing these values for us. The market demand for these improved crops is a desired demand which reflects the value of additional yield and the marginal costs of harvest and distribution. Mishan (1971) provides several examples of the application of CBA to public sector capital investment.

Finance control and accountability

The concept of accountability is crucial to the operation of both public and private sector enterprises. As far as the public sector is concerned, Johnson (1971, p. 283) points out that the emphasis 'in Britain has been almost exclusively on procedures which would enable Parliament to exercise a *post facto* check on the manner in which monies have been spent for the purposes approved by (but not proposed by) Parliament'. This view is supported by Normanton (1971) who points out that public accountability should be capable of much more. Public sector accountability means that those charged with drafting and/or carrying out policy should be obliged to give an explanation of their actions to their electorate. In the public sector there have been many recent developments to improve both the quality of financial management and the quality of information provided to management, politicians and the public at large. The key emphasis in these reforms is to achieve greater value for money from public expenditure. By the term 'value for money' we mean providing *economic* and *efficient* services and programmes that are also *effecive* in terms of predetermined objectives.

These three terms can be defined as follows:

1   *Economy* – acquiring resources of an appropriate quality for the minimum cost.
2   *Efficiency* – seeking to ensure that the maximum output is obtained from the resources devoted to a department (or programme), or conversely ensuring that only the minimum level of resources is devoted to a given level of output.
3   *Effectiveness* – ensuring that the output from any given activity is achieving the desired results.

A lack of economy could occur, for example, when there is over-staffing or when overqualified staff or other overpriced inputs are used. An operation could be said to have increased in efficiency either if fewer inputs were used to produce a given amount of output, or a given level of inputs resulted in increased output. Inefficiency would be revealed by identifying the performance of tasks that serve no practical purpose, or the accumulation of an excess of (or unnecessary) material and supplies. Note that there is an important distinction between the terms efficiency and productivity. Productivity is the arithmetical ratio between the amount of goods and services produced and the amount of resources used in the course of production – the ratio between output and input. Efficiency, on the other hand, is the relationship of actual output/input (productivity) to a performance standard. Very often government produces what it terms efficiency measures when it actually provides less useful, productivity measures.

Effectiveness is evaluated by establishing that approved/desired goals have, or are, being achieved. This is not necessarily a straightforward procedure; some goals may not be initially apparent since government legislation is often produced with expected benefits imprecisely defined. Effectiveness indicates whether results have been achieved, irrespective of the resources used to achieve those results. It could be that an efficiently managed programme fails to produce effective results. Assessing the effectiveness of government programmes in a systematic and regular way is the newest and most difficult area of work that public sector management have to adapt to.

Central government

The main platform for recent financial reform arose initially with a government White Paper, *The Reorganisation of Central Government*, (Cmnd 4506) issued in October 1970. This White Paper instituted three basically administrative procedures for facilitating political decision making. These measures were the development of the Public Expenditure Survey Committee (PESC); the establishment of Programme Analysis and Review (PAR) and the creation of the Central Policy Review Staff (CPRS). In the words of Cmnd 4506 (p. 3):

> The administration has pledged itself to introduce a new style of government. More is involved than bringing forward new policies and programmes: it means ... improving the efficiency of the machinery to achieve the aims it sets itself ....
>
> The review of government functions and organisations which have been carried out ... is intended to lay the necessary foundations.
>
> The aims in that review have been:
>
> (i) To improve the quality of policy formulation and decision-taking in government by presenting ministers, collectively in Cabinet and individually within their departments, with well defined options, costed where possible, and relating the choice between options to the contribution they can make to meeting national needs. This is not confined to new policies and new decisions, but implies also the continuing examination, on a systematic and critical basis of existing activities of government.
>
> (ii) To improve the framework within which public policy is formulated by matching the field of responsibility of government departments to coherent fields of policy and administration.
>
> (iii) To ensure that the government machine responds and adapts itself to new policies and programmes as they emerge, within the broad framework of the main departmental fields of responsibility.

The need to undertake expenditure forecasts was recognized by the Plowden Committee Report (1961) on the *Control of Public Expenditure* (Cmnd 1432). PESC is chaired by a deputy secretary to the Treasury, and its three-year forecasts are published twice a year, under Schedule 5 of the 1975 Industry Act. PESC does not embody detailed analysis of policy operations; its purpose is primarily for macro-economic planning. For each year of the forecast the previous year's level of service is taken as the base, that is then modified by additions representing new policies, and subtractions reflecting closure of activities, that have already been agreed to during the year. Proposals over and above the levels so indicated constitute new policy proposals yet to be approved. This process implies that forecasts become effectively the annual Budgets.

Since 1982/3 cash planning has replaced the previous system of constant prices. The change of cash planning arose, in part, because estimates in constant prices implied that cash had to be provided, regardless of the rise in prices, in order to maintain the agreed levels of services in real terms. In a time of rising inflation this had the potential of depriving the government of control over cash expenditure. While PESC is an important instrument of demand management and financial control it has two important limitations. First, it does not call for explicit statements of the objectives of public sector expenditure and, second, it cannot reconcile a detailed analysis of existing programmes with alternative strategies. These deficiencies were supposed

Figure 20.1   Key elements in scrutinies

The aim is greater value for money by improving the efficiency and effectiveness with which departments deliver policies, programmes and services
The focus is priorities for improvement
The Permanent Secretary supervises the process in association with the Minister
The scrutiny takes nothing for granted but looks directly at what actually happens at all levels of the area under study
The examining officer comes from within the department but not from the area to be reviewed
The examining officer is independent and reports direct to the Minister and Permanent Secretary
The scrutiny process has a tight schedule and is in four parts, investigation; action plan; implementation; implementation report
The action manager converts the report into results and delivers a report on what has been achieved within two years of the start of the process
The Efficiency Unit will be involved throughout the process

Source: Efficiency Unit

to be remedied by PAR studies. The responsibility for preparing a particular PAR report rested with the particular department, the Treasury, the CPRS, and any other affected government department.

PAR reports, as with so many other government reports, are classified and are not generally available except to a limited number of ministers and senior civil servants. The objectives of PAR were generally considered to be rather too ambitious. In 1979 the government formally abandoned PAR and instituted an alternative strategy of *scrutinies* under the (then) direction of Sir (later Lord) Derek Rayner. The third measure, instituted by the 1970 White Paper, was the establishment of the CPRS colloquially referred to as the 'Think Tank'; a small multi-disciplinary unit that still remains as part of the Cabinet Office. The major role of the CPRS is to overview the totality of government policies. Its members initiate inter-departmental studies and are closely involved with the work of the PESC.

The Rayner scrutinies led to the formal establishment of the Efficiency Unit, also part of the Cabinet Office. The scrutiny approach involves selecting subjects or programmes for examination, typically over a ninety-day time scale. The examining officer in a scrutiny is a member of the department in which it is to take place, not a member of the Efficiency Unit. Figure 20.1 outlines the key elements in scrutinies, while Figure 20.2 outlines the five stages involved in a scrutiny.

A by-product of this programme of scrutinies, for there have been well over 300 carried out since 1979, was the establishment of the MINIS system, initially in the Department of the Environment. MINIS is the catchphrase used to describe the process of developing a management information system for ministers. While other depart-

Figure 20.2   Stages in a scrutiny

1   Setting up a scrutiny

The Minister	Approves subject for scrutiny
Permanent Secretary	Identifies the action manager Chooses the examining officer Issues the specification
Scrutiny Liaison Officer	Informs the relevant staff and the trade union side Coordinates the starting brief

2   Doing the investigation

Study Plan

Examining Officer with support and advice from the Efficiency Unit	Plans the scrutiny Approves the team Drafts the study plan Consults those concerned including trade unions Circulates the study plan within fifteen working days of starting the scrutiny
Minister and Permanent Secretary	Review the study plan with the scrutiny team
Fieldwork Examining Officer with support and advice from the Efficiency Unit	Collects evidence Organizes team
Action Manager	Assists the examining officer
Synopsis Examining Officer with support and advice from Efficiency Unit	Prepares the synopsis after sixty working days Discusses the synopsis with the Permanent Secretary Consults the trade union side on emerging findings affecting staff
Permanent Secretary	Reviews the synopsis with the scrutiny team
Report Examining Officer with support and advice from the Efficiency Unit	Drafts report Informally consults interested managers Issues report to the Minister and Permanent Secretary
Permanent Secretary	Discusses the report with the scrutiny team
Efficiency Unit	Comments on the report
Minister	Accepts the report

3   Action plan

Action Manager	Prepares the action plan Consults trade unions and other interested bodies
Minister and Permanent Secretary	Decide on recommendations Decide whether and how to publicize Approve the action plan
Efficiency Unit	Comments on the action plan

Figure 20.2   Stages in a scrutiny (contd.)

4 Implementation	
Permanent Secretary	Is responsible for implementation
Action Manager	Ensures approved recommendations are implemented
Scrutiny Liaison Officer	Acts as Permanent Secretary's agent
5 Implementation report	
Action Manager	Prepares final implementation report within two years
Permanent Secretary	Ensures that implementation report is accurate and implementation is achieved
Efficiency Unit	Comments to the Minister on results achieved
Minister	Accepts implementation report

ments have developed their own versions of MINIS there remains no comprehensive approach that could be adopted by all central government departments. Lord Rayner resigned his post in 1983 and was succeeded by Sir Robin Ibbs, a former head of the CPRS. Like Rayner, Ibbs had an industrial background. Rayner is a Marks and Spencer's executive director and Ibbs had a similar appointment with ICI.

A more recent development has been the establishment of the Financial Management Initiative (FMI) which was launched in May 1982 as part of the government's response to the Treasury and Civil Service Select Committee's third report (HC 236, Session 1981–2). Paragraph 94 of this report, entitled *Efficiency and Effectiveness in the Civil Service* called for a common framework of analysis for the proper management and evaluation of programmes together with the establishment of clearly defined objectives and targets for which ministers and permanent secretaries would be answerable to parliament. The government's response to those recommendations were contained in a White Paper also entitled *Efficiency and Effectiveness in the Civil Service*, Cmnd 8616. Paragraph 13 spelt out three clear principles for management reform:

The aim of the financial management initiative is to promote in each department an organization and system in which managers at all levels have:

(a)   A clear view of their objectives and means to assess and, wherever possible, measure outputs or performance in relation to their objectives.

(b)   Well-defined responsibility for making the best use of resources, including a critical scrutiny of output and value for money.

(c)   The information (particularly about costs), the training and the access to expert advice that they need to exercise their responsibilities effectively.

In line with these principles, each department was required to develop and define a plan which, on completion, was to be sent to the Treasury and the Management and Personnel Office, which is yet another section within the Cabinet Office. The central task of the FMI is to alter the way in which decisions are made about public expenditure, particularly through the creation of line management responsibility. The Financial Management Unit, more recently redesignated the Joint Management Unit, was established to assist departments with the implementation of FMI. Although the FMI is a relatively new strategy there is a growing literature which makes it clear that it is a general approach rather than a standard one (see, for example, Cmnds 8616, 9058, 9297 and Cassels 1983(a), (b)). However, in the longer term, for the FMI to be effective it must integrate not only with each department's decentralized management structures but also with overall strategic planning mechanisms such as PESC.

Gray and Jenkins (1986) conclude that while the FMI has enhanced the status and operation of certain aspects of financial management, this has tended to be at the expense of the integration of strategic management and even of accountability itself. They note that the FMI represents a particular view of what accountable management means. Whereas in the 1970s efficiency meant the maximization of outputs for given levels of input, the language of the FMI (and for that matter other associated developments) in the 1980s indicates that the code of accountable management now in use emphasizes a responsibility (and accountability) for reducing inputs regardless of output. Little is heard about policy effects or outcomes.

The National Health Service

Until the 1974 reorganization, the expansion of the National Health Service (NHS) was haphazard and unplanned. In 1974 the management of the NHS was divided into regions, areas and districts. Since 1982 area authorities were removed as an unnecessary administrative layer. There are now fourteen regional health authorities whose role is to interpret the policies of the DHSS for the 191 district health authorities. The 1974 reorganization also saw the establishment, by the DHSS, of the Resource Allocation Working Party (RAWP) which reported in 1976. This development was felt necessary as there was no overall policy for equalizing the scale and accessibility of health-care resources across the regions. The RAWP proposed that funds should henceforth be allocated across the regions according to a formula designed to establish an equitable criteria for need. RAWP targets are provided for both revenue and capital expenditure so that some redistribution can take place in order to upgrade the provision of service in under-provided regions. A detailed account of the RAWP formula provision is contained in *Sharing*

Resources for Health in England, the report of the Resource Allocation Working Party (DHSS, 1976) and the *Advisory Group on Resource Allocation* (DHSS, 1980). The original hope had been that resource equalization might be achieved nationally by the late 1990s. This target would now appear to be far too optimistic.

The report of the Körner Committee (DHSS, 1984) seeks to make available improved financial information to assist management to more competently manage their resources. The aim of Working Group F (which dealt with the provision of financial information) was to provide more refined and meaningful cost information. The working group highlighted five criticisms of NHS financial information systems:

1   Financial information did not provide patient treatment costs (i.e. translating the *input* of resources into the *outputs* of health care).
2   Those costs that were produced tended not to reflect budget responsibility.
3   Hospital classification, under the costing system, did not account for substantial variations in case-type which existed between hospitals of the same type.
4   Financial information was of suspect validity, particularly when apportionment was required to produce patient care analysis.
5   Lack of timeliness of information for control purposes.

Working Group F recommended the development of speciality costing to provide a minimum data set of some twenty specialities. A speciality cost can be defined as the average cost of treating patients within a speciality or group of specialists. Work is currently underway to develop the recommendations of Working Group F.

A third development in the NHS has been the attempted development of management budgeting which arose from a recommendation of the Griffiths Report – the NHS Management Enquiry (DHSS, 1983). It is an approach to budgeting which has the following characteristics:

- The unit (i.e. a division of a District Health Authority) should be the focal point for management delegation.
- Clinicians should be involved in the budgeting process.
- Clinicians' budgets should include costs directly controlled by the clinicians, and charges (at standard cost) for the use of other services.
- All budget holders would have limited ability to reallocate a proportion of any cost saving that they might achieve.
- The system developed should emphasize management and not accounting.

A number of pilot schemes were undertaken with mixed success. Outside of these schemes most hospital budgets continue on a primarily functional basis – nursing, pharmacy, catering etc.

Local government

Since World War II local authorities have lost many of their functions to central government. Some, such as those originally provided by the Poor Law (1934, 1947), most civil airports (1945), electricity (1947), gas (1948) and water (1974) were transferred to public corporations; some of these have since been privatized. Others such as trunk roads (1946), hospitals (1947) and most remaining local health services (1974) have been transferred to central government. Table 20.1 summarizes the main functions carried out by local authorities in England and Wales.

With the introduction of PESC, successive governments have taken the view that all local government expenditure, not merely grant aided, should form part of the public expenditure planning process. The UK trend is more and more towards central control of local authority spending with the unfortunate effect that management become discouraged from long-term planning. This approach can be contrasted to that adopted by the United States and a number of European countries where there is no detailed control of local government spending.

All local authority spending has to be authorized by statute or subordinate legislation. Such legislation can be divided into two broad categories: that which imposes an obligation on local authorities to do something (mandatory legislation); and that which permits local authorities to provide certain limited additional services at their own discretion (permissive legislation). Annex 12 of the Layfield Committee Report (Cmnd 6453, 1976) usefully illustrates the classification of services into these two categories. The only exception to this principle is provided under the Local Government Act 1972 (Section 137) whereby authorities may undertaken limited discretionary spending. Local government expenditure accounts for about one-quarter of all public spending in the UK.

The principal funding of local authorities is presently provided by rates, a property tax based on the rateable value of property (see Glynn 1987, Chapter 8). In addition local authorities can borrow funds. Their power for this is contained in the Local Government Act 1972 (for England and Wales) and the Local Government (Scotland) Act 1973. However, since the Planning and Land Act 1980 stricter controls have been imposed on the ability of local authorities to raise capital expenditure. These provisions are detailed in a DOE circular (No. 9/83) issued in 1983, and reflect government's desire to restrict what it deemed to be, hitherto, excessive levels of expenditure. A further two circulars, DOE 6/84 and 9/85 have updated the guidance given in DOE 9/83. An Audit Commission report, *Capital Expenditure Controls in Local Government in England*, published in 1985 criticized the present system and offered several suggestions for the improvement of capital controls.

Under the new proposals the government intends to abolish domestic rates and substitute, instead, a community charge. It is also proposed to convert non-domestic rates from a tax varied at local discretion to a tax set by central government at a uniform level throughout the country.

Table 20.1   Main functions of local authorities as at 1985

Function	England and Wales metropolitan		Non-metropolitan		London		Scotland	
	County	District	County	District	GLC¹	Borough	Region	District
Consumer protection	×		×			×	×	×
Education		×	×		(Inner London)	×	×	×
Environmental health		×	×	×	×	×	×	×
Fire service	×		×		×		×	
Housing		×		×	×	×		×
Industrial development	×	×	×	×	×	×	×	×
Libraries		×	×			×	×	×
Passenger transport	×		×		×		×	
Planning								
Structure plans	×		×		×		×	
Development control		×		×	×	×		×
Police	×		×		(Central government)		×	×
Rate collection		×		×		×	×	
Recreation	×	×	×	×	×	×	×	×
Refuse disposal	×		×		×		×	×
Social services		×	×			×	×	
Transport and highways								
Policy and principal roads	×		×		×		×	
Non-principal roads	×	×	×	×		×	×	×

1 Since disbanded

The aim of this list is to give a brief summary of the distribution of the main functions. There are many footnotes possible in a list of this type and a detailed summary can be found in Byrne (1981).

Source: Holtham (1986), p. 45

The arguments on which the government based its proposals were given in the 1986 Green Paper (Cmnd 9714) *Paying for Local Government*. This was the fourth in a series of Green Papers since 1971 to have addressed the problem of rating reform. The principal objective of this latest Green Paper was to bring about a reduction of local government spending. Thus it was proposed to reduce what government regarded as excessive expenditure by some local authorities and to provide for a system of income generation that enhanced local accountability.

Despite the widespread unpopularity of rates as a form of taxation, little is known of their economic effects, far less the effects of any possible alternatives. The government has, as stated, tended to focus much of the debate on the question of local accountability. Cmnd 9741 cites what government believes to be three weaknesses with the rates system:

1 The fact that over half of those eligible to vote did not pay rates, whereas a poll tax would be paid by nearly all adults.
2 The fact that on average some 54 per cent of rate base expenditure was met by non-domestic rates, with the non-domestic contribution rising in some authorities to as much as three-quarters of the income raised locally. Local authorities were therefore in the position of increasing expenditure on services for voting domestic ratepayers largely at the expense of the non-voting, non-domestic ratepayer.
3 Problems with the administration and equity of the grant system when supporting locally determined rates which conceals the real cost of services from the electorate.

In some respects the government's proposals represent an about-turn of policy since the very notion of a poll tax was rejected by government in the Rates White Paper of 1983. There are however two reasons which explain this. First, the Audit Commission published an extremely critical report on the block grant distribution in August 1984. Some authors have argued that this report encouraged renewed pressure from critics of the system both outside and, more significantly, within government. In October 1984, the Secretary of State for the Environment announced the setting up of an inter-departmental inquiry which coincided with the second reason – the widespread protest against rate increases which erupted in Scotland following a revaluation which had its impact on Scottish households with the arrival of rates bills in April 1985.

The main reforms proposed are fourfold:

1 The replacement of domestic rates by a flat-rate community charge/poll tax which would be levied on all adults. The level of charge, while the same for each adult within a local authority, will vary according to the spending level of each authority. The aim is therefore to spread the cost of local government more widely among those who benefit from its services.
2 The conversion of non-domestic rates from a tax levied at variable

rates by different local authorities according to their spending requirements into a nationally uniform tax with the proceeds distributed to local authorities on an equal amount per adult basis.
3 The simplification of the grant system by conversion of the present
block grant into two lump sum grants a 'needs grant' to compensate
for differences in assessed spending needs per adult between local
authorities and a 'standard grant' to provide an additional sum from
national taxation towards the cost of local services.
4 A simpler formula for assessing the 'needs grant' which is to be
based on fewer key indicators.

Local authority finance officers will face a number of challenges to
implementing these proposed reforms. Their first job will be to compile
a register of those required to pay the community charge/poll tax and to
institute measures that seek to locate those that may seek to evade the
charge by failing to register. The method of collecting rates from council tenants has traditionally been along with their rents. It will be
impossible to collect this new charge in the same way because:

1 Information on the number of eligible taxpayers at any time will not
be readily available.
2 The tenant is not liable for payment of all the poll taxes in his/her
household.

Tenants of privately rented accommodation who previously paid an
inclusive rent will be similarly affected. Some financial officers have
voiced concern that the number of summonses for non-payment will be
far higher than under the rates system as individuals move on without
settling their tax bills. It may very well be that these proposals are very
much more costly for local authorities to administer.

The implementation of a community charge/poll tax is supported by
government on the grounds that it will improve local accountability.
However critics have condemned the scheme as being: regressive or
unfair to those on low incomes; difficult to administer; and likely to
increase the potential for the central control of local finances. No other
European country has such a tax.

No national reforms have been undertaken to harmonize local authority financial control but efforts are currently underway to improve the
quality of local authority annual reports (see Glynn, 1987, Chapter 8).

Nationalized industries

Nationalized industries represent those industries taken into public
ownership for a variety of economic, political and social reasons. They
have generally been thought of as comprising those industries that
dominate four strategic sectors of economic activity: energy; public
transport; communications; and iron and steel. Nationalized industries

are expected to follow best commercial policy with respect to both financial reporting and accounting.

Government control of nationalized industries has taken the form of setting financial targets set by the relevant minister of each industry's sponsoring department. Industries can control their own pricing policy. The 1978 White Paper, *The Nationalised Industries* (Cmnd 7131) withdrew guidelines established in a 1967 White Paper (Cmnd 3437), whereby nationalized industries were instructed to adopt long-run marginal cost pricing policies. (This instruction was qualified by an insistence that accounting costs should be covered in full and that financial targets should be met.) Paragraph 68 of Cmnd 7131 states, in part, that:

> ... the government believes that it is *primarily* for each nationalised industry to work out the details of its prices with regard to its markets and its overall objectives, including its financial target.

Financial targets usually take one of the following main forms: a return on net assets calculated on a current cost basis before the deduction of interest and tax; a self-financing ratio; a percentage return on turnover; or a target profit or loss. The first measure, the return on net assets, is the most common measure. Labour-intensive industries such as the Post Office tend to be asked to achieve a percentage return on turnover, while historically ailing industries, such as British Rail, are required to meet a target level of profitability.

Since 1976 a cash limit has been set annually for each nationalized industry's external financing requirements. Because the normal practice is that loans are guaranteed by the government they are therefore counted as part of government financing despite the fact that the funds do not come directly from public funds. With overseas borrowings the Treasury operates a scheme, for which industries pay a premium, whereby they are insured against losses arising if sterling depreciates against the foreign currency in which the loan was taken out.

Privatization

Privatization, since 1979, has become an integral part of government policy. Privatization is not a phenomenon peculiar to the UK since it is now adopted policy in many countries including Australia, Finland, Malaysia, Mexico, New Zealand and the Philippines. In the first eight years of privatization policy the government has raised more than £25 billion and the number of private shareholders has risen from 2 million, in 1984, to 9.4 million in 1987. Initially the government's privatization programme began slowly with the sale of 5 per cent of British Petroleum, it is now geared up to produce £5 billion a year. Flotations such as British Telecom and British Gas have been very successful. British Telecom attracted 2.3 million UK investors, including 230,000 Telecom employees. When dealings opened on the London stock market, the shares traded at an immediate 90 per cent premium which brought criticism from the opposition that the shares were some £1.3 billion undervalued. Another criticism has been of the costs associated with launch costs, currently in excess of £500 million. Not all share offers have proven so attractive. The planned £7.2 billion British Petroleum share offer, the world's biggest single flotation, coincided with the international stock market crash. At the very time that the shares were offered for sale, share prices on Wall Street and in London, Japan and Hong Kong plummeted in an unprecedented slide sparked off by computer programmed 'sell-offs' in New York as investors became increasingly concerned about the deficit position of the US economy. Table 20.2 shows the 1987 numbers of shareholders in thirteen privatized companies.

The privatization programme is not just about stock market flotations. Since 1979, the government has sold more than one million houses (either local authority, new town or housing association properties). Current government plans envisage another one million house sales over the next five years. No official figures for the gross receipts of these sales are available. Treasury statistics suggest that the market value of those properties already sold exceeded £20 billion but that receipts were something less than £15 billion. This shortfall is principally due to the generous discounts offered to tenants/buyers to encourage home ownership.

Many assets have been sold by tender. The 1982 sale of the National Freight Corporation was by means of a management/employee buyout. Management buyouts have also been a feature of a shipbuilding industry. Such names as Vosper Thorneycroft, Swan Hunter and Vickers Shipbuilding and Engineers were all management buyouts. So too were Unipart and Leyland Bus. These last two examples illustrate another facet of this policy – the sale of subsidiaries. British Rail provides another illustration since it has had to sell off Sealink, its prestigious hotel chain and its Doncaster Wagon Works.

Contract tendering, whereby a number of state or local authority service functions are now contracted out to the private sector, represents yet another form of privatization. The government's contention is that competitive tendering for service contracts such as refuse collection, laundry and catering will prove cheaper and more efficient. It remains to be seen if this will be the case. Probably the most extreme example of competitive tendering surrounds the new private sector management which has recently taken over the running of the Devonport and Rosyth naval dockyards.

The recent history of privatization in the UK can be classified as one that has followed no consistent rationale. The transfer of ownership per se provides no clear path to increased efficiency. British Telecom has, after all, simply changed from being a state monopoly to being a privately owned monopoly. It has also to be remembered that while the receipts of privatization reduce the public sector borrowing requirement this is a one-off effect.

Table 20.2 Shareholders in privatized industries

Company (year privatized)	Successful applicants 1st issue	Successful applicants 2nd issue	Successful applicants 3rd issue	Current number of shareholders	Date	Percentage decrease
Amersham International (1982)	65,000	n/a	n/a	5,940	30.9.87	−91
Associated British Parts (1983)	45,500	8,000	n/a	9,666	30.9.87	−79
BAA (1987)	2,187,500	n/a	n/a	≃1,500,000	19.10.87	−31
British Aerospace (1981)	155,000	260,000	n/a	102,788	6.10.87	−36
British Airways (1987)	1,100,000	n/a	n/a	404,000	6.10.87	−57
British Gas (1986)	4,407,079	n/a	n/a	3,000,000	30.9.87	−32
British Telecom (1984)	2,300,000	n/a	n/a	1,417,905	31.3.87	−38
Britoil (1982)	35,000	450,000	n/a	178,600	31.7.87	−63
Cable and Wireless (1983)	26,000	35,137	218,588	174,758	6.10.87	−38
Enterprise Oil (1984)	13,695	n/a	n/a	11,100	30.6.87	−19
Jaguar (1984)	125,000	n/a	n/a	34,918	30.9.87	−72
Rolls Royce (1987)	2,000,000	n/a	n/a	1,250,000	19.10.87	−27
TSB (198)	3,000,000	n/a	n/a	1,970,000	2.10.87	−34

Source: Adapted from an original table in *The Observer* – Privatization Survey, Sunday 25 October 1987, p. 63

References

Audit Commission, *Capital Expenditure Controls in Local Government in England*, HMSO, 1985.

Baumol, W. J., *Economic Theory and Operations Analysis* (2nd edition), Prentice-Hall, 1968.

Brown, C. V. and Jackson, P. M., *Public Sector Economics* (2nd edition), Martin Robertson, 1983.

Cassels, J., *Review of Running Costs*, Management and Personnel Office, 1983a.

Cassels, J., *Review of Personnel Work in the Civil Service*, HMSO, 1983b.

Cmnd 1432, *Control of Public Expenditure*, HMSO, 1961.

Cmnd 6453, *Local Government Finance*, HMSO, 1976.

Cmnd 7131, *The Nationalised Industries*, HMSO, 1978.

Cmnd 8616, *Efficiency and Effectiveness in the Civil Service*, HMSO, 1982.

Cmnd 9058, *Financial Management in Government Departments*, HMSO, 1983.

Cmnd 9279, *Progress in Financial Management in Government Departments*, HMSO, 1984.

Cmnd 9714, *Paying for Local Government*, HMSO, 1986.

DHSS, *Sharing Resources of Health in England*, HMSO, 1976.

DHSS, *Advisory Group on Resource Allocation*, HMSO, 1980.

DHSS, *Report of the NHS Management Inquiry*, Chairman: Roy Griffiths, HMSO, 1983.

Glynn, J. J., *Value for Money Auditing in the Public Sector*, Prentice-Hall, 1985.

Glynn, J. J., *Public Sector Financial Control and Accounting*, Basil Blackwell, 1987.

Gray, A. G. and Jenkins, W. I., 'Accountable Management in British Central Government: Some Reflections on the Financial Management Initiative', *Financial Management and Accountability*, Autumn 1986.

H. M. Treasury, *Investment Appraisal in the Public Sector: A Technical Guide for Government Departments*, 1984.

Holtham, C., in Henley, D., Holtham, C., Librieman, A. and Perrin, J. (eds) *Public Sector Accounting and Financial Control*, Chapters 4 and 5, Van Nostrand Reinhold (UK), 1986.

Johnson, N., 'Financial Accountability to Parliament', in Smith, B. L. R. and Hague, D. C. (eds), *The Dilemma of Accountability in Modern Government*, Chapter 13, St. Martins Press, New York, 1971.

Layard, R. (ed.), *Cost Benefit Analysis*, Penguin Books, 1972.

Mishan, E., *Cost-Benefit Analysis*, Allen and Unwin, 1971.

Normanton, E. L., 'Public Accountability and Audit: A Reconnaissance', in Smith, B. L. R. and Hague, D. C., *The Dilemma of Accountability in Modern Government*, Chapter 14, St. Martins Press, New York, 1971.

Prest, A. R. and Turvey, R., 'Cost-Benefit Analysis: A Survey', *Economic Journal*, Vol. 75.

Index